China's Pension Reforms

Existing literature has looked at many factors which have shaped Chinese pension reforms. As China's pension reform proceeds in an expanding and localising fashion, this book argues that there is a pressing need to examine it in the context of China's political institutions and economic transformations. The book takes a unique approach by looking at political institutions of the Chinese state and the changing conditions of the Chinese economy, which rarely receive proper treatment in the current analysis of China's pension reforms.

Ke Meng is Assistant Professor at the School of Public Policy and Management, Tsinghua University.

China Policy Series
Series Editor: Zheng Yongnian
East Asian Institute, National University of Singapore

China's Global Quest for Resources
Energy, Food and Water
Edited by Fengshi Wu & Hongzhou Zhang

China's New Public Health Insurance
Challenges to Health Reforms and the New Rural Co-operative Medical System
Armin Müller

China-Africa Relations
Building Images through Cultural Co-operation, Media Representation and on the Ground Activities
Edited by Kathryn Batchelor and Xiaoling Zhang

China's Authoritarian Path to Development
Is Democratisation Possible?
Tang Liang

Foreign Policies toward Taiwan
Shaohua Hu

Governing Environmental Conflicts in China
Yanwei Li

Post-Western Sociology
From China to Europe
Edited by Laurence Roulleau-Berger and Li Peilin

China's Pension Reforms
Political Institutions, Skill Formation, and Pension Policy in China
Ke Meng

For more information about this series, please visit www.routledge.com/China-Policy-Series/book-series/SECPS

China's Pension Reforms

Political Institutions, Skill Formation and Pension Policy in China

Ke Meng

Routledge
Taylor & Francis Group
LONDON AND NEW YORK

First published 2019
by Routledge
2 Park Square, Milton Park, Abingdon, Oxon OX14 4RN

and by Routledge
605 Third Avenue, New York, NY 10017

First issued in paperback 2020

Routledge is an imprint of the Taylor & Francis Group, an informa business

British Library Cataloguing-in-Publication Data
A catalogue record for this book is available from the British Library

Library of Congress Cataloging-in-Publication Data
A catalog record for this book has been requested

ISBN 13: 978-0-367-50437-3 (pbk)
ISBN 13: 978-1-138-48089-6 (hbk)

Typeset in Galliard
by Apex CoVantage, LLC

The book is dedicated to my parents, MENG Qiliang (蒙启良) and WU Duanduan (吴端端), and my wife, JIN Xiangyi (靳相宜), for their patience, support and sacrifice.

Contents

Figures

Tables

Acknowledgements

I am most grateful to my supervisors at Oxford University. First, Professor Robert Walker's seminar "Social Policy in China" showed me the possibility of studying the Chinese welfare state through the lens of Western theories. Secondly, Dr. Adam Saunders led me into the field of comparative political economy of the welfare state. Finally, Professor Martin Seeleib-Kaiser's guidance for my MPhil degree helped lay the foundation for the book. Their enthusiasm and support have been essential during this work.

I give my deep thanks to my examiners, Professor Eric Thun and Professor Marius R. Busemeyer, whose advice on how to push forward this project has been most valuable.

I would like to express my sincere gratitude to the assessors for my Transfer of Status and Confirmation of Status, Professor David Soskice, Professor Duncan Gallie, Dr. Stuart Basten and Dr. Erzsébet Bukodi. Without their guidance, insight and encouragement, the completion of this book would not have been possible.

I am indebted to Dr. Xin Liu and Dr. Yu Tao for many stimulating discussions. Their devotion to recording China's past and present gives me faith in my generation.

Finally, I would like to thank Lam Yongling and Samantha Phua at Routledge. Their enthusiasm and professional advice has been most helpful in publishing this manuscript.

This book is supported by the National Social Science Foundation of China (16CGL045), Tsinghua University Initiative Scientific Research Program (2015THZWJC09), and Cyrus Tang Foundation Young Scholar Awards.

1 Introduction

Learning about China through its pension reforms

The first decade of the twenty-first century witnessed the rise of an expansive yet localised pension system in China. This book formulates a theoretical framework to explain two puzzling characteristics of the Chinese pension system, namely its rapid expansion in the absence of electoral pressures and persistent localisation despite an authoritarian central government. The framework focuses on the complementarities between political institutions, the pension system and labour markets in China. The central argument is that the Chinese political institutions shape an expansionary and localised pension system by driving municipal authorities to compete with each other in generating specific skills in local labour markets. To be more precise, China's pension reform coincided with two structural changes in the Chinese economy, that is, industrial upgrading and labour market tightening. The two trends raised the need for the training and retaining of workers with specific industrial skills. An expanding and regionally fragmenting pension policy encourages workers to invest in the acquisition of skills that are specific for local industries by insuring them against lifetime income loss, and serves to keep the industrial workers in the locality by limiting the cross-regional portability of their pension packages. The implementation of pension policy falls within the domain of local government. The incentive of the municipal authority to adopt the expanding and localising pension policy is structured by the Chinese political institutions, which award promotions to local officials who outperform their counterparts in promoting local industrialisation. Under this incentive structure, the office-seeking Chinese municipal bureaucrats engage in an economic competition and in the process implement the expansionary and localising pension policy, which is beneficial for skill formation and hence local industrial expansion. The result of the Chinese political institutions, in the context of industrial upgrading and labour market tightening, is the expansive and localised pension regime.

By demonstrating the interconnections between political institutions, social policy and labour markets in the Chinese context through the study of the Chinese pension system, this book contributes to three sets of literature. First, it adds to the Varieties of Capitalism theory by testing its hypothesis in the Chinese context that social protection enhances the formation of specific skills (Estevez-Abe et al. 2001; Iversen and Soskice 2001; Iversen 2005). Secondly, it complements the Statist account of welfare state development (Flora and Alber 1981; Orloff and Skocpol 1984; Skocpol and Amenta 1986), which shows that political concerns appease challenging social interests and drive state actors to expand the welfare state. This book argues that in addition to such political anxieties, economic consideration, especially that regarding skill formation, can also be one important motivation behind state bureaucrats' push for welfare state formation. Finally, this book contributes to the institutionalist model of welfare politics (Lijphart and Crepaz 1991; Iversen and Soskice 2006, 2009, 2010; Estevez-Abe 2008), by revealing in an authoritarian setting how institutional arrangements shape political competition and the nature of the welfare state.

This introductory chapter proceeds in four sections. First, it starts with a brief introduction of China's pension reform, identifying the two puzzling features of the resultant pension system. Then it contextulises the Chinese pension reform, focusing on the economic and political environment in which the reform unfolds. Finally, before outlining the structure of the book, it discusses how a political-economic account of the Chinese case contributes to the literature on the comparative political economy of the welfare state. This book, in short, utilises the issue of pension reform as a policy case to show the political-economic logic in the formation of the Chinese welfare state, thereby improving our understanding of the political economy of the welfare state in general.

Chinese pension reforms through historical and comparative perspectives: two puzzles about China's pension system

The Chinese welfare state is pension-dominant. Government spending on public pension far exceeds that on other major social insurance programmes, making pension the most important component of the Chinese welfare regime (Figure 1.1). Welfare states in advanced economies are dominated by healthcare spending in addition to pension expenditure (Moran 1999), while in China spending on medical care cannot even remotely rival those on pension programmes. Given the country's stage of development, the rise of a pension-dominant welfare state in China is "sudden and exceptional" (Frazier 2006: 3). One cannot make sense of the Chinese welfare state without understanding its pension system.

China's pension system, in the broadest sense, is a three-part government-sponsored arrangement. It constitutes a mandatory pension insurance system for urban residents, a voluntary old-age insurance system for rural residents and non-contributory special occupational schemes for civil servants and soldiers. The pension system for the urban areas, or urban basic old-age insurance as it is named in China, is a multi-pillar system which entails: a mandatory pay-as-you-go pension insurance (Pillar 1); a compulsory defined contribution individual account (Pillar 2); and optional pension insurance which enterprises and individuals could purchase (Pillar 3). Under this system, Pillar 1 is financed solely by employer contributions of 20 percent of wages, while Pillar 2 is funded by employee contributions of 8 percent. As we shall see below, the regional fragmentation of the pension system means that in practice specific contribution rates

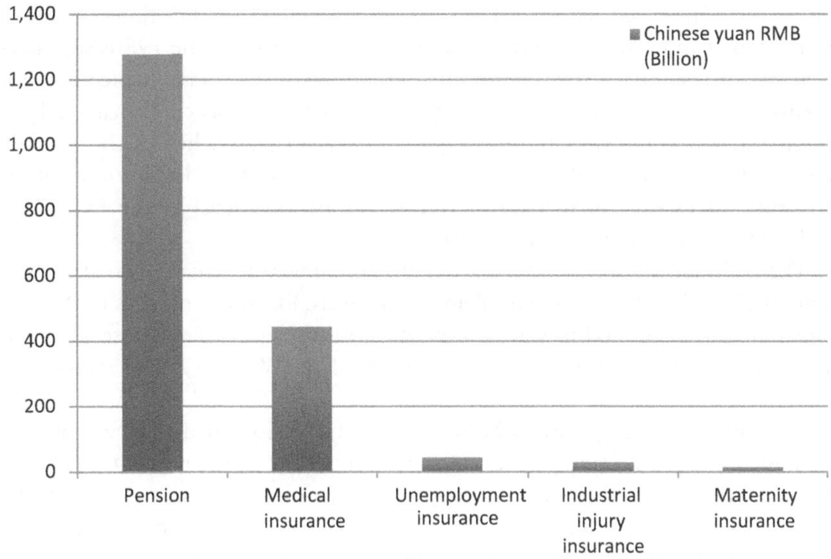

Figure 1.1 Public expenditure on major social insurance programmes (2011)

Source: China Statistical Yearbook (2012)

are chosen by the provinces and municipalities, with the wages used to calculate the contributions being subject to a minimum of 60 percent and maximum of 300 percent of average wages in the locality. On the precondition that contributions have been made for at least 15 years, an individual reaching retirement age (60 for men and 50 for women) is entitled to receive a pension funded from a "social pool" and his or her individual account. Pension benefit is calculated on the basis of a locality's average salary, the individual's indexed contribution salary and the individual account balance. The focus of this study is the pension system for urban workers and residents, especially its government-run, mandatory components (Pillar 1 and 2). This book does not cover voluntary pension insurance for firms and individuals (Pillar 3) because it is still in its adolescence. In 2008, the share of firms that purchase optional pension schemes for workers was only 1 percent, while the proportion of workers who participated in such occupational pension programmes was just 1.3 percent (Zheng 2010: 6).

This system has gone through several reforms to reach its current form. The foundation of China's pension system was laid by the 1951 *Labour Insurance Regulations*, which was enacted by the State Council two years after the founding of People's Republic of China. It covered urban workers in public and private factories with more than 100 employees. With the accomplishment of the socialist transformation of urban industries in 1957, in which private companies were collectivised and incorporated into state-owned enterprises, few urban firms were left with fewer than 100 employees. This transition, combined with the 1958 modification to the 1951 Regulations, which abolished the threshold of 100 employees, effectively achieved full pension coverage for all full-time workers at state-owned and urban collective enterprises. Regulations in the 1950s stipulated that labour insurance programmes including pension should be financed by firm contributions of 3 percent of the wage bill, which was collected, managed and pooled across enterprises by municipal and sectorial branches of the ACFTU (All-China Federation of Trade Unions). Thirty percent of local contributions to pension fees were further transferred to the national level by the ACFTU to redistribute across regions and industrial sectors.

The Cultural Revolution that started in 1966 however virtually dismantled this system. ACFTU officials at central and local levels, like other officials in the state apparatus, were purged in waves of political movement during those turbulent years (1966–1976). ACFTU then fell into paralysis. With no one to manage the collection and distribution of labour insurance, in 1969 regulations were formulated calling for enterprises to be solely responsible for financing pension programmes and distributing pension benefits. Under the new arrangement China's pension system ceased to be a pay-as-you-go type of social insurance that makes intergenerational transfers from current workers to retirees. Instead, pensions became enterprise operating expenses. State enterprise managers were left alone in charge of pension distribution to retired workers according to broad guidelines drawn up by state regulations. And the generosity of the pension package depends on the financial situation of the enterprise. The result was an enterprise-based pension system.

After the Chinese leadership initiated market-oriented reforms in 1978, the welfare arrangements under the planned economy were thought to be incompatible with a market economy. In particular, the enterprise-based welfare system, where state enterprises were required to be solely responsible for financing pension programmes and distributing pension benefits, was held accountable for imposing too much financial burden on firms and causing economic inefficiency. In 1986, with the aim of easing the social burdens on the state sector, tentative reforms took place in several localities, asking pension contributions to be shared between the state enterprise and its employees and pooled within the locality. This signified the beginning of the end of the enterprise-based pension arrangement and the start of a "social insurance type" pension system in China.

These early local experiments with pension reform were adopted as national policy in 1991 by the central government (State Council Document 33 [1991]), which transferred the authority of pension provision and administration from the state enterprise to the local government. In 1995, the central government (State Council Document 6 [1995]) asked all localities to complement the mandatory pay-as-you-go pension insurance with a compulsory defined contribution individual account for all urban enterprise employees (i.e., workers in both state and private sectors). This arrangement is called "the combination of social pools and individual accounts" (*tongzhang jiehe*) and has become the basic setting for China's urban pension system. In 1997, the piecemeal reform measures that had been taken before were consolidated and reaffirmed by the central government in the State Council Document 26 [1997], which has since served as the guiding regulation on China's national pension policy. Subsequent development mainly saw the extension of its principles to cover more segments of the society (for example, State Council Document 38 [2005] required the coverage of the pension system to further extend to urban workers in self-employment and flexible employment, notably migrant peasant workers).

The development of the Chinese pension system in the reform era, when put in a comparative perspective, shows two puzzling characteristics. The first puzzle is about the reform approach. Most large developing countries chose to protect privileged segments of the workforce by preserving corporatist welfare arrangements when they reformed their pension systems in the last quarter of the twentieth century. By contrast, China abolished its socialist "mini welfare states" run by state-owned firms under the enterprise-based arrangement (Gu 2001), which once only covered privileged industrial workers in the pre-1978 Maoist period, and replaced them with an urban-based old-age insurance arrangement with increasingly extended coverage (see Figure 1.2). In this respect one can compare

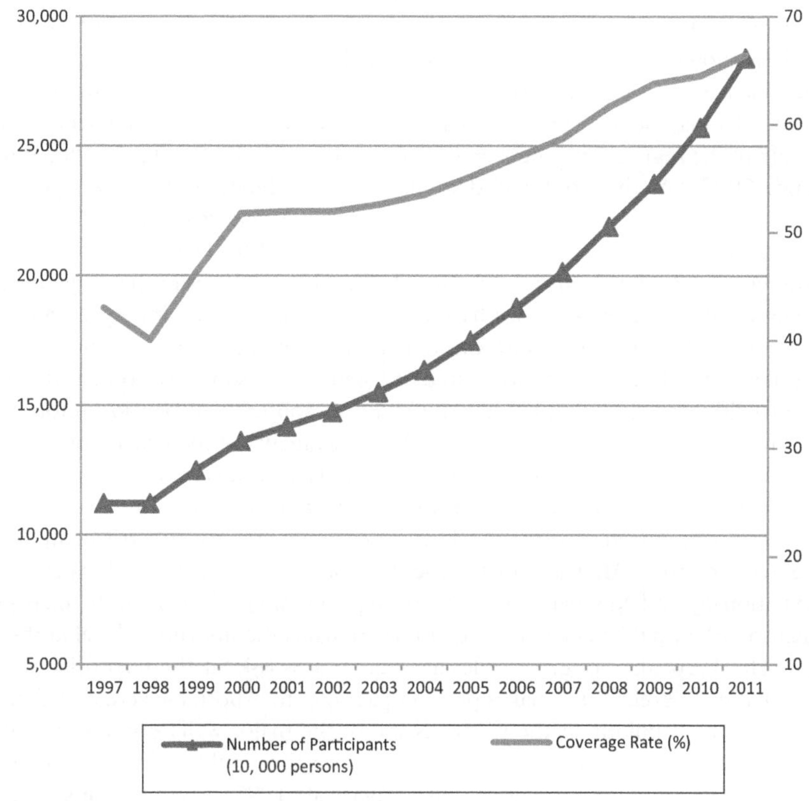

Figure 1.2 Number of participants and coverage rates of urban pension programmes (1997–2011)

Source: China Statistical Yearbook (2012). Pension coverage rates are measured as the ratio of participants of urban pension programmes to the urban workforce.

China with two large developing countries, Brazil and India. The three are members of the club named "BRICs" (Brazil, Russia, India, and China), denoting today's four most vibrant emerging economies (O'Neill 2001). Rudra (2002) puts forward a typology of welfare states in less developed countries, which distinguishes between protective welfare states and productive welfare states. While in productive welfare states social policies are directed to nourish a productive workforce demanded by the capital, so the economy can prepare to compete in the world market, protective welfare states seek to insulate domestic industries from international competition, making social rights reserved for a small, politically influential clientele. Rudra's cluster analysis classifies India and, to a less extent, Brazil as protective welfare states. This echoes the conclusions of other researchers, who report that the protective or corporatist features of the Indian and Brazilian welfare systems have persisted despite several reforms since the 1980s. For example, Allianz International Pensions (2013: 3) reports that the Indian pension system, which consists of various targeted plans for different occupation and earning groups, is "reminiscent of the country's traditional caste system". Ferrera (1996) conceptualises the welfare regime in Latin America countries, including that of the Brazil, as "clientelistic welfare state". On the other hand, Rudra's analysis shows East Asian Tiger economies like South Korea and Singapore are identified as having productive welfare states. Although Rudra's analysis does not include China, theorists on East Asian welfare states have increasingly seen China as one of the region's productivist welfare regimes (Holliday 2002; Holliday and Linda 2003). As this book will demonstrate, the Chinese state utilises pension policy as a tool to facilitate skill formation and economic growth, a defining feature of the productive welfare state. Frazier (2010: 176–182) also discerns the different approach to pension reform in China compared with other large developing countries. Therefore, we have a puzzle: While the developing world sees its democracies cater to the interests of narrow segments of society with selective social policy, China, an authoritarian party-state that is supposed to be less sensitive to citizens' needs, applies a more inclusive approach to pension reform by expanding the pension system to cover larger segments of the urban population. In the absence of genuine electoral pressures, what motivates the Chinese government to respond to the social needs for old-age income security?

The second puzzle about the Chinese pension system is its territorially fragmented structure. After almost two decades of pension reforms, China still has no nationally unified scheme for its pension programmes. In China, the management of urban public pension programmes remains the domain of local authorities. This keeps the pooling of old-age income loss risks at the territorial rather than national level, and it makes pension packages non-portable across localities. This pattern is unique in the world: None of the major welfare states, whether they are unitary or federal, large or small, have their public old-age insurance systems fragmented on a regional basis (Agarwala 1998). Despite being federal democracies where sub-national political actors tend to block national redistributive endeavours by forming coalitions to exercise their veto powers (Beramendi 2012; Obinger 2005; Tsebelis 2002), large developers such as Brazil and India

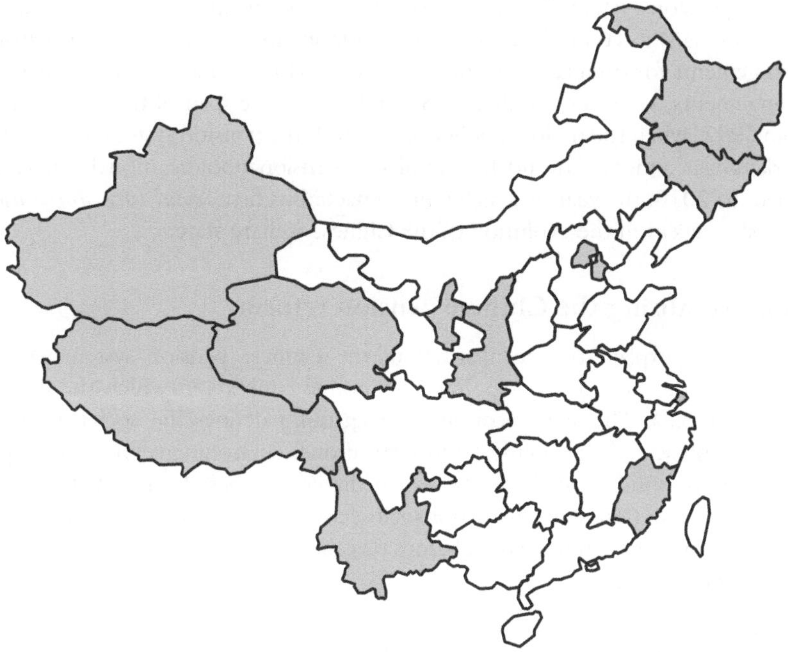

Figure 1.3 Provincial jurisdictions with provincial-level integrated pension schemes (2011)

Source: National Audit Office (2012)

have achieved the national integration of their public pension systems. China, a constitutionally unitary country with an authoritarian central government, fails to have its basic pension schemes unified at the national level. China has five levels of government. Descendingly they are the national government (i.e., the central government), province, municipality, county and township (for a more detailed introduction to the territorial structure of the Chinese state, please see Appendix 1). By 2011, of the 31 provincial-level jurisdictions in mainland China, only 13 had their pension schemes consolidated at the provincial level, while the rest of the provinces still had authority over pension provision and administration left with municipal governments (see Figure 1.3, where the 13 provinces are shaded). This presents a second puzzle, namely that while China's authoritarian central government has attempted for the past decade to achieve national pension integration, the country's pension system is still deeply fragmented along regional lines and firmly controlled by local governments.

This book therefore aims to develop a unified explanatory framework, which highlights the political-economic interaction between political institutions, pension policy and labour markets, in order to answer the question of why China's pension system is expansive and localised. Some clarifications about the research topic should be made at the outset. First, as mentioned earlier, this study focuses on the pension system for urban workers, i.e., municipal basic old-age insurance, especially its compulsory, state-run components, rather than on the pension arrangements for rural residents or civil servants (for an analysis on rural pension arrangements, see Cai et al. 2012). Secondly, the time span of this study ranges from 1997, when the national policy to establish the pension system for all urban workers was announced and the municipal pension pooling model was established, to 2010, the year in which China enacted its first *Social Insurance Law*, a watershed event in the evolution of the Chinese welfare state.

Contextualising the Chinese pension reform

One cannot explain the peculiarities of the Chinese pension system without understanding the particular political-economic contexts in which the pension reform unfolds. The socio-economic background defines the social needs for pension policy, and the political and institutional environment affects how policymakers respond to such needs, which directly shapes the resultant pension system. This section starts with the socio-economic contexts in which China's pension reform was implemented before revealing the reform's political and institutional underpinnings.

Socio-economic contexts

China's pension reform, fully implemented since 1997, unfolds against the backdrop of two structural changes in the Chinese economy in the first decade of this century: industrial upgrading and labour market tightening. The popular image of China as the world's workshop producing cheap, low-end commodities like toys and umbrellas has become increasingly outdated since the beginning of the twenty-first century. With China's accession to the WTO in 2001, the pouring into the Chinese market of foreign direct investment and technological know-how, combined with reforms on domestic regulatory frameworks on market entry according to WTO rules, injected great stimulus into the process of industrial upgrading of the Chinese economy by providing financial and technological resources as well as competition pressures. As Brandt et al. (2008: 624) observe, "ongoing domestic reform facilitates deepening engagement with global markets, and therefore promotes continued upgrading and capacity-building among Chinese manufacturers". The industrial upgrading of the Chinese economy is evident in the shift in China's export mix. As can be seen in Figure 1.4, which shows the share of different types of export commodities in China's total exports to the world in value terms, the proportion of low value-added products, like textiles and processed materials, has kept falling since the late 1990s, while the increase of the share of products at the higher end of the value chain, like electronics and heavy manufactures, has been steady and accelerated since 2001. Whereas China's exports were dominated by low-end commodities like raw materials and processed textile products a decade ago, in 2010 more than 60 percent of

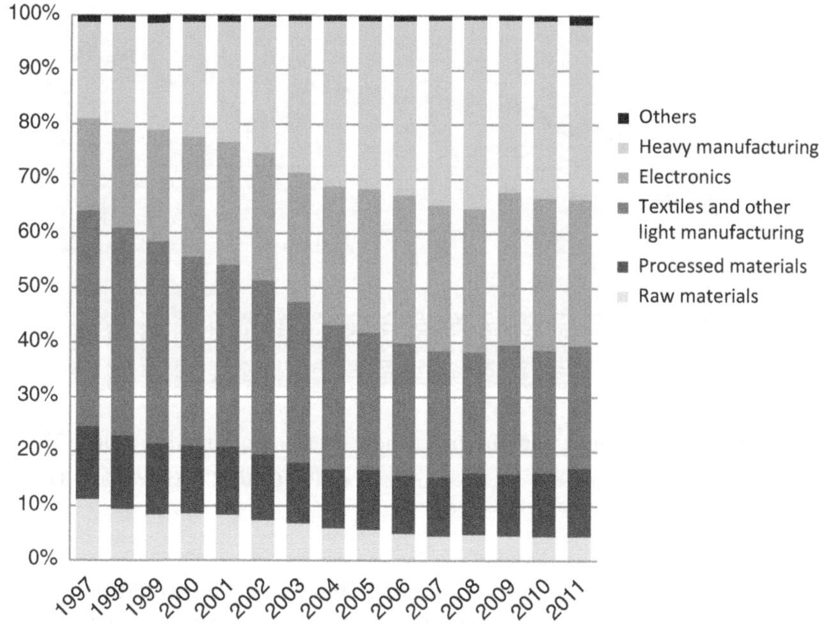

Figure 1.4 The composition of China's exports by product type (1997–2011)
Source: UN Comtrade (http://comtrade.un.org)[1]

Chinese export value came from more technologically sophisticated products (see also Brandt and Thun 2010; Herrigel et al. 2013). The fact that China now can compete at the relatively high end of the world product markets indicates the industrial structure and technological levels of the Chinese economy have seen considerable progress over the past decade.

Industrial upgrades required a corresponding skill upgrade of the Chinese workforce, and this skill upgrade coincided with the tightening of labour markets. The conventional view is that with a large population China enjoys an abundant supply of cheap labour force, which gives the country a "demographic dividend" and thus fuels its economic rise in the last three decades. This is no longer the case. Demographic transition, which is the natural result of China's rapid modernisation but also accelerated by the government's one-child policy, has led to an ageing population, with the growth of people at working age (15–64) slowing down since the early 2000s (Cai and Wang 2010). When the slow growth of working age population is met with a booming economy, the result is a tightening labour market. As shown in Figure 1.5, the ratio of job vacancies to people seeking jobs in China's urban labour markets has kept firmly increasing since 2001, only meeting brief setbacks in the recent financial crisis before bouncing back strongly in 2009. As the labour market tightens, the competition

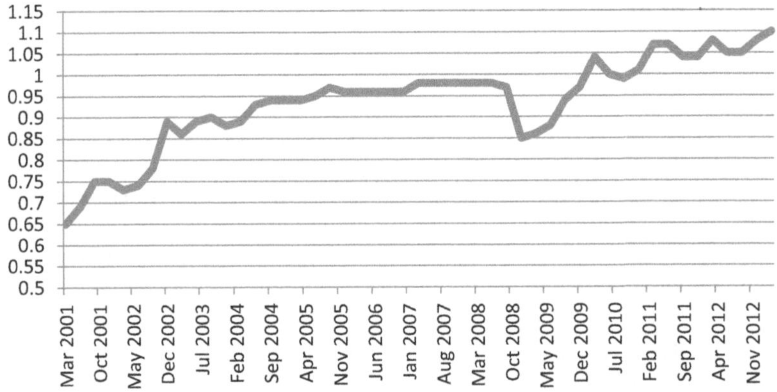

Figure 1.5 Demand-supply ratio in the Chinese urban labour market (2001–2012)

Source: Ministry of Labour and Social Security, from the CEIC China Premium Database (http://dev.ceicdata.securities.com/China.html)

for labour force is likely to intensify among employers, who would outbid each other to offer competitive compensation packages to attract and retain workers (Nee and Opper 2012). Drawing on China Household Income Project (CHIP), John Knight et al. (2011) find that even migrant workers, the traditionally least paid segment of the Chinese urban workforce, saw their real wage increase by an annual rate of 7 percent on average during the period of 2004–2009. The past decade marks the beginning of the end of cheap Chinese labour (Rein 2012).

The changing socio-economic conditions, notably industrial upgrading and labour market tightening, have profound implications for the role of social protection programmes, like pensions, in the economy and the social policy preferences of economic actors such as workers and employers. First, with the process of industrial upgrading raising the demand for a workforce with a higher level of industrial skills, social protection schemes become increasingly important in terms of facilitating skill formation. According to the literature of Varieties of Capitalism, which will be discussed in Chapter 2, comprehensive social protection programmes encourage individuals to acquire specific industrial skills by assuring them about the stability of future income. To the extent that social protection helps bring about income stability and secure the sufficient supply of skilled labour force, Chinese workers and employers, especially those who rely on specific skills for production, require expansionary social policies like the extending of the coverage of public pension programmes.

Secondly, in addition to its positive impacts on skill formation, China's social insurance system, with its localised structure, also serves to regulate the labour market competition. The tightening of labour markets intensifies the competition for skilled workforce among Chinese employers, and poaching is rampant (Li and Sheldon 2010; Sheldon and Li 2013). To retain workers, which is meant not only to have a stable workforce but also to protect employers' investments in the skill development of workers, employers have to offer higher-than-equilibrium wages. An especially effective form of such wages is the deferred benefits. As Swenson (2002: 27) argues, "insurance-type benefits, like pension, take the form of 'deferred wage', further inhibiting turnover by inducing workers to stay long enough to qualify for and then receive them". This book argues that the localised public pension scheme can serve the purpose well. It discourages labour mobility by making pension package non-portable across regions. This in turn deters poaching activity by raising the amount of money the outside employer has to offer to the poached employee, whose loss of pension rights has to be compensated. With the excessive competition in labour markets curtailed and the problem of poaching addressed, the employer then has an incentive to fund training programmes for employees, which assist skill improvement to meet the demand of industrial upgrading.

Political and institutional foundations

Socio-economic changes determine the economic functions of social protection and social policy preferences of the Chinese workers and employers (for examples of new socio-economic conditions giving rise to new demand for social policies, one can see Armingeon and Bonoli (2006), Bonoli (2007), Iversen and Wren (1998), Iversen and Cusack (2000), Emmenegger et al. (2012) and Fleckenstein et al. (2011)). But citizens' policy preferences never automatically translate into government policy. Whether policy outcome reflects citizens' preferences depends on how political institutions align the preference of policymakers with that of the populace. In other words, it is the incentive structure facing policymakers that determines whether they will make policy choices that correspond to citizens' preferences. Then who are the decision makers in China's pension reform, and what incentive structure do they face?

The major policy actor in China's urban pension reform is the leader of the municipality (Frazier 2010), and the political institution that structures his incentive is the "decentralised authoritarianism" (Landry 2008). Despite a façade of a constitutionally unitary state, China never specifies in formal rules how the centre and the locality should interact with each other. This ambiguity leaves ample room to local authorities to pursue their own developmental strategies and to manoeuvre for a position of power in their relations with the central government. In fact, the local state in China has so much autonomy and political influence that central leaders, from Mao Zedong to Deng Xiaoping, often ally with local authorities to form political coalitions in elite competition, a strategy called "playing to the province" (Shirk 1993: 162). Given the prominence of regions in the Chinese political life, one should not be surprised to find the Chinese state is characterised by a high degree of decentralisation of decision-making. As shown in Figure 1.6, the local government accounts for over 70 percent of overall public expenditures by the Chinese state, while when it comes to social policy, the local state is responsible for 86 percent of total social expenditures (including

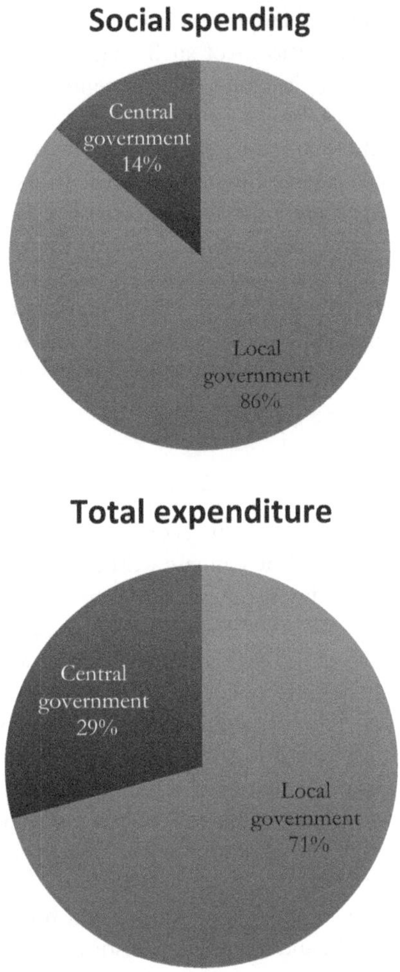

Figure 1.6 Share of central and local government spending (2000–2011)
Source: China Statistical Yearbooks (2001–2012)

the spending on social security, pension, healthcare and employment policies). Political scientists have coined various terms like "market-preserving federalism" (Weingast 1995; Qian and Weingast 1997), "Chinese style federalism" (Montinola et al. 1995) and "de facto federalism" (Zheng 2007) to capture the highly decentralised nature of the Chinese state.

With regional authorities granted such autonomy, how does the Chinese central government control them? This leads to the notion of authoritarianism. China is an authoritarian state in the sense that public officials are selected, not on the basis of competitive election, but through a rigorous cadre evaluation and promotion system tightly controlled by the party-centre and the central government (Lieberthal 2004: 208–219). It is this system that incentivises Chinese local leaders, who are office-seeking and concerned about their career advancement, to utilise their autonomy according to local conditions to achieve developmental goals set by the central government, rather than to get their own way.

One crucial feature of this "decentralised authoritarianism" (Landry 2008) is the bureaucratic promotion tournament (Edin 2003; Tsui and Wang 2004; Li and Zhou 2005), in which the central government awards the municipal leaders who perform best in achieving developmental targets like local economic growth by promoting them to higher-level government offices. The implication of the bureaucratic promotion tournament is twofold. First, Chinese local leaders are motivated to increase the likelihood of being promoted by pursuing pro-growth economic strategies to expand the regional economy of their jurisdictions. This explains the "entrepreneurial" and "developmental" behaviour of the Chinese local state (Oi 1992; Walder 1995; Blecher and Shue 1996; Duckett 1998). Secondly, local leaders are also incentivised to decrease the promotion chances of their competitors by adopting non-cooperative sabotage measures like local protectionist policies. This is the reason why leaders of Chinese local states can act like "economic warlords" who keep a tight control over access to economic resources in their own jurisdictions, be it customers, capital, or labour force (Wedeman 2003). In short, a local leader may win the competition for promotion by making himself look good and others look bad.

The other important facet of China's decentralised authoritarianism is that the central government's commitment to award the winning local officials in the promotion tournament is not always credible. The authoritarian nature of the Chinese central government means that no mechanism exists that ensures it is committed to its promise to promote the best-performing municipal leader to top provincial posts. In particular, under the arrangement of what I call "Chinese-style political decentralization", such promise is not equally credible across all regions. The credibility of the Chinese central government's commitment to promote municipal leaders can be revealed by studying the insider/outsider profile of provincial leadership. In provinces where provincial leading posts are traditionally held by home-grown insiders rising from municipalities, such commitment is much more credible and hence more motivational than in provinces that are often governed by outsiders parachuted from Beijing or elsewhere. Authors like Tsai (2007) and Persson and Zhuravskaya (2012) have reported, through case studies and statistical analysis, that a Chinese locality being governed by home-grown leaders tends to be associated with a higher level of public goods provision in the locality. They explain this by arguing that home-grown cadres have some intrinsic attributes that will make them more inclined to serve the local people through public goods provision. This study differs from them in that it sees background of local leaders not as an indication of any personal attributes, but as an indication of an incentive structure that affects the incentives of lower-level officials to provide public goods. That is to say, background of provincial leaders suggests the incentive structure facing municipal officials.

Considering the combined effects of the two institutional settings of decentralised authoritarianism in China, i.e., bureaucratic promotion tournament and Chinese-style political decentralisation, it can be inferred that the incentive of Chinese municipal leaders to adopt pro-growth policies and to engage in local protectionist activities is a function of the credibility of the central government's commitment to promotion. These two political institutions provide the basic incentive structure that shapes municipal leaders' behaviours. Then the issue becomes what pension policy this incentive structure motivates the office-seeking Chinese municipal leaders to choose in the context of industrial upgrading and labour market tightening, where a large pool of skilled labour force is a major component of the competitiveness of local economy. This book, in Chapter 3, will formulate a political-economic theory on how Chinese municipal authorities, driven by the political institutions to engage in an economic competition among them, make pension policy to facilitate the acquisition of industrial skills and the retention of industrial skilled workers.

Theoretical implications

How does a study of the Chinese case of pension reform improve our understanding of the political economy of the welfare state in general? Drawing on China's experience in pension reform, this research attempts to add to three streams of literature. The first one is the literature on the economic benefits of social protection in terms of its positive impacts on skill formation (Estevez-Abe et al. 2001; Iversen and Soskice 2001; Iversen 2005; Cusack et al. 2006). The second strand of literature is the one that investigates how state agency shapes the development of the welfare state (Heclo 1974; Weir and Skocpol 1983; Skocpol and Amenta 1986). Finally, this study tries to contribute to the literature on the institutional underpinnings of welfare politics (Birchfield and Crepaz 1998; Lijphart and Crepaz 1991; Iversen and Soskice 2006, 2009, 2010).

Mainly formulated under the Varieties of Capitalism paradigm (Hall and Soskice 2001), it has been argued that social protection can be beneficial for economic development because it gives workers incentive to invest in human capital, which is conceptualised as productive skills co-specific for both employers and employees (Estevez-Abe et al. 2001). This study tests this hypothesis in the Chinese context. On that basis, this study explores how the expansion and fragmentation of the Chinese pension system is linked with the competition between political actors on developing local economy through the training of a skilled workforce.

The Chinese case is ideal for demonstrating that economic considerations may play a crucial part in the development of the welfare state (Iversen and Soskice 2009; Mares 2001, 2003; Martin and Swank 2012). When arguing this in the settings of OECD countries, where trade unions are likely to have political leverage, it is difficult to tell whether the enactment of social legislation is a response to the pressure from the organised labour that is concerned about redistributive equality, or if it is the result of the support of social interests like employers who care more about economic efficiency (for example, see Mares 2001, 2003; Swenson 2002). In other words, with the presence of politically strong trade unions, the welfare state can always be interpreted as the product of labour playing redistributive politics against the market forces (Esping-Andersen 1985), thereby making it a daunting task to demonstrate the argument that in addition to serving the redistributive cause the welfare state also facilitates the well-functioning of the market economy through, for example, dealing with market failure in skill formation (for the debate on this issue, please refer to Korpi (2006) and Iversen and Soskice (2009)).

Compared with the cases of advanced democracies, the Chinese context makes it relatively easy to isolate and demonstrate the economic rationale behind the welfare state. The necessary organisations for the working class to use their political muscle to pursue redistributive goals, as identified in the power resource literature (for example, see Lenski 1966; Korpi 1983; Huber and Stephens 2001; Korpi and Palme 2003), are leftist parties, which are able to take part in competitive elections, and trade unions, which are independent from the state. China has neither of these. China is a one-party state, where the existence of any party other than the ruling Communist Party and the seven "political consultative parties" is illegal. In addition, Chinese unions are subservient to the Party, which is manifested in several institutional arrangements, such as that the Chairman of All-China Federation of Trade Unions must be a member of the Standing Committee of the Communist Party Politburo (Metcalf and J. Li 2005). Surely it would be oversimplifying to describe the Chinese labour movement as weak or incompetent. Labour may be mobilised in a different, non-institutional way in the Chinese context than in the historical context of the West. Indeed, authors like Ching Kwan Lee (2007: 229) and Mingwei Liu (2010) find out that unlike its Western counterpart, labour activism in China tends to be cellular and localised and vary in union strategies according to regional socio-economic conditions. But at least for the period this research studies (1997–2010), there has been no evidence showing the Chinese way of labour mobilisation, if there is any, has equipped the Chinese labour with sufficient strength to challenge the government or the capital. Even Ching Kwan Lee (2007) herself admits that the central theme for the regional economic development is one of "local accumulation" by acquisitive local officials and businessmen. Therefore, the institutional environment of China allows a possibility to rule out the impact of unions in social policymaking and focus on the economic considerations in the making of welfare policy.

Revealing the economic functions of social policy brings us new insights into the literature on the role of the state agency in welfare state development. Thanks to the contribution made by state-centred theorists (Evans, Rueschemeyer and Skocpol 1985; Skocpol and Amenta 1986), the state has been brought back onto the centre stage of public policymaking and the comparative political economy more generally, and the agency of state actors has been assigned an important role in the process of welfare state formation. The state-centred theory helps to balance the power resource theory of welfare politics, which is dominated by the analysis of social interests such as the organised labour (Korpi 1983; Korpi and Palme 2003; Esping-Andersen 1985; Hicks 1999; Huber and Stephens 2001), by exploring how state actors and ruling bureaucrats utilise social policy as a means to appease challenging social groups (see also Offe 1984), as was in the case of Bismarckian Germany and Hapsburg Austria (Flora and Alber 1981) and post-Communist Eastern European countries (Vanhuysse 2006). In short, the Statist model of welfare politics attributes the building of the welfare state to the political benefits of social policy to state actors.

But the benefits of social policy to state actors can also be economic. Drawing on the Chinese case of pension reform, this study argues that economic considerations in terms of facilitating skill formation can loom large when state actors make social policies. As will be demonstrated in this study, the political actors who make the economic calculation in China's urban pension reform are state bureaucrats, especially those working as municipal leaders. They are engaging in an economic and promotion competition in which officials seek to enhance promotion chances by outperforming one another in generating economic growth. This study shows how state actors' concerns about economic issues like skill formation shape their policy actions on welfare state building. Therefore, this study makes a contribution to our understanding of welfare state development by linking the Statist model of welfare politics, which focuses on the role of state agency in welfare state formation, with the Varieties of Capitalism theory, which reveals the economic benefits of social policy with respect to skill formation. It shows that to appease the challenging social interests is not the sole concern of state actors when they make social policy, as the Statist account of the welfare state often argues. Through social policy, the state agents also try to foster industrialisation by addressing the market failure in the formation of industrial skills, as one can see in the Chinese pension reform. From the perspective of the state, the raison d'être of social policy is not just political, but economic as well.

Examining the role of the state actor in welfare politics from the perspective of Varieties of Capitalism also contributes to the model of welfare politics that is based on economic benefits of social policy. Drawing on economic implications of welfare programmes, this model of welfare politics, termed as the cross-class alliance model (Swenson 1991; Estevez-Abe 2008), challenges the power resource theory by introducing the active participation of employers in social policymaking. In light of the business preferences for social policy, which are based on social policy's economic functions in terms of insuring against risks and containing labour management costs, it has been argued that employers may have a shared interest with the unions in the enactment of social legislations and regulations (Martin 1995, 2000; Swenson 1991, 2002; Mares 2001, 2003). That is to say, the essence of welfare politics should be accurately captured by the notion of "politics of markets" (Iversen 2005), which argues the strategic interaction among various market participants such as employers and unions shapes the welfare state in a way that enhances the efficiency of the market economy, rather than the idea of "politics against markets" (Esping-Andersen 1985), which interprets the welfare state as the organised labour's effort to wield political power to counteract the market force. By revealing the social policy preferences of the Chinese employers through analysing their statements, presented in Chapter 6, this study articulates the "politics of markets" in the Chinese context and therefore contributes to the cross-class alliance model of welfare politics.

Although it directs theoretical attention to social policy preferences of employers, the cross-class alliance theory fails to incorporate political power into the model of welfare politics. Indeed, this theory focuses on the economic calculation of societal actors such as employers and trade unions and hence their active involvement in the process of social policymaking. There is no account of the participation of political actors, such as elected politicians and state bureaucrats. This book, on the other hand, by studying the economic considerations of the Chinese state actors in pension politics, demonstrates that it is possible to build a model of welfare politics based on the economic functions of the welfare state that take political power into account.

A theory of welfare politics that incorporates political power has been provided by the new institutionalist model of social policymaking. This model understands institutions as the rules that regulate political interactions. Institutions affect policy outcomes by shaping agents' preferences, forming actors' expectations about the response of others and structuring their choices of actions. A particular focus of this set of literature is on the impact of electoral rules, which are able to shape the electoral strategies and hence the redistributive preferences and policy actions of office-seeking politicians. Most notable is that proportional representation leads to large welfare states because it structures political competition in a way that biases more social spending (Katzenstein 1985; Birchfield and Crepaz 1998; Lijphart and Crepaz 1991; Iversen and Soskice 2006, 2009; for the impact of electoral system proportionality on skill formation, see Iversen and Soskice 2010). Focusing on different types of welfare provision rather than different levels of social spending, Estevez-Abe (2008) draws on the Japanese case to demonstrate various distributive biases that emerge under different electoral rules, especially district magnitude and personal vote, which shape the competition strategies and distributive preferences of politicians. The institutional underpinnings of political competition, therefore, are an important factor shaping the pattern of welfare provision.

Although Estevez-Abe (2008) discusses the institutional constraints on the behaviours of Japanese bureaucrats, the majority of the literature on the institutionalist model of social policymaking primarily looks at electoral competition, in which politicians compete for votes in order to win electoral campaigns and get elected to the legislature. It rarely studies the bureaucratic competition, in which bureaucrats in the executive branch of the government compete for promotion to higher-ranking positions in the administrative hierarchy. This research supplements the institutionalist theory of welfare politics by studying the competition among state bureaucrats in the pension reform of China, an exemplar country in terms of bureaucratic politics. It asks the following questions: If the shaping of the Chinese pension system is driven by the competition among local state officials for economic performance and promotion opportunities, then what are the institutional underpinnings of such competition? In other words, what institutional arrangements motivate Chinese local bureaucrats to compete with each other for economic performance and career advancement, which in turn leads to competition in training a labour force with industry-specific skills through expansive and fragmenting pension policy? This book will demonstrate that in the absence of Western-style electoral competition in China, social policymaking has been shaped by bureaucratic competition that is regulated by political institutions. This, therefore, enriches our understanding of how political institutions structure political competition, manifested as electoral competition in advanced democracies and bureaucratic competition in China, which in turn shapes patterns of welfare provision.

Studying China's welfare politics from the viewpoint of institutionally shaped political competition broadens the possibility of studying the Chinese case in a comparative framework. China, because of its peculiar political system (i.e., an authoritarian regime led by a hegemonic party), has long been denied a place in the comparative political economy theories of the welfare state, which are mostly formulated on the basis of the historical experience of advanced democracies. This prevents a deeper understanding of the Chinese case with the help of the comparative political economy literature. It also denies this set of literature the opportunity to develop and enrich itself by drawing on the experience of the world's second largest economy. We can get out of this unfortunate situation by going beyond the democracy/authoritarianism dichotomy and finding a common ground on which China can be compared with other countries. Applying the notion of institutionally shaped political competition to China can be a first step to finding such common ground. China is not a member of the club of liberal democracies. But this does not mean there is no institutionally regulated competition among political actors in China. As will be shown in this study, China's political institutions give rise to bureaucratic competition among local officials, and this has profound implications for the shaping of the Chinese pension system. If we go beyond the democracy/authoritarianism contrast and place our investigation on a higher level of abstraction, then we can see that in the sense of having institutionally shaped political competition with distributive consequences, China is no different from other industrialised democracies. What we need to do is to identify which institutions regulate political competition in China and to discover how the competition affects the design of its welfare provision. After that, we may examine to what extent welfare politics in China can be compared with that in other countries and whether China can be incorporated into the comparative political economy literature on the welfare state. This study presents the first step in the efforts to situate China in the landscape of the comparative studies of the welfare state.

To summarise, building on the notion of social policy facilitating skill formation, this study formulates an institutionalist account of the pension policy actions of China's local state actors. It argues that the institutionally shaped competition between state agents to utilise the economic benefits of pension schemes leads to the expansion and fragmentation of China's urban pension system. This study therefore first contributes to the Varieties of Capitalism literature by testing its thesis in the Chinese context that social protection programmes assist skill formation. Then by revealing the Chinese state actors' economic considerations in pension policymaking, this study adds to the literature on the role of state agency in welfare state development. Finally, this study contributes to the institutionalist theory of welfare politics by demonstrating how political institutions structure the competition among Chinese state actors, which in turn shapes their pension policy preferences and actions.

Structure of the book

This study adopts mixed methods that combine quantitative approach with qualitative analysis. It is structured to reflect this methodological choice. Theoretical insights are first to be drawn from the literature. On the basis of these insights, a theory will be formulated, showing the interrelationship between political institutions, agency of state actors in the making of pension policy and skill formation on the part of workers and employers. To assess the validity of this theory, quantitative approach will be applied to test its observable implications, while qualitative analysis will be conducted to evaluate to what extent its assumptions about political and economic agents' preferences and behaviours accurately reflect the reality in China. Qualitative analysis also serves to provide micro-foundations for the macro-level statistical analysis. Only with the predictions surviving the quantitative tests and assumptions supported by qualitative materials can we demonstrate the validity of our theory.

Following this introductory chapter, Chapter 2 provides a literature review, discussing how theories on welfare state development can improve our understanding of China's pension system building. It shows that the literature on the impact of political institutions on social policymaking is especially helpful in highlighting the central role in China's pension reform played by state actors, especially those at the municipal level, and the institutional arrangements that make the interaction among them competitive and non-cooperative. The interests of Chinese municipal state actors in getting actively involved in pension reform rest with the economic benefits of pension policy in terms of facilitating the formation of productive industrial skills, as emphasised in the Varieties of Capitalism literature and the labour economics theories on individual's human capital investment.

Drawing on the insights from the literature, Chapter 3 formulates a theory from the perspective of rational choice institutionalism, which, according to Hall and Taylor's (1996) categorisation of institutionalism, refers to the institutionalist approach that examines how institutional settings shape rational actors' strategic calculation and interaction. The theory aims to show how the equilibrium of the interactions between political and economic agents leads to the expansion and localisation of China's pension system. This theory generates two predictions on the policy behaviours of the Chinese municipal leaders, namely *Expansion Hypothesis* and *Localisation Hypothesis*, and two predictions on the human capital investment decisions by workers and employers, namely *Schooling Hypothesis* and *Training Hypothesis*.

Having a theory and its predictions in place, Chapter 4 sets out to discuss the methods to be used to assess the validity of this theory. This study applies a mixed methods research strategy, combining quantitative approach with qualitative analysis, to have a comprehensive assessment of the theory. The quantitative approach is aimed at utilising statistical manipulations of large amounts of data to have systematic testing of the implications derived from the theory. The quantitative data come from statistical yearbooks on Chinese provinces, which are treated as the unit of analysis in the statistical analysis. The qualitative analysis, on the other hand, is meant to substantiate the theory by providing micro-foundations and to evaluate the theory's assumptions about agents' preferences and behaviours.

The following two chapters apply the mixed methods to assess the validity of our theory. Chapter 5 examines the impact of political institutions on pension policy behaviours of political agents. After showing the pension policy preferences of Chinese municipal leaders through their conference speeches, it tests the *Expansion Hypothesis* and *Localisation Hypothesis*, which argue that the regional variations in institutional arrangements should cause regional variations in pension policy choices by municipal leaders. Chapter 6 explores how such choices of pension policy in turn affect human capital investment decisions by economic agents. It draws on survey data and qualitative newspaper data to reveal economic agents' preferences for pension programmes, before quantitatively testing the *Schooling Hypothesis* and *Training Hypothesis* to see how workers and employers make human capital investment decisions in response to local pension arrangements.

While the venture of this research is rooted in academic scholarship, it also wishes to speak to policy debates ongoing in China today. So Chapter 7, in addition to summarising the preceding chapters, concludes this book by discussing how the political-economic framework of this research can improve our understanding of wider economic issues in China. This study comes at an uncertain point in the trajectory of China's economic rise, when the slowing economic growth due to the global recession has exposed the greatest weakness of the Chinese economy, namely the imbalanced growth model. This model is characterised by the unusual prominence of the export-led manufacturing sector and the equally uncommon lagged development of the service economy. In offering insights into how China's welfare state is embedded in the developmental strategy of supplying a workforce with industry specific skills, the political-economic framework formulated in this study provides an institutionalist explanation of China's imbalanced economic growth model: The expansive Chinese welfare state, which rises in a political context of interregional competition, favours the growth of the manufacturing sector by subsidising the production of industrial specific skills, and constrains the expansion of the service economy by imposing heavy social security taxes. The net result is the imbalanced growth formula. This study, therefore, not only contributes to the literature on the service economy expansion and its relationship with the welfare state by applying the literature's theoretical insights to the Chinese case (for examples of this set of literature, see

Iversen and Soskice 2010; Wren 2013), but also engages with the policy debate in today's China on how to rebalance the Chinese economy by offering a fresh perspective of the causes of the imbalanced growth model.

Note

1 Following the procedure used by Australian Treasury (www.treasury.gov.au), this study classifies export products coded as the two-digit product classification codes of the HS classification system into the following high-level product groupings. Raw materials: refers to the sum of: live animal product (01–05); vegetable product (06–14); animal or vegetable fat or oil (15); mineral product (25–27); and wood and article, and charcoal (44–46). **Processed materials**: refers to the sum of: prepared foodstuffs, beverage and tobacco (16–24); product of chemical or allied industry (28–38); plastics, rubber and article thereof (39–40); pulp of wood, paper, and paperboard (47–49); and articles of stone, cement or glass (68–70).**Textiles and other light manufacturing**: refers to the sum of: raw hide, skin and leather (41–43); textile and textile articles (50–63); footwear, headgear and umbrellas (64–67); and miscellaneous manufactured articles (94–96). **Electronics**: refers to the sum of: electrical equipment (85); and optical equipment, clocks and musical instruments (90–92). **Heavy manufacturing**: refers to the sum of: vehicle, aircraft, vessel and transport equipment (86–89); arms and ammunition (93); nuclear reactor, boiler and machinery (84); and base metals and articles thereof (72–83). **Other**: refers to the sum of: pearl, precious stones and metals (71); art, collector's piece and antiques (97–98); and commodities not classified according to kind (99).

2 Explaining pension reform in China

The relevance of welfare state development theories

This chapter reviews three sets of literature. They are the literature on the logic of industrialism in welfare state development, the Statist account of social policymaking and the theories on the positive impacts of social policy on skill formation. The literature on industrialism and late-industrialisation highlights the central role of the state in the process of welfare state modernisation in late-industrialising countries such as China. The discussion of the literature on the role of state institutions in social policymaking suggests that institution matters in shaping the social policy behaviours of political agents. In the Chinese context, the political agent that plays a leading part in China's pension reform is the Chinese local state at the municipal level, which competes against its counterparts to promote local economic development. According to the labour economics literature and the Varieties of Capitalism theory, one instrument that could be employed by Chinese local leaders to foster regional economy is social security policy, which facilitates the formation of specific industrial skills. Such economic function of social protection makes it crucial for local industrialisation and economic expansion. These insights constitute the basis on which this book formulates its theory on the political-economic logic of the Chinese pension system.

Logic of industrialism

Many would attribute the development of the Chinese pension system to China's rapid economic expansion and increasingly ageing population, echoing the argument of industrialism logic. One can distinguish between the old and new "logic of industrialism". The first generation of "industrialism logic" draws on the modernisation paradigm to explain the rising social expenditures throughout the industrialised nations in the early postwar years. It is argued that industrialisation generates the social risks that traditional social institutions, like kinship and patrimonial arrangements, are inadequate to deal with (Kerr et al. 1960). This renders vulnerable those who are unable to participate in and generate incomes from capitalist labour markets, such as the old and the sick (Pampel and Weiss 1983). This requires the state to step in to increase public spending on social programmes, which is made possible by the material wealth generated from industrial expansion (Wilensky and Lebeaux 1958). The result of the "logic of industrialism", therefore, is the growth of the welfare state.

Cutright (1965) and Wilensky (1975) were among the first to test empirically the industrialism account of welfare state development. The study by Wilensky (1975) is especially important for two reasons. First, Wilensky's quantitative analysis identifies economic growth and population ageing to be the most crucial factors that contribute to welfare state expansion. This is central to subsequent studies, in which GDP per capita and the share of the elderly in the population become default controls in empirical testing of theories on welfare state development. Secondly, Wilensky (1975: 24) argues "economic growth is the ultimate cause of welfare state development". This implies that all nations, with their economies reaching a similar stage of development, would eventually converge at comparable levels of welfare state maturity. This view constitutes what Myles and Quadagno (2002) call the strong version of the industrialism theory on welfare state expansion.

This version of industrialisation theory, which predicts a convergence of national welfare states, is later developed into a "new logic of industrialism" (Pierson 1996: 148). In this theory, the economic determinism is found not in the force of industrialisation, but in the weight of globalisation. It is argued that economic integration of the world market, especially that of capital markets, constrains fiscal and monetary policy options of national governments, which now have to engage in tax competition in the increasingly globalised world economy (Rodrik 1997; Steinmo 1994; Strange 1996; Tanzi 1995). The implication for the welfare state is clear: With the national government's control over tax bases weakened, social transfers and services, which are funded by national taxes, have to be rolled back (Schwartz 1994). Unlike the old logic of industrialism, which predicts an upward convergence of national welfare efforts, the new version of industrialism logic expects to see a downward trend among welfare states in an era of globalisation.

This relates to the "social dumping" thesis. The term "social dumping" refers to the situation where national governments reduce social benefits and employment protection to enhance the competitiveness of their economies, anticipating firms would choose to operate at or relocate to countries with low social costs in the global market (Alber and Standing 2000: 99). The result of every government doing so is a "race to the bottom", a metaphor originally made by William Cary (1974) to describe the regulatory competition among U.S. states, which is updated in the social policy literature to refer to a convergence towards very rudimentary national welfare states. The "social dumping" thesis is applied in the context of increasingly intensified international competition, which can result from incorporation of less developed countries into the world market (Sinn 2001), integration of EU single market (Mosley 1995) and EU eastern enlargement (Vaughan-Whitehead 2003).

In addition to failing to explain the timing of the first adoption of the social security programmes (Collier and Messick 1975), the logic of industrialism is also unable to explain the non-convergence of the welfare states in the developed world. Indeed, to the contrary of what this theory predicts, being at comparable levels of economic development does not lead industrialised countries to spend the same proportion of their national wealth on social programmes. In fact, the discrepancy in welfare efforts of the developed nations has persisted, if not increased, since the early postwar years, with the Nordic countries and the Anglo-Saxon nations at the two ends of the spectrum (Lindert 2004). As for the "race to the bottom" argument, the other version of the convergence thesis, no statistical evidence has been found to support it. Instead, authors have observed a continuation of national differences in spite of the supposedly levelling effects of globalisation, which is attributed to the cross-national differences in domestic political and institutional factors (Garrett 1995, 1998; Rhodes 1996; Swank 1998). Although the logic of industrialism is not successful in explaining cross-national differences between rich democracies, it is generally believed this argument "explained broad social policy differences between rich and poor nations" (Pierson 1996: 148). But as will become clear later, when we assess the industrialism logic argument in the Chinese context, this thesis is actually not more helpful in explaining the situations of social policy in developing countries such as China, due to its neglect of the historical condition of late-industrialisation.

The logic of industrialisation literature identifies the social demands generated by industrialisation and economic growth, and the Chinese story to some extent is consistent with this logic. Over the past three decades, China's economic growth has been almost uninterrupted, averaging at around 10 percent a year, which consequently makes China the second largest economy in the world in terms of nominal GDP (The Economist 2010a). With economic prosperity comes the improvement of human wellbeing and then the heavy burden of caring for the elderly people. According to World Health Organisation (2011), life expectancy of the Chinese people now reaches 76 years (74 years for men and 77 years for women). The average annual growth rate of the population aged over 60 is 3 percent, three times the natural increase rate of the national population. As a result, the trend of population ageing puts the pension system under great pressure. In 1978, the ratio of the number of pensioners to the number of active contributors in China was 1:30. This figure changed dramatically to 1:5.4 in 1989 and 1:3.5 in 2001 and is projected to reach 1:1.69 in 2050 (Ministry of Labour and Social Security 2001). Population ageing therefore constitutes an important backdrop to China's pension reform.

From this demographic perspective, voluminous analyses of the Chinese pension system are produced to offer policy recommendations on how the government should respond to the financial burden posed by the demographic pressure (for example, see World Bank 1997; Finer 2003). *The Graying of the Middle Kingdom* by Jackson and Howe (2004) documents and predicts the trend of demographic transformation in China caused by falling fertility and rising longevity, and warns about a likely financial crisis for China's pension system half a century later unless the Chinese government, first and foremost, pumps more funds into this system and makes the individual account fully funded. West (1999) reports several government-led reforms on the pension arrangement in responses to the ageing Chinese population, arguing that the decision to dismantle the enterprise-based welfare system was made on the grounds that the old system would be financially unsustainable to meet the challenge posed by a declining worker-retiree ratio.

These studies, though quite informative in documenting demographic statistics and innovative in offering reform measures, "tend to take for granted the capacity of states to implement ambitious and complicated new schemes for the provision of old-age income to pensioners", as Mark Frazier (2004: 45) criticises. Indeed, most studies, often commissioned by international development organisations like the World Bank, deal with the reform of old-age income security arrangements in developing countries and transition economies, where limited state capacity is usually a defining feature due to the strength of social forces, as Midgal (1988) finds in several African countries, and due to the fragmented structure of the state, as we shall see in the Chinese case. The policy-oriented studies based on the industrialisation/demographic transition perspective are correct in pointing out that if we would take proper actions the ageing population would not become a time bomb. But this does not mean the demographic pressure would translate automatically into certain state actions like those they recommend. Without taking into account the limited state capacity of developing countries, these studies often offer unrealistically ambitious policy options, like that "the foundation of the retirement system must be a universal floor of protection" (Jackson and Howe 2004: 23), and make the pension reform measures actually taken in practice puzzling, like the Chinese pension system's low level of risk pooling, which should have been heightened years ago given the mounting financial pressure caused by a declining worker-pensioner ratio. Paying no attention to the actual ability of the state is the first drawback of the literature on China's pension reform inspired by the industrialism and demographic perspective.

A second drawback of this set of literature is its ignorance of the specific historical situation in which developing countries like China are caught, that is, the late-industrialisation. Industrialisation alone cannot account for the demographic pressure on China's pension system. Despite its sustained economic growth, China's GDP per capita has only reached the level of Japan in the early 1960s (Hubacek et al. 2007). China, therefore, with a developing country economy, has already become one of the fastest ageing countries in the world, confronted with the problem of population ageing that is expected to be found only in developed economies. Another way to illustrate this is to note that China's population ages faster than the industrial countries historically did. For example, it took Belgium more than 100 years to have the share of the population over 60 increase from 9 to 18 percent. The same transition would take only 34 years in China (World Bank 1994: 2). One may hold the one-child policy responsible for China's faster-than-usual demographic transformation. After all, the policy was launched in 1979, it clearly has profound depressive effects on fertility rates and therefore it should be contributing to China's population ageing which has accelerated since its implementation (White 2006; Zhang and Goza 2006). This may to some extent account for China's faster transition to an ageing society, but it cannot explain the demographical transition of other developing countries that have never had any birth control policy. For example, Venezuela will take even less time than China, that is, 22 years, to double the percentage of the population over 60 from 9 to 18 percent. It is clear that the logic of industrialisation is unable to explain why developing countries have to deal with the demographic pressure that is expected to only come at a higher economic development stage. Then why do developing countries grow old before they get rich?

This is because what developing countries are experiencing is not industrialisation but late-industrialisation. What matters is not only what you do but also when you do it. Difference in timing could be crucial. Building on the historical analysis by Gerschenkron (1962), Amsden (1989) formulates the late-industrialisation theory. Amsden argues that late-industrialisers, i.e., countries that had not started industrialisation until the twentieth century, such as South Korea and India, borrowed technologies and institutions from the pioneer modernisers to upgrade their production procedures, thereby catching up with the leaders in the industrialised Western world. This book argues that the advantage of backwardness in learning from pioneers is not confined to the field of productive technology and industrial policy; it can also exist in the field of welfare-related technologies, policies and institutions. For example, the transfer of medical technology and equipment from the former Soviet Union to China during the 1950s and 1960s helped greatly to improve the health and wellbeing of the Chinese people (Zhang et al. 2004). The World Bank (1994) reports that the massive diffusion of medical knowledge contributes to the population ageing trend in developing countries. The point here is not to fully discuss the role of backwardness advantage in welfare state development in the developing world, but to make it clear that the logic of industrialisation, mainly drawing on the historical experience of the pioneering industrialised countries in the West, is inadequate to explain the demographic pressure confronting developing countries. Instead, the development of welfare programmes of developing countries should be put in the context of late-industrialisation, in which countries like China once exploited the backwardness advantage to achieve a relatively high degree of human development but now has to deal with the demographic pressures resulting from their former success at a low stage of economic development.

A further implication of late-industrialisation is that it gives the state a prominent role in the society's resource allocation process. As Gerschenkron (1962) observes, most late-developers, if they are to catch up with industrialised pioneers, have to concentrate their limited amount of capital to invest in some pivotal industries, the so-called commanding heights of the national economy. This was what the Germans did for the chemical and electronic manufacturing industries in the late nineteenth and early twentieth centuries and what the Japanese did for the ship-building industry in the interwar period. The only actor with the interest to do this is the state. Other social sectors, like the business sector, however organised and powerful they might be, represent a mere fragment of the society. Only the state, being the legitimate monopoly of political power over a territory in the Weberian sense, has the interest and willingness in such nationwide investment. The prominence of the state in late-industrialisers' catching-up strategy and modernisation project, pension programme being an important component, is a historical necessity.

This tells us why developing countries including China struggle with the modernisation of their pension systems. Being late-industrialisers means they have to rely on the state to do this daunting task, which is made even more difficult by their "growing old before getting rich" through backwardness advantage. But being developing countries means they often lack necessary economic resources to strengthen the state capacity through institution building and staff training. A state is weak when and where it is most needed. This is probably the root of many social and political problems in the developing world. To be sure, being late-industrialising and being developing are two faces of the same coin. However, it is this coin that the industrialism theory and the numerous studies inspired by it tend to overlook when they deal with issues in developing countries.

Similar to the late-industrialisation argument, the logic of industrialism theory also points to the necessity of state intervention in modernisation programmes like social welfare provision. The traditional social institutions like the family are inadequate to deal with the social risks in an industrial era. Tu et al. (1989) trace the changes of average household size in Mainland China throughout the twentieth century and find it in constant decrease (reaching 4.43 person per family in 1982), meaning that the traditional extended family has been gradually replaced by the modern nuclear family. The one-child policy put in place since the late-1970s in particular has a serious consequence, which is the "4–2–1" family. It refers to the situation where the only grown-up child has to shoulder the responsibility of taking care of the two parents and the four grandparents (Leung 2003). It is obvious that such a nuclear family is unable to take the responsibility to care for the elderly in China. Clearly here is a family failure.

Then how about the market? Authors like Esping-Andersen (1999) have given strong theoretical accounts to explain why markets are ultimately insufficient to deal with social risks. For example, problems of adverse selection and moral hazard rampant in the market render the private annuity market unable to distinguish between people likely to be long-lived and people likely to be short-lived, whereby the annuity prices are driven up, resulting in inefficient market outcomes (also see Barr 1989). These theoretical arguments hold for China. Furthermore, with highly underdeveloped financial markets, China is in an even worse position to utilise the market to deal with its social risks. According to a Goldman Sachs report, for example, China's stock markets are the "most immature" in Asia (Bloomberg 2010). The structure of Shanghai equity market, China's most dynamic and capitalised equity market, is still relatively undeveloped by regional standards as Chinese regulators have taken a gradualist approach to market development. For example, the free float level at Shanghai's share market, which is only 30 percent, is the lowest among the benchmark stock exchanges in most Asian-Pacific nations, dwarfed by, for example, Australia and Japan, which have the levels of free float at 91 and 76 percent, respectively (Bloomberg 2010).

Likewise, China's bond market is immature, where failure to honour both corporate bonds and local government bonds often upset not only the purchasers but also the central bank, and it only develops slowly as a share of financial intermediation (Keidel 2009). It seems that at least in the near term, China's financial markets seem unable to handle the tremendous task of financing the insuring of the ageing Chinese society.

The implication of the family failure and the market underdevelopment is that the government should step in to provide and administrate a public pension system. This is also consistent with the argument of the late-industrialisation literature, which emphasises the important role of the state in late-industrialising countries in their modernisation projects. Then why do researchers studying China's pension reform through the lens of the industrialism paradigm often fail to take the state capacity into account when offering policy prescriptions? This may be due to a Eurocentric perspective, which takes the administrative capacity of the state found in Europe as given in other countries (for a critique of the Eurocentricity of western modernisation theories, see Mehmet 2002). Or maybe the researchers are dazzled by the achievements of the Chinese state in the past three decades in terms of generating economic growth and therefore assume it is naturally having a "getting things done" quality. In later chapters, this study will open the black box of the Chinese state and show how it is constrained by several institutional arrangements in pension reform, thereby dismissing the popular myth of the omnipotent Chinese party-state.

Although acknowledging the central role of the state in pension reform, both of the industrialism and late-industrialisation literature stop here. Neither of them step further to ask important questions concerning the implication of the territorial structure of the state: Which level of government should take the responsibility of pension policymaking? Why do some countries have pension administration controlled by the national government while in others the authority to administer pension programmes resides with sub-national authorities? How is this arrangement affected by the institutions that govern the relations between the central and regional governments? These questions are of particular relevance for China where pension administration is the domain of provincial and municipal governments. To tackle these questions, one therefore needs to review the literature on the relationship between state institution and welfare state development.

State institutions

As put forward by Skocpol (1985) in *Bringing the State Back in*, the state in the state-centred literature is conceptualised in two senses. First, viewed from the Weberian perspective, the state is treated as an independent political actor, capable of "fully autonomous state actions" (Skocpol 1985: 15). In other words, the state ceases to be merely reflective of the interests of social classes or just an instrument through which social groups realise their goals. Instead, the state has its own aims, the raison d'état, and is armed with necessary personnel and organisational resources to achieve these aims free from the pressures of the society.

Secondly, the state is understood through the Tocquevillian lens as "configurations of organization and action that influence the meanings and methods of politics for all groups and classes in society" (Skocpol 1985: 28). That is to say, the state itself, with its own institutions and the policy environment it creates, constitutes a field in which all actors, state bureaucrats and social groups alike pursue their goals, interact with each other and shape the political outcome. The majority of the Statist literature follows either of the two perspectives.

Let us start with the Weberian approach, which examines the state as an autonomous political actor. This thrust of the state-centred theory has identified the state bureaucracy as an active and crucial element in the process of public policymaking. Heclo (1974) compares the policy formation process in Britain and Sweden, two countries with highly centralised bureaucracy, and finds that civil servants were quite important in the initiating of policy innovations. In the American context, Skowronek (1982) dispels the assumed weak state image of the United States and highlighted bureaucratic expansion at the turn of the twentieth century. For example, administrative autonomy can be discerned in Social Security Administration, where programme administrators, although constrained by the policy guidelines of the ruling party, are able to define and implement policy priorities for the public old-age assistance programme (Cates 1983; Derthick 1979). This approach helps to overcome the drawback of T. H. Marshall's (1950) social citizenship theory as identified by Mann (1987) as over-emphasising the role of social interests like the rising bourgeois and proletariat at the expense of overlooking the strategy of the ruling class implemented through the state apparatus. Indeed, in the history of the welfare state too often social legislations were initiated by the ruling monarchist rather than by any social forces in opposition, as in the case of Bismarckian Germany and Hapsburg Austria, and an analysis of the administrative capacity of the ruling class enabled by the state apparatus helps to explain why that was the case (Flora and Alber 1981).

The state bureaucracy is an important actor in the formation of social policy. Obviously, it operates and interacts with other policy actors within the constraints of state institutions. This brings us to the Tocquevillian perspective of the state, which views the state as a set of institutional arrangements and policy settings that structure domestic politics (Skocpol 1985: 28). In the case of social policymaking, it is argued that social policy is shaped by the institutional configurations and policy legacies of the state (Skocpol and Amenta 1986). This approach first leads to the state capacity thesis, which, with the state capacity indicated by the centralisation and bureaucratisation of the state apparatus, argues "strong states are likely to produce strong welfare states" (Pierson 1996: 152). In a comparative study of the health insurance reform in Sweden, Switzerland and France, Immergut (1992) shows successful reforms depend upon the centralisation of the state executive. Orloff and Skocpol (1984) demonstrate that the lagged development of the bureaucratisation of the American state explains the late introducing of social policy initiatives in the United States, especially when compared with Britain, which developed a centralised state bureaucracy before mass democratisation. On the other hand, state institutions that reduce the administrative cohesion and capacity of the state, like federalism and separation of powers, tend to impede welfare state development. For example, the Canadian federalism, by fragmenting political authority and providing multiple accesses to the social policymaking process, facilitates minority groups to block unfavourable social legislations (Banting 1987), even though the strong party discipline in the Canadian parliamentary system is often able to thwart the lobbying effort of social groups (Maioni 1998). Likewise, in the United States, the federal structure of the American state allowed Southern politicians to bring racial divide as a salient issue into the making of American social policy until the 1960s (Quadagno 1988).

Apart from shaping welfare policy by imposing state institutions on social policymaking, the state also affects welfare state development through its policy legacies. Two themes emerge following this line of logic. First, social programmes created by the state in the past, by generating their own constituents, affect the formation of interest groups, which in turn influences welfare politics in the future. This leads Pierson (1996, 2001) to portray the politics of containing social benefits as "new politics of the welfare state", in which beneficiaries of past social programmes make the retrenchment difficult, contributing to the "frozen welfare state landscape" that exhibits stable social spending (Esping-Andersen 1996: 24).

The second theme of the policy legacy thesis puts an emphasis on policy learning. As Heclo (1974: 315) puts it, "policy invariably builds on policy, either in moving forward what has been inherited, or amending it". That is to say, in explaining today's policy, one has to look at previous governmental efforts dealing with similar social problems, which impose policy and cognitive constraints on state activity afterwards (Shefter 1977; Skocpol and Finegold 1982). For example, in the United States, the making of the Social Security Act of 1935 was affected by the prior social legislation initiatives made by the state government in the old-age pension and unemployment insurance (Skocpol and Ikenberry 1983). This understanding of policy as a result of building on previous government actions echoes the path dependence theory, which argues past circumstances may accumulate over time to constitute long-term equilibria (David 1985; Pierson 1993, 2000). A less researched aspect of the policy learning argument is the possibility that the welfare state can get its institutional form by adopting practices from other policy areas. Gordon (1988), in documenting the evolution of the industrial relations in Japan from 1835 to 1955, reveals that the institutional settings of the enterprise-based labour management system were imitated from the state bureaucracy newly established after the Meiji Restoration. In a similar vein, Bian (2009) traces the origins of China's bureaucratised workplace-based welfare arrangement to the bureaucratic traditions of the late Chinese imperial dynasties, thereby refuting the conventional view that the Soviet practice on state welfare provision inspired China's socialist enterprise-based welfare regime.

The policy learning argument is based on one assumption. The analysis of this assumption will help to reveal one theoretical pitfall of the state-centred approach. By focusing on the impacts of previous state activity on governmental action, the policy-learning argument makes an assumption about the preferences and behaviours that the state actors have. Policymakers, as assumed in the policy learning thesis, base their actions on prior state policy. That is to say, state actors do not derive their behaviours from any internal preference or external social pressure. Instead, they form future goals and actions on the basis of what they did before. In this way, public policymaking is an "inherently historical process", in which the dependence on the past path becomes the self-reinforcing dynamic (Quadagno 1987: 119). The preferences of the state actor, accordingly, become irrelevant. The problem with this view is that it does not apply to times of crisis or rapid social change. Indeed, during normal times, when the past practice is still believed to be viable, learning from previous decisions could be a feasible model of policymaking. But when policymakers are caught in times of crisis, like the Great Depression in the 1930s, or in times of radical social change, like China's post-socialist transition, they tend to repudiate the past, and the policymakers' preferences matter greatly in determining what new policies they will choose. For example, comparing the experiences of the United States and Sweden in the 1930s and 1980s, Blyth (2002) shows politicians' policy preferences, which primarily came from the economic ideas they held, had causal impacts on the two states' policy reactions to economic crises. Therefore, when we look beyond normal times, the preferences of state actors become important in explaining public policymaking. Unfortunately, there is no consensus in the state-centred literature about state bureaucrats' preferences. Sometimes they try to maintain social stability (Flora and Alber 1981) or ensure regime survival (Johnson 1982). At other times the state officials simply seek to guard their administrative turf (Cates 1983) or manage larger budgets and administrative organisations (Skocpol 1995). The Statist literature falls short of providing theoretical foundations of the state actor's preferences. This is one major drawback of this set of literature.

A remedy to this pitfall is provided by the rational choice theory. While it can be traced to philosophers in the social contract tradition like Thomas Hobbes and John Locke (Monroe 2001), the modern rational choice approach to social and political science was developed by a group of economists through the 1950s to 1960s (Ordeshook 1990), based on the conviction that individuals are the ultimate unit of social analysis, a position termed as methodological individualism which will be discussed in detail in Chapter 4. Kenneth Arrow's (1951) seminal contribution puts forward the impossibility theorem, demonstrating the inherent conflict between the individual and collective rationality in democratic society. Anthony Downs's (1957) *An Economic Theory of Democracy*, assuming political actors to be rational maximisers of individual utility as opposed to social welfare, makes the proposition that self-interested politicians seek to maximise votes in electoral competition. This inspired later development in the spatial model of voting, in which rational electoral candidates compete for voters' support by converging to the centre point of the ideological space (Shepsle and Bonchek 1997). The assumption about the individual rationality of political actors is also adopted by other prominent rational choice theorists. Buchanan and Tullock (1962: 305) assert that each participant in the political game seeks to further their own interests "at the expense of others if this is necessary". Mancur Olson (1965: 65), in his theory on collective action, argues actors are rational in the sense that their interests are pursued by means "that are efficient and effective for achieving these objectives". William Riker (1962: 22), one of the pioneers in the application of rational choice approach to political science, states boldly that "politically rational man is the man who would rather win than lose, regardless of the particular stakes".

The individual rationality assumption sets a starting point for analysing the preferences and hence the behaviours of state actors. On this basis, the rational choice approach develops its theory of the state. Margaret Levi (1988), drawing on historical cases from the Roman Republic to French Revolution, applies game theoretical language to show how self-interested public officials bargain with subjects and citizens to expand the state capacity to extract fiscal resources from the society. Writing in the tradition of Douglas North (1986), who applies the neoclassicial economics approach to the analysis of the state, Yoram Barzel (2002), in his book *A Theory of the State*, gives the most theoretically informed account of the nature of the state, which is understood as a solution to the problem of enforcing property rights in a world of economic transactions among rational individuals. Based on game theory, Masahiko Aoki (2001) develops a general framework for comparative institutional analysis, in which different kinds of institutions, including the state, are rules of the games in equilibrium.

The most renowned theorist who applies the rational choice approach to the state bureaucracy is William Niskanen (1971). As the title of his book *Bureaucracy and Representative Government* indicates, Niskanen explores how elected politicians control permanent civil servants. Adopting the individual rationality assumption, Niskanen argues state bureaucrats are self-interested, rational actors. Specifically, they are budget maximisers, seeking to obtain the largest possible budget in their negotiation with the politicians (the sponsor) to enrich themselves (in the form of higher salary, better benefits, bigger office buildings, etc.). Here Niskanen formalises the assumption implicitly recognised in the Statist literature that bureaucrats seek to run larger budgets (for example, see Skocpol 1995). This revenue-maximising assumption proves influential, becoming the standard assumption about the preferences of bureaucrats in many later analyses (Mueller 2003). Bureaucrats' efforts to maximise budgets are taken responsible for the rapid expansion and the low efficiency of the bureaucratic machine. Subsequent literature is devoted to alter the parameters of the Niskanenian model, like the assumption on the negotiation process (Romer and Rosenthal 1978; McGuire et al. 1979) and the assumption on the informational asymmetry between the bureaucrat and the politician (Miller and Moe 1983). Few efforts have been made to assess the budget-maximising assumption, suggesting its wide acceptance as an accurate description of the preferences of the state bureaucrat. As we shall see below, this assumption only has very limited applicability in the context of China's bureaucratic politics.

It is such unquestioning acceptance of its bold assumptions that often puts the rational choice theory at risk of making unrealistic arguments. As Green and Shapiro (1994) point out, rational choice theorists have the ambition to formulate universal theories of politics. This is commendable, but it often leads to "a debilitating syndrome in which theories are elaborated and modified in order to save their universal character" (Green and Shapiro 1994: 7). This is why rational choice theorists often make bold general assumptions about the preferences and behaviours of political agents, which are necessary for building universal theories, but which may not capture the reality correctly. One may need to use extra caution when applying the rational choice theory to a non-Western context like China. Indeed, despite its universalist aspiration, the rational choice theory is formulated on the basis of the experiences of Western democracies. The universalist assumptions it makes seldom conform with varying national contexts of different democracies in the West, not to mention the context of China. This requires us to assess the applicability of the rational choice theory of the state bureaucracy and the Statist approach in general in the Chinese context.

The Statist approach, by putting the state in the centre of public policymaking, is of great relevance for studying China. This is because in this country the state is often the single most important agent in the policymaking process. China was characterised by Dr. Sun Yat-sen, Father of Modern China, as "a heap of loose sand", meaning that the Chinese society has a class structure in which "all classes are weak" (Meisner 1999: 16). Consequently, Chinese social interests have little power over the making of public policy, leaving the state in the centre of the stage. Indeed, an undemocratic state without the check of any powerful social interests, the Chinese state exemplifies the notion of "strong state". Thus, the welfare reform that the Chinese state undertakes should serve as a most-likely-case of the state capacity argument discussed above. In other words, if there is any empirical case for the state capacity thesis, then it should be China. However, despite all the success and impressive performance in other aspects of economic reform, in the area of social policy the Chinese state's efforts to transform a localised pension system into a more unified one have only achieved very limited progress. Then the Chinese case seems to cast some doubts on the state capacity literature. What prevents the Chinese state from wielding its seemingly omnipotent power?

This leads us to the dilemma the Chinese polity is caught in. The Chinese state has to maintain control over a country with a vast geographical extension and great ethical and regional diversities. One cannot rule a country like this simply from Beijing. Instead, one has to delegate. So the Chinese state adopts a highly fragmented and decentralised structure (Landry 2008; Lieberthal and Lampton 1992). This is not simply to generate administrative efficiency from division of labour. More importantly, this is meant to ensure the local government's responsiveness to local needs and interests, hoping to gain the performance legitimacy, a type of state legitimacy which is crucial for the legitimation of the Chinese state but which Weber ignores when he formulates his theory of domination (Zhao 2009). Paradoxically, the decision of the central government to decentralise, aiming to realise efficiency and to acquire political legitimacy, creates powerful political interests that sometimes are even challengers to the central state itself. Such political interests are the territorial authorities.

Although formally declared as a unitary state in the Constitution, China never specifies in formal rules how the centre and the locality should interact with each other (Goodman 1986; Zheng 2007). This ambiguity leaves ample room to local authorities to pursue their own developmental strategies and to manoeuvre for a position of power in their relations with the central government (Florini et al. 2012). The Chinese provincial government enjoyed considerable autonomy even in the Maoist years (Granick 1990: 73). This decentralised structure has been further fostered since the post-Mao market transition through a series of institutional innovations, including the introduction of the public finance system that shared taxation and other important government revenues between the central and the provincial governments. Against this background, the province has been playing an increasingly important role in the Chinese political economy, as have been documented in many studies. For example, local experimentations by regional governments that prove effective are often borrowed by the central government to formulate nationwide reform directives (Oi 1999; Walder 1995). In the area of macroeconomic policymaking, Huang (1996) examines several rounds of economic overheating during the early reform era (1978–1993) and finds that this is largely caused by the "investment hunger" of the provincial government, which defied the central command to curtail government projects and continued to invest in order to stimulate the regional economy. Huang's multivariate regression analysis of a panel of data on 27 provinces during this period shows a significant association between the willingness of provincial officials to implement austerity policy and the number of posts they take in the Central Committee of Chinese Communist Party. In a similar vein, Shih (2008) argues that the inflation cycle is shaped by the competition among intra-party factions with conflicting preferences over pro- or anti-inflation monetary policies. Shih effectively pushes Huang's argument one step further by exploring the possibility that central leaders ally with provincial officials to form influential political coalitions, echoing Shirk's (1993: 162) observation that in Chinese politics "playing to the provinces" is a major strategy to mobilise political support in the central elite political competition.

Unfortunately, in the field of Chinese social policy, the role of local government remains under-explored. Indeed, only with a few exceptions like Frazier (2010), the majority of the researches on China's social policy follow the literature on the Western welfare state and take the settings of the nation state for granted, effectively leaving the role of territorial authorities and the politics of central-local relations out of the analysis (for the discussion of the inapplicability of the "nation-state assumption" to studying the Chinese welfare system, see Shi 2009). The absence of local government in the study of China's welfare reform will surely impede a comprehensive understanding of this process, given the importance of territorial governments in the area of social policy in China, which is evident in the fact that, as we have seen in Figure 1.5, the Chinese local government accounts for more than 85 percent of public social spending in the first decade of this century.

Studies on the political dynamics of China's pension reform are rare. Even rarer are the studies that look at the role of local government in the reform of the Chinese pension system. Indeed, when Bland and Yu (1999: 3) tried to fill the gap in the literature on China's welfare system when they found "no theoretically informed account on the politics of Chinese pension reform has yet been published", they put "decentralisation and limited administrative capacity" as the number one factor that affects the politics of the Chinese pension reform. Their article is more of a theory-oriented research agenda than an empirical study. This agenda, unfortunately, seems to have not received much academic attention since its publication. One decade later, authors like Shih-Jiunn Shi (2009: 2) still note that "[g]iven the rising importance of local governments, however, their role in the social policymaking has regrettably caught scant attention from the scholarship of Chinese welfare studies". But his efforts to fill this gap in his article is hardly satisfactory, not only because he only provides limited empirical evidence of local authorities' actual input into China's social policymaking, but also due to his treatment of the local government as a mere vehicle of innovative ideas on pension reform rather than the stakeholder pursuing its own interests within the confines of institutional settings of the Chinese state.

A recent contribution along this line of research is Mark Frazier's *Socialist Insecurity* (2010). This book provides us with a comprehensive picture of China's pension reform since the early 1990s and argues that the urban government is a major actor dismantling the old enterprise-based welfare arrangement and expanding the new social insurance programmes. The incentive driving urban officials in the pension reform, according to Mark Frazier, is their hunger for pension funds, which clearly echoes Niskanen's assertions about bureaucrats being budget maximisers. As will become clear later in this study, this is too simplistic an assumption about local officials' preferences. If municipal officials are craving pension funds, then in every province we should expect to see their resistance against the pension provincial integration, which will effectively take away from the municipal government the ownership rights to the funds in local pension pools. But then how can we explain why some provinces have a pension arrangement integrated at the provincial level while others have not? In other words, Frazier's account fails to answer questions about the regional variation of pension reform. This failure reflects the limited applicability of Niskanen's supposedly universal budget-maximising assumption. Only with the exception of one chapter, Mark Frazier relies too much on the evidence from two cities, Beijing and Shanghai. He seems especially preoccupied with the 2006 Shanghai social security scandal in which local officials misappropriated millions of social insurance funds, which probably leads him to follow Niskanen to assume Chinese local officials to be maximisers of public funds. Nevertheless, *Socialist Insecurity* is by far the most informative and insightful publication on the involvement of local governments in Chinese pension politics. One particular insight it has is the notion of "local coalition between urban officials and crony capitalists" (Frazier 2010: 173). This study will take this idea forward to further investigate the possibility of Chinese employers forming coalitions with the government in pension reform.

As argued above, Frazier's (2010) view that Chinese local officials' pension policy preferences are determined by their pursuit of pension funds is problematic. According to an institutionalist understanding of political actor's policy preference, one can assume what in general motivates political actors, but when it comes to preferences in particular policy areas, the policy preferences cannot simply be assumed but have to be examined in light of the relevant institutional arrangements. In other words, how political actors' motivations are translated into concrete policy preferences is not given. Instead, they are shaped by the institutional settings in which the actors are caught (Thelen 1999). Then in order to know what pension policy preferences the local government has, we should examine the institutional environment in which Chinese local officials form preferences and make decisions. The starting point is the institutional underpinnings of the Chinese political economy. China's impressive economic performance since the 1980s poses a great puzzle for social scientists. Indeed, the contribution of North (1981) to our understanding of the institutional foundations of economic growth makes the Chinese case very intriguing. The kinds of institutions North and others working in the field of neo-institutional economics associate with good economic performance are rule of law, representative government and property rights. China is famous for none of them – hence the puzzle: Why has the Chinese economy grown against all odds?

The search then starts for the Chinese functional equivalents of the economy-friendly institutions. These institutions can enhance economic performance because they are able to "make the incentive right" (Easterly 2001). In other words, they can give agents credible incentives to consume, save and invest in a way that will stimulate economic growth. The expansion of the Chinese economy should be explained by the existence of such institutions in China no matter how unorthodox they may be. One institution held responsible for the phenomenal Chinese growth by many prominent political economists is the so-called "market-preserving federalism", which is characterised by fiscal decentralisation (Oi 1992; Montinola et al. 1995; Qian and Weingast 1997; Weingast 1995). According to this argument, the driving agent of China's economy is the Chinese local state. Local governments in China promote regional economy by adopting pro-business policies in order to maximise government revenues to which they have residual claims guaranteed by intergovernmental fiscal revenue-sharing contracts under the fiscal decentralisation arrangement. This explains why the Chinese local government usually has a "helping hand" in economic development instead of a rent-seeking "grabbing hand" often observed in developing and transition economies (Krueger 1974; Frye and Shleifer 1997). Indeed, compared with other countries at a similar stage of economic development, the extent of fiscal decentralisation in China is larger, as shown in Table 2.1. This fiscal federalism argument has received ample empirical support (Jin et al. 2005), mostly by the provincial-level data, and thus become the dominant explanatory framework in the political economy of the Chinese growth since the late-1990s.

Table 2.1 Expenditure/revenue of central government and inflation rate in selected countries

Countries	*Central expenditure as a share of GDP (%)*	*Central revenue as a share of GDP (%)*
China	10.2 (1990–91)	6.1 (1990–91)
Developing countries	26.4 (1985)	22.7 (1985)
Low-income countries	20.8 (1985)	15.4 (1985)

Source: Cited in Huang (1996: 72)

It is worth noting that Mark Frazier clearly writes within this framework. His *Socialist Insecurity* (2010) also assumes Chinese urban officials to be revenue-seeking and therefore expanding the pension programmes to collect more pension contributions.

The problem with the "market-preserving federalism" paradigm is its failure to capture the fluid nature of Chinese politics. First, in practice the revenue-sharing contracts between the central and local government are often subject to ad hoc changes made unilaterally by the central government. In other words, the promise of the central government to give its local agents residual claim to fiscal revenues is actually not credible, which may not be surprising given the fickle character of the Chinese state. Despite this, local governments nevertheless pursue economic development passionately, as documented by the fiscal federalism literature itself. Secondly and most importantly, put forward in the mid-1990s, the fiscal federalism paradigm fails to keep up to date with the post-1994 development in China's fiscal system. In 1994 the central government re-centralised the authority over government revenue, thereby increasing the share of central revenue to total government revenue from 25 percent to 55 percent (see Figure 2.1). This change in the intergovernmental fiscal relations, according to the fiscal decentralisation argument, should have slowed down China's economic growth. But this is not what actually happened. In fact, the average GDP growth rate during 1994–2000 was 8.1 percent, the same as that in the period of 1987–1993. And there is no sign of the ceasing of local competition for economic development. Having been deprived of the rights to revenue generated from local economic expansion, why does the Chinese local state continue to foster regional economy? All the above discussion suggests there may be other source of local officials' motivation. But what is it?

This is where the model of bureaucratic promotion tournament comes into play. In this model, which is based on the seminal work by Lazear (1981), Chinese local officials are not assumed to be revenue-maximising. Instead, they are assumed to be office-seeking, meaning they want to be promoted to higher government positions. The rules of promotion are set by the central government, which chooses officials from a large amount of candidate local leaders to fill a limited number of senior government posts. Since the number of positions is much larger than that of candidates, the local officials have to compete against

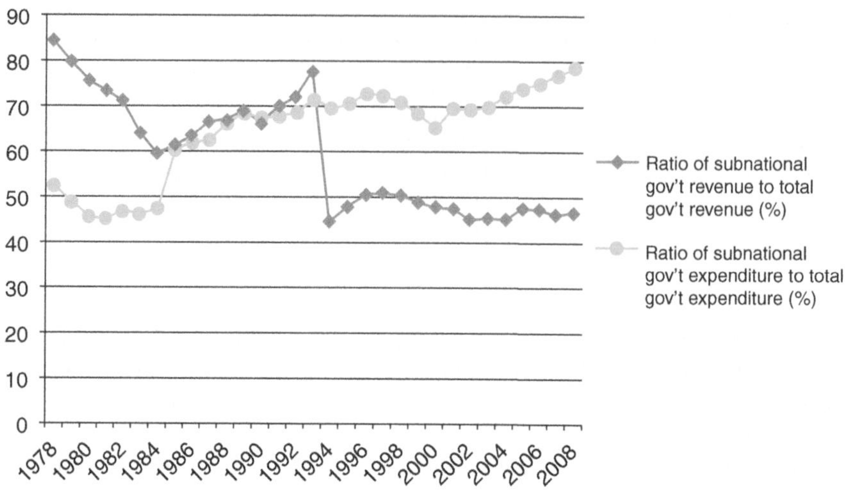

Figure 2.1 Ratio of sub-national government revenue/expenditure to total government revenue/expenditure, 1978–2008 (%)

Source: China Statistical Yearbooks 2000 and 2009

each other, outperforming their counterparts in demonstrating their capacity to achieve the developmental goals like economic growth set by the central government. Only the winner of the competition can get promoted. It is the promise of the central government to promote the tournament competition winner, which is assumed to be credible, that motivates Chinese local leaders (Edin 2003; Li and Zhou 2005; Tsui and Wang 2004).

Chapter 3 will discuss the bureaucratic promotion tournament perspective in detail and apply it to develop this thesis's own theoretical approach. Here we compare this argument with the fiscal federalism thesis. The model of bureaucratic promotion tournament is said to have more explanatory power than the fiscal federalism argument in accounting for the behaviour of Chinese local state because it can explain what may appear incomprehensible under the fiscal decentralisation paradigm. First, the promotion tournament theory argues that with the hope of being promoted local governments are motivated to foster regional economy by enhancing local competitiveness, building a business-friendly environment, investing in local infrastructure projects, etc. This explains why the local hunger for economic development persists after the centralisation of authority over fiscal revenue, which the fiscal federalism argument fails to understand. This persistence simply reflects the continuation of the promotion tournament. A second implication of the bureaucratic tournament model is the difficulty of cooperation between local governments. Because only the winners emerging from the local economic competition can be promoted, the competition between local governments is non-cooperative. In other words, the highly competitive promotion tournament makes the interaction between localities a zero-sum game, meaning that one municipal leader's gain in the likelihood of being promoted is the loss of the other. A rational local leader then should avoid anything that would better his competitors more than himself. Therefore, it is very difficult for two municipalities to take cooperative action even if this can enhance the economic efficiency of both parties. This is perplexing under the perspective of fiscal federalism. Indeed, if local governments are solely concerned about government revenues generated by economic expansion, then the one thing we are sure of them doing is being cooperative and exploiting each one's comparative advantage to have mutual gains. What we really observe in the Chinese political economy, however, is rampant local protectionism. Local protectionist policies range from setting up all kinds of trade barriers to copying the industrial development plans from neighbouring localities regardless of one's own comparative advantage, merely to make sure its neighbours do not enter the market under its jurisdiction (Wedeman 2003). This can be easily explained by the promotion tournament model: The local officials simply cannot afford for their competitors to grow strong and get ahead of them and thus are willing to do everything to prevent this from happening, even if it means to have something they do not really want (as in the case of building industries in which they do not have comparative advantages). Therefore, the promotion tournament model, with its two implications, one about the local passion for economic growth and the other about the local protect against neighbours, has more explanatory power than the fiscal federalism argument. Chapter 3 will build on the promotion tournament model to formulate a theory to explain why China's pension system is expansive and localised.

To summarise this section, the state-centred approach to welfare politics highlights the crucial role of the state actor in welfare state development. The rational choice theory of the state formalises and specifies the preferences of the state actor by assuming them to be self-interested, and more specifically, revenue-maximising. This assumption is adopted in the analysis of the behaviours of Chinese municipal officials, as in the market-preserving federalism thesis. This approach, however, fails to account for the possibility that local leaders' pension policy preferences are constructed by the institutional arrangements of the Chinese state. This requires us to analyse the institutional environment that shapes Chinese municipal leaders' developmental strategies and policy decisions, which will be conducted in Chapter 3. Before that, we must examine how social policy, and pension policy in particular, is linked with local leaders' economic development strategy. This leads us to the literature on how social policy can benefit skill formation.

Social policy and skill formation

A seminal contribution to our understanding of the role of social policy and the welfare state in the functioning of the modern capitalist economy comes from the Varieties of Capitalism paradigm (Hall and Soskice 2001). It highlights the relationship between social protection and skill formation (Estevez-Abe et al. 2001). The starting point of the Varieties of Capitalism paradigm is the notion of institutional complementarity (Aoki 1994). According to Hall and Soskice (2001: 17), institutional complementarity refers to the mutual reinforcement of the efficiency of two or more institutions. Built on this idea, the concept of a production regime is formulated by Hollingsworth, Schmitter and Streeck (1994: 76) to refer to a constellation of institutionally complementary institutions and policies, including employer organisations, labour market institutions, financial regulation and macroeconomic policy, etc. (also see Soskice 1999; Stephens and Huber 2001). Hall and Soskice (2001: 21–33) explore the components of the production regime and examine the configuration of five spheres of strategic relationships the firm has to deal with, which are industrial relations, vocational education and training, employee relations, corporate governance and inter-firm relations. Two types of capitalist economies emerge, namely the liberal market economies (LMEs) and the coordinated market economies (CMEs). The two are differentiated on one fundamental dimension, that is, coordination. In a liberal market economy, coordination is achieved through market mechanisms, thereby preferring investment in transferable assets and radical innovations. In a coordinated market economy, coordination is done by non-market, strategic means, which then favour investment in specific assets and incremental innovations. This is the original formulation of the Varieties of Capitalism theory.

The importance of social policy in production regimes becomes clear when one considers the production strategies of firms that depend on different types of skills (Estevez-Abe et al. 2001). A fundamental decision a firm has to make is on which production strategy to take. It must decide whether to have a flexible production strategy, which needs an army of workers with transferable skills that would ensure management autonomy to reduce labour costs, or a production strategy that focuses on niche segments of the market, which requires a highly cooperative workforce with skills that are specific to the relevant industries and even firms. Clearly, the skill here is conceptualised on the basis of the dichotomy made by Gary Becker (1964), which makes a distinction between general and specific training. General training is devoted to equipping workers with general skills that are productive in a wide range of firms and industries, while specific training provides workers with specific skills that are only valuable for particular industries and employers. Social protection, therefore, is hypothesised to be complementary to a firm's specialised production strategy because it gives workers incentive to acquire specific skills by providing income support in adverse situations like unemployment, to ensure the returns to such human capital investment. In other words, by dealing with the risks associated with making investment in specific skills, social protection solves the market failure in the formation of industry- and firm-specific skills and facilitates firms to adopt specialised production strategy. Therefore, social policies, especially employment protection, unemployment benefits and wage protection – which aim to achieve income maintenance by curtailing management's power to lay off workers, providing income support during unemployment and upholding employee wages above certain levels – are the cornerstone of the "welfare production regime", which refers to the configuration of employer production strategies, employee skill profiles and supportive socio-political institutions (Estevez-Abe et al. 2001: 146). Recent studies focus on the skill formation component of production regimes in advanced economies (Busemeyer and Trampusch 2012). Researchers are particularly interested in the variation of institutional arrangements of vocational education and training within the group of coordinated market economies (CMEs) such as Sweden and Germany, arguing that CME countries' skill formation regimes can be further differentiated on two dimensions, namely the vocational orientation of the education system and the firms' participation in vocational education and training (Busemeyer 2009; Thelen and Busemeyer 2012). The varieties of skill regimes within the group of coordinated market economies suggest that the positive link between social protection and skill formation can be articulated differently in various national contexts.

The Varieties of Capitalism paradigm, along with its implications about the economic benefits of social policy in skill formation, has become prominent in the comparative political economy literature since the 2000s. But the application of this paradigm to China has only started in recent years. It mainly deals with the question of what kind of capitalism China has. Wilson (2006) suggests that we may not have an unambiguous answer to this question because the Chinese economy, being in the process of post-Communist transition, is characterised by a dualism between the state and private sector, each of which has a distinctive mode of coordination. State enterprises, especially those national champions in pillar industries, rarely face market competition. Instead, they are subject to bureaucratic and political types of coordination that one would expect to find in the Keiretsu of Japan and the Chaebol of Korea (see Soskice (1999) for the Japanese and Korean cases). But the close collaboration between the government and large enterprises in key industries is not a justification for grouping China and Japan and South Korea together into any sort of Asian model of capitalism (Bruno 2003). So while Redding and Witt (2008: 381) predict that "[t]he present South Korean business system is probably the closest equivalent among the existing major forms of capitalism to what the Chinese business system may look like in the next 10 or 20 years", Naughton (2007) provides a counter-argument, which focuses on the separation between the public and private sector in China. For the foreseeable future, the Chinese Communist Party (CCP) is likely to maintain its primacy and hence control over the commanding heights of the national economy. So CEOs of state enterprises in pivotal industries will continue to be appointed by the Central Committee of CCP, which would never happen in Japan or South Korea. For the private sector, the mode of coordination is much more market-based. But when it comes to corporate finance, the situation becomes something uncaptured by the analytical framework of the Varieties of Capitalism theory. Because the state enterprises have a monopoly on access to loans from banks, which are mostly owned by the state, the private enterprises have very limited access to formal bank loans (Allen et al. 2008: 517; Walter and Howie 2012). They also confront discriminating regulations when they try to raise funds from the capital market. As a result, entrepreneurs in the private sector have to rely on unofficial financial arrangements like loans from friends and family and unlicensed private banks to get their firms and projects financed (Naughton 2007). Given the unique context (i.e., the dualism during transition and the one-party state), the Chinese capitalism, which is still in the making, is a hybrid of different coordination mechanisms. Indeed, Krug (2012) discerns a wide range of institutional diversity in the Chinese economy. The lack of institutional coherence in the Chinese case poses one major challenge to the study of the country's institutional complementarity and business system (Storz et al. 2013; Witt and Redding 2013). The theorisation of Chinese capitalism therefore requires further scholarly efforts in the future.

This study does not seek to categorise China into either of the ideal types of market economy identified by the Varieties of Capitalism theory (hereafter VoC). Instead, it attempts to engage with the VoC hypothesis on the role of social policy in skill formation and test it in the Chinese context. But before we set out to do the testing, we have to know to what extent this VoC argument is relevant for China. In particular, we should ask the question of how important skill is for the Chinese economy. Needless to say, the VoC argument is formulated in the context of an advanced capitalist economy. The Chinese economy may be capitalist but it is not advanced. So one may well argue that at the current stage of development, a highly skilled labour force may not be as much a driving force for the Chinese economy as it would be in the OECD countries. This view misreads the Chinese situation. Without an army of industrial skilled workers, the industrial upgrading of the Chinese economy, as has been indicated in Chapter 1, would have been impossible. This is clear evidence of the importance of industrial skills to economic growth in China. But even before the industrial advancement gained momentum, human capital had played a crucial role in China's economic success. It is commonly believed that China's economic takeoff is fuelled by the massive, low-skilled, hence cheap, migrant workers. This assumption does not do justice to the Chinese workers. If a massive labour force could lead to economic expansion, then why can't the equally populous India, with an even younger population, perform as well as China in economic terms? The crucial difference is not how many labourers a country has, but how employable they are. The 1990 World Development Indicator shows that the literacy rate for the Chinese adult population was 77.8 percent while it was only 48.2 percent in India. The literacy rate for Indian women was even lower, 33.7 percent, while the rate for women China was 68 percent. The contrast is even more stunning when one realises the difference between the definition of literacy in the two countries. In China, the definition of being literate is one's ability to read and write 1,500 Chinese characters, while the Indian definition is the ability to write one's own name in any language he or she happens to speak. The investment in human capital under the leadership of Chairman Mao has paid off in the post-Mao era, in which the expansion of labour-intensive, export-oriented industries has made China the world's second largest economy. The better economic performance of China compared with India could be explained by the advantage China has over India in human capital resources (Dreze and Sen 2013; Kohli 2012), which gives China a comparative advantage over other developing countries in the world market competition. Therefore, in the developing world, at a relatively low economic stage, simply being literate counts as a skill that could make someone employable and productive. This is the reality in today's Global South, which is hard to imagine for those from OECD countries, where raising literacy rates is an issue that was solved decades ago. But if we look at today's developed countries one and half century ago, as Iversen and Stephens (2008) do, public education and basic public health measures like epidemic disease control in early welfare states greatly contributed to the growth of the modern economy by shaping nations of healthy and well-educated citizens and workers. Clearly the same logic is repeating itself in the developing world today.

After the economic takeoff, skill and human capital has become increasingly important to developing economies like China. Paul Romer (1986) and Robert Lucas (1988) incorporate human capital into Robert Solow's (1956) exogenous growth theory to construct a growth model with endogenous technological change driven by human capital accumulation through schooling. Using school enrolment rates as a proxy for human capital, Barro (1991; 1996) finds initial human capital is positively related with the growth rate of GDP per capita in around 100 countries during the period of 1960–1990. Evidence from 120 developing countries from 1975 to 2000 also supports a positive relationship between economic growth and human capital, whose accumulation can be attributed to government social spending (Baldacci et al. 2008). In the Chinese context, human capital is especially hypothesised to have a direct impact on production, among other positive effects, via generating skills necessary for workers to adapt to market transition and technological innovation (Lin 2003). Having the growth of total factor productivity (TFP) controlled for, a significant proportion of China's economic growth from 1952 to 1999 can still be attributed to the stock of human capital, approximated by the average years of schooling per capita for the population in the age group of 15–64 (Wang and Yao 2003). Applying a different measure of human capital, which is the percentage of the population with either a college degree or senior high school certificate, Fleisher et al.'s (2010) cross-provincial study of the period of 1985–2003 shows that provinces with more human capital enjoy higher industrial output and productivity growth, after controlling for other pro-growth factors such as infrastructure and foreign direct investment. The study by Qian and Smyth (2006), with a smaller sample covering 27 provinces from 1990 to 2000, yields similar results. The above empirical studies, though relying on different measures of human capital, suggest a positive role of human capital and education in the economic development of the world and China in particular.

Human capital is positively associated with economic performance in China. But does this mean the Chinese local state will rely on the accumulation of human capital to foster regional economy? After all, Chinese local officials have other means to promote the development of regional economy. For example, they can invest in local infrastructure projects, which will stimulate the local economy on a massive scale. Heckman (2005) shows that the Chinese state favours physical capital investment over human capital investment in forms of training and schooling. This view, which may have a point for China's early development stage, neglects the complementary relationship between human capital and physical capital, which has become increasingly evident with the industrial and technological progress of the Chinese economy. With economic development comes a higher requirement for human capital because new industries with sophisticated technologies need a high quality labour force. As Justin Lin Yifu (2003: 288) puts it, in China "human capital becomes increasingly complementary to physical capital in the new, frontier industries/technologies". This complementarity may be reflected in the decision on the geographic locations of investment by foreign investors. Shen and Tian (2002) examine Chinese provinces as recipients of foreign direct investment (FDI) in the late 1990s and find that after controlling for other factors that may affect the investor's choice of investment location, the regions with abundant stock of human capital attract more FDI. Using the data in 1992, Broadman and Sun (1997) report that adult literacy has a positive and statistically significant impact on the spatial distribution of FDI while the level of wages unexpectedly shows no significant effect, suggesting the quality of labour force counts more than its costs in investors' decision on the location of their investment. Therefore, even if Chinese local officials prefer to invest in physical capital, they cannot afford to ignore the accumulation of human capital given the increasingly close link between the two.

If a pool of skilled labour force is important to the performance of the local economy, then how can social policy in general and pension programmes in particular contribute to the accumulation of labour force with productive skills? As will become clear in the following discussion, the literature suggests two mechanisms through which social protection programmes facilitate the local accumulation of skilled labour force. The two mechanisms correspond to two kinds of human capital investment decisions. The first type of human capital decision is made by the student, who has to divide their educational investment between general education and vocational education (Estevez-Abe et al. 2001; Iversen 2005). As we shall see in the labour economics literature, social protection programmes can encourage students to attend vocational schools to acquire specific skills by assuring them about the security of future income. This is consistent with the VoC argument that the welfare state is conducive to the formation of specific skills, but the labour economics elaborates the micro-foundations underlying this association, thereby supplementing the VoC argument on the role of social policy in skill formation. The second kind of human capital decision is made by the employer, who has to decide what levels of on-the-job training programmes are to be provided to employees so the latter can acquire productive skills that are specific to the employer's industry. Insights into what determinants affect this decision are also drawn from labour economics, which argues the social protection programme that can serve to limit workers' job turnover should induce employers to provide on-the-job training programmes that aim to equip workers with specific skills. This is because by limiting worker mobility, social programmes offer a solution to the "poaching problem" in skill formation, where employers, worried about workers being poached by other firms after the training programmes finish, will under-invest in the training of employees. The two mechanisms are discussed in detail in following paragraphs.

First let us look at students' schooling decisions. Human capital theory in labour economics conceptualises schooling and education as an investment in one's human capital, which increases individual productivity and hence labour market income (Becker 1962, 1964). Rational individuals are assumed to calculate their lifetime income before committing themselves to a certain period of schooling. So individuals make their schooling decisions by weighing the marginal benefit of an additional year of schooling (i.e., increased labour market income) against its marginal cost (i.e. the sum of spendings on the education and the earnings forgone while studying). Drawing on this theory, Mincer (1974) constructs the human capital earnings function, a regression model with a linear schooling term, to calculate the private rate of returns to education. Mincer's function has become the most commonly employed empirical model in labour economics when it comes to investigating individual educational investment (Heckman 2011; Lemieux 2010).

The human capital theory focuses on the level or magnitude of education, which is operationlised as years of schooling in Mincer's wage equation. It seldom pays attention to the types of education, which can be divided as general education and vocational education (Charlot et al. 2005; Decreuse and Granier 2007). This is understandable if we realise that the labour market in human capital theory is assumed to be perfectly competitive. That is to say, in the labour market there are no job-matching frictions, which are the factors obstructing the match between job applicants and vacant positions, including the low rate of job destruction, wage stickiness, skill mismatch and inefficient matching process as a result of labour market institutions (Fujita and Ramey 2009; Hall 2005; Marimon and Zilibotti 1999). Since matching frictions for individuals can come from the kinds of skills the individual acquires from different types of education, in a theory that does not account for such labour market imperfections, the examination of different kinds of education becomes irrelevant to analysis. Therefore, one must drop the assumption of perfect labour market competition to investigate the factors affecting individuals' schooling decisions on the types of education to receive.

Subsequent theoretical development seeks to use labour market imperfections to explain economic agents' educational investment, especially incomplete information and the resulting job-matching frictions, a situation where job matching is no longer instantaneous as in a perfectly competitive market, but becomes time-consuming and costly due to labour market institutions like employment protection. The result is a large body of literature that examines the impacts of matching frictions in the labour market on human capital investment. The effort to theorise the interrelationship between matching friction, labour market institutions and the decision to choose vocational over general education started with Rosen's seminal work in 1981. Like labour economists after Becker and Mincer,

Rosen works within the theoretical framework that incorporates labour market imperfections, and he is interested in how matching frictions affect individuals' decisions on human capital specialisation. Rosen draws on Adam Smith's idea that the degree of division of labour, which is in essence a specification of human capital in a certain production area, depends upon the scope of the market for the end product and hence the skills to manufacture this product. Rosen argues that the larger the scope of the market for a skill, which means there are more employers whose production needs such skill and therefore more opportunity for workers to utilise this skill, the more willing are workers to make human capital investments to specialise in this skill.

Rosen's argument implies that when labour market ceases to be perfectly competitive and there are situations of job-matching frictions, where one is unable to employ his skills during the employment interval, workers will be discouraged to engage in human capital specification and the level of human capital investment will be suboptimal from the society's perspective. This is consistent with the prediction of Acemoglu's (1996) model that unemployment, which means a considerably high level of matching frictions, is detrimental to the incentive of workers to invest in education. This prediction, however, fails to account for the European experience of the 1970s and 1980s, when a rising level of unemployment coexisted with an increase in the duration of schooling years, as Charlot et al. (2005) point out. To explain this puzzling case, Charlot and his colleagues borrow insights from Nelson and Phelps (1966) and present a two-dimensional concept of education, which makes a distinction between vocational education, aimed to deepen the productivity of workers in one or a few specific technologies, and general education, meant to broaden the scope of the technology the worker can use and thus to improve the adaptability of the worker's skills. In light of this perspective, the conclusion of Rosen (1981) and Acemoglu (1996) becomes more applicable to the type of education that intends to increase the worker's productivity in one certain industry, i.e., vocational education. Indeed, the model constructed by Charlot et al. (2005) shows that in a purely vocational education setting, unemployment will lead the worker to under-invest in human capital. But if education is general, designed to improve the applicability of the worker's skills across a wide range of industries, then in times of unemployment the worker will turn to the general education because it will equip them with transferable skills that can increase their contact rates with employers and hence the chances of exiting unemployment. In fact, the worker will over-invest in general education to a socially suboptimal level. This echoes the conclusion of one prominent theory in labour economics, that is, the signalling model (Arrow 1973; Spence 1973), which argues that people's heavy investment in obtaining a university degree is not meant to improve his productivity but is intended to make signals to employers about his inner, unobservable ability. In the model of Charlot et al. (2005) the divide between vocational education and general education is fixed. Decreuse and Granier (2007) make the choice between the two kinds of education endogenous when they model a student's decision on which type of education to get. Their model synthesises earlier findings, showing that in the presence of matching friction, workers prefer transferable skills to specific skills (for a similar analysis, see Wasmer 2006).

The implication of the theories discussed above is clear. To encourage the acquisition of skills that improve the worker's productivity in one or a few industrial sectors, one has to address the problem caused by job-matching frictions. This is where social policy comes into play. As the theories suggest, job-matching frictions lead to employment intervals when the worker cannot utilise his skill to generate incomes, and consequently encourage people to choose general education over vocational education because the former can give them transferable skills that would better help them get out of the employment interval so they can make earnings. It then follows that if social and political actors, such as the employer or the state, step in to provide income support during those intervals, then the returns to and hence the attractiveness of having transferable skills will diminish and people will be willing to acquire productive skills specific to certain industries through vocational education, without worrying about income sources during employment intervals caused by matching frictions. This advances the efficiency of the overall economy not only by improving the worker's productivity but also by preventing people over-investing in general education simply for signalling purposes. Therefore, the literature of labour economics, especially its theories on the relationship between job-matching friction and human capital investment, provides an economic rationale for the welfare state by highlighting the positive role of social policy in dealing with problems caused by matching friction and hence in promoting the formation of productive industrial skills.

This is consistent with the argument of the Varieties of Capitalism theory. The seminal work by Estevez-Abe et al. (2001) formulates the concept of welfare-skill formation nexus. It draws upon Gary Becker's (1964) conceptualisation of skills and makes a distinction between general skills, industry-specific skills and firm-specific skills. It assumes that individuals care about their lifetime income when making schooling decisions. In other words, "people calculate overall return to their educational/training investment before deciding to commit themselves" (Estevez-Abe et al. 2001: 149). It then uses the comparative pattern of national economies in advanced countries to show the tight coupling between a strong welfare state, especially one with strict employment protection and generous unemployment protection, and the national workforce's skill profile characterised by a dominance of industry-specific and firm-specific skills. In a similar vein, Iversen (2005: 9) argues that a generous welfare state contributes to the formation of what he terms a "specific skills system", because it can encourage workers to make investments in skills that are specific to firms or industries by making "implicit agreements for long term employment and real wage stability".

Although the original argument of Estevez-Abe et al. (2001) does not relate skills to pensions but to various labour market policies, the Varieties of Capitalism approach takes pensions as "deferred wages" and implicitly recognises the role of pension programme in skill formation. Indeed, pension constitutes an important part of people's lifetime income. While in the neocorporatist literature pension is understood as the "social wage" alongside other kinds of social benefits like healthcare and unemployment benefits (for example, see Molina and Rhodes 2002), in the Varieties of Capitalism literature it is a wage that is "deferred to the future" (Iversen and Soskice 2001: 876). In the words of Iversen (2005: 79), "those who are most fearful of losing the labour market power of their skills, and, hence, their ability to secure good health and pension plans through employers, will also be most concerned about guaranteeing a high level of benefits, even if the benefits are 'deferred' to the future". The workers, as described in Iversen's remarks as having the highest stakes in holding the market value of their skills and thus in having generous social benefits even if the benefits are only received in the future, like pension, are those with specific skills. Therefore, it then follows that by guaranteeing a level of a deferred wage and hence the stability of lifetime income, the presence of generous pension programmes should affect individuals' schooling decisions in a way that encourages the acquisition of specific industrial skills through vocational training.

The schooling decision, which is made by students on whether to get a general or vocational education, is one facet of human capital investment. The other dimension of human capital investment this book studies is the training decision, which is made by the employer on whether or not to provide training programmes for employees to equip them with specific industrial skills. Indeed, individuals acquire specific skills not only through vocational education at schools but also through vocational trainings at workplaces. On-the-job training sometimes is entirely funded by the employer, while in other cases the training costs are shared between employers and employees (Becker 1962, 1964). The participation of employers, therefore, is important for the provision of on-the-job training programmes. Then what affects employers' willingness to provide such training programmes? The following paragraphs will review the labour economic theories on private sector training. The literature will show that poaching externality, which exists especially in the case of industry specific skills, will lead to an under-provision of training programmes by employers (Stevens 1996). Therefore, the institutional arrangements that limit the worker's job turnover and thus offer a partial solution to poaching will encourage employers to provide training programmes.

The literature on training decisions, like that on schooling decisions, starts with Gary Becker's human capital theory. As discussed earlier, Becker (1964: 33–50) dichotomises training into general training, which gives workers the productivity that is the same for the training company and the market, and specific training, which endows workers with the productivity that is only valuable to the training firm. In a perfectly competitive labour market, employers have no incentive to provide general training programmes; since the labour market is competitive, the training firm cannot reap any of the returns on the general training. The returns will go entirely to the worker in the form of a higher wage, which in a competitive labour market has to be equal to his marginal productivity, which has now been increased due to the training. If the training firm turns down the worker's pay raise request, then the worker will leave the training company and join another firm that will pay him according to his marginal productivity. Since there is no chance to reimburse the costs of training, the employer will not fund any general training in the first place. When it comes to specific training, the situation is completely reversed. Since specific training equips the worker with skills that are of value only to the training company, the firm can reap all of the benefits of the training programme. This, therefore, gives the firm incentives to finance the training (Becker 1964: 44–48).

Up to this point, Becker's analysis of general training seems to echo the analysis of the same issue by Arthur Pigou (1912), who also sees the incapacity of the firm to capture the returns on general trainings as a major factor that deters employers from providing such training programmes. This incapacity is the result of the fact that "workpeople are liable to change employers" (Pigou 1912: 153). This phenomenon is termed by later economists as "poaching externality" (Moen and Rosen 2004; Gautier et al. 2010), which means that the tendency of outside firms to hire away trained workers discourages all firms from funding training programmes and thus leads to an under-investment in the worker's human capital. Therefore, in the presence of the poaching externality, the level of human capital investment made by employers is socially suboptimal. Pigou's idea was widely accepted in the first half of the twentieth century as one explanation for the failure of Britain to produce a workforce that had a high level of skills comparable to that of the German labour force.

Unlike Pigou, Becker rejects the notion of "poaching externality". The drawback of Pigou's analysis, Becker would argue, is that it neglects the worker's willingness to fund the general training programme. Knowing that they will not be able to get the returns on general trainings, employers do not want to finance them. But the employer is not the only party that can provide the funding. The worker, anticipating that he will reap all of the returns from general trainings, will have the incentive to pay for such training programmes themselves. Then the question becomes how the payments are arranged. Becker argues that the employee can pay for the trainings by receiving reduced wages during the training period (Becker 1964: 40). This explains why workers often start their career with a period of apprenticeship when they learn from their senior colleagues and get under-paid. Workers will calculate and weigh the earnings forgone during training against the returns on training. Since the training costs and benefits are all internalised by the worker, there is no externality resulting from poaching. In equilibrium, human capital investment reaches a socially optimal level. In other words, the perfect labour market competition ensures efficient investment in human capital. Therefore, by focusing on the worker's incentive to pay for trainings, Becker disproves the existence of poaching externality and reaches a strikingly different conclusion, compared with Pigou's analysis, that only workers fund the general trainings and the resultant human capital investment is socially optimal.

Becker's analysis of on-the-job training decisions, which argues that the worker will bear the full costs of general trainings while the employer will finance specific trainings, has been influential since it publication. Later theoretical developments expand Becker's model and enhance its explanatory power. This model has been greatly improved thanks to the contribution by Hashimoto (1981), who formalises Becker's model and introduces into the model transaction costs of evaluating workers' productivity. The two-stage interaction between the employer and the worker is set as follows: At the start, when the two parties are uncertain about the worker's productivity after trainings, they sign a fixed contract specifying the level of wages and trainings, a contract which is not re-negotiable. When the training is completed, the productivity of the worker is revealed to the employer, while alternative wages in the market is revealed to the worker. The two parties, then, will compare their respective benefits from the training with the terms in the pre-determined contract and decide whether or not to end the employment relationship (i.e., the employer will fire the worker if the worker's productivity is lower than the agreed wage, while the worker will quit if the wage is lower than the market value of his productivity). Hashimoto's model shows that with the transaction costs of performance evaluation and contract negotiation, in the case of specific trainings, secession can be inefficient from the perspective of the society. To have an efficient solution, Hashimoto argues, training costs of specific trainings will be shared between the employer and the worker. This arrangement is necessary given the fact that the non-investing party will be able to capture part of the returns on the specific trainings, which will effectively give it more bargaining power in the negotiation process and thus lead to socially suboptimal negotiation results. This phenomenon is later termed by Williamson (1979) as a "hold-up". By identifying the "hold-up" problem in the investment decision and modelling its solution, Hashimoto (1981) modified Becker's original model and explains a usual arrangement in the design of specific training scheme, that is, the cost sharing between employers and employees.

Although its explanatory power for specific trainings has been improved by subsequent theoretical development, Becker's model still fails to explain an important phenomenon in economic life that firms often provide general trainings that have value for other firms. As discussed earlier, Becker's model makes the prediction that employers have no incentive to provide general trainings because they cannot reap any of the returns on such trainings. But in reality we have ample evidence showing that private firms do provide general trainings for their employees, ranging from giving on-the-job trainings designed according to industry standard to paying tuitions fees for MBA courses. Loewenstein and Spletzer (1999: 710), using National Longitudinal Survey of Youth (NLSY) and Employer Opportunity Pilot Project (EOPP) survey, find that workers and employers report that "most of the skills learned in training are useful elsewhere". Similarly, Barron et al. (1999) examine the 1993 National Assessment of Vocational Education survey, which explicitly asked employers: "How much of skills learned on-the-job by new employees in this job are useful outside of this company", and report that over 70 percent of employers considered most or almost all of the skills gained by new workers were general skills. It is true that employers may overestimate the generality of the trainings they provide. But focusing on the perspective of the training recipient, Booth and Bryan (2002) use the British Household Panel Survey (1998–2000) and find that participants in workplace training programmes financed by employer view the trainings as general. More importantly, Booth and Bryan apply statistical techniques to analyse the survey data, showing that with other personal characteristics being controlled for the trainings, employees receive increased wages in the training firm and in the outside firm alike, which supports training recipients' perception of the trainings as general.

If workplace training tends to be general, then how is it financed? Will it be fully financed by workers who accept a reduced wage at the starting stage of the employment, as Becker's model predicts? There is not much evidence for the expected negative relationship between employee starting wage and the incidence of on-the-job training. Barron et al. (1989) consider the process of matching heterogeneous workers to jobs and test their model with the Employer Opportunity Pilot Project (EOPP) data, finding no statistically significant relationship between the workers' starting salaries and trainings. Barron et al. (1997) analyse a different dataset, the Small Business Association Survey, and report a significant and negative association between entry-level wages and on-the-job trainings. But the negative effects of workplace trainings on starting wages are so small that it hardly indicates the worker bearing a significant proportion, not to mention all, of the training costs, as Becker predicts. Loewenstein and Spletzer (1998) report similar findings of a negligible impact of trainings on starting wages after analysing the National Longitudinal Survey of Youth (NLSY). It seems that the bulk of general training costs falls on employers.

Empirical studies show firms do provide and finance general trainings, which is in striking contrast with the prediction of Becker's model. How can we explain this? Why do employers have incentives to invest in the worker's general skills? This question has motivated recent theoretical models that drop the core assumption of Becker's model, that is, the perfectly competitive labour market. Acemoglu and Pischke (1999) assume an imperfect labour market with job-matching frictions. Matching and search costs make the market wage offered by alternative employers lower than the worker's marginal productivity, thereby giving the firm that employs the worker a de facto monopolistic bargaining power. With such power, the firm can currently hire the worker with the market wage and yet exploit his productivity that is higher than the market wage. The same logic applies when the worker receives what Acemoglu and Pischke call "technologically general training" and thus has higher productivity. The firm with a monopolistic bargaining power then can enjoy the increased productivity without paying the employee wages equal to this productivity. Since employers can reap some of the returns on the technologically general training, they have incentives to finance such training.

Acemoglu and Pischke's (1999) model does not specify sources of labour market imperfections. A substantial amount of literature is devoted to examining the origins of labour market imperfections and their implications. Of particular relevance to this study is the analysis by Stevens (1994, 1996), who sees labour market imperfections as contingent upon the types of skills. Stevens evaluates Becker's conceptulisation of skills, arguing that the concept of general skills only applies to a perfectly competitive labour market, in which there are numerous buyers (i.e., employers) for such skills that are of the same value to all buyers, while the notion of specific skills is only suitable for a purely monopolistic labour market, where there is only one buyer who values this particular kind of skills. The type of skills that sits in between these two extreme cases is not a mixture of general skills and specific skills, Stevens argues. Instead, such middle-ground skills should be conceptualised as "transferable skills", similar to Acemoglu and Pischke's (1999) "technologically general skills" or Esteves-Abe et al.'s (2001) "industry specific skills", which are valuable to some firms but not to others. Since the number of buyers is more than one but not numerous, the nature of the market for industry specific skills is not perfectly competitive, nor purely monopolistic, but incompletely competitive. This means a worker with industry specific skills is paid a wage that is above his reserve wage (paid in purely monopolistic market for firm-specific skills) but below his marginal productivity (paid in a perfectly competitive market for purely general skills). In other words, the returns on industry specific skills will not be taken entirely by the firm (as in the case of specific skills), nor will be reaped solely by the worker (as in the case of general skills), but will be shared between the employer and the employee. This is what the Varieties of Capitalism literature means when it argues some assets like industry specific skills are "co-specific" for both employers and workers (for example, see Hall and Soskice 2001: 17). It is the prospects of acquiring some of the benefits from industry specific skills that gives firms incentives to invest in the trainings on such skills. This explains why firms often fund trainings in what appears to be general skills, which in fact are of value to the industry.

An important implication of the above analysis is the reemergence of poaching externality. As discussed earlier, Becker (1964) dismisses the existence of poaching externality by focusing on the purely ideal skill types in a perfect labour market. But in the situation of incomplete labour market competition, as argued by Stevens (1996), poaching externality reappears. This is because if the possibility that firms can reap part of the premiums of industry specific skills gives employers incentives to make investment in industry specific trainings, then it should equally motivate employers to poach skilled workers from the training firm. In other words, if a firm hopes to benefit from industry specific skills, making investments in training its own employees is one way to achieve this. Another way, which may be more convenient, is to poach from elsewhere workers that have completed the training programme paid by other companies. This creates an externality because training benefits and costs are not assumed by the same firm. Anticipation of the poaching possibility will lead all firms to under-invest in training programmes that will equip workers with industry specific skills. The level of human capital investment of the society, therefore, is suboptimal, due to the market failure resulting from poaching externality.

One may argue that the validity of Stevens's argument about the existence of poaching externality depends upon how much knowledge the outside firms have about the productivity and training experience of the worker they intend to poach. As authors like Katz and Ziderman (1990) and Chang and Wang (1996) would argue, one of the defining characteristics of an incompletely competitive labour market is informational asymmetry. Between the worker's current employer and alternative employer, there exists an informational asymmetry about the worker's unobservable ability and actual trainings the worker receives. The uncertainty about the worker's genuine productivity, it then follows, would deter outside firms' poaching activities. Such uncertainty, if we follow the argument of Hashimoto (1981), will constitute transaction costs in the job-matching process and reduce the wages the worker will receive from the poaching company, which will lower the worker's willingness to do job-hopping. Informational asymmetry, therefore, reduces poaching externality.

Stevens's theory could be improved if it took informational asymmetry about the worker's productivity into account. But this does not mean one cannot defend this theory within its own framework. The focus of Stevens's argument is the industry specific skills, which are of value to some firms but not to others. They are, in other words, transferable across firms within the same industry. There are technical and institutional reasons for the fact that they are transferable within an industry. With respect to technology, for example, the process for machinery operation and production should be standardised if the industrial skills involved are to be transferable. Such transferability should also be ensured by institutional arrangements like certified qualification systems for skill levels acknowledged industry-wide (Acemoglu and Pischke 2000; Casey 1991). Without these technical and institutional supports, it is hard to imagine the industrial skills can be standardised and hence transferable within the industry. The same technical and institutional supports, this study argues, can reduce uncertainty about the worker's skill levels and productivity by standardising and recognising the worker's skills. This will reduce the severity of the informational asymmetry problem between the worker's current employer and the alternative employer and thus make poaching an attractive strategy for the latter. Poaching, in other words, is a viable option for firms in the case of industry specific skills. This explains the phenomenon highlighted in the Varieties of Capitalism literature that in Germany collective wage bargaining between employer associations and trade unions is often set at the industry level. The rationale behind this arrangement is that "by equalising wages at equivalent skill levels across an industry, this system makes it difficult for firms to poach workers" (Hall and Soskice 2001: 25). Stevens (1996: 23) also cites surveys by Britain's Training Agency as evidence to show employers' concerns about the problem of poaching when they provide on-the-job trainings. Poaching, therefore, is a problem that truly exists. It cannot be easily assumed away by citing uncertainty about the worker's capacity or informational asymmetry between different employers. It has to be dealt with.

This leads to an important policy implication of Stevens's theory. If the problem of poaching, which impedes employer-sponsored training and leads to suboptimal human capital investment, is caused by the failure of an incomplete labour market, then the solving of this problem may require certain institutional infrastructures. We have discussed one type of institution: industry-level collective wage bargaining. This study argues that the poaching problem can also be solved by the institutional arrangement that directly limits the worker's mobility, like China's localised pension system. Indeed, the problem of poaching externality, in essence, is the employer's fear that workers might leave the company after the training programme completes. As Stevens (1994: 541) argues, one important source of poaching externality is the "uncertainty about labour turnover". It then follows that the arrangement that serves to reduce labour turnover and facilitate labour retention should help relieve employers' worries about poaching and thus induce them to invest in on-the-job trainings.

The idea that some arrangement could reduce job turnover and serve the purpose of labour retention relates to the notion of efficiency wage. In labour economics, the efficiency wage theory argues that a worker's productivity is positively related with the wages he or she receives (Cahuc and Zylberberg 2004: 353–360). Several variants of this theory are developed to explain why this is the case. The first model emphasises the role of the higher-than-equilibrium wage in discouraging shirking (Shapiro and Stiglitz 1984). It is argued that a higher wage increases the cost of losing one's job, which therefore reduces the worker's inclination to shirk. The second model looks at the firm's recruitment strategy (Weiss 1980, 1990). A wage higher than the labour market equilibrium level will attract more job applicants to the firm, thereby allowing the firm to select better employees from a bigger pool of labour force. A final model examines the impacts of higher wages on job turnover (Stiglitz 1974). A wage higher than that offered by other firms means the worker is less willing to leave the current employer, which thus reduces the turnover rate and saves the firm the costs of recruiting and training new workers. Apart from the above economic interpretations, a sociological understanding of efficiency wage is also put forward by Akerlof (1982, 1984), which sees a higher wage as a gift from the employer to the worker, who is then expected to return this favour by putting more effort into their work.

The turnover model of efficiency wage is most relevant to this thesis. It argues that efficiency wage serves as an incentive mechanism for labour retention. A specific form of efficiency wage with such function is deferred payments. Lazear (1979, 1981) analyses the employee's age earnings profile. His deferred payments model argues that the workers with less seniority, for example those at the entry-level, get paid below their marginal productivity and the workers with more seniority receive wages that are above their marginal productivity in forms of higher salary, bonus or pension. This arrangement encourages newly recruited workers to furnish the skills required by the firm and to stay with the firm long enough to qualify for those deferred benefits. A steep pay scheme, in other words, motivates and retains workers (Shapiro and Stiglitz 1984). The deferred payments model explains a notable phenomenon in labour markets, which is the return to seniority (Buchinsky et al. 2010; Kotlikoff and Gokhale 1992; Lazear and Moore 1984). The implication is clear: Deferred payments, like pension, can be designed to serve the purpose of labour retention.

This is why occupational pension programmes can have the effects of reducing labour mobility – an argument that has received ample empirical support. Using the data from the 1984 Survey of Income and Programme Participation (SIPP) conducted by the U.S. National Bureau of Economic Research, Gustman and Steinmeier (1993) finds job turnover rates to be lower in occupational pension-covered groups, no matter what the type of pension scheme is, DB (defined benefits) or DC (defined contribution). This is consistent with an earlier study by Mitchell (1982), who, after conducting probit analysis of workers' decisions on changing jobs on the basis of a panel dataset from the US-wide Quality of Employment Survey in 1973 and 1977, reports that fringe benefits offered at the firm level significantly reduce the likelihood of workers changing jobs. In the Chinese context, a similar story can be told of the socialist enterprise-based welfare system. The occupational welfare programmes, which were offered by state-owned enterprises (SOEs), served as an obstacle to labour mobility, preventing skilled labour force in SOEs from moving to the vibrant, emerging private sector (Naughton 1995).

In terms of limiting labour mobility, regional pension programmes resemble the occupational pension schemes. This is evident in the literature on the impacts of pension portability on intra-EU mobility. EU citizens have the legal right to work wherever they choose in the European Union. To prevent the lack of portability of social rights from becoming an obstacle to EU citizens enjoying the right to free movement within the Union, European Council Regulations No. 1408/71, No. 574/72 and No. 883/2004 were created to coordinate social rights granted under different member states' national legislation (Verscheuren 2009). So in theory EU citizens should be able to take their social benefits' entitlements anywhere in the EU. Legal analysis by social policy lawyers normally assumes so (Andrietti 2001; Forteza 2010; Whiteford 1996), but empirical research proves otherwise. The Eurobarometer wave 75.1 of 2001 asked respondents multiple-choice questions about their perceived obstacles to mobility. The result shows that among the 13 options, "social security abroad" ranks sixth as the most relevant "practical difficulty" in relocating to another Member State, after language barriers, family concerns, bureaucracy involved, job opportunities and cultural differences (d' Addio et al. 2013: 9). This micro picture is consistent with the macro-level findings from Fenge and Weizsäcker's (2010: 264) study on public pension systems in EU-15 that "some inherent mobility distortions survived directive 1408/71". This is confirmed by many other studies, which show the difficulty with transferring public social security packages across nation states will decrease the propensity of citizens to make cross-border relocation (Avato et al. 2009; d' Addio et al. 2013; Holzmann et al. 2005; Holzmann and Koettl 2012).

Although it is not entirely appropriate to draw a parallel between the European case of fragmented welfare systems and China's localised public pension arrangement, the message is clear: If the European Union, even with the help of EEC directives to coordinate the national welfare schemes, could not ensure full labour mobility, then it is reasonable to expect that the localised Chinese pension system, without such coordination mechanism, is more likely to see labour mobility impeded by the non-portability of pension rights. Indeed, under the localised structure of the public pension system, instead of being managed by the national government, the public programmes that cover workers are administered by individual geographical units, which are municipalities (or at best provinces), as the occupational pension schemes are run by individual employers. Under the localised pension schemes, workers and their employers contribute to the pension pool of the locality, and the benefits depend on the amount and length of contributions from employees and employers. This greatly limits the portability of pension rights accrued under such an arrangement, if not making the pension package entirely non-portable. This locality-based pension programme is very much like the firm-based occupational pension, which also limits the portability of pension packages. So it makes sense to hypothesise that by incurring potential loss of pension benefits to workers who try to move out of the locality, the Chinese public pension schemes deter the workers from doing so and consequently lead to prolonged employment and decreased labour mobility.

It follows that with labour mobility constrained, employers become more willing to provide and fund training schemes for employees. The reason is simple: If a worker changes jobs and moves from one municipality to another, he risks losing his previous contribution to his pension plan he made when he worked for the previous city. It means the outside firm may need to pay a higher wage, which has to offset the worker's forgone pension contributions, if it chooses to poach a skilled worker elsewhere. This should deter poaching activity and, according to Stevens (1994, 1999), will consequently give current employers incentives to invest in trainings on industry specific skills. In short, Chinese workers covered by the public pension programme should be more likely to receive trainings from their current employers because this programme reduces their mobility. Chapter 3 will draw on this insight to inform the theoretical building of this book, which explores how the deferred payments made on the basis geographical units, like China's localised pension benefits, help to retain the labour force within the locality in a context of labour market tightening.

To summarise, this section starts by demonstrating the crucial importance of productive skills to the Chinese economy. With the ongoing industrial upgrading, which results in an increasing complementarity between physical and human capital, China has become more and more dependent on a workforce with industrial skills to bolster its economy. Social protection programmes and pension in particular can meet the economy's requirement for skilled workers through its contribution to skill formation. Drawing on the literature of the Varieties of Capitalism theory and labour economics, this section identifies two mechanisms through which social protection programmes can facilitate the formation of specific industrial skills. First, by ensuring the stability of lifetime income, the public pension system encourages the student to choose vocational education, which will equip him with specific productive skills. Secondly, by partly addressing the poaching problem through reducing labour turnover, the arrangement that limits the portability of benefit packages motivates the employer to make investments in employee training programmes, which will improve the worker's specific skills. The two hypotheses on how expansive and localised pension systems impact the individual's schooling and training decisions will be incorporated in this study's theoretical framework in Chapter 3.

Summary

This chapter has reviewed three streams of literature, each of which provides insights into this study of China's pension system. The industrialisation literature, with a focus on the social needs to deal with structural pressures that come with secular trends like modernisation and demographic ageing, rightly highlights the need for the state to step in to provide old-age income security. This is especially true for China, a late-industrialising country where the state intervention assumes an even more important role in socio-economic development. However, this literature treats the state as a holistic entity and therefore falls short of identifying with which administrative level of the state the responsibility of pension provision and administration resides, while this is a highly salient issue in China's pension reform. In a vast country like China, where a top-down approach to governing is simply not feasible to ensure the government's responsiveness and administrative efficiency, local authorities are granted ample autonomy. This gives the regional government a vital role in the nation's political and policymaking process. Pension policy, in particular, lies in the authority of the municipal government. To understand the dynamics of China's pension reform, one has to investigate the policy behaviours of the political leaders of the municipalities, which are shaped by the political institutions of the Chinese state.

This leads to the state-centred literature on the impact of state institutions on welfare state development. This literature explores how the agency of state actors is structured by political institutions and how such an institutionally shaped agency is articulated in the process of social policymaking. To explain state bureaucrats' social policy behaviours, one must specify their policy preferences. The rational choice theory of the state offers a way to model state actors' policy preferences by assuming them to be revenue-maximising. This approach, when applied to the Chinese case, successfully identifies the economic competition between Chinese municipalities. But the revenue-maximising assumption, in its application to the Chinese pension reform, fails to take into account China's particular political and institutional environment, which shapes Chinese state actors' pension policy preferences. Chapter 3 will formulate a theory that examines the institutional underpinnings of Chinese local leaders' pension policy behaviours.

Finally, this chapter investigates the role of social policy in skill formation, which has been extensively discussed in the literature on Varieties of Capitalism and labour economics. The Varieties of Capitalism paradigm offers us a macro picture at the national level that the developed welfare state is institutionally complementary to the specific skills system. Labour economics provides the micro-foundation of this broad picture. According to the two sets of literature, social protection programmes such as public pension are conducive to the formation of specific industrial skills for two reasons. First, a pension programme encourages students to attend vocational schools by dealing with labour market risks (i.e., the risks of income loss) that are likely to come along with specific skills. Secondly, it can induce employers to provide on-the-job trainings by limiting the portability of the pension package and thus offering a partial solution to the "poaching externality".

Given the positive impacts of social protection on skill formation and the policy behaviours of Chinese local leaders shaped by China's political institutions, it follows that the inter-municipal economic competition will drive municipal leaders to extend the coverage of pension programmes to induce the training of workers with specific industrial skills that are crucial to local economic development, and at the same time keep the pension programmes at the municipal level so the skilled workers can be retained within the jurisdiction of the municipality. This is the reason why China has an expansive and yet localised pension system. All of these insights will inform the theoretical foundation of the next chapter.

3 Political institutions, economic conditions and pension policy in China

A theoretical argument

This chapter formulates a theory on the interconnections between political institutions, pension policymaking and labour market behaviours in China's pension reform. This theory examines how institutional arrangements of the Chinese state, notably bureaucratic tournament promotion and Chinese-style political decentralisation, shape the pension policy actions of municipal leaders, and how the resultant pension policy affects human capital investment decisions by workers and employers in labour markets. This theory builds on Edward Lazear's (1981, 1989) seminal work on tournament competition in organisations, but it extends Lazear's model by relaxing his assumption that the principal can make credible commitment to award the agent who wins the tournament competition.

Drawing on Treisman's (2007: 27) three-stage formalisation of the political process, the theory is structured into three parts, which combined together constitute a political-economic equilibrium. The first phase is the leadership selection stage, in which bureaucratic tournament promotion and Chinese-style political decentralisation structure the incentives of Chinese municipal leaders. The second stage is the policymaking stage, in which the incentive structure shapes municipal leaders' pension policy choices. In this stage predictions are generated on under what conditions municipal leaders will expand the coverage of pension programmes and resist the integration of the pension system. The final stage is the economic decision-making stage, which shows how economic agents such as workers and employers make human capital investment decisions in response to the local pension arrangement. It generates predictions on which type of skills, general skills or specific skills economic agents will acquire in the presence of local pension schemes.

As this theory shows, the choices of economic agents facilitate the formation of industry specific skills that are crucial for local economic development. This reinforces municipal leaders' tendency to implement an expansive and localising pension policy. It is in the sense of such positive feedback that the three-stage process comprises a political-economic equilibrium whereby the expansive and localised features of the Chinese pension system can be sustained. Before formulating the theory, this chapter starts by discussing its foundational theoretical perspectives, namely methodological individualism and rational choice institutionalism.

Methodological individualism and rational choice institutionalism

Methodological individualism is a theoretical position that asserts social phenomena should be explained in terms of individual choices that are to be aggregated into the phenomena of interest. "The elementary unit of social life is the individual human action", Elster (1982: 463) points out when he discusses the essence of methodological individualism. "To explain social institutions and social change is to show how they arise as the result of the actions and interactions of individuals" (Elster 1982: 13). In this way, theories based on methodological individualism are different from theories that see social phenomena as the function of impersonal historical forces, like the modernisation theory and other structural-functionalist theories, or theories that attribute social changes to the agency of collective actors, like the various kinds of interests group explanations (Tsebelis 1990).

Adopting the position of methodological individualism, this study maintains that China's pension system, the social institution we seek to make sense of, should be understood with reference to the individual choices made by political and economic agents (i.e., local bureaucrats, workers and employers) and to the interactions among them. Therefore, theories that hold structural pressures like industrialisation and demographic transition as causal factors shaping the Chinese pension system, which have been discussed in Chapter 2, become competing hypotheses to the central argument of this study and thus have to be taken into account when our main hypotheses are being tested.

Under the perspective of methodological individualism, individual agents are assumed to be rational, making choices on the basis of rational calculation. This is why methodological individualism is naturally linked with rational choice theory. Here rationality is instrumental, simply referring to the "optimal correspondence between means and ends" (Tsebelis 1990: 18). Hall and Taylor (1996: 944) see this as a fundamental characteristic of rational choice theory's behavioural assumptions: "[t]he relevant actors have a fixed set of preferences or tastes (usually conforming to more precise conditions such as the transitivity principle), behave entirely instrumentally so as to maximise the attainment of these preferences".

Drawing on this theoretical position, this study assumes the political and economic agents involved in the process of China's pension reform to be rational preference-maximisers. Then what are these preferences? For economic agents like workers and employers, it is normally assumed that they try to maximise their utility, which refers to income in the case of workers and profit in the case of employers. But when it comes to the preferences of political agents, fewer consensuses are found in the literature. Persson and Tabellini (2000: 10) identify two types of motivation in the literature of rational choice theory. Politicians can be partisan, who cater to the interests of a fragment of society. Or alternatively, political actors can be opportunistic, who care about attaining office (office-seeking) and/or extracting rents to enrich themselves (rent-seeking). As we have seen in the last chapter, studies on contemporary Chinese politics generally assume bureaucrats in China to be opportunistic, while there are debates on which kind of opportunistic behaviour, office-seeking or rent-seeking, better capture the motivation of Chinese bureaucrats. Given the evidence of local official behaviours presented in Chapter 2, this study argues that the notion of office-seeking is a better approximation of the reality of Chinese politics.

In rational choice theory, the calculations made by agents are not only rational, meaning that it aims to maximise actors' preferences, but also strategic, which means that the calculations are made in anticipation of the bahaviours of other agents. Such strategic calculation, in turn, is structured by institutions. This emphasis on the central role of institutions in shaping strategic interactions among agents and hence in determining political outcomes is the essence of rational choice institutionalism. As Hall and Taylor (1996: 945) put it, "an actor's behaviour is likely to be driven, not by impersonal historical forces, but by a strategic calculus and, . . . this calculus will be deeply affected by the actor's expectations about how others are likely to behave as well". Then what shapes agents' expectations about others' behaviours and responses? The answer is institution. Institution is conceptualised as a set of formal and informal rules that govern social interactions (North 1990). By providing rules of games and channelling information about the likely responses of other actors, institutions help the agent to anticipate others' behaviours and to devise one's own strategy accordingly. Institutions, in a word, have an impact on political outcomes by affecting the strategic interactions among the participating actors. This is the most important insight that rational choice institutionalism offers to the study of politics.

This study formulates a rational choice institutionalist theory to explain why China's pension system is expansive and localised. This theory shows how political institutions of the Chinese decentralised authoritarianism give rise to this system by structuring the strategic interactions between municipal leaders and the central government. It demonstrates the role of institutions to affect municipal leaders' expectations about how likely the central government is to award their efforts to promote regional economic development, and hence to influence municipal officials' efforts to pursue local economic expansion through pension policy that is conducive to local human capital investment. The implications of this theory, as will be discussed in detail later, are that the regional variation in the expansion and localisation of pension schemes should be caused by the regional variation in the relevant institutional settings that shape municipal officials' expectations about their promotion prospects. In addition to explaining the behaviours of political actors in pension policymaking, our theory also explores how economic agents make human capital investment decisions in response to the pension schemes installed by municipal leaders. In short, the strategic interactions between political and economic agents generate a political-economic equilibrium that makes the Chinese pension system expansive and localised.

Stage one: leadership selection

Adopting the theoretical positions of methodological individualism and rational choice institutionalism, the first part of our theory models how political institutions incentivise Chinese municipal leaders. The starting point is the leadership selection process. At this stage, the model of bureaucratic promotion tournament is applied to analyse the impacts of promotion prospects on the behaviours of Chinese local officials. This model is originally formulated by Lazear and Rosen (1981), who examine the motivation mechanism applied in the situation where one party (the agents) acts on hehalf of another (the principal). They point out that the tournament competition is an instrument used by the principal to provide incentive to its agents to carry out the orders given by the principal. To be more precise, the principal gives orders to agents, examine how their jobs are done and reward them not by assessing their performance in absolute terms but by comparing the performance of agents and choosing the agent with the best performance to be the only recipient of the prize. In other words, the agents, carrying out the same task given by the principal, are in a tournament competing to be the best player and the sole winner of the principal's award. The advantages of the tournament competition as an incentive mechanism are twofold. First, if the reward is a job vacancy that has to be filled by someone anyway, then in the eyes of the agents the promise made by the principal to give this reward is credible because when the tournament finishes the principal has no incentive to renege its promise since it is simply not in its interests to do so. Secondly, the tournament competition is cost-effective because the assessment process only involves comparison between the performances of agents rather than designing a system of index and collecting massive information to measure the agent's absolute performance. Two conditions have to be met if the tournament competition is to function well as an incentive mechanism. First, agents should carry out the same task, otherwise there will not be any true comparison between their performance. Secondly, agents should be able to have an impact on the result desired by the principal, otherwise the results will not reflect the ability of the agents.

These two requirements are present in the Chinese case. In China, local governments are given the same task, which is to promote the local economy, and they are granted by the central government with administrative means and fiscal resources to do so. Therefore, based on the insights from the literature on principal-agent theory and on tournament competition in particular, the bureaucratic promotion tournament model is constructed as a competing hypothesis of the fiscal decentralisation argument (Edin 2003; Tsui and Wang 2004; Li and Zhou 2005). Unlike the fiscal federalism paradigm where Chinese local officials are seen as revenue maximisers, the bureaucratic promotion tournament theory assumes local leaders to be office seekers, aiming to get promoted to higher-ranking bureaucratic posts. The scenario here is a Chinese version of tournament competition: The principal, which is the central government, delegates the task of fostering economic development to its agents at local levels with the promise that the best developer in generating economic growth will be promoted.

Empirical findings have lent support to this model. For example, Li and Zhou (2005) examine the bureaucratic career of provincial party secretaries from 1979 to 1995. Their regression model, employing turnover data of these top provincial leaders, shows that the chances of being promoted are positively associated with the economic performance of a leader's province. Chen et al. (2005) enlarge the sample to cover the period of 1979–2002 and discover similar findings. The relationship between economic performance and bureaucratic career not only exists at the provincial level but also holds for municipal leaders. Mei (2009) finds that in the Zhejiang province the likelihood of a municipal leader getting promoted is dependent on the GDP growth rate of his or her municipality, while in the province of Hubei it is the share of municipal GDP that counts.

The problem with the promotion tournament theory, when applied to the Chinese context, is its assumption that the principal can make credible commitment to award the winning agent in the promotion tournament. The original tournament competition model formulated by Lazear and Rosen (1981) assumes the potential recipients of the reward offered by the principal are restricted to the agents the principal hopes to motivate, which renders the promise made by the principal credible to these agents. Accordingly, the bureaucratic promotion tournament model, when applied to the case of Chinese bureaucratic politics, assumes that the local officials are the only candidates for the higher ranked bureaucratic posts for which they are willing to compete for promotion. In the multilevel governance structure of the Chinese state, this assumption does not hold. In China, for any office within one jurisdiction, candidates come from four sources in most cases, as listed in the following Table 3.1 with simplistic examples for illustrative purpose.

Table 3.1 Sources of candidates for bureaucratic offices

	Scenarios	*Example*
Source 1	Promotion from the lower level of government within the same jurisdiction	Mayor of municipality A of province X gets promoted to be the governor of province X
Source 2	Transfer from the same level of posts within the same jurisdiction	Mayor of municipality A of province X gets transferred to be the mayor of municipality B of province X
Source 3	Promotion from the lower level of posts in other jurisdictions or in central government	Mayor of municipality A of province X gets promoted to be the governor of province Y Director of a department of a central ministry gets promoted to be the governor of province Y
Source 4	Transfer from the same level of posts in other jurisdictions or in central government	Mayor of municipality A of province X gets transferred to be the mayor of municipality B of province Y. Minister of a central ministry gets transferred to be the governor of province Y

It is clear from the above table that a given office, for example the provincial leadership post, is not only open to the lower-level officials like municipal mayors within this province, i.e., insiders, but also to officials from other provinces and central ministries, i.e., outsiders. In other words, the reward offered by the central government in the form of promotion is not restricted to the group of local agents in a given jurisdiction. Therefore, to the municipal mayors within one province the promise made by the central government that the reward of promotion to provincial posts is dependent on municipal economic performance is not necessarily credible. This requires us to relax the credible principal assumption in the model of bureaucratic promotion tournament. Given the fact that municipal leaders are the major policymakers and implementers of sub-provincial policies, relaxing the credible principal promise assumption and allowing the credibility of central principal to vary will enable us to examine how the variation in central credibility will affect policy outcomes at local levels. Such variation in the credibility of the central government can be indicated by the profile of the provincial leadership, i.e., whether they are locally recruited insiders or parachuted outsiders. The following paragraphs further explain the working of this arrangement, which is called "Chinese-style political decentralisation" in this study.

The term "Chinese-style political decentralisation" may seem odd at first glance. Indeed, we are used to thinking of China as a politically closed party-state where the political power is highly concentrated at the Party centre, no matter how administratively and fiscally decentralised it may be. This view has some truth as we shall see below, but it is over-generalised and too simplistic to allow us to see some institutional settings that grant de facto political power to localities. One of such institutional arrangements, as I shall show, is one under which the provinces are governed by insiders, i.e., home-grown officials who build their entire bureaucratic career from grassroots within the province, as opposed to being ruled by outsiders sent from Beijing. This arrangement, combined with the tournament promotion, constitutes an important incentive structure, because it affects local officials' perceptions of the credibility of the promise on promotion made by the central government. Given its profound policy implications, this often-overlooked institution should be taken seriously. Let the analysis begin with a discussion of the prevalent view on how politically decentralised China is.

Despite the term "market-preserving federalism", China is not formally structured as a federal polity. Regardless of various measures to decentralise administrative authorities over local affairs during the last three decades, there has not been any serious push for political decentralisation in China,[1] that is, to enfranchise local people and empower local congress to share political power with the local party-state and the central authority. In fact, authors have offered evidence that supposedly shows the centre has tightened its political control over the regions in the reform era. For example, Huang (1996) traces the changing length of provincial leadership tenures since the founding of People's Republic of China. He finds that the post-1978 provincial officials serve a much shorter term than their predecessors (see Table 3.2), suggesting that the central government has been reshuffling provincial appointments more frequently to prevent the latter from

Table 3.2 Average tenure of provincial leaders in China, 1949–1995 (years)

	1949–67	*1977–81*	*1982–95*	*Ratio: 82–95/ 49–67*
Provincial party secretary	6.23	3.86	4.05	0.65
Provincial governor	6.43	3.28	3.84	0.60

Source: Cited in Huang (1996: 106)

making alliance with (or being captured by) local interests and using their newly gained administrative power in the decentralisation process to defy central orders. This leads Huang to conclude that in post-1978 China political centralisation had to go hand in hand with administrative and fiscal decentralisation, because the former is necessary to sustain the central control to prevent the disintegrating tendency that is often associated with the latter.

This view actually echoes the popular wisdom that political reform in China is lagging far behind economic and administrative reform. Economically China may have become more open, but politically it is still the country we used to know. Is it really the case? Has China no political decentralisation? Surely we can see a declining tenure length of regional leaders in the post-1978 era. But it is rather hasty to jump to the conclusion that China has become more politically centralised, because simple numerical summation of provincial tenures leaves out important information on the qualitative differences among provincial leaders. Without such information, one cannot discover the real constraints facing the central government when it selects provincial leaders. That is to say, the central government does not choose provincial leaders at will. Instead, as shall be shown below, the candidate pool could be limited to very specific groups of cadres with certain quality. So, even if the central government could reshuffle provincial officials more frequently, the fact that each time its choice on the successors is under meaningful constrain implies a less powerful centre than one would expect from the simple observation of decreasing provincial tenure length. Then what kind of quality of provincial leader should be identified if we are to assess the actual extent of political centralisation in China?

This research suggests looking at provincial leaders' career paths. As we have seen in Table 2.2, a provincial official, before appointed to this provincial-level post, may have either of the following three career paths: either he is transferred/promoted from another province, or from one central ministry,[2] or he is promoted from within the same province like from the municipal leadership. If the provincial leader has either of the former two career paths, then he is rendered as an "outsider" to this province. If he rises from one of the municipalities within the same province, then he is counted as an "insider" in the provincial politics. Table 3.1 (with the blue line) depicts the share of years when the provincial governor was an insider for each of the 18 provinces (selected on the basis of presentational economy). It also includes the average tenure length of provincial governor in each province, as shown with the height of the red bars.

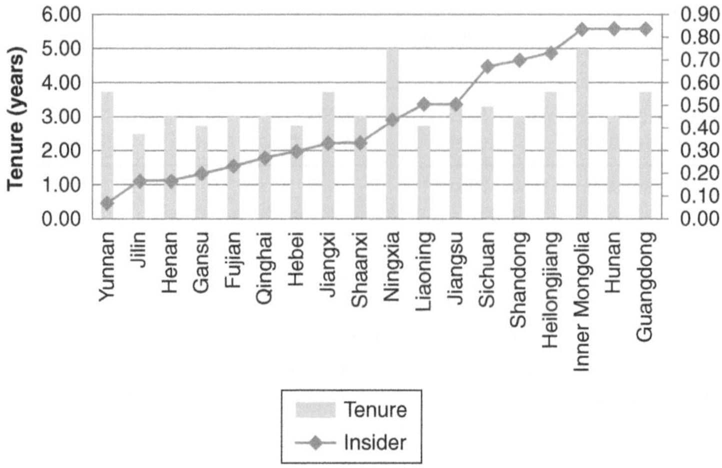

Figure 3.1 The share of insider-dominant years and the average tenure of provincial governors in 18 provinces (1978–2008)

Source: Career paths of provincial governors are derived from their resumes, which can be obtained online from the official website of the Chinese central government (www.gov.cn/) and the official websites of the selected provincial governments.

Figure 3.1 shows for the selected 18 provinces the insider indicator has a much larger variation than that of the tenure. Some comparisons of individual cases would be helpful to illustrate the point that the indicator of qualitative difference among provincial governors should be more important than their tenure in assessing the degree of de facto political decentralisation in China. Take Shandong and Fujian for example. Governors in both of the provinces have a similar length of tenure (i.e., around three years), but in Shandong the insiders governed for 21 years in the 30-year reform period while the number for Fujian was only seven years. In other words, it seems that when the central government chooses Shandong governors the candidates have to be limited to the insiders, while the scenario in Fujian is very much the opposite. In this case, can we still say that, on the basis of their similar governor tenure, Shandong and Fujian are equally "centrally controlled" by the party centre, as Huang (1996) would suggest? Or should we say that Shandong enjoys much more de facto local political power because the centre's action could be constrained by the local influences, the influence which the centre could not easily dismiss as it would do in Fujian? The latter interpretation seems more accurate. This is what I call the "Chinese-style political decentralisation", that is, regional politics being dominated by insiders and the will of the central government being checked when it tries to intervene in the local affairs.

One important implication of the Chinese-style political decentralisation is that this arrangement is likely to motivate local officials to respond to local needs. This idea is best summarised in Lily Tsai's book titled *Accountability without Democracy* (Tsai 2007). In her book, Tsai studies public goods provision in Chinese villages. She compares villages where public goods like roads and irrigation systems are well provided with those where these public goods are under-provided. Her findings from extensive fieldwork show that a crucial factor to explain the willingness of the village officials to provide public goods is whether village officials are recruited from "encompassing solidary groups" in village, like clans. It is argued that in these solidary groups to which officials belong, in order to gain influence, a kind of soft power as conceptualised by Tsai, the village official is likely to provide public goods and avoid any kind of behaviour that would be denounced by his or her peers in the group. Here what Tsai has demonstrated is that in China, an undemocratic policy where free elections are absent, accountability of local officials is enforced not through formal rules like competitive election but through informal ties (like the solidary group) that link officials with the society. Then how does one discern such informal ties? As Tsai has shown, it can be done by examining an official's background, especially where he is recruited and how he builds his career. The usefulness of this approach is not limited to the study of the governance at the village level. In fact, it has proved fruitful when applied to the higher level of government. Using a panel of data on 31 Chinese provinces over 26 years, Persson and Zhuravskaya (2012) show that the background of top provincial leaders has considerable impact on the provision of regional public goods. Provinces led by party officials who build their careers within the province enjoy a better business environment and higher level of public goods provision than the provinces governed by cadres transferred from outside the province. The impact of "home-grown" provincial leaders is evident even after other inter-provincial variations like fiscal constraints and macroeconomic conditions are controlled. As Dani Rodrik (2005: 981) notes, the success of China should be attributed to that "unorthodox institutions worked precisely because they produced orthodox results". This seems to be the case when China manages to ensure the responsiveness of local government to social needs, not through political decentralisation in a liberal democratic fashion, but through its own style of political decentralisation.

It is clear now that the Chinese polity is not only administratively and fiscally decentralised, but also politically decentralised in an unorthodox way, which is the Chinese-style political decentralisation. Following the institutionalist logic, this decentralised structure should have profound implications for the preference and behaviour of local government. Then how exactly does the political decentralisation in China have such policy impacts? Persson and Zhuravskaya (2012) show that officials recruited locally tend to provide more public goods than those parachuted from outside. Their explanation for this is that local insiders are more likely to be assimilated into, if not "captured" by, the circle of local elites and therefore to have the preference of these elites. In other words, the de facto political decentralisation affects local officials' preferences by making this preference that of local elites. This book argues this is not the mechanism through which the politically decentralised structure shapes local governments' preferences.

Indeed, one cannot derive this from the evidence provided by the above study. The dependent variable of Persson and Zhuravskaya's study is the public spending on education and healthcare. The independent variable is the background of provincial leaders. The problem is that the majority of education and healthcare spending happens at the sub-provincial level, i.e., at the municipal and county levels. In other words, the provincial leaders do not directly make decisions on the aggregate level of social spending of a province, which is hardly surprising given the localised structure of the Chinese welfare system. So even if provincial leaders' preferences can be aligned with that of the local elites, they simply lack the legal authority to dictate how much should be spent on municipal welfare programmes. The best we can do, if we are to save Persson and Zhuravskaya's argument, is to argue that insider provincial leaders would increase fiscal transfers to municipal governments that are stipulated to be spent on social programmes. But then one has to show how provincial leaders can monitor sub-provincial officials and ensure these transfers are really spent on the right programmes if they do not want another Shanghai social insurance funds scandal exposed in their jurisdiction. Are insider provincial leaders more willing to take a firm hand in the case of public funds embezzlement than outsiders? Probably not. After all, they build their careers within the province and these municipal leaders are their power resources, if not protégés. Insider provincial leaders would be reluctant to punish any of them. Knowing the bottom line of their provincial party bosses, municipal officials, driven by a sort of moral hazard, could be even more audacious than they would be under the provincial leadership composed of outsiders. Therefore, Persson and Zhuravskaya's interpretation seems invalid. But their regression analysis does show a statistically significant association between provincial leader background and the overall level of public goods provision. Why is this the case if it is not because of the alignment between the preferences of insiders and those of local elites as Persson and Zhuravskaya claim? Can we have a better explanation of this?

By linking together two institutional settings, which are bureaucratic promotion tournament and Chinese-style political decentralisation, here I offer a parsimonious explanation without distorting the reality of Chinese politics. Following the promotion tournament model, I assume local officials, instead of being revenue-seeking, to be office-seeking. That is to say, municipal officials are eager to climb up the bureaucratic ladder. And the next step they want to take is the government post one level higher than the municipal post, that is, the provincial post. The decision of who are to be provincial leaders is made by the central government. The central government then employs the tournament competition to motivate the municipal leaders, promising that the promotion to provincial posts hinges on municipal economic performance. This promise, however, is not equally credible across provinces. If a province has long been governed by officials promoted from the municipality, which means municipal leaders working in this province have a good chance of getting the provincial post, then the promise by central principal is credible. But if a province frequently has leaders sent from Beijing, then the municipal leaders in this province know they may not be promoted to the provincial leadership no matter how well their municipalities perform in economic terms, suggesting that the central promise of promotion is not credible. The credibility of the central government can greatly shape the preference and hence the behaviour of municipal officials. For those municipal leaders who are fortunate to serve in an insider-dominant province, motivated by the credible promise from central government, they work their hardest to promote local economic development, which is the main criteria when assessing cadres' performance, in order to squeeze into the candidate pool for the future provincial leadership. Such motivation however is much lower for those municipal leaders who work in an outsider-led province, because in such a province the promise of rewarding the best economic champion is not credible, meaning that municipal officials know no matter how well they perform in their job they are unlikely to get the attention from the central government, which will parachute an outsider to the province anyway. Surely, these unlucky municipal leaders may still have chances of getting a job in the provincial government. But at the very best they can only be one of the seven or eight vice-governors (which are by no means reserved for municipal leaders and are also open to outsiders). But even this may count as nothing in the eyes of some ambitious bureaucrat compared with the provincial leadership, especially when it comes to the possibility for office holders to be further promoted to the party centre. Indeed, only the provincial leader (not the deputy leaders) can serve in the Chinese Communist Party's Politburo, the true core of the Chinese political power. The point here is not that municipal leaders in outsider-dominant provinces would have no incentive to do anything, which is simply untrue. Rather, they do have motivation but their motivation to perform well is much lower than their counterparts serving in insider-led provinces where the promise made by the central government is more credible in terms of municipal leaders having greater chances of getting the provincial leadership posts.

The implication of the above story, therefore, is that the motivation of local officials to compete against each other to promote regional economy and enhance local competitiveness, whether it is through business-friendly policies or protectionist measures, is a function of the credibility of the central government on bureaucratic promotion in the province. With this knowledge, we can re-interpret the findings of Persson and Zhuravskaya (2012). The backgrounds of provincial leaders do not reflect certain inherent qualities of them, as assumed by many scholars examining Chinese leaders' resumes, like Persson and Zhuravskaya. Instead, it is an indicator of the central government's credibility and hence the incentive structure in which local officials calculate and behave. Being office-seeking may be the same for every local official. But this universal preference has to be mitigated through institutional settings so it can be translated into local officials' concrete preferences over public policies. Such institutional arrangements, as has been shown, are the bureaucratic tournament promotion and the Chinese-style political decentralisation. These institutional settings, through affecting officials' chances of promotion and the credibility of the central government on promotion, shapes municipal leader's preferences and hence behaviours regarding local developmental strategies. Municipal officials in insider-dominant provinces, motivated by the credibe promise of the central government, are more likely to adopt policies that would create a better business environment and provide more public goods to foster socio-economic development. By contrast, municipal bureaucrats in outsider-dominant provinces, frustrated by the prospect that their efforts would not earn them a prominent provincial post which the party centre will always fill with an outsider, tend to be less motivated, if not predatory, in local economic development, compared with their counterparts in insider-dominant provinces. That is why we can see, as in Persson and Zhuravskaya's article, a positive relationship between provincial leaders being insiders and local provision of public goods. Bureaucratic tournament promotion and the Chinese-style political decentralisation, being incentive structures constraining local governments, shape local officials' policy behaviour.

Having revealed the impacts of the Chinese-style political decentralisation, it is worthwhile to explore its causes, i.e., what brings this institutional arrangement into being? To answer this helps us explain a seeming paradox: If the central government wants economic growth, then why does it, instead of appointing insiders to every province, which should give the municipal leaders more incentive to pursue economic expansion, assign outsiders to provincial leading posts in some cases, which tends to discourage the sub-provincial leaders from promoting local economic development? In other words, why do some provinces have insiders as their provincial leaders while others have outsiders? This study argues that while it is true that the central authority asks for economic performance, the varying geographical and historical conditions of Chinese provinces may compel the central authority to have political considerations rather than purely economic calculations when it decides which one, the insider or the outsider, to appoint as provincial leader. Two political considerations are prominent. The first is the need to control the minority ethnic groups. The Chinese central government is highly alert to any separatist tendency, which is most likely to come from ethnic minority groups such as the Tibetans and Uyghurs. So in provinces with sizeable minority communities, like Tibet, Xinjiang, Gansu, Qinghai and even Yunnan, provincial leaders are often outsiders, who are sent there by the central government to excise a firm grip on the locality. The second political consideration stems from the need to maintain the reform-minded coalitions between the central and local political elites. As mentioned in Chapter 2, "playing to the province" is a major strategy employed by the political elites at the central level to mobilise political support from the locality in the power struggle with other factions in the party centre. After the death of Chairman Mao, this strategy was applied by market-oriented reformers, notably Deng Xiaoping, in the battle with the conservatives who sought to retain the Maoist regime. Deng allied with the provinces that had suffered the most under the Maoist radicalism, who thus were most willing to embrace changes to form a reform-oriented coalition, which successfully brought him to the status of paramount leader. In the process he granted the provinces much autonomy, including the implicit political autonomy to have their home-grown officials (i.e., insiders) as their provincial leaders, to "give local officials an incentive . . . to join his political coalition for reform" (Shirk 1993: 21). This is why many of the provinces that pioneered China's market transition, like Guangdong, Shandong, Zhejiang and Sichuan, are often governed by insiders in the reform period, while the strongholds of the planned economy, like Jilin and Liaoning, are more likely to be led by outsiders, who are there to keep in check the local officials and citizens reluctant to abandon Maoist practices. A province's affinity with Maoism, in turn, is determined by how it was incorporated into the Communist regime during the process of the Chinese Communist Revolution (Yang 1996; Kung and Lin 2003; Anderson 2010). Therefore, the geography and history of a province often shape the central government's decision on the appointment of its provincial leaders. Geography and history matter, but this does not suggest that the economic logic ceases to work. It just means the possibility of economic calculation to dominate the appointing decision is reduced by other structural factors. Since the central government's personnel decision is shaped by historical and geographical factors, which are decided outside our theory, the credibility of the central authority on bureaucratic promotion (as indicated by the composition of provincial leadership) is treated as exogenous in our theory.

The above disussion about the leadership selection process can be summarised and encapsulated in the following parsimonious way. This study makes the following assumptions about Chinese bureaucrats' preferences:

1 Bureaucrats are rational maximisers of their own utilities.
2 Bureaucrats derive utilities from holding offices.
3 Offices that are higher in the administrative hierarchy generate a higher degree of utilities.

The logical implication of the above three assumptions is that Chinese bureaucrats maximise their utilities by climbing up the bureaucratic ladder. In other words, Chinese bureaucrats are office-seeking. The municipal officials, therefore, try to maximise their utilities by pursuing the provincial offices, whose administrative status is one level higher than that of the municipal posts.

The municipal leaders' pursuit of provincial posts is regulated by two institutional settings. The first institutional arrangement is bureaucratic tournament promotion. The central government appoints provincial leaders. The number of provincial posts is limited. The municipal officials have to compete against each other for the promotion to the provincial office. The winner of the intermunicipal competition is decided on the basis of municipal economic performance. That is to say, the municipal leader who performs best in terms of delivering economic growth wins the competition. This arrangement motivates municipal officials to enhance their chances of winning the competition by, on the one hand, promoting economic development within their own jurisdictions through economy-friendly policies, and on the other, sabotaging the economic growth of their competitors through non-cooperative local protectionist policies. This is easy to understand: One can win the competition by making himself look good and others look bad.

The second institutional setting is termed as Chinese-style political decentralisation. Due to the authoritarian nature of the Chinese central government, there is no mechanism that can make the central government committed to appointing the best-performing municipal officials to be provincial leaders. The credibility of the central government's commitment to award the wining municipal officials provincial posts is not equal across all regions. In some provinces, municipal leaders that emerge winning from the tournament competition get the provincial posts, but in other provinces the provincial positions are filled with outsiders from elsewhere like central ministries or other provinces, which resembles the hiring practice whereby employers recruit from the external labour market rather than promoting internally.

The two institutional arrangements have profound implications for policy choices of the municipal leaders. The bureaucratic tournament promotion drives municipal officials to make efforts to foster local economic growth and to compete with each other by adopting non-cooperative or even sabotaging actions. The likelihood of municipal leaders having those behaviours is in turn dependent upon the credibility of the central government's commitment to award the tournament winner, which is dictated by the Chinese-style political decentralisation. Therefore, the more credible the central government's commitment to award the inter-municipal competition winners provincial posts is, the more effort the municipal leaders will make to develop regional economy and implement local protectionist policies. This is how the institutional arrangements of the Chinese state, namely bureaucratic promotion tournament and Chinese-style decentralisation, govern the leadership selection process and hence constitute the incentive structure that shapes the behaviours of the office-seeking municipal leaders.

Stage two: social policymaking

The incentive structure given rise by the institutional settings in the leadership selection process has great implications for municipal leaders' policy behaviours. First, motivated by realistic prospects of promotion, local leaders foster regional economy by enhancing local competitiveness through various policy measures including building a business-friendly environment and investing in local infrastructure projects. A second implication of the institutional arrangements is the difficulty of cooperation between local governments. Because only very few winners of local competition can be promoted, the competition among local governments is non-cooperative. In other words, the highly competitive promotion tournament makes the interaction between localities a zero-sum game, meaning that one municipal leader's gain in the likelihood of being promoted is the loss of the other. A rational local leader then should avoid anything that would better his competitors more than himself. Therefore, it is very difficult for two municipalities to take cooperative action.

The above logic is articulated in the area of pension policy as follows. As we will see later at the economic decision-making stage, by reducing labour market risks of lifetime income loss, pension policy can be conducive to the formation of specific industrial skills, which are crucial for local economic expansion in the context of industrial upgrading and labour market tightening. In this case, if municipal leaders are motivated by a credible commitment of the central government regarding bureaucratic promotion to foster the development of regional economy, then they will expand the coverage of pension programmes so more workers and employers can be encouraged to acquire industry specific skills, a kind of production factor that is crucial for local industrialisation. The central government's credible promise will also incentivise municipal leaders to keep the pension programmes localised at the municipal level, a kind of local protectionist policy, because this can make the pension package non-portable and therefore prevent skilled workers from moving to and benefiting other municipalities. The credibility of the central government's commitment regarding bureaucratic promotion is indicated by the historical composition of the provincial leadership. If a province traditionally has insider leadership that is promoted from its municipalities, then the central government's promise to award the winner of the inter-municipal tournament competition is credible to the municipal leaders within this province. Such promise becomes less credible to municipal officials if the province usually has outsider leadership, which is not promoted locally but transferred from Beijing or elsewhere. The above logic then generates the following two hypotheses:

1 *Expansion Hypothesis*: The province more often governed by insider leadership will have a higher level of pension coverage because its municipal leaders are motivated to spare more efforts to promote local economic development by expanding the coverage of pension programmes.
2 *Localisation Hypothesis*: The province more often governed by insider leadership is less likely to have its pension scheme integrated at the provincial level because its municipal leaders have the incentives to keep the pension programmes localised along the municipal border.

Stage three: economic decision-making

After municipal leaders install the pension programmes, how will economic agents such as workers and employers respond? In particular, will they respond to the presence of the local pension programmes by making human capital investment decisions in a way that favours the acquisition of specific skills? Following Gary Becker (1962, 1964), this study conceptualises human capital as two types of skills. They are general skills, which are valuable in a wide range of sectors, and specific skills, which are productive in only a small number of industries. This study focuses on the human capital investment decisions made by two types of economic agents. The first type of economic agent is the student, who has to make the schooling decision on which kind of education to pursue: general education that offers general skills or vocational education that teaches specific skills. The second kind of economic agent is the employer, who makes the on-the-job training decisions on whether or not to provide training programmes for employees that equip them with specific skills.

Our model on how these two types of economic agents make human capital investment decisions builds on three assumptions about individuals' preferences and behaviours:

1 Individuals are rational maximisers of lifetime income, which is composed of wages and pensions.
2 Individuals invest in human capital to acquire skills that will generate the highest expected lifetime income.
3 Individuals are risk averse.

The question then arises: Which type of skills, general skills or industry specific skills, will individuals choose to maximise their expected lifetime income? General skills are of value to a large number of industries and firms, whereas industry specific skills are valuable to only one or a few industries. Different skill specificity leads to different income loss risks. During a time of unexpected economic downturn or technological change, workers with general skills will face fewer risks of income loss because, given that their skills can be utilised in a large number of industries, general-skilled workers will have higher contact rates with potential employers and hence better chances of exiting unemployment if they are made redundant, and the transferability of their skills will ensure that they will earn the same level of wage if they get reemployed. The situation is reversed for workers with industry specific skills. These workers will face more income loss risks during economic downturn. This is because, if they get laid off, the high specificity of their skills greatly limits the number of their potential employers and makes it difficult for them to be hired at the same wage if they are back to work. Compared with general skills, specific skills entail higher risks of income loss.

Such risks have implications for the accumulation of wealth in preparation for retirement, i.e., pension. Pension can be understood as "deferred wage" (Iversen and Soskice 2001: 876; Iversen 2005: 79). It is closely associated with the employment status and earning ability of the workers before retirement. If a worker is made redundant and his skills are left idle, then his income drops, so does his financial input into his pension plan, be it in the form of savings, taxes or old-age income insurance contributions. The contribution to his post-retirement plan will decrease even more if such contribution requires the input from the employer. Therefore, the loss of income at working age, which we have associated with specific skills, means the loss of pension after retirement and hence the loss of lifetime income.

The implication is clear: If the risks of lifetime income loss are more likely to come with specific skills than compared with general skills, then any risk-averse individual will choose to acquire general skills to maximise his lifetime income and shun the investment in specific skills, provided there are no outside interventions to alter individuals' human capital investment decisions.

If we bring in outside factors like social protection programmes, then the picture will be different. A social protection programme is the institutional arrangement that insures workers against the risks of income loss during times of unemployment, disability, old age, etc. It has many institutional manifestations. Of particular relevance to this study is the public old-age income insurance. By providing pension benefits, the state assures the individuals about the stability of their lifetime income. The lifetime income of workers, in other words, becomes less dependent upon their employment status and earning ability, compared with the case where there is no such state input on the pension programme. The public pension scheme then constitutes an insurance against the risks of lifetime income loss. Without the public pension programme, such insurance would be provided by general skills, which minimises the income loss risks with the help of skill transferability. With a public pension programme in place, the necessity to acquire general skills to maximise lifetime income diminishes. Without worrying about the loss of lifetime income, individuals, when they are students who have to choose between general education and vocational education, then are not deterred from acquiring specific skills through vocational education. That is to say, students are more likely to attend vocational schools when there is a more comprehensive public pension system. This is the first implication.

If workers care about pension benefits for the sake of lifetime income, then the portability of pension package should have an impact on their labour market behaviours. The Chinese public pension system is regionally fragmented along municipal and provincial borders, which makes pension package non-portable across regions. Workers cannot move from one locality to another without incurring the loss of some or all of the accumulated pension benefits. This therefore deters labour mobility. One implication of the reduced workforce mobility is that employers become less concerned about the problem of poaching. Poaching across regions becomes more expensive in the presence of a localised pension system because outside firms have to pay more to the poached workers so that the lost pension benefits can be compensated. In this sense China's pension system deters poaching. Being less worried about their workers being poached, employers become more willing to invest in employee training programmes that will equip workers with industry specific skills. This is our second implication.

Therefore, on the basis of the assumptions made about individual preferences and behaviours, two hypotheses are generated, which combined together argue that China's pension system contributes to the formation of specific skills because it encourages students and employers to invest in the acquisition of such skills. These two hypotheses are:

1 *Schooling Hypothesis*: If social protection programmes like pension can encourage students to acquire industry specific skills, then regions with higher pension coverage rates should have higher enrolment rates in vocational schools.
2 *Training Hypothesis*: If localised pension programmes can limit job turnover and hence alleviate the problem of poaching, then workers covered by pension programmes should have longer job tenure and thus be more likely to receive trainings offered by employers.

Summarising discussion: China's localised pension system as a beneficial constraint

This study adopts the position of methodological individualism, arguing that China's pension system should be understood in terms of individual choices made by local leaders, employers and workers. The theoretical perspective of rational choice institutionalism is then applied to build a three-stage theory on how political institutions of the Chinese state shape the strategic interactions between rational agents and eventually lead to an expansive and localised pension system. The starting point of this theory is the interaction between the central government and the municipal leaders in the leadership selection process. At this stage, under the institutional arrangements of bureaucratic promotion tournament and Chinese-style political decentralisation, municipal leaders make calculations based on their expectations on how likely they are to be awarded by the central government, and accordingly choose the degree of efforts to promote local economy and the level of hostility against other municipalities. The incentive structure formed in the leadership selection process shapes the pension policy choices of municipal leaders in the policymaking stage. When the commitment of the central government to promote the winner of the inter-municipal tournament is credible, municipal leaders tend to implement an expansive pension policy and resist the integration of pension programmes beyond the municipal level, in the hopes that this could induce the training of a locally retained workforce with productive industrial skills. Whether such belief is grounded in facts depends on the outcome of the economic decision-making process, where economic agents like workers and employers respond to municipal leaders' pension policy by making decisions on human capital investment. The interactions between political and economic agents in this three-stage process generate a political-economic equilibrium in the sense that political institutions create policy and the policy leads to economic outcomes that in turn reproduce the policy and the institutions by providing positive feedback. Only by putting it in the perspective of this equilibrium can we explain the continuing expansion and persistent localisation of China's pension system. To have a comprehensive assessment of the validity of this theory requires its predictions to be tested and its assumptions evaluated. This asks for a mixed methods approach that combines the quantitative methods with the qualitative analysis. This is to be discussed in Chapter 4.

Before discussing the methodology applied to test this theory, it is helpful to discuss how the theoretical framework of this book engages with two prominent notions in the literature of the comparative political economy of the welfare state, namely "beneficial constraint" and "welfare magnet". This thesis's argument that China's localised pension system facilitates skill formation conforms to the idea of "beneficial constraint". This concept is formulated by Wolfgang Streeck (1997) in his discussion on the capacity of institutions to constrain the voluntaristic choices of rational actors so beneficial outcomes can be generated for the society as a whole. In particular, this concept refers to the institutional underpinnings of the market economy that restrain actors from doing what they believe is in their best interests, implicitly forcing them to choose alternative strategies they would not otherwise have considered, and (unintentionally) enhance the overall economic efficiency. It is articulated on the basis of the historical experience of the forging of the German production regime in postwar years. During that period, with the disgracing of right-wing parties due to their shameful wartime record, the German business sector was tamed by leftist parties and strong unions. As a result, a co-determination system that limits managerial power and an expensive welfare state funded by employer contributions were imposed on German capitalists, who did not want these restraining institutions but had to give up resistance and accept them given the political circumstances. Faced with the resulting situations of an expensive workforce, German firms had to give up the competition strategy that relied on mass production of low-quality commodities, a relatively easy strategy they would have chosen if there were no institutional constraints on managerial prerogatives and production flexibility. Instead, they were forced to take a difficult "high way", climbing up the value chain of industrial production and focusing on the niche segments of product markets. Meanwhile, to make the best use of the expensive labour force, German employers had to invest significantly in their employees' skill development, thereby contributing to the formation of a high-skilled workforce. The resultant production mode is what Streeck calls "diversified quality production", which has since served as the cornerstone of the postwar German economic efficiency. The economic success of the German economy, therefore, is not the result of any intelligent design. On the contrary, it should be seen as the largely unintentional outcome of the institutional settings given rise by the political circumstances in early postwar years, which restrained the capitalist's production strategy choice but eventually upgraded the structure of German industries and enhanced the overall efficiency of the German economy.

A similar story can be told of the Chinese case of public pension inducing employer investment in worker skills. As will be clear from the qualitative materials presented in Chapter 6, which deal with social policy preferences of employers, some segments of Chinese employers, especially those pursuing industrial upgrading like Geely Automobile, support expansionary social policies and urge the government to impose stricter regulations on the employers who gain cost advantages by evading social insurance contributions. The employers who can afford to evade social insurance contributions and use cheap, unskilled labour force, arguably, should be producing in low-end industrial sectors. China's extensive public pension system, this study argues, forces these employers to climb up the value chain to survive the market competition. The reason for this is as follows. The politics of inter-municipal competition for bureaucratic promotion give rise to a localised pension system. With the support of employers who need to retain skilled workers for industrial upgrading, this system is expanded and imposed on all employers, including those whose production strategy requires a mobile, low-skilled workforce. The expensive pension programme, on the one hand, levies a financial cost in the form of pension contributions on these low-skill-intensive Chinese firms. This forces these employers to compensate the extra human capital costs (i.e., social insurance contributions) by increasing workers' productivity through vocational trainings designed to improve their skills. On the other hand, the localised pension scheme discourages voluntary mobility of workers by incurring the loss of pension benefits when workers move across localities. The reduced labour mobility, due to the institutional restraints, gives employers assurance that their workers will not easily job-hop and therefore encourages employers to make investments in workers' skill development. The net result of the expensive and localised pension system, therefore, is that employers have to give up low-end, low-skill-intensive competition strategy, which they would have voluntarily followed if labour costs had not been raised by social insurance contributions, and to pursue a high-skill-intensive production strategy by investing in the skill upgrading of employees, an investment that they would not be willing to make if job turnover rates were not reduced by the non-portability of pension packages. The expansive and localised Chinese public pension system is restrictive in terms of curbing the voluntary mobility of workers and the competition strategy choices of employers. But it is at the same time beneficial in the sense that it facilitates the pursuit of the alternative production strategy that would improve the skill profile and hence the productivity of the whole economy. China's localised pension system, therefore, by generating beneficial outcomes for the society as a whole with constraints on voluntaristic choices of workers and employers, articulates the logic of "beneficial constraint".

While the notion of "beneficial constraint" lends theoretical support to our theory, the idea of "welfare magnet" is a competing hypothesis to our argument. It has been argued that social protection programmes like pension can facilitate the production of specific skills by encouraging workers and employers to make investment in the acquisition of those skills, which implies that local officials who are concerned with the industrialisation of local economy will get actively involved in pension reform. But there is an alternative argument as to why Chinese local leaders may have an interest in social problems like providing pensions. One may have a "welfare magnet" argument that generous social benefits can serve as a magnet that attracts skilled workers to move from elsewhere to the municipality. Indeed, under the constraints of a short tenure length, making investment to train their own skilled workers may be time-consuming in the eyes of municipal leaders. Then to have a quick solution to the issue of human capital and investment and accumulation, local leaders may consider increasing social spending to build a working environment that is attractive to skilled workers. Therefore, a locality with comprehensive social protection programmes can have a large pool of skilled workers, not because those programmes encourage the human capital investment by local citizens as argued earlier, but because those programmes attract skilled workers from elsewhere. Do Chinese social protection programmes have such magnetic effects? To answer this question requires us to review the literature on the "welfare magnet" hypothesis and evaluate it in the Chinese context.

A large body of literature on migration examines how the generosity of social programmes affects migrants' location choices. It has been hypothesised that a high level of social benefit generosity will attract migrants. In other words, localities, whether they are countries, states or any other jurisdictions, will be "magnets" that draw migrants in if they offer generous social benefits. This hypothesis has been formulated and extensively tested in the context of the United States, where the concern of international migration often stirs major public debates. In an influential article, George Borjas (1999) examines whether location decisions made by international migrants who come to the United States can be affected by the variation in welfare benefits across the states. International migrants, assumed by Borjas to be wealth maximisers, are a self-selected sample of people who are willing to bear the fixed costs of migration, which means the marginal cost for them of choosing the "right" state with high social benefits should be low. The implication is that the states that have higher levels of welfare generosity should see more international migrants who receive welfare benefits. This hypothesis receives empirical support from statistical analysis of the 1980 and 1990 Public Use Microdata Samples (PUMS) of the U.S. census. This then leads Borjas (1999: 635) to conclude that inter-state differences in immigration patterns can be partially explained by the variations in welfare benefits across states. This conclusion is supported by a recent study by McKinnish (2007), who examines the same U.S. Census data with a research strategy that synthesises approaches of previous welfare migration literature. McKinnish provides further support for the magnetic welfare argument by showing those residents closer to the state borders are more likely to engage in welfare migration.

In the Chinese context, will generous welfare programmes have a similar magnetic effect in serving as a force that pulls mobile workers to work in a locality? Chen and Coulson (2002), using a dataset of 223 Chinese cities covering 1995 to 1999, investigate the causes of the growth rate of urban residents in the non-agricultural sector minus the natural growth rate of the urban population (i.e., births minus deaths). After controlling for factors that may attract migrants to urban areas, such as economic growth and service sector development, they find a positive association between government fiscal expenditure and the rate of migration to cities. The authors explain this association with reference to the attactiveness to mobile workers of better local schooling, which tends to be associated with high public spending. Then why can better local schooling affect the Chinese worker's location choice? This is because workers may move to localities with better schools for their children to have better education, and educated workers are more likely to do so than their less educated counterparts. Never underestimate what Chinese parents can do for their children especially when they are only allowed to have one child. In an interesting paper on the impact of the birth control policy on the investment in human capital in China, Rosenzweig and Zhang (2009) report a trade-off between the number of children and the quality of children in terms of health condition, school grades and college enrolment chances. The heavy investment in child nutrition and education may be induced by the fact that most Chinese parents only have one child to rely on when they get old. So as rational individuals, following Gary Becker's reasoning, in order to secure the future of the child and hence their own post-retirement life, parents will do anything for their only child, including moving to a nice city.

The "welfare magnet" argument has one drawback. It pays no attention to the policy and institution that governs the migration flow, which is termed as "migration regime" by Razin and Wahba (2011). This is not surprising. Empirical testing of the "welfare magnet" hypothesis is often conducted within one country, be it the United States or China, where sub-national jurisdictions have the same migration regime. This certainly helps to control for the impact of migration policy, which is important to empirical testing. But the price is that it gives researchers no chance to investigate the impact of migration regime when it comes to theoretical building. Migration regime appears unimportant in a single country research strategy simply because it is the same everywhere at the sub-national level, but this does not mean it is not important for welfare migration.

Razin and Wahba (2011) take on this pitfall of previous "welfare magnet" literature and set out to examine how welfare state's magnet effect is mediated by different migration regimes. Their research strategy is to compare and contrast countries with different migration regimes. Two types of migration regimes are identified: the free migration regime, where the state recognises an individual's right to reside and work freely regardless of his personal characteristics, and the restricted migration regime, where there is no recognition of the rights to free movement. Razin and Wahba assess the different effects of the two regimes on international migration by comparing the free movement within European Union (plus Norway and Switzerland) and the restricted labour movement from non-EU countries. Their statistical results show that welfare state generosity has different impacts on the skill composition of migrants, depending on which type of migration regime is in place. When there is free migration regime, low-skilled workers will be attracted to the country and end up living on welfare benefits, while high-skilled people will be deterred from moving to this country because of the fear that they may have to shoulder a heavy financial burden to fund the welfare state due to welfare dependency. Under a restricted migration regime, the generous welfare state is still a public good that is appealing to everyone, regardless of skill levels, but there is no such worry about financial burdens for skilled workers. This is because a restricted migration regime, by giving the government policy tools to keep at bay unskilled workers that are likely to be welfare dependents, offers the skilled workers a credible promise on the sustainability of the welfare state and hence the stability of future taxation. This motivates the entry of skilled migrants, who are more than welcome in the country because the government knows skilled migrants will be net contributors to the generous, expensive social programmes. In a word, the effects of the "welfare magnet" on migration are contingent upon migration regimes. While a free migration regime shifts the pattern of migration towards an unskilled one, a restricted migration regime leads to the migration of skilled workers.

The argument of Razin and Wahba (2011) may lead one to conclude that under China's internal migration regime, generous social programmes should encourage the migration of skilled workers. Indeed, the institution in China that regulates interregional migration, called the Household Registration System or *Hukou*, is highly restrictive and selective. At every sub-national level, it discriminates against migrants from other localities who have no or few productive skills, but at the same time favours the migration of better educated migrants (for a discussion on China's education-based selective migration, see Pan 2012). Clearly Hukou is similar to the kind of restricted migration regime identified by Razin and Wahba (2011). Under such migration regime, will a Chinese locality with better social protection programmes attract more skilled workers? If we follow the argument of Razin and Wahba (2011), then the answer should be "yes". But this study does not think so.

Razin and Wahba are right to bring in the institutional arrangements that regulate migration. But they have only focused on the institutions of the host country, that is, the country where migrants move to. Their study pays no attention to the policies and institutions of the source country, that is, the country where the migrants come from. The outflow of skilled workers, who are attracted by generous welfare systems in other countries, means "brain drain" for the source country. The source country will have policy responses to prevent such "brain drain". These preventive measures then should affect the features of migration. This idea is especially relevant for the Chinese case. Chinese local governments view a skilled workforce as a crucial component of local competitiveness. They will not sit aside and watch their skilled workers leave. In fact, Chinese local authorities extensively intervene in the labour market to keep skilled workers from leaving their jurisdictions, by, for example, retaining skilled workers' personnel files (Wang 2008; Liao and Qing 2011). Such intervention also includes the localising pension policy, which, as will be demonstrated in Chapter 6, reduces job turnover and thus limits labour mobility. Because of local states' intervention, skilled workers may not be able to leave a locality without incurring high costs (like the loss of accumulated pension funds) in the first place. This is why the "welfare magnet" argument, which pays no attention to the preventive measures by source countries that limit labour mobility, will not be applicable to the Chinese context. This also explains why Chinese localities have to train their own skilled workforce as opposed to trying to poach them from elsewhere. Such training, as we have argued, will have to be facilitated by the expansion and localisation of pension programmes.

Notes

1 The only progress in political decentralisation seems to be limited to the introduction of village-level elections. The efforts to push for free elections above that level are rare (O'Brien, K. J. and L. Li 2000).

2 In some cases, he serves in managerial positions in strategically important state-owned enterprises. As these enterprises are controlled by certain central ministries, these officials are included in the group of ministry-transferring cadres and thus coded as "outsiders".

4 Research methodology

How do we study China (and its pension system)

To evaluate the theory formulated in the previous chapter, this study employs a mixed methods research strategy. It combines the quantitative approach, which is deployed to test hypotheses generated by our theory, and the qualitative approach, which is dedicated to substantiate the theory and assess its assumptions about agents' preferences and behaviours. The first section of this chapter presents the research design of this book. After a critical review of major branches of social science methodology, this section justifies the selection of China and its pension system as the focus of this book. It also explains why this study adopts a sub-national research design and chooses province as unit of analysis. Disaggregating China into sub-national units enlarges the number of cases, which allows this study to use the statistical method to test the implications of our theory. This quantitative approach should be coupled with the qualitative analysis because this is the way through which we can have a comprehensive assessment of the validity of our theory.

Advocates of the rational choice approach argue that a theory should be justified on the capacity of its predictions to survive empirical tests rather than on the accuracy of its assumptions (Friedman 1953). This study agrees with the stance that one should assess a theory on the basis of the explanatory power of its implications, and in accordance with this position, this book utilises a quantitative approach to systematically test the hypotheses derived from our theory. But this study is cautious with the assertion that the accuracy of the assumptions bears little relevance in determining the validity of a theory. In fact, avoiding examining the accuracy of assumptions is potentially dangerous. As Hall and Taylor (1996) point out, generating predictions on behaviours from rational choice theory is sensitive to the assumptions made about agents' preference structures. If these assumptions are made arbitrarily or without empirical support, then one can never know whether the theory inspired by the rational choice approach shows anything concrete about social life, nor one can have genuine confidence in the predictions based on such assumptions, even though the predictions may have ample explanatory power in terms of being able to pass empirical tests. The failure to make behavioural assumptions a reasonable approximation of social reality becomes one of the major "pathologies" of rational choice theory (Green and Shapiro 1994).

To avoid the error of making unrealistic assumptions, this study employs a qualitative approach to interpret and understand the preferences and behaviours of political and economic agents. This study reveals the actors' perspectives on pension policy and skill acquisition by citing their own words in speeches collected in fieldwork and interviews derived from newspaper data. This is meant to examine to what extent the assumptions made in the rational choice account of this study reflect what agents genuinely think about issues concerning pension policy and human capital investment. The close resemblance between the theoretical assumptions made by the researcher and the actual belief and behaviour of the agents should demonstrate the validity of the assumptions and hence the validity of our theory.

Therefore, the need to have a comprehensive assessment of our theory, which not only examines its implications but also evaluates its assumptions, requires a mixed methods research strategy that couples quantitative techniques with qualitative methods. On the basis of assumptions about the preference and behaviours of political and economic agents, this study formulates a rational choice institutionalist theory to explain the expansive and localised characteristics of China's pension system, which generates observable implications to be tested. The quantitative methods of statistical analysis are then used to test these implications, while the qualitative approach is deployed to evaluate the assumptions about actors' preferences and behaviours. Only by combining the quantitative and qualitative approach can we fully assess the validity of the theory. The following sections present the research design of this book and discuss further methodological issues involved in the application of the two approaches.

Research design

A fundamental question a researcher must ask himself, according to de Vaus (2001: 1), is whether he aims to discover what is going on (descriptive research) or he seeks to explain why it is going on (explanatory research). If the research belongs to the latter camp, then a further question emerges as to whether it aims at theory-building, which uses inductive reasoning so observations are generalised into a theory, or theory-testing, which applies deductive reasoning to construct a theory before using empirical evidence to assess it against competing theories (de Vaus 2001: 5). This book is clearly an explanatory study since it attempts to explain why the Chinese pension system is expansive and localised. In addition, it aims at theory-testing, because in the preceding chapter we have applied the rational choice approach to build up a theory on the bahaviours of political and economic agents in China's pension reform. In this case, the purpose of research design for this book is to choose a research strategy among various options that will best serve the goal of theory-testing.

Lijphart (1971) provides a framework to categorise different research strategies, which often serves as the point of departure for many subsequent discussions on social science methodology (for example, see Collier 1993). This framework identifies four branches of methodology in social science. All of them aim to realise the *ceteris paribus* condition, which means holding other variables constant, because this is the only way to identify causal relationships and formulate scientific explanations (Lijphart 1971: 683).

The first method for scientific inquiry identified by Lijphart (1971) is the experimental method. It achieves *ceteris paribus* by comparing one group of observations exposed to a stimulus (the experimental group) with the other group (the control group) that is identical to the former group in every way except that it is not affected by the stimulus. This allows the researcher to attribute any difference in the result to the presence of the stimulus, thereby identifying a causal relationship. The condition of two groups being equivalent in every aspect can be achieved through the procedure of randomisation, which randomly assign subjects to research groups to avoid selection bias by eliminating systematic preexisting group differences (Bloom 2008). In the settings of social research, however, this often meets ethical or practical impediments. So researchers have devised alternative ways to apply the experimental method. One approach is the quasi-experimental design, which observes a time series of data interrupted by some discreet event, like the introduction of a new public policy, and compares the observations before and after this event to assess the event's causal effect (Campbell and Stanley 1963). This approach counts as an experimental design in the sense that the interrupting event is treated as a form of experimental intervention that occurs in a natural setting. The quasi-experimental design is often criticised for its lack of randomisation (Achen 1986), which may lead to incorrect estimation of the causal effect of the interrupting event because subjects may differ in certain prior attributes that may affect the impacts of the event. Nevertheless, it is widely applied in studies that assess the effects of public policy (for a recent example of its application, see Dube et al. (2013), who examine the impacts of the 2004 expiration of a U.S. federal gun law on gun-related crimes).

The practical and ethical constraints limit the application of the experimental method in social research, but the idea of experiment has been influential in social science methodology in the sense that every social research method aiming at establishing general empirical proposition must have in it "the essential logic functions of experiment" (Nagel 1961: 452). This is why Lijphart (1971: 685) calls the comparative method, the second branch of social science methodology identified in his framework, the "substitute" for the experimental method. The comparative method seeks to approximate the logic of experimental control by conducting two strategies originally formulated by Mill (1843), that is, the most-similar-system design, which compares cases that are equivalent in all ways except for a few aspects of theoretical interest and holds these differences responsible for any variation in the outcome, and the most-different-system design, which identifies same correlations between cases' characteristics across a number of otherwise completely different cases (also see Hopkin 2002). The comparative method conceptualised by Lijphart (1971) deals with a small number of cases in order to give empirical explanations. Subsequent developments in the comparative methodology see a renewal of interpretive historical analysis. This can be seen in Skocpol's (1979, 1984) work on comparative historical sociology, which examines long-term historical process in the comparative perspective, and in Ragin's (1987) contribution to the "holistic" approach to comparison, which, following Verba's (1967: 112) treatment of cases as "configurative wholeness" rather than aggregations of several analytic aspects, puts an emphasis the holistic nature of cases and examines the model of causality in this setting, namely conjunctural causation, meaning that factors can have their causal effects only in combination with other factors. New development also sees the number of cases the comparative method can handle increased, thanks to the application of fuzzy sets and set theory to the comparative methodology (Ragin 2008; Schneider and Wagemann 2012), which now allows the researcher to conduct in-depth analysis of a modest number of cases (20 or so).

Having said this, the number of cases the comparative method can deal with is still limited. This leads to what Lijphart (1971: 686) thinks is the major problem facing the comparative method, that is, the problem of "many variables, small number of cases". This problem occurs when the limited number of cases greatly constrains the researcher's ability to control for many variables simultaneously, which makes it difficult to achieve the *ceteris paribus* condition and assess his or her theory against alternative ones. Therefore, although hypothesis-testing is seen as a primary goal of the comparative method (Skocpol and Somers 1980), in practice it is not always easy to assess several competing hypotheses with this approach. Lijphart (1971) suggests two primary ways to deal with this "too many variables, too few cases" problem. First, one may reduce the number of variables by applying the most-similar-system design. Indeed, when focusing on largely similar cases, which are "comparable cases" in Lijphart's (1971: 687) words, one may treat these similar aspects as constants and therefore can isolate the associations between those dissimilar characteristics. This solution, however, is criticised for causing a problem of "overdetermination" (Przeworski 1987: 38), meaning that too many similarities between cases deny the researcher the opportunity to assess competing theories, and therefore the dependent variable is "overdetermined" by the researcher's hypothesised causal factor. Instead, Przeworski (1987) suggests that the most-different-system design should be used for hypothesis-testing. This suggestion, however, is rejected by Geddes (2003: 89). She argues that because the most-different-system design selects cases on the basis of the value of the dependent variable, it causes a lack of variance on the outcome and introduces a selection bias. Other theorists like King et al. (1994: 129) also ask researchers to avoid selection on the dependent variable.

If reducing the number of variables is likely to cause extra problems, then to address the issue of "many variables, small number of cases" one may have to increase the number of cases, which is Lijphart's (1971) second strategy to deal with this problem. An enlarged sample of observations gives the researcher enough degree of freedom to conduct statistical manipulation. This leads to the third branch of social science methodology identified in Lijphart's framework, that is, the statistical method. This method achieves *ceteris paribus*, i.e., the controlling for variables, by means of partial correlations, which essentially divides the sample into groups and focuses on the correlations between variables within each group. The statistical method can approximate the logic of experimental design to the extent that authors like Lazarsfeld (1955: 119) even assert the experimental method can be seen as a special approach to the statistical design. Although the statistical method is widely applied in all fields of social research, statisticians like Freeman (1987, 1991) suggest that researchers use caution when conducting quantitative analysis of social phenomena, primarily because the data collected and employed in the social sciences often fail to meet the assumptions underlying the statistical approach. Fortunately, innovations in statistical techniques help social researchers to deal with these problems. One example is the development of "robust" statistical procedures, which prevent the regression coefficients being distorted by deviant or extreme values, a problem that often occurs when the analysis only includes a few hundred country and region cases (Hampel et al. 1987; Mosteller and Tukey 1977). Ragin (1987) argues the assumption in statistical analysis that causal relations are homogeneous across cases does not hold in the social world, where "conjunctural causation" are often encountered, meaning causal effects vary with contexts. This problem can be addressed by adding interaction terms into the regression equation, which allows researchers to examine how the impacts of a certain independent variable change depending on the value of another explanatory variable (Jackson 1992). The application of interaction terms in political economy has proved fruitful, as one can see in the debate on how corporatism affects major European countries' economic performance, where the strength of the unionised labour and the power of left-wing parties are interacted in the quantitative analysis to examine the impacts of the two factors on economic growth (Lange and Garrett 1985; Jackman 1987, 1989; Hicks and Patterson 1989). Having solved the methodological problems such as those mentioned above, the statistical method is a powerful tool for theory-testing. That is why Lijphart (1971: 485) makes the comments that for the purpose of making scientific generalisations one should "generally use the statistical method instead of the weaker comparative method".

The final branch of social science methodology highlighted in Lijphart's (1971) framework is the case study method. Unlike the statistical method, which studies many cases, or the comparative method, which is applied to at least two cases, the case study method focuses on one single case, and by examining it intensively gains an in-depth knowledge of this case. Lijphart (1971: 106) thinks a single case cannot serve as the basis for disproving a generalisation, and therefore the major function of the case study method is not so much to test established theories as it is to inform researchers for the purpose of theory-building. Likewise, Earl Babbie (1992: 24) argues that since it includes only one case, the case study method offers little variation in the outcome to be explained and hence no chance of disconfirming a hypothesis, a situation which he calls "the problem of ex post facto hypotheses".

For other authors, that the case study method is not fit for theory-testing is one major yet common misunderstanding about this method (Flyvbjerg 2006; Yin 2009: 47). A strategy to realise the potential of the case study method for theory-testing is offered by Campbell (1975). He argues that a given theory can generate many implications for different facets of one case, and therefore examining whether these implications are supported by the evidence collected from this case multiplies the researcher's opportunities to test the theory. This strategy is termed by Campell (1975) as "pattern matching". It is echoed by King et al. (1994: 48), who are aware that simply increasing the number of cases, an approach recommended by Lijphart (1971), may not add new information and thus suggest the researcher should increase the number of implications derived from his theory, which allows the researcher to test the theory from different angles and enhances the causal inference. Another strategy aimed at enhancing the ability of the case study method to test a theory is what George and McKeown (1985: 34) call "process-tracing". Through this strategy the researcher closely studies the sequential unfolding of the events, which occurs over time within the case, in an effort to assess to what extent the causal process suggested in the theory is reflected in the actual dynamics of change. Like Campbell's (1975) "pattern matching", the process-tracing approach also seeks to explore the multifaceted nature of the case. The difference is that it focuses on examining this along the timeline. Other theorists concerned with the possibility of the case study method to test hypotheses, like Eckstein (1992), suggest analysing a "critical case", the case which the researcher expects to best fit the hypothesised causal story. A critical case tends to be either a "least likely" or "most likely" case, that is, the case which is likely to either strongly verify or clearly falsify the theory to be tested. An exemplary analysis of a "least likely" case is given by Robert Michels's (1962) study of oligarchy in organisations. It chooses to study a horizontally organised association with strong democratic ideals, which should be unlikely to become oligarchical, in order to test and demonstrate Michels's iron law of oligarchy. Whyte (1943), on the other hand, gives a classical example of the "most likely" case design, by studying a Boston Italian slum community, where existing theory expects to see social disorganisation but, in fact, finds that order and social integration emerged.

This book is a case study, focusing on the Chinese pension system. Why study China? The rationale for this case selection is twofold. First, as discussed in Chapter 2, this book engages with the Statist approach to welfare state development, which argues that the authority and capacity of the state contributes to the formation of the modern welfare state. The Chinese state, given its unitary structure and authoritarian nature, has the political authority and administrative capacity necessary for welfare state building, which is rarely found elsewhere. Therefore, if the Statist thesis is right, then we should expect China to have a modern welfare system that matches its state capacity. In other words, China serves as the most likely case for the Statist theory of welfare state development. But as Chapter 1 has revealed, despite more than a decade's efforts, China still has no nationwide integrated pension system that one would expect to see given the tremendous authority and capacity of the Chinese state. To explain this puzzle, therefore, will contribute to the Statist theory of welfare state. Secondly, this book engages with the Varieties of Capitalism theory and seeks to test one of its implications that economic considerations, especially those regarding skill formation, can be an important rationale behind the expansion of the welfare state. As discussed in Chapter 1, in the Western context, the presence of the unionised labour, which pursues redistribution, makes it difficult for researchers to separate the quest for economic efficiency from the pursuit for social equality when examining the motivation behind welfare state development. The Chinese case, where the trade unions are politically weak, offers better opportunity to focus on the concerns about economic efficiency in social policymaking and demonstrate the Varieties of Capitalism argument on the economic role of social policy.

This efficiency argument leads to the reasons why this book chooses to study the pension system. As Figure 1.1 has shown, pension provision is the most expensive component of the Chinese welfare state. One cannot make sense of the Chinese welfare system without understanding its pension component. This is one rationale behind the selection of pensions as the focus of this study. More importantly, since pension provision is the most expensive component, it imposes the heaviest social costs on employers. This should harm economic efficiency and drive employers to resist pension expansion. If concerns about economic efficiency take a central place in China's social policymaking, as this book argues, then pension should be the last social programme that Chinese policymakers would like to actively expand, because this would impose too expensive a financial burden on the market. In other words, pension is the least likely case of our economic efficiency argument. If we can demonstrate that even in the case of pension political actors, in fact, passionately expanding pension programmes to pursue economic growth and employers actually supporting such expansion, then our thesis that economic considerations loom large in China's social policymaking can be better supported.

This book being a case study poses challenges to the testing of the theory formulated in Chapter 3. Indeed, how can we test a theory on one single country case? This book argues this can be done by using disaggregated data, which can be collected on sub-national units. King et al. (1994: 48–49) give an example of disaggregating data to increase the observable implications and hence the opportunities to test a theory. They suggest that when examining how economic variables such as the unemployment rate affect the outcome of the U.S. presidential election, the researcher should disaggregate presidential election results and unemployment rates to the state level because this offers "many more observations of the implications of our theory than does the aggregate rate for the nation as a whole". This book applies this strategy, disaggregating data to China's sub-national units. Therefore, the decision to examine sub-national units is made not only because our theory predicts what policy actions the local government will have, but also because of the methodological requirement for theory-testing in the single case study, which asks the researcher to examine as many facets of this case as possible (Campbell 1975). The sub-national variation is one important facet of the Chinese case.

While political science has traditionally focused on national-level phenomena and hence comparisons across nations, a "sub-national turn" can be clearly discerned in recent years (Rithmire 2014: 166; also see Snyder 2001). Sub-national research design, in which researchers draw on cases at the sub-national level to build and test theories, has gained considerable popularity. This research strategy proves especially fruitful in single case studies. One can see its application in studies that cover a diverse range of topics, including the democratisation dynamics in authoritarian settings in Brazil (Hagopian 1996) and Mexico (Cornelius et al. 1999), ethnic conflicts between religious groups in India (Varshney 2002; Wilkinson 2006) and public goods provision in China (Tsai 2007). It is interesting to note that the sub-national research design is most likely to appear in studies on large developing countries with a high level of internal disparity, such as Brazil, India and China. Indeed, in the field of contemporary China studies, sub-national research design is a major strategy for researchers to make empirical generalisations about the Chinese case. For example, Thun (2006) compares the approaches to the development of automobile industry in three Chinese regions and from the comparisons derives general patterns of China's industrial policy in the auto sector. This approach is also used by Segal (2003) and Breznitz and Murphree (2011), who demonstrate their arguments about the development of the Chinese IT industry through comparisons between some of China's most economically vibrant regions such as Shanghai and Guangdong. In addition to the comparative method, the statistical method equally features in sub-national studies on China. Authors like Huang (1996) and Shih (2008) utilise time-series-cross-section analysis of data on Chinese provinces to test theories on the political determinants of China's macroeconomic stability and inflation cycle. This book follows these studies to apply the sub-national research approach to the Chinese case.

If this book is to be a sub-national research design, then the question arises as to which level of sub-national jurisdiction it is to use as unit of analysis. The theory we are to test argues that the institutional arrangements of bureaucratic promotion for municipal leaders, which are indicated by the insider/outsider composition of the provincial leadership, serve as an incentive structure for municipal officials in this province and hence should have an impact on their efforts to expand pension coverage and resist pension integration. Our theory involves two levels of government, that is, the municipality and province. Which one should we use as unit of analysis? This book chooses the province as unit of analysis for the following three reasons. First, according to Przeworski and Teune (1970), the logic of scientific inquiry and the comparative method in particular can work at two levels, that is, at the level of systems (for example, the nation state) and at the within-system level (for example, the individuals within the nation state). The analysis can be conducted at either of the two levels, depending on what the research is about. If the research is about how systems affect the behaviour of units within them, then the research can be designed as follows: The independent variable is measured at the level of system, and the researcher can also measure the dependent variable as the system level variable by aggregating the properties of within-system units to the system level (Przeworski and Teune 1970: 49). Since both the independent and dependent variables are measured at the system level, the unit of analysis is the system. This book follows this design. In the case of this study, the system-level unit is the province, the within-system level unit is the municipality, the independent variable is the provincial-level incentive structure and the dependent variable is the municipal leaders' pension policy choices, which are aggregated into the observed provincial-level policy outcomes in terms of pension coverage rates and the level of risk pooling. This design decides that the province should be used as unit of analysis.

Secondly, using province as a unit of analysis allows us to examine the provincial-level incentive and sanction arrangements that affect the policy actions of the municipality. This study focuses on the incentive mechanism that motivates Chinese local leaders to implement pension reforms. But clearly the policy behaviours of municipal leaders hinges not only on the carrot offered by the promotion arrangement, but also on the stick wielded by their provincial bosses. In other words, what matters in shaping municipal officials' policy action is not only the incentive arrangement, which awards the officials if they succeed in achieving certain policy goals, but also the sanction mechanism, which exerts pressures on municipal officials to take policy actions. If we are to isolate and examine the effects of the incentive arrangement, we have to control for the impacts of the sanction mechanism. The pressures municipal leaders receive come from the provincial government. The Chinese state has a "one-level-down" cadre management system, in which each sub-national government is solely accountable to its immediate superior, i.e., the next higher-level government (Joseph 2010: 232). For example, the central government has the authority to appoint provincial government heads, which can appoint or discharge municipal leaders without seeking approval from the central government. The implication of this dependence on one's immediate superior is that the provincial government can credibly force municipal leaders to carry out its favoured policies (Perry and Goldman 2007). Therefore, variables measured at the provincial level can indicate such pressures imposed by the provincial government on municipalities. For example, the elderly dependence ratio of a province can suggest the urgency for the provincial government to deal with the problem of population ageing, which will then translate into the pressures faced by municipal officials to carry out pension reform measures dictated by the provincial leadership. Since the sanction mechanism confronting municipal leaders resides at the provincial level, one has to choose province as the unit of analysis if he or she wants to control for the impacts on municipal officials of such a mechanism.

Finally, choosing the province as the unit of analysis helps us to overcome constraints on data availability. The majority of publicly available data on sub-national jurisdictions in China are collected at the provincial level. As shall be seen in next section, provincial statistical yearbooks are published on many topics, ranging from economic development to social security. They contain the data on all major variables examined by this book. By contrast, data on Chinese municipalities are available from only one source, that is, *China City Statistical Yearbook*. This source, however, does not report data on social security or vocational education issues such as pension coverage rates and vocational school enrolment rates, which are crucial for this study. The limited availability of municipal data, therefore, prevents this book from using municipality as the unit of analysis.

To summarise this section, a review of the four branches of social science methodology in light of Lijphart's (1971) framework reveals that the statistical method should be the general choice in theory testing. This is because it is more practical and bears fewer ethical constraints than the experimental method, and it deals with the problem of "too many variables, too few cases" better than the comparative method. This book being a case study of the Chinese pension system requires us to apply a sub-national research strategy because this is the way to increase the number of observations and hence the opportunities to test our theory. Given that both of the incentive and sanction mechanisms facing municipal leaders are at the provincial level, the province is chosen over the municipality as unit of analysis. In this way, we follow the two-level research procedure for the comparative method, and we take both of the incentive and sanction arrangements into account so the latter can be controlled for when we examine the effects of the former. In addition, choosing province as the unit of analysis allows us to ensure data availability for our analysis. Therefore, the best way to study political agency at the municipal level is to look at the provincial-level institutional environment that shapes municipal leaders' behaviours. This sub-national research design will be implemented through a mixed methods strategy that combines quantitative approach with qualitative analysis. This is to be discussed in following sections.

Quantitative approach

Using province as unit of analysis facilitates us to apply a quantitative approach to test our theory. The reason for this is twofold. First, armed with an increased number of cases under a sub-national research design, this study is able to employ TSCS (time-series-cross-section) regression techniques because it has ensured enough degrees of freedom for statistical manipulation. All of China's 31 provincial-level jurisdictions are incorporated in this study. Ideally, 31 provinces across 10 years (2000–2009) can yield a dataset of 310 cases, decent enough for conducting TSCS (time-series-cross-section) regression analysis. Secondly, given that the Chinese provinces are in similar historical, cultural and socio-political contexts, the conceptulisation of variables can be both connotatively precise and applicable to all cases. This is because the comparability between provinces helps us to avoid the problem of "conceptual stretching". This problem refers to the situation where comparativists, in order for their concepts to be applied to all cases that are in different contexts (for example, nation states in varying socio-economic contexts), have to stretch the concepts so much that these concepts may become rather vague or even hallow. In Satori's (1970: 1035) words, one can "cover more only by saying less". One can avoid this however by examining comparable cases such as the Chinese provinces. Finally, the comparability of data can be ensured because the data collection and process procedure is standardised across the Chinese provincial jurisdictions.

To apply the quantitative approach and the TSCS strategy in particular to test our theory, we have to deal with two issues. First, what statistical techniques will be used? Secondly, how is the availability and reliability of data? Let us begin with the first issue. The TSCS design has been widely used in the last two decades in the comparative political economy because this strategy helps researchers to overcome the "too few cases" problem discussed in previous section. Traditional cross-sectional and time-series analyses cover only a limited number of spatial units and available data over time. The small sample size constrains the degree of freedom necessary for modelling the association between the explanatory and outcome variables. By contrast, TSCS design allows the researcher to relax this restriction, because in such design the cases become "country-year", which start from the country *i* in year *t*, then the same country in year *t+1*, and all the way through to the last country in the last year of the period. With a greatly enlarged sample size, the researcher can conduct multivariate analysis without worrying about the number of independent variables exceeding that of the cases (Schmidt 1997: 156). The TSCS design has a wide application in substantive research on some of the most important issues in the comparative political economy (for an introduction to TSCS methodology and its applications, see Janoski and Hicks 1994: 167–242). One can see this application in empirical works on the institutional determinants of macroeconomic performance (Alvarez et al. 1991; Swank 1992), on the socio-political causes of the welfare state expansion (Pampel and Williamson 1989; Huber et al. 1993) and on how political and economic factors affect the openness of domestic financial markets (Alesina et al. 1994; Quinn and Inclan 1997), just to cite a few examples.

The TSCS design builds on the standard ordinary least square estimator (OLS), and this raises several methodological issues. In particular, when applied to the TSCS setting, the OLS estimator tends to be insufficient and biased and therefore produces insufficient coefficient estimates and biased standard errors. This is because the OLS estimator makes specific assumptions about the error structure, asking that all the errors are independent of each other and that they share the same variance (homoscedasticity), while the data structure of the TSCS design violates these assumptions in several ways (Hicks 1994: 171). For example, the errors in TSCS design tend to be serially correlated and contemporaneously correlated, meaning that they are not independent from one period to the next and from one unit to another. This is not surprising given that values measured across time (for instance, the same economy's size over time) are temporally interdependent and that units closely interconnected with each other (like the Scandinavian countries) cannot be independent for one another. Also, in TSCS design the errors are likely to be heteroscedastic in the sense that they tend to have different variance across units. To give an example of this problem, Hicks (1994: 172) makes a comparison between the United States and Switzerland. The U.S. has a large heterogeneous workforce and hence very volatile unemployment rates, and therefore the variance in the U.S. unemployment rates tends to be greater than in smaller, more homogeneous countries like Switzerland, which has less volatile unemployment rates.

Further statistical techniques are developed to address these problems. Building on the works by Parks (1967), Kmenta (1971) formulates the generalised least squares estimation (GLS). This estimator deals with the problems arising from the data structure of TSCS design by making two assumptions. First, the error covariance matrix is known. Secondly, the elements of the error covariance matrix are correctly specified. In practice the first assumption is kept but the second one is often dropped, which yields the estimator of feasible generalised least squares (FGLS). The Parks-Kmenta method was arguably the most widely used technique for TSCS design in the comparative political economy until the mid-1990s (for examples of its application, see Alvarez et al. 1991; Huber et al. 1993).

Things have changed since Beck and Katz (1995) published their seminal article on an alternative approach to TSCS analysis. This article criticises the application of FGLS because, due to its assumption that the error covariance matrix is known, it tends to underestimate the true variability of the standard errors of the estimated coefficients. In other words, FGLS would cause the inflation of standard error, thereby misleading the researcher to call some variable statistically significant when the opposite might be the case. To address this problem of standard error inflation, Beck and Katz (1995) suggest a different approach. Since in TSCS analysis the OLS estimates of coefficients are consistent but its estimates of the standard error are inaccurate, one can use OLS in settings of TSCS design as long as the issue of standard error estimation is addressed. Therefore, Beck and Katz propose to keep the OLS estimator but replace OLS standard errors with panel-corrected standard errors (PCSE), which take into account the contemporaneous correlation and heteroscedasticity of the TSCS error structure. As for the issue of serial correlation, Beck and Katz suggest it can be dealt with by either estimating autoregressiveness or including a laggard dependent variable in the right-hand side of the equation. Utilising Monte Carlo analysis Beck and Katz demonstrate their technique of ordinary least squares with panel-corrected standard errors (OLS-PCSE) is able to produce accurate estimation of standard error variability in TSCS analysis. Since Beck and Katz's (1995, 1996) study, OLS-PCSE has become the most utilised approach for TSCS analysis in comparative politics and political economy (for example, see Brady et al. 2005; Oatley 1999; Quinn and Inclan 1997).

For TSCS analysis, therefore, this book uses Beck and Katz's (1995) OLS-PCSE with a first-order autocorrelation correction and a panel-level heteroscedastic errors correction to address the issues of serial and contemporaneous correlation and heteroscedasticity. This approach applies when the dependent variable is continuous, as in our *Expansion Hypothesis* and *Schooling Hypothesis*, which deal with continuous dependent variables such as pension coverage rates and vocational school enrolment rates. When the regression has a binary dependent variable, as in the case of *Localisation Hypothesis*, which examines whether or not the province has its pension arrangement integrated at the provincial level, the appropriate statistical technique is the ordinary logit model (Menard 2010). One of the assumptions underlying the OLS estimator is that the error variances are normally distributed. This assumption is violated when the dependent variable is dichotomous, in which case the error variances tend to follow a logistic distribution (Pampel 2000: 36). This error structure should be modelled by ordinary logit regression, which estimates the probability of an outcome happening. The outcome is measured as a binary variable, with a value of 1 indicating the occurrence of the outcome and a value of 0 representing its nonappearance. Compared with other statistical techniques that deal with continuous dependent variable, the logit model is less utilised in the comparative political economy of the welfare state, whose primary interest such as government social spending is often of a continuous nature. Yet a recent renewal of interest in explaining social policy preferences, which are often measured as binary or mutilnominal variables (for example, individuals' policy preferences are indicated by their responses to questions such as "Do you support or not support government redistribution?"), has seen an increasing application of the logit model (Busemeyer et al. 2011; Busemeyer 2013; McCall and Kenworthy 2009).

These studies that apply the logit model in the comparative political economy of the welfare state primarily deal with cross-sectional data, which report for example respondents' policy stances in one given year (for example, an often used dataset is the International Social Survey Programme (ISSP) 2006 "Role of Government IV"). They do not have to deal with the complexity that results from the TSCS (time-series-cross-section) design. Beck et al. (1998: 1262) term the time-series-cross-section data with a binary dependent variable as BTSCS data and point out that it shares "all the standard characteristics" of continuous dependent variable TSCS data. This means the analysis of BTSCS data, as in the case of the testing of this study's *Localisation Hypothesis*, is faced with similar methodological problems that arise from the error structure of TSCS data as discussed earlier. A particularly serious issue is the problem of temporal correlation, meaning that errors in BTSCS data are likely to be interdependent across time. This violates the assumption of the ordinary logit estimator that errors should be serially independent. Therefore, applying the ordinary logit model to BTSCS data would lead to incorrect estimates of standard errors. For example, Poirier and Ruud (1988) report that in logit and probit models standard errors tend to be wrongly estimated in the presence of temporally correlated errors. Likewise, Beck and Katz (1997) demonstrate that in BTSCS settings the problem of temporal correlation is likely to cause an underestimation of the variability of standard errors. In practice this problem is mostly encountered in the study of international relations, especially in the literature on conflict studies, which uses BTSCS data to examine the occurrence of war or militarised conflict across time (for example, see Farbera and Gowa 1997: 397). Oneal and Russet (1997: 283) admit that in statistical analysis of BTSCS data the "greatest danger arises from autocorrelation".

Beck et al. (1998) proposes a simple approach to deal with the issue of temporal correlation in BTSCS data. They suggest that the researcher include a series of period dummy variables (usually year dummies) as controls to the logit model specification. This solution is based on the idea that BTSCS data are essentially equivalent to grouped event history data. Event history analysis examines the length of elapsed time until the occurrence of an event (for example, the breakout of war), that is, the length of a "spell" (for an introduction to event history analysis, see Blossfeld et al. 2007). It models the hazard rate, which is an indication of the likelihood of the event occurring, as a function of independent variables. If the hazard rate does not depend upon the length of the spell, then the hazard is "duration independent". On the other hand, if the hazard rate changes with the duration of the spell, then the hazard is "duration dependent". Durations can be measured continuously so the hazard rate varies continuously. Alternatively, duration data can be "grouped" into one point so it only tells us whether a unit has experienced the event at some discrete point in time (for example, a certain year). This is the case in BTSCS data, which codes the happening of an event as 1 (that is, the hazard rate is equal to 100 percent) and assigns the occurrence to a certain year so we know the specific point at which the event occurs (for conducting event history analysis for longitudinal data, see Allison 1984). It is in this sense that Beck et al. (1998) argue BTSCS data is grouped duration data. This idea allows them to apply the technique used in event history analysis to deal with duration dependent hazard in the settings of BTSCS to correct for serially correlated errors. This technique is the inclusion of period dummy variables. This book will apply the same method to deal with the problem of BTSCS temporal correlation when testing the *Localisation Hypothesis.*

A final note on statistical techniques concerns the inclusion of unit dummy variables. A convention in TSCS analysis is to add unit dummies to the right-hand side variables to control for unobservable cross-unit heterogeneity. This book does not follow this procedure. Instead of adding unit dummies, which in the case of this study are province dummies, this book adds region dummies, which indicate the macro-region (eastern, interior or western region) in which the province is located. Province dummies are not included for three reasons. First, the use of unit dummies is most defensible when we are not sure about whether certain cross-sectional variance arising from history and geography would have impacts on the outcome of interest. In Peter Kennedy's words (1998: 227): "The dummy variable coefficients reflect ignorance – they are inserted merely for the purpose of measuring shifts in the regression line arising from unknown variables". So it is reasonable to add unit dummies in a cross-national study, where the variance in national history, for example, is great and hard to control for without adding country dummies. The problem of ignorance, however, is far less severe in a study comparing Chinese provinces, the difference among whom is much less than that among nation states. Secondly, as Plumper et al. (2005) point out, "the use of unit dummies can lead to the absorption of most of the theoretical interesting cross-sectional variance". They especially remind researchers that unit dummies should *not* be included if the theory being tested implies level effect. This effect refers to the situation where in addition to changes in the level of the independent variable, the level of the independent variable itself could theoretically affect the level of the dependent variable. Adding unit dummies to the equation will absorb such effect in the sense that this effect will be reflected not in the coefficient of the independent variable we are interested in but only in the coefficient of the unit dummies. Thirdly, testing the *Localisation Hypothesis* with a binary dependent variable requires using the logit model. Adding unit dummies would easily make the model fail to achieve convergence. This problem also confronts Yumin Sheng (2010: 171) when he estimates his probit model of Chinese provincial leaders' characteristics. He then gives up controlling for the provincial-level fixed effects. This book will choose to do the same. Therefore, province dummies are not to be added. As an alternative, this book adds region dummies, which can capture the major unobserved cross-provincial differences without suppressing too much interesting variance among provinces.

Having discussed the statistical techniques for our TSCS analysis, we now move to the second issue of data availability and reliability. Data used for the quantitative analysis are publicly available. The independent variable, i.e., the insider composition of provincial leadership, is constructed on the basis of the career paths of provincial party secretaries and governors (for a detailed discussion on the measurement of the independent variable, see Chapter 5). One can study provincial leaders' career trajectories by investigating their resumes, which are available on the official website of the Central People's Government of People's Republic of China (www.gov.cn) and the official websites of the provincial governments of the 31 provincial-level jurisdictions. Data for other variables come from the statistical data collected and compiled by relevant government bodies like the National Bureau of Statistics of China, Provincial Bureau of Statistics and All-China Federation of Trade Unions, etc. China Statistical Publishing House publishes most of the statistical yearbooks. Detailed data sources are provided in Table 4.1.

This study takes measures to ensure the data used for the quantitative analysis are reliable. The reliability of the data provided by the Chinese government has often been questioned. Indeed, there is a saying in China that "officials produce

Table 4.1 Data sources

Variables	*Data sources*
Pension coverage rates	China Population and Employment Statistics Yearbook (2001–2010) China Labour and Social Security Statistics Yearbook (2001–2010)
GDP per capita	China Statistical Yearbook (1997–2010)
Elderly-dependency ratio	China Population and Employment Statistics Yearbook (1997–2010)
Inter-municipal disparity	Provincial Statistical Yearbook of 31 provincial jurisdictions (1997–2010)
Fiscal transfer from the central government	China Finance Yearbook (1997–2010)
Employment share of the manufacturing sector	China Industry Economy Statistical Yearbook (1997–2010)

statistics, and statistics produce offices". In a bureaucratic state where promotion is dependent on quantified performance, officials have every incentive to manipulate statistical data to get a better chance of promotion along the bureaucratic ladder. However, as Chen (2010) argues, there is no need go to the extreme of being paranoid about the reliability of the Chinese data. State-generated data, in fact, can be of great use if the user stays clear-headed about how it is produced and, most importantly, who produces it. The data most likely to be distorted are those generated by local officials, which tend to report and publish inflated data to impress their superiors. Therefore, this study avoids using the data from subnational government whenever possible. That is why most of the variables are measured using data collected by national agencies like the National Bureau of Statistics of China. This reduces the possibility that these data are subject to the manipulation of local officials. Only in the case of measuring the variable of inter-municipal disparity, this book uses data collected at the provincial level (i.e., the municipal GDP per capita). But even this would not distort the overall picture. If the provincial government is prone to inflate data on its economic performance, then all provincial governments should have equal incentive to do so. So such inflation will not change the relative ranking among provinces on this variable. Therefore, the data used for measuring inter-municipal disparity, though subject to the risk of being manipulated by local officials, can yield a generally reliable picture.

Although the quantitative statistical analysis is useful for exploring associations between macro factors, it falls short of determining the causal mechanism underlying those associations. It is especially unable to reveal the micro-foundations of the general tendency, i.e., preferences and choices of individual agents that are aggregated into the macro phenomenon. This is where the qualitative approach comes into play. By investigating different actors' preferences on pension policy and how they perform according to their views, we are able to uncover the complexity in the process of China's pension reform. This complements the relatively parsimonious statistical results. Moreover, by discovering whether the agents really calculate and behave in the way hypothesised in this study, it helps to assess the validity of competing interpretations of the statistical association and verify the causal mechanism of our theory.

Qualitative approach

The rationale for applying a qualitative approach in this study is twofold. First, the qualitative approach is employed to evaluate the accuracy of our theory's assumptions about the agents' preferences and behaviours. This is important because the validity of a rational choice theory, as discussed earlier, depends on not only how well its predictions can survive empirical tests, which can be determined through quantitative analysis, but also on how accurately its behavioural assumptions reflect the social reality, which has to be found out by uncovering the actual preferences and behaviours of agents through qualitative methods. Secondly, in the process of discovering the actual preferences and actions of relevant actors, the qualitative analysis will reveal the contexts in which agents form their preferences and make choices. This contextualisation of preferences and decisions uncovers the socio-economic conditions that affect preference-forming and decision-making. These socio-economic situations are not included in our theory, because it focuses on the institutional constraints that shape the behaviours of agents and leaves other relevant conditions out of the model in order to be parsimonious. So the revealing of relevant socio-economic conditions through qualitative analysis complements the parsimonious theory, and in the process the theory gets contextualised and substantiated. Therefore, by uncovering the actual preferences and behaviours of political and economic agents, the qualitative analysis in this study aims to evaluate the theory's assumption about agents' preferences, which is important for assessing the validity of the theory, and to contextualise actors' desires and beliefs, which complements the theory.

Then how can we know the preferences and beliefs of the relevant agents in our theory? For economic agents like workers and employers, the answer is pretty straightforward: We can know about their viewpoints by listening to what they have to say about pension policy and skill development. What they say can be taken as expressing their genuine views because normally they have little incentive to lie about their situations and they are unlikely to face external constraints that would refrain them from telling the truth (especially in the case of talking about non-politically sensitive issues like pension). This study uses journalistic materials from major Chinese national and regional newspapers that cover interviews with workers and employers on issues of public pension, vocational education, labour retention and firm-funded training. It applies a strategy of purposeful sampling to select the relevant materials. As Pattern (2002: 230) points out, "[t]he logic and power of purposeful sampling lies in selecting information-rich cases for study in depth. Information-rich cases are those from which one can learn a great deal about issues of central importance to the purpose of the enquiry". In other words, with purposive sampling the researcher chooses the materials that offer the best information to serve the research purpose and answer the research question. In particular, this study adopts one of the subcategories of purposive sampling (Pattern 2002: 235), namely maximum variation sampling, which aims at "capturing and describing central themes that cut across a great deal of variation" (Markula and Silk 2011: 221). That is to say, this study selects and analyses newspaper articles that reflect contrasting policy views. For example, it covers stories of workers willing and unwilling to join pension schemes and employers willing and unwilling to contribute to pension funds. In this way it is hoped that an unbiased account of worker and employer preferences concerning relevant policy issues could emerge from the qualitative analysis.

Anyone using Chinese newspaper data for qualitative analysis is confronted with the issue of press censorship. Indeed, it is generally believed that the Chinese government tightly controls the mass media to make sure everyone keeps the "party line" (Young 2012). This could have a direct impact on which views would appear in the media and which would not, thereby compromising the quality of the Chinese newspaper data. This conventional view, however, is challenged by a recent study by Gary King et al. (2013), which, on the basis of computer-assisted content analysis of online text posts, shows that the Chinese authority is not more likely to curtail criticism of the state and its policies. Rather, it is the comments that mobilise citizens for collective action that are more likely to be silenced. This finding regarding the Chinese government's Internet censorship practices echoes earlier studies, which show that newspapers have more leeway in discussing policy issues in their online editions (for example, see He and Zhu 2002). Issues like pension policy and vocational education are not likely to spur social mobilisations. So it is reasonable to think that views regarding these issues expressed in newspapers, especially in their online editions, are not distorted too much by the government's censorship. Therefore, this study primarily draws on online editions of major national and regional newspapers for newspaper articles that are subject to qualitative content analysis. Having said this, censorship may still have an impact on what we read in the mass media in a subtler way by, for example, making individuals in interviews (interviewees and reporters alike) censor themselves, i.e., conforming to the official discourse (Tong 2009). The issue of self-censorship is inevitable in a country where freedom of speech is highly regulated, if not curtailed. This study acknowledges it and uses caution when interpreting peoples' views expressed in the mass media.

While one can interpret the preferences of workers and employers from their interviews, when it comes to revealing the preferences and perspectives of political agents like Chinese local bureaucrats, interviews may become less useful in documenting what they really think. Indeed, when speaking to the public media or the researcher, politicians may have incentive to promote a rosy picture of the situation. It may not necessarily be that politicians would lie about the actual situation – it is just that politicians' desires to look good will affect how they frame policy issues when they give interviews to the media or the researcher. This problem is universal, but it may become even more severe in China, where the political culture does not encourage open policy debate, especially between policymakers and the public. In the case of this study, what we hope to reveal is the policy preferences and beliefs of the municipal leaders. They are no ordinary government staff but party secretaries and mayors of the municipal party-state, so they have even higher stakes when giving interviews, which will make them more cautious in making comments on policy. Researchers would find what they say differs little from the official document or the publicly stated policy line. In short, it would be difficult, or at least very time- and energy-consuming,[1] for researchers to induce Chinese bureaucrats in local leadership to talk about their genuine views on policy issues.

This study has to solve this problem because to understand the policy preferences of municipal leaders is important to its analysis – but how? This study suggests looking at the internal speeches by municipal leaders. Internal speeches are speeches addressed by municipal leaders (i.e., the municipal party secretary, mayor and vice-mayor, who are in charge of specific policy areas) at work conferences (i.e., the conferences that are dedicated to discussing concrete policy issues) to their subordinates (i.e., the sub-municipal cadres such as county leaders who are charged to implement the policies made by the municipal government). Such speeches are called "internal" because when they are delivered they are not open to the public or the media. Nor are they required to be submitted to the municipal leaders' superiors in the provincial government for approval. Without the need to look good to the public or to please their provincial boss, municipal leaders are relatively free to express their policy opinions at those work conferences behind closed doors. Internal speeches of municipal leaders are dedicated to offering diagnoses of social problems, providing policy solutions and mobilising lower-level cadres for policy implementation. By analysising internal speeches addressed by municipal leaders at economic work conferences and pension reform work conferences, the researcher can get to know municipal officials' relatively genuine policy preferences on pension provision and their views on the economic role of pension policy. By revealing the actual pension policy preferences and behaviours of municipal leaders, one can evaluate the assumptions made in our theory and substantiate the causal story it tells.

There are several ways through which the researcher gets access to those internal speeches. First, during the fieldwork in China the researcher contacted local social insurance agencies to collect the speeches. Because speeches of leading municipal officials made in work conferences are treated as policy guidelines, normally they are dispatched to related functional agencies that are in charge of policy implementation. Such a functional agency like the social insurance agency is a major source of the internal speeches. I was able to get in touch with them when I made two field trips to China, one from December 2010 to January 2011 and the other from July 2012 to January 2013. I visited local social insurance agencies in five provinces – Shaanxi, Liaoning, Fujian, Guangdong and Guizhou (see Figure 4.1) – to collect internal speeches by leading municipal officials. The provinces were selected to reflect China's inter-provincial diversities in geographical and socio-economic terms. As one can see from Figure 4.1, three provinces are located on the coastal line while two are in the inland areas, which allows us to take into account the historical "coastal-interior divide" in China (Saw and Wong 2009: 2). Among the selected coastal provinces, two are economic stars that rose in the post-1978 reform era (Guangdong and Fujian), renowned for their vibrant private sector economies, while the two Northern provinces, Liaoning and Shaanxi, are home to many state-owned enterprises, most of which were established in the socialist years. Including these provinces in the case selection provides the opportunity to control for diverse historical and economic conditions.

The second source of the municipal speeches is the Internet. Months after the delivery of the internal speeches, some of them are posted on municipality's governmental website as archives. So searching the municipal government's official websites is another way to collect its leaders' internal speeches. Finally, sometimes local official newspapers publish leaders' speeches delivered at work conferences after those speeches are declassified. Those local newspapers are archived by databases for Chinese journals and newspapers, notably the China Knowledge

Figure 4.1 Locations of fieldwork sites

Resource Integrated Database (CNKI). These databases then allow researchers to get access to municipal internal speeches.

In total, this study collected 36 pieces of municipal internal speeches. They are then subject to qualitative content analysis, which is a standardised "sense-making effort that takes a volume of qualitative material and attempts to identify core consistencies and meanings" (Patton 2002: 453). Three approaches to qualitative content analysis are identified by Hsieh and Shannon (2005) on the basis of to what extent inductive reasoning gets involved in the process. The first approach is conventional qualitative content analysis. It is purely inductive, used for ground theory-building, which hopes to let coding themes emerge from the raw data. The second approach is termed "directed content analysis". It is theory-informed, deriving the coding categories from a theory or previous relevant studies, with the aim to "validate or extend a conceptual framework or theory" (Zheng 2010: 2). The final approach is summative content analysis, which synthesises the quantitative and qualitative perspectives of content analysis, combining the counting of manifest themes (i.e., words) with the interpreting of latent meanings.

In light of the typology formulated by Hsieh and Shannon (2005), the qualitative content analysis of this study falls into the second camp, namely directed content analysis. Its purpose is to evaluate and validate our theory's assumptions about agents' preferences and behaviours, which means it is theory directed. So the qualitative content analysis in this study is conducted in a manner that follows the procedure of directed content analysis (Schreier 2012): After the qualitative data are prepared, individual themes, rather than linguistic units (for example, words and sentences), are defined as units of analysis. The themes or categories (like "inter-municipal competition" or "economic benefits of pension programmes") are informed by our theory. Also derived from the theory is the coding scheme, which mainly decides the rules for assigning category codes to contents. The coding scheme is then tested on a sample of nine municipal internal speeches. An additional coder, with Chinese language skills, is invited to code the same sample. The inter-coder agreement is 93 percent, suggesting a high level of consistency. Then the coding scheme is applied to all the speeches. In the process new themes emerge that are not covered by our theory (hence not included in the coding frame) and yet are relevant to this study. So new coding categories are added and presented to the additional coder to check their consistency. After all the qualitative data are coded, the author then sets out to explore the properties of categories and uncover the patterns of relationships between them. The findings from the qualitative content analysis are reported in Chapter 5 and 6 as the micro-foundations of the macro-level statistical associations.

Although the priority of qualitative research is not to be representative, this study tries to avoid the results of its qualitative analysis being distorted by particular cases, which is possible if the qualitative data were collected from a biased selection of cases. This is why, as discussed earlier, the locations of the fieldwork site are chosen in a way that covers as much of the interregional diversity in China as possible. As Sidney Tarrow (2004: 176) points out, "[t]he representativeness of qualitative research can never be wholly assured until the cases become so numerous that the analysis comes to resemble quantitative research". So to ensure the representativeness of qualitative studies, he suggests a strategy of "framing qualitative research within quantitative profiles", which means to situate the qualitative research on a few cases in a context of the large-N dataset, as Charles Tilly (1993) does when he bases a narrative of revolutions in Europe on a collection of more than 700 revolutionary events in the last five centuries. It would be ideal for this study to collect qualitative data from all Chinese provinces across a long time span. But this clearly exceeds the capacity and scope of an individual project. So this study chooses the second-best strategy, selecting the cases purposefully to take into account China's internal disparity. This, admittedly, is a compromise. But the author believes this would not be a serious problem. After all, the purpose of the qualitative analysis of this research is not to build up a new theory inductively, which would require the qualitative data to be drawn from a representative selection of cases. Rather, it is meant to validate an already-built theory by examining whether the agents view the world in the way assumed by the theory. This is a modest goal and can be achieved without making a high level of demand for representativeness.

In short, the qualitative approach applied in this study aims to reveal the preferences and behaviours of political and economic agents, especially those of municipal leaders. By doing so, the behavioural assumptions made in our theory can be evaluated, the causal story told by the theory can be substantiated and the theory's statistical implications can be complemented with micro-foundations. In the case of Chinese municipal leaders, this study suggests applying the directed qualitative analysis approach to analyse their internal speeches delivered at various kinds of work conferences to discover their policy views and behaviours.

Summary

This study adopts a mixed methods research strategy. It has formulated a rational choice institutionalist theory on the expansion and localisation of China's pension system, focusing on how political institutions shape the pension policy actions of Chinese municipal leaders and how the resultant municipal pension schemes affect economic agents' human capital investment decisions. The quantitative approach is applied to test implications of the theory with statistical techniques of time-series-cross-section analysis. In addition, qualitative methods are employed to uncover the policy preferences and behaviours of municipal leaders, employers and workers, so that the assumptions made by our theory can be assessed and the theory itself can be contextualised and substantiated. The next two chapters will implement this research strategy to assess our theory.

Note

1 My experiences of fieldwork in China suggest that only when the researcher has strong personal ties with the politician can the official trust the researcher and talk frankly in interviews. Nourishing such personal ties requires considerable interaction, which is too time- and energy-consuming for a DPhil study to manage.

5 The economic story

How does the Chinese pension system help economic growth through skill formation and labour retention

The theory of this book, i.e., the political-economic logic of China's pension system, has two parts. The first part deals with the influence that public pension policy has on economic agents' decisions on human capital investment. The second part is about the effect of political institutions on Chinese municipal leaders' pension policy choices. This chapter explores the first, which discusses what economic results an expansive and localised pension scheme can generate. It is argued that an urban pension programme facilitates the formation of industry specific skills. This is done through two mechanisms. First, by dealing with labour market risks associated with specific skills and thus ensuing the stability of lifetime income, the urban pension programme encourages students to acquire such skills by attending vocational education. Secondly, by limiting labour mobility and hence addressing the poaching problem, the pension system induces employers to make investments in on-the-job training programmes that will equip workers with specific skills. The net result is that a workforce with industry specific skills is trained under the extensive and localised pension system.

Hence, we have the following hypotheses, which are to be tested in this chapter. First is the *Schooling Hypothesis*: If social protection programmes like pension can encourage students to acquire industry specific skills, then regions with high pension coverage rates should have high enrolment rates in vocational schools. The second is the *Training Hypothesis*: If localised pension programmes can limit job turnover and hence alleviate the problem of poaching, then workers covered by pension programmes should have longer job tenure and therefore be more likely to receive trainings offered by employers. In addition, this chapter tests a third hypothesis, which is the implication of the first two hypotheses: If urban pension programmes induce individuals like students and employers to invest in the acquisition of specific skills, then workers with such skills should be clustered in regions with high pension coverage rates.

This chapter has the same structure of the following Chapter 6. It first provides micro-foundations by revealing agents' preferences and behaviours, and then tests the associations between macro-level phenomena. To be precise, the first section of this chapter examines economic agents' preferences concerning pension programmes, i.e., how workers and employers view urban pension schemes, by analyzing the CGSS2006 (Chinese General Social Survey),[1] an opinion survey of Chinese workers, and comments made by employers. After providing the micro-foundations, the rest of this chapter tests the macro-level associations. The second section tests the *Schooling Hypothesis*, which, drawing on the idea that a strong presence of social protection programmes like pension reduces the risk of acquiring industry specific skills and thus encourages students to attend vocational schools, predicts a positive association between pension coverage rates and vocational education enrolment rates. The third section tests the *Training Hypothesis*, which argues that localised pension programmes, by making the pension package non-portable and hence job changing across regions costly, discourages labour turnover and therefore encourages employers to provide on-the-job training programmes. This section starts by exploring the effects of pension programmes on labour mobility, and then it examines how this affects the training decisions made by employers. The fourth section extends the analysis to test further theoretical implications. If China's urban public pension system encourages students and employers make human capital investments in ways that facilitate the formation of specific industrial skills, as argued by our theory, then we should expect to observe a geographical concentration of workers who possess specific skills in regions with a high coverage rate of pension programmes. This hypothesis is tested in the fourth section, which uses workers' occupations as a proxy for skill specificity on the basis of the harmonisation of China's national classification of occupations with the 1988 version of the International Standard Classification of Occupation (ISCO-88).

Micro-foundations: pension policy preferences of workers and employers

Preferences of workers

Are Chinese workers' preferences concerning social protection programmes related to the types of skills they possess, as assumed in the Varieties of Capitalism theory? Following the literature, this section uses Chinese data to evaluate the validity of this assumption in the Chinese context. In other words, this section replicates the procedure used in the literature on social policy preferences in the Chinese case.

At the outset, it is helpful to clarify the rationale for studying Chinese citizens' policy preferences. One may wonder why it is relevant to understand individual pension policy preferences in China. Indeed, China is not a liberal democratic country and its pension policymaking is not based on its citizens' policy preferences. Indeed, as we have shown in Chapter 5, the Chinese pension system is shaped by the bureaucratic competition, which is structured by political institutions in China. In other words, China's pension policymaking follows a top-down approach, in which political actors make policies to cater to their own interests, rather than a bottom-up route whereby citizens' preferences are aggregated by electoral competition into public policy. If this is the case, then why should we care about Chinese citizens' policy preferences? This book argues that citizens' preferences matter even in an authoritarian setting because the sustainability of government policy depends on to what extent the policy fits with the citizens' preferences. Citizens' policy preferences reflect their needs for government action in certain policy areas. The government may impose a policy without any concern of the needs of the populace. If such policy does not require much contribution from citizens, then people may just accept it in a passive way. If, however, such policy requires citizens' contribution, as in the case of a pension policy where employers and workers have to put a considerable share of their income into the pension funds, then popular preferences/needs for this policy become important in terms of ensuring the sustainability of the policy. If citizens have few needs for that policy, then there will not be much popular contribution to its implementation. If the government chooses to coerce citizens into making the required contributions, then costs of monitoring and punishing will increase. Either way, the policy's long-term financial and political sustainability will be jeopardised. In the case of pension policy, if Chinese bureaucrats simply impose expensive pension schemes that no one wants, then the evasion of pension contributions will be rampant, which will ultimately bring down the pension system. But, in fact, what we observe is the growth, rather than the death, of the Chinese pension system. This very fact suggests that there must be segments in the society that support pension expansion in China and therefore provide positive feedback to the continuation of the Chinese pension system. Therefore, to fully understand the long-term sustainability and continuing existence of this system, i.e., to what extent the Chinese pension system constitutes a political-economic equilibrium, one has to uncover which segments of the populace need and support public pensions in China. In other words, one has to examine Chinese citizens' pension policy preferences. This will be done in the following analysis, which applies the method used by the literature on individual social policy preferences to the Chinese case.

How does the existing literature examine the determinants of indivudal social policy preferences and the impact of skills on such preferences in particular? In the literature (for example, see Iversen and Soskice 2001; Fleckenstein et al 2011), the independent variable, i.e., workers' skills, is proxied by occupations, which are classified according to International Standard Occupation Classification (especially its 1988 version, i.e., ISCO-88). For the dependent variable, i.e., workers' attitude towards social protection programmes, the literature utilises cross-national social surveys, notably the rounds of the International Social Survey Project (ISSP) that are themed on citizens' perceptions on the appropriate role of government, to examine individuals' support (or non-support) for redistributive social spending. The literature then investigates whether the two variables are linked with each other, i.e., whether the specificity of a worker's skills can affect his or her attitude towards government intervention in the area of social security. The underlying hypothesis, as discussed in detail earlier, is that workers in occupations that require specific skills should be in greater need for public social security programmes and hence be more likely to support the government's involvement in welfare provision because the limited transferability of their skills makes them more likely to face income loss risks during economic downturn.

Testing this hypothesis in the Chinese context requires us to replicate the above approach as much as possible using Chinese data. Let us start with the dependent variable, workers' attitudes towards social policy. As discussed above, to measure this variable the literature draws on the data from ISSP, especially the ISSP rounds with the theme of the role of government. China only participated in ISSP2009 (Social Inequality IV). So China is not covered by the 2006 round of ISSP that focuses on the role of government. In other words, we cannot draw on ISSP2006 (Role of Government IV) to examine Chinese citizens' viewpoints on social policy.

Given that there is no ISSP data on how Chinese citizens view the role of government in public welfare provision, this study relies on another social survey, which is the Chinese General Social Survey (CGSS). CGSS is the Chinese equivalent of the General Social Survey, a widely used survey on societal trends nainly within the U.S. that has been conducted since 1972. An annual or biannual survey of Chinese households designed to collect longitudinal data on social trends, CGSS is the first and most important continuous national social survey project in mainland China. CGSS started in 2003 and its first five rounds (in 2003, 2004, 2005, 2006 and 2008) have been made available to the public. Of all the publicly available CGSS data only the 2006 wave asked questions on ideological and political attitudes. In CGSS2006 the only question about citizens' view on the role of government was the question that asked respondents to rank government spending priorities among several areas. It is framed like this: "Assuming that there is a large amount of public funds available to the government, in which areas would you like the government to spend it? Please choose three areas from the provided options and rank them according to their importance to you". The questionnaire offers 11 options, including public pension. This study takes choosing pension as the first preference, indicating a great need for more government involvement in the provision of old-age income security. The hypothesis therefore is that those who exhibit such need should be concentrated in the occupation groups that require specific industrial skills.

This leads to the measurement of the independent variable, the worker's skill specificity. As discussed earlier, the existing literature measures this variable by examining the respondent's occupation, which is often classified according to the 1988 version of the International Standard Occupation Classification (ISCO-88). In particular, of the nine major occupation groups of ISCO-88, Fleckenstein et al. (2011) define ISCO-88 major groups 1, 2 and 3 as occupations requiring high-general skills, major groups 4, 5 and 9 as posts needing low-general skills and major groups 7 and 8 as professions with specific skills. This study follows this approach to measure Chinese workers' skill specificity, so Chinese workers' occupation should be coded on the basis of ISCO-88.

Unfortunately, CGSS does not apply ISCO-88 to record Chinese citizens' occupations. Instead, it uses China's own National Classification of Occupation, which was put into use in 1999 (NCO-99). This requires us to use ISCO-88 to recode the occupation data in CGSS. In other words, we have to convert China's NCO-99 into ISCO-88. Compared with ISCO-88, which distinguishes four levels of skills and consists of nine major groups of occupation, under which there are 28 sub-major groups, 116 minor groups and 391 unit groups, NCO-99 defines three levels of aggregation of occupations, consisting of eight major groups, 66 minor groups and 413 unit groups. With these differences notwithstanding, NCO-99 and ISCO-88 are not two separate, totally unrelated systems. In fact, the making of NCO-99, which started in November 1994, borrowed many conceptual and practical ideas from ISCO-88. As Peter Elias documented in 1997,

> China has now also commenced plans to introduce a version of ISCO-88 as its national classification. This process was started with a programme of training for key officials and statisticians associated with the production and use of occupational information, studying the conceptual basis of ISCO-88. . . In preparation, key industrialists and statisticians have participated in training sessions organised by the ILO Turin Training Centre.
>
> (Elias 1997)

The fact that NCO-99 shares the same conceptual and theoretical basis with ISCO-88 makes it possible to achieve the harmonisation between the two occupation classification systems. This study converts NCO-99 into ISCO-88. The conversion is carried out at the lowest level of aggregation of these two systems, i.e., the unit group of occupation. That is to say, the 391 unit groups of ISCO-88 are used to recode the 413 unit groups of NCO-99. A detailed discussion on the conversion is provided in Appendix 2.

Having the occupation of each respondent in CGSS2006 recoded to ISCO-88 and knowing each respondent's view on the priority of government spending, we can examine the relationship between individuals' skill specificity and his or her pension policy preference. The assumption to be evaluated is that compared with other workers, workers in specific skilled occupations should be in greater need for public pensions and therefore be more likely to support government involvement in the provision of pension programmes. The purpose here is to assess the assumption about the pension preferences of Chinese workers. This study will first follow the approach used in Fleckenstein et al. (2011) and utilise descriptive statistics to illustrate the relationship between skill specificity (indicated by occupations) and the need for public pension programmes before applying the multivariate regression technique to analyse Chinese workers' pension policy preferences in a more systematic and rigorous way.

Figure 5.1 shows the percentage of workers in each ISCO-88 major occupation group who agree that public pension programmes should be the most important area where the government should spend public money. Clearly, the occupation that sees the highest share of workers expressing strong support for a public pension scheme is major group 8, the plant equipment operators, a specific

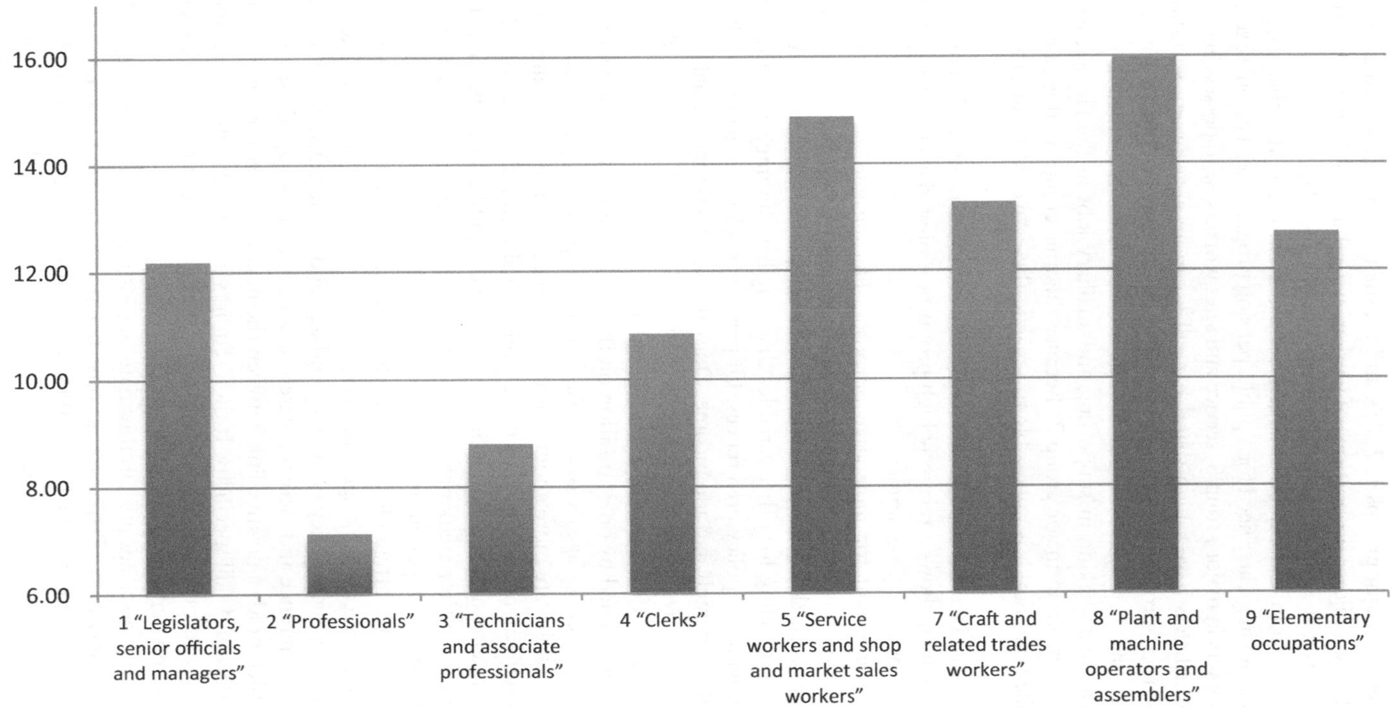

Figure 5.1 Share of Chinese workers in isco-88 major groups who agree public pension should be the most important public expenditure item (2006)

Source: Chinese General Social Survey 2006

skilled occupation group. Compared with other occupation groups that require general skills (i.e., major groups 1, 2, 3, 4 and 9), the two specific skilled groups, group 7 and 8, see higher proportions of workers who think public pension provision should be at the top of the government's policy agenda.

What we find from CGSS2006 is largely consistent with the idea that specific skilled workers are in greater need for a public pension programme. The only exception is the workers in major group 5, service and sales workers, who possess general skills but nevertheless have a high share that call for more government spending on public pension programmes. The reason for this is that in China's national occupation classification system, NCO-99, the service worker is a broad category. It includes workers working in supporting and auxiliary jobs in the factory, who should have been put in major group 7. Because the unit groups in this category are not detailed enough, it is impossible to separate these "would-be-in-group-7" workers from the true service workers with general skills. So major group 5 covers many specific skilled workers that should have belonged to major group 7. This may be the reason why it shows a relatively high proportion of workers that have great need for public pension programmes.

Despite being useful for illustrative purposes, Fleckenstein et al.'s (2011) approach has clear drawbacks. It mainly relies on descriptive statistics to show the correlation between skill specificity and social policy preferences, and therefore falls short of controlling for other variables that may have an impact on the formation of individuals' policy preferences. Of particular relevance to our analysis are two variables, namely age and income. Drawing on data on individual preferences for redistributive government spending from 14 OECD countries, Busemeyer et al. (2009: 196) show that "individual attitudes towards social policies are not only determined by one's position on the income scale, but also by one's position in the life cycle (age)". In the case of pension provision, it is reasonable to argue that people care more about pensions when they get older because they are closer to retirement age and thus more likely to gain from the redistribution of the younger generations, and that people prefer more public spending on pension provision when they are poorer because they stand to gain more from redistributive government expenditures in the form of public pension provision. It is then hypothesised that the individual need for (i.e., support for) public pension spending should increase with age and decrease with income. The positive association between pension policy preference and age and the negative relationship between such preference and income, therefore, are competing hypotheses to our argument, which holds a positive link between the need/support for public pension programmes and skill specificity. It then requires us to hold constant age and income, along with other variables, when we examine the relationship between skill specificity and pension policy preferences.

To this aim, this book adopts a multivariate regression approach. The dependent variable, *Pension Policy Preference*, is constructed as an ordered response variable using the aforementioned CGSS2006 question on government spending priority. It has four ordered values, coded as 0 if the individual does not choose public pension as a government spending priority and as 1/2/3 if the individual ranks public pension as the third/second/first government spending priority. That is to say, the larger the value of the variable of *Pension Policy Preference*, the greater the individual's need/support for public pension programmes. The independent variable, *Skill Specificity*, is measured as a binary variable following Fleckenstein et al.'s (2011) operationalisation of specific/general skills. If the individual is in ISCO88 major group occupation 7 or 8, then he is thought to have specific skills and thus is coded as 1 for the variable of *Skill Specificity.* If the individual works in one of the other ISCO88 major group occupations (1, 2, 3, 4, 5 and 9), then he is coded as 0 for the variable of *Skill Specificity*, indicating that he has general skills. Our hypothesis is that there should be a positive relationship between *Skill Specificity* and *Pension Policy Preference.*

The two alternative arguments to our hypothesis, as discussed above, concerns the role of income and age in the formation of individuals' pension policy preferences. The control variable of *Income* is measured as the individual's monthly wage in decile terms. It shows at which decile the individual's monthly earnings are in the income distribution (with 1 being the lowest decile and 10 being the highest). The other crucial control variable is *Age*, which simply refers to how old the individual was in the survey year (2006). Besides these two variables, we have to control for other individual characteristics. These include *Gender* (1 = Male, 0 = Female), *Marital Status* (1 = Currently in marriage, 0 = not in marriage), *Education* (dummy variables indicating whether the individual receives his highest educational attainment from vocational education), *Ethnicity* (dummy variables indicating the individual's ethnic background) and *Religion* (dummy variables indicating the individual's religious belief). The model also includes *Contract* (1 = The respondent had signed labour contract with his employer, 0 = No labour contract) and *Hukou Status* (1 = The respondent having a urban household registration, 0 = The respondent having a rural household registration), with the aim to capture the difference in policy preferences between labour market insiders (i.e., those who hold local household registration and labour contracts) and outsiders (i.e., those who do not) (Rueda 2007). Finally, the analysis controls for the variable of *Region* (dummy variables indicating where the individual lives, in the western, central or eastern region), trying to control for any unobserved regional level cultural/socio-economic factor that may affect individual social policy preference.

Given that the dependent variable is ordinal, our analysis applies ordered logit regression as the estimation method. It is an extension of the logistic regression model and can model more than two (ordinal) response categories. The result from the model of pension policy preference is presented in the first column of Table 5.1 (Model 1). Our discussion focuses on three variables, namely *Skill Specificity*, *Income* and *Age.* We can see that after controlling for other individual characteristics including income decile and age, there is a positive and statistically significant association between the individual's skill specificity and his support for public expenditures on pension programmes. This supports our hypothesis that compared with general skills, specific skills, by entailing a higher level of labour market risks, will lead the individual to require more government involvement in

Table 5.1 Determinants of individual social policy preference: public pension and redistribution (2006) Ordered logit regression

	Model 1 (dependent variable: pension policy preference)	*Model 2 (dependent variable: social policy preference)*	*Model 3 (dependent variable: redistribution preference)*
Skill specificity	.1352291**	.1177276**	.1490182**
	(1.144799)	(1.124938)	(1.160694)
Income	–.0446365***	–.0609382***	–.0454158***
	(.9563451)	(.9408814)	(.9556)
Age	.0275271***	.0118831***	.0023937
	(1.027909)	(1.011954)	(1.002397)
Gender	–.2051233***	–.131727**	–.1062083*
	(.8145469)	(.8765803)	(.8992373)
Contract	–.1298598**	–.117714*	–.0681025
	(.8782185)	(.8889503)	(.9341648)
Hukou status	.1085104	–.1901766	.2388231***
	(1.114617)	(.8268131)	(1.269754)
Marital status	.0800153	–.0337091	.0027556
	(1.083304)	(.9668528)	(1.002759)
Education	Yes	Yes	Yes
Ethnicity	Yes	Yes	Yes
Religion	Yes	Yes	Yes
Region	Yes	Yes	Yes
Observations	4774	4774	4628
Probabilty > Chi-square	0.000	0.000	0.000
Log likelihood	–5349.4569	–4476.8608	–5011.9662

*, **, ***, stand for $p < 0.1$, $p < 0.05$ and $p < 0.01$ two-tailed test. Odds ratios are in parentheses.

the ensuring of old-age income security. The significance and signs of the coefficients of the variables of *Income* and *Age* are also consistent with our expectation: The negative relationship between income decile and pension policy preference supports the thesis that an individual has more to gain from the redistributive public pension spending when he steps down the income scale, while the positive association between age and the need for government pension expenditure suggests that being closer to retirement age will lead to higher likelihood of gaining from inter-genearational redistribution and therefore will induce more support for such redistribution in forms of public pension spending.

To have a sense of the magnitude of the effects of the variables, we have to look at their proportional odds ratios, which are shown in parentheses underneath the coefficients in Model 1. The odds ratio of the variable *Skill Specificity* is 1.145. This means that holding other variables in the model constant, compared with the worker with general skills, the odds of the specific skilled worker thinking of public pension as the government's first priority versus the combined second/third/non-priority categories are 1.145 times greater, and that the odds of the combined first/second priority categories versus the combined third/non-priority categorites are 1.145 times greater, etc. In other words, other things being equal, compared with individuals having general skills, individuals with specific skills are 14.5 percent more likely to demand public pension spending. Likewise, the odds ratio of the variables of *Income* and *Age* are 0.956 and 1.028 respectively, which means other things being equal, an individual is 4.4 percent less likely to support public pension programmes when his income level climbs up by 1 decile in the income distribution, and he is 2.8 percent more likely to favour government involvement in pension provision when he gets one year older, holding everything else constant. It is clear that after controlling for income level, seniority and other individual characteristics, skill specificity still shows a sizable, if not greater, impact on individual pension policy preferences.

Our skill specificity thesis can do more than explain pension policy preference. It can also shed light on the formation of Chinese citizens' preferences regarding social policy and redistribution in general. Besides public pension, the CGSS2006 question on public spending priority mentioned earlier lists other policy areas for respondents to choose as a government priority. Among them are healthcare, education, poor relief, unemployment assistance and active labour market policy. This book takes these policy areas, along with public pension, as a broad concept of social policy. Drawing on this information, we can construct an ordinal response variable, *Social Policy Preference*, coded as 0 if the individual chooses none of the social policy areas as a government spending priority and as 1/2/3 if the individual takes any of the above social policies as the third/second/first government spending priority. CGSS2006 also provides an opportunity for us to examine Chinese citizens' preferences regarding redistribution, by asking about the respondents' attitudes towards the view that "The government should collect more taxes from high income groups to help the poor". To indicate the individual's support for income redistribution, we use this question to construct another ordinal response variable, *Redistribution Preference*, which is coded as 0/1/2/3 if the respondent is strongly against/against/agreeing with/strongly agreeing with this stance.

Using *Social Policy Preference* and *Redistribution Preference* as dependent variables, we can apply the ordered logit model to examine the determinants of Chinese citizens' preferences. The independent variable is still *Skill Specificity*, coded as 1 if the individual is in specific skill occupation and as 0 if he works in general skill jobs. The hypothesis to be tested is that individuals with specific skills should be in greater need for social policies and therefore more likely to support government redistribution. The control variables, including *Income* and *Age*, are the same set of variables we include in the pension policy preference model. The regression results are shown in Table 6.1 (Model 2 and 3). One can see that *Skill Specificity* has significant and positive impacts on the individual support for social expenditure and redistribution. To put it in odds ratio terms, other things being equal, in comparison with people with general skills, individuals who have specific skills are 12.5 percent and 16 percent more likely to support social spending and government redistribution, respectively. *Income* still has expected impacts, consistently showing negative effects on the support for social policy and redistribution. *Age*, on the other hand, is positively related with support for social spending, as expected, while it ceases to be significant in the redistribution preference model. The literature of the comparative political economy of the welfare state rarely assesses the relative importance of skill specificity, income and age in the shaping of individual social policy preferences (with the exception of Busemeyer et al. (2009), which however mainly focuses on income and age and does not pay much attention to skill specificity). Our analysis here should be a starting point for future research in this direction.

In the three models presented in Table 5.1, skill specificity shows consistent and expected impacts on the formation of Chinese citizens' social policy preferences and pension policy preferences in particular. This is strong evidence demonstrating the crucial role of skill specificity in shaping Chinese workers' need for social protection programmes like public pension. This therefore lends ample support to the argument that Chinese workers with specific industrial skills need public pension programmes more than workers with general skills, which suggests that this hypothesis is a valid one in the Chinese context. It is on the basis of this argument that we have the *Schooling Hypothesis*, which predicts that a comprehensive public pension programme encourages students to choose vocational education over general education and thus to acquire specific skills. Here it is helpful to deal with two possible counter-arguments, one concerning whether Chinese students have a choice between vocational and general education and the other regarding the degree of rationality involved in the making of this choice.

As the first counter-argument, one may argue that the actual decision on education investment depends not only on one's preference but on one's ability as well. For example, if the education system has a strict tracking arrangement and sets a high standard required for progressing to the next level of academic study, as is the case in the German education system, then the student who fails to meet the standard would simply not be allowed to pursue further academic education and therefore would be "tracked" onto the path of vocational education. In this case, the education institution, with its tracking system, translates the limited academic ability of the student into the constrained choice over education investment. With an education system as such in place, there is simply no need for incentive to encourage people to get a vocational education. The tracking system in education will do the job.

However, there is no such strict tracking arrangement in China's education system. This system in China, simply speaking, works as follows. All Chinese citizens are required by law to attend the nine-year compulsory education (from age 6 to 15), which consists of six years of primary education and three years of junior secondary education (or middle school). What serves as the bridge between the nine-year compulsory education and higher education are three years of senior secondary education (or high school), where one may attend the general high school that leads to academic university or the vocational high school that leads to higher vocational colleges. Which kind of high school one is to attend after the nine-year compulsory education, the general or vocational high school, is mainly decided by one's performance in the Senior High School Entrance Examination at the age of 15. This is similar to the German tracking system, but it has two crucial differences. First, the tracking in China's education system happens when students turn 15 years old, rather than around 10, which is the case in Germany. Secondly, and most important, in China the severe competition for a place in general high schools only occurs in the very top high schools, which set high-level entrance requirements. For the rest of the local general high schools, the admission requirement is fairly low. In other words, the majority of students taking the Senior High School Entrance Examination would have sufficient scores to enter these average-level general high schools. For example, in 2013, a 15-year-old student in the city of Nanchang would have to score 569 points (out of a total of 600 points) to get into the very best general high school in the municipality, while it would only take 320 points to get admitted by one of the average general high schools and 300 points to enter the vocational high school (*Jiangnan Metropolis* 2013). In terms of the entrance requirement, the wide gap between the top and the average general high schools and the narrow distance between the average general high school and the vocational high school suggests that Chinese students do have a wide range of choices between general and vocational education. Then the question becomes what factors students would consider to make such a choice. This book argues that if specific skilled workers are in greater need of social protection, as we have seen from the analysis of CGSS2006, then the presence of a comprehensive social protection system, with public pension provision as its most important component, will encourage students to get a vocational education. In other words, social security and pension arrangement in particular will affect individuals' schooling decisions.

This argument may invite criticism, which leads us to the second counter-argument, concerning the role of rationality in an individual's education investment decision. Indeed, one may challenge that even though specific skilled workers are generally in greater demand for the public pension programme, it is hard to believe it would be the agent that makes the student's, or parents', schooling decision, or that students could be so farsighted and rational to take public pension into account when making the decision on which type of education to get, decades before retirement. In other words, the assumption simply seems too demanding that people are rational to the extent that they think about their retirement life when they make decisions at an early age.

This study contends that we do not have to impose a demanding rationality assumption on agents to argue that the presence of a public pension programme can have an impact on one's schooling decision. People may not possess the degree of rationality to take everything into account and process all the information when they make decisions, but they do have the capacity to observe the situations of others and to make choices on the basis of what they learn from them. This is the basic human capacity to learn, imitate and adjust. An individual may not have pension programmes in his mind when he makes the decision of whether or not to attend vocational school and to become an industrial worker. But he will look around and make an assessment of the living standards of industrial workers before he makes the choice of whether or not to become one of them. If a young person learns that the life of a worker with specific skills is satisfactory, thanks to comprehensive social protection programmes such as public pension, which insures him against the risks of lifetime income loss, then there is a good chance he would like to become an industrial worker. But if it turns out an industrial worker often has to suffer income loss, due to the absence of a comprehensive social protection system, then the young individual may be deterred from stepping onto the same path and therefore shun vocational education. Limited individual rationality may not allow the presence of comprehensive public social protection programmes to ***directly*** enter people's calculations in making schooling decisions, but the presence of social protection systems will nevertheless ***indirectly*** affect people's human capital investment decisions through the "watch and learn" process described above.

This mode of decision-making, to make decisions on the basis of others' experiences, is common among Chinese parents. As Mr. Lin, from the city of Lanzhou, explained to a reporter of *Lanzhou Morning Post* (2010) why he would not let her daughter get a vocational education,

> There is no way I send my daughter to the vocational school . . . Many of my colleagues had their kids go to vocational school. After graduation they become workers. The wage is low, benefits are bad, and the job is not stable. I will not put my child on this road.

It is reported that Mr. Lin then sent his daughter to a high school to get a general education, even though it meant he had to pay an extra 3,000 RMB for tuition fees. Clearly, largely based on what other people who had chosen vocational education ended up with, Mr. Lin made a decision on which type of education his child would have. The low compensation and job insecurity of an industrial worker, which is likely to be the result of the inadequacy of the Lanzhou municipal social protection system, reduces the attractiveness of vocational education for the citizens of Lanzhou. So the appeal of vocational education mostly comes from the treatment one gets from working in industrial factories in terms of the compensation and social benefits received. This is consistent with our earlier findings from CGSS2006 that workers in occupations requiring specific industrial skills are in greater need for social protection programmes like public pension. Chinese policymakers, in both the local and national government, are clearly aware of that. When asked by the authors of *China Vocational & Technical Education* (2009) what determines the attractiveness of vocational education, Li Zhong'an, member of the Standing Committee of National People's Congress, China's legislature, gave the following remarks

> The attractiveness of vocational education is in essence the attractiveness of the career path [it leads you onto]. You can choose the general high school and go to the college, or you can attend vocational school and step on the path to become a skilled talent. In some extent, it is the contrast between to be a worker or to be a cadre [i.e. management] . . . Whether or not to choose the path of vocational education, is directly dependent upon whether the prospective job will entail a good position, a good compensation package, and a high social status . . . The more people can expect from vocational education, the more attractive vocational education will be.

At the end of the interview, Li Zhong'an acknowledged that to improve the attractiveness of vocational education is something "that cannot be achieved by the vocational education system itself alone", because to improve the appeal of vocational education, the attractiveness of the career path of workers has to be improved, which can only be achieved through the efforts of the whole society and the government. In a similar vein, local officials, like Zhao Weiliang, vice president of the Municipal Board of Education of the city of Chongqing, attributed "the treatment for skilled workers" as "the most crucial and important condition for bringing about the attractiveness of vocational education" (*China Vocational & Technical Education* 2009). Unlike Li Zhong'an, who thought the improvement of the treatment for skilled workers would depend on the efforts of the whole nation, Zhao Weiliang gave a more realistic view that we should count on the "attention and support of the leading cadres". This corresponds to the argument of this study that the efforts of local leaders, who are motivated by the prospects of career advancement, to a large extent determine whether a locality can have a comprehensive social protection system, which in turn shapes the livelihoods of industrial workers and hence the attractiveness of vocational education. The positive impact of the treatment for skilled workers on the appeal of vocational education are captured by this study's *Schooling Hypothesis*, which argues that regions with a comprehensive public pension programme will see higher enrolment rates of vocational education.

Preferences of employers (1): labour retention and the poaching problem

We have seen how Chinese workers view social protection programmes like public pension and how this view is related to individual decisions on human capital investment. Then how about the views of employers? The *Training Hypothesis* of this study predicts a positive relationship between the provision of employer-provided on-the-job training and the coverage of a public pension programme, because by charging extra costs to those who job hop the localised pension system can discourage the practice of poaching and thus reduce employee turnover rates. This hypothesis is based on the assumptions that Chinese employers make their social policy preferences based on the human resource management need of labour retention, and that the poaching problem deters Chinese employers from investing in the skill development of their employees. The following analysis evaluates whether these assumptions accurately portray certain aspects of the reality in the Chinese business world.

The most used employer survey in China is the China Privately-Owned Enterprise Survey (CPOES). It is a biannual nationwide survey conducted since 1991 by the Chinese Academy of Social Sciences in collaboration with All China Industry and Commerce Federation. Unfortunately, CPOES focuses on the socio-economic background of employers, the networks among them, their participation in social and political activities and their self-assessment of their social and political status. There is no survey question on Chinese employers' view on the role of social protection programmes. Therefore, we have to draw on qualitative data, mostly statements made by employers in interviews with academics and journalists, to illustrate the social policy preferences of Chinese employers.

As discussed in Chapter 5, China has experienced labour market tightening since the early 2000s. The analysis of speeches by municipal leaders has revealed that the situation of labour shortage alerts Chinese local leaders, who then urge employers to treat employees better so the workers will stay. This is exactly what Chinese employers have done in a tightening labour market. To retain the workforce, they raise labour compensation. Enterprises that would have evaded their social insurance contribution now can no longer afford to do so, because without a full social insurance package workers simply would leave. As Bei Jianying, owner of a manufacturing factory in the province of Anhui, told *China Economic Weekly* (2011), "to solve the problem of labour shortage, the enterprise has to better workers' treatment, so we can keep our workers". One measure to improve the treatment of employees, according to Mr. Bei, is to pay the full amount of employers' share of social insurance contributions to employees' accounts, which has ensured "little labour mobility" of his factory workforce since the measure was taken. Other employers from Anhui province, like Xie Jun and Zhang Jianfa, expressed similar views to the reporter of *China Economic Weekly*. "We buy our employee all five kinds of social insurance [i.e., pension, unemployment, healthcare, maternity and work injury]", says Mr. Xie, "If workers have [participated in] social protection programmes, then our workforce becomes obviously more stable". Likewise, Mr. Zhang, a manager in the city of Fuyang, Anhui province, adopted a similar strategy for labour retention. "We keep our employees stable by improving their treatment", Mr. Zhang comments, "We encourage everyone to join in social insurance programmes, to reduce [labour] mobility".

It is revealing to note that the above news story from *China Economic Weekly* came from the province of Anhui, an inland province. Anhui is often thought as having a net outflow of labour force, which pours into the coastal provinces to fuel the growth of the export-led manufacturing industries. If even employers in interior regions have to raise labour compensation for labour retention, then we can have an idea of the situation in more developed, more labour-hungering areas. Nee and Opper (2012) interviewed more than 100 employers during 2006–2011 in the Yangtze River Delta, China's most dynamic economic area, and found that "tight labour markets in which firms must compete to recruit and especially to retain their employees have led to a rapid improvement of employment conditions" (312). For example, the owner of a Ningbo-based office equipment producer reports in 2011,

> Labour shortage is now a serious problem. There used to be a lot of workers coming to us from the provinces of Jiangxi and Anhui. But now their provinces are developing, and they are no longer willing to work away from home . . . My old workers now have their own houses, and do not want to work for me anymore.
>
> (Nee and Opper 2012: 312)

The measure taken by the employer in Yangtze River Delta to retain workers, again, is to offer a competitive compensation package. A producer put it quite clear, "as long as the salary and benefits are all right, workers will certainly not run away" (Nee and Opper 2012: 370). This will surely increase labour costs, but it is based on careful cost-benefit calculation. As another producer reasoned, "once the skillful workers leave, it is hard to train new workers" (Nee and Opper 2012: 370). Therefore, one aim of labour retention, which is mainly achieved through competitive labour compensation, is to protect employers' investment in workers' skills.

This leads to the discussion on the positive impact of labour retention on employers' willingness to provide on-the-job trainings for employees. It has been argued that employers will be discouraged to offer training programmes if their workers tend to job-hop or be poached by other companies. In other words, high job turnover, which can be caused by the problem of poaching, reduces the incentive of employers to fund on-the-job training programmes. Is this a fair description of what happens in China? On this point, the China Privately-Owned Enterprise Survey (CPOES) does not provide information on employers' considerations in employee skill development. So, again, we have to draw on employers' statements from journalistic sources.

In 2009, the Shenzhen Logistics and Supply Chain Management Association surveyed all companies in the logistics industry in the city of Shenzhen, and found that 79 percent of the surveyed firms would like to have in-house training schemes for employees, but the majority of them actually did not have any (*Modern Logistics* 2010). One of the reasons why employer-funded trainings were so rare in this industry, according to one interviewed employer, is the threat of poaching. This employer took his own experience as example,

> I have always thought human capital is crucial for the development of the firm, so I put a huge amount of resources into employee training. But unlike what I had hoped, after the training finished many employees did not stay with the firm and grow with the firm. Instead, they jumped to other firms

> that offered higher salaries. My guys that I put so much effort to cultivate ended up able lieutenants of my competitors. This made me very frustrated. Since then I gave up training and learnt to poach.
>
> (*Modern Logistics* 2010)

When everyone is afraid of poaching, poaching becomes rampant. It is a self-fulfilling prophecy. As another interviewed manager put it, "now we logistics firms fall into a vicious cycle where all want to make it quick. Whenever firms need someone, the first thing they can think of is not to improve their training schemes so employees can meet their needs, but to poach from other firms" (*Modern Logistics* 2010).

Therefore, in a tightening labour market, where employees have more options and more bargaining power, the problem of poaching is severe. The most important measure Chinese employers take to deal with the poaching problem is to offer a better compensation package. As we have seen earlier, to offer a competitive wage package is a major strategy to retain workers in a tightening labour market. The social insurance component of the compensation package is particularly useful for labour retention. This is because the localised structure of Chinese social insurance programmes like pension, by rendering the social insurance package non-portable and therefore incurring extra costs to cross-regional labour mobility, reduces job turnover and deters poaching activity. Therefore, being covered in social insurance programmes, for instance public pension, will reduce the likelihood of a worker being poached by outside employers and therefore prolong his employment relationship with his employer, which in turn will encourage the employer to fund on-the-job training programmes. This is the *Training Hypothesis*, which will be tested quantitatively later in this chapter.

Preferences of employers (2): regulation of labour market competition

The discussion above shows that Chinese employers see better compensation packages, which include salary and social benefits, as useful to retain workers, and this is a prerequisite for employer investment in the long-term skill development of the employee. Then on the basis of this can we form an understanding of Chinese employers' social policy preferences, i.e., why they may support more state intervention in social insurance and the establishment of a more comprehensive welfare state. At first glance, to derive the social policy preferences of Chinese employers seems straightforward: If social protection programmes like pension help employers to retain labour and improve employee skills, then surely they will ask for more state involvement in welfare provision, which would entail more subsidies to social insurance programmes. This is true, but it does not tell us the whole story. The real incentive of employers to support welfare expansion is subtler. It is not just about the retention of the labour force, but also about the regulation of the competition in labour markets.

It has been shown that workers, especially those in occupations requiring specific skills, are in need of social protection programmes like pension. And the fact that employers use generous compensation packages, which include social insurance benefits, for labour retention also demonstrates employees' demand for social security programmes. But all of these only concern one aspect of the Chinese social insurance system, which is its function to provide social security. It does not consider this system's other function, which is to limit labour mobility through its regionally fragmented structure. When the non-portable nature of the Chinese social insurance packages is taken into account, the simplistic picture that has emerged from the above analysis becomes more complex. Indeed, a better social insurance package means higher income security. This is surely attractive to employees, especially those with specific industrial skills. But on the other hand, the social insurance schemes limit workers' mobility, which make offers less attractive and even can drive workers away to other employers whose production strategies rely on labour market flexibility and who will allow workers to keep their mobility by ignoring state regulations and not joining the social insurance programmes. In other words, workers need social insurance programmes to ensure income security, but some segments of the workers, especially those with general skills, also want to have labour mobility. If in this security-mobility trade-off the general-skilled workers prefer the latter to the former, then a generous social benefit package simply cannot work to attract and retain the labour force. Instead, the package probably could drive them away to other firms that also need unconstrained labour mobility. This is the problem that Mr. Zhang, a food factory manager at Xining in Qinghai province, faced. Zhang told *Xihai Metropolis* (2012),

> Our firm wants to buy [social] insurances for employees, first to secure their future life, and secondly to use social protection to keep them stay . . . But they are not willing to cooperate with the firm [to join the social insurance programme]. The reason is simple: They are just afraid that the firm uses social insurance to chain them up so they cannot jump ship.

In other cases, employers' insistence on participation in social insurance programmes can force workers to leave. In a steel factory in the city of Zibo, Shandong province, 40 employees left because they did not want to follow the employer's instructions to join the local social insurance scheme (Dazong Daily 2008). The firm had to give in to another three workers, who threatened that "If you force me to buy social insurance, then I will quit to shift to a firm that does not buy [social insurances]". When asked why they were unwilling to join the social insurance programmes, one of the workers who threatened to quit answered:

> We come from another locality to work here. If we pay social insurance fees here, then it will cost us more than 1000 yuan a year. But it [the social

insurance package] cannot be taken to our hometown if we go back home to work there. So what's the point [of buying social insurance here]?

The fact that the firm gave in to the demand of the three workers who refused to join local social insurance programmes suggests that their threat to move to another factory is credible. Indeed, some employers in China, especially those whose competition strategy requires flexibility in labour management, often ignore the stipulation in *Labour Law* that all urban employees should join social insurance programmes. They even help the employees (and ultimately themselves) to evade the social insurance contribution. This clearly gives them a cost advantage compared to those firms that hope to achieve industrial upgrading through investment in workers' skill development, which requires the solving of poaching problem and nourishing of the long-term employment relationship, which can be attained by having the employees join the mobility-limiting public social insurance programmes. The latter group of employers, with a production strategy that relies on technological upgrading and skill improvement, therefore has every incentive to call for state intervention in the area of social policy to impose social insurance programmes on all employers and employees. This is why Li Shufu, automobile magnate and owner of Geely Automobile, proposed a motion to the National Committee of the Chinese People's Political Consultative Conference in 2011 when elected as its member, a motion that is titled "Guaranteeing Labour Rights, Achieving Enterprise Transformation and Upgrading".[2] The aim of this motion is to urge the national legislature to pass what Li calls "Regulations on the Guaranteeing of Rights of Enterprise Employee". Li highlights the importance of his motion in a context of labour shortage and industrial upgrading,

> Labour shortage has become more and more severe: It is not a temporal phenomenon after the Chinese New Year. Nor is it only confined to the South Eastern and Southern provinces. Some of the interior and Western regions have the same problem. Labour shortage has become a social problem. It has started to affect the development of enterprises. It is harmful to the ongoing enterprise transformation and upgrading, to the nourishing of Chinese global brands, and to the building of a harmonious society. We have to pay great attention to this problem.

Next, Li sets out to propose his strategy to tackle this problem,

> I think for China to have global brands and for Chinese enterprise to achieve the goal of transformation and upgrading, the first and foremost thing to do is to improve the business environment, especially to make sure workers can enjoy their labour rights, including the rights to pension, social insurance, healthcare, public housing, and vocational training.

It is noteworthy that Li equates a business-friendly environment with an environment where workers enjoy various labour rights. It is in striking contrast with the conventional wisdom that Chinese companies benefit from a human resource management regime that sees excessive labour rights abuses. To be sure, many Chinese employers do rely on abusing labour rights to keep labour costs low. These employers are exactly whom Li fights against. He calls for the authority to impose tougher regulations on them,

> Surely our government has paid great attention to issues like social protection reform, healthcare reform, and pension reform, etc. The enforcement of *Labour Law* has also been strengthened. All of these undoubtedly are of crucial importance to the guaranteeing of labour rights. Then why can we still see many violations to employees' rights and interests? Why many firms cannot have a stable workforce and have to deal with the problem of labour shortage?
>
> The answer is that many of the government's measures to protect employees' rights and interests have not been fully translated into action. Some firms adopt human management practices that are against the law, and they can do so without being punished heavily, thereby enjoying a low cost of law breaking and feeling free to violate employees' rights.
>
> To change this, I urge the relevant central ministries, especially All China Federation of Trade Unions, to make the "*Regulations on the Guaranteeing of Rights of Enterprise Employee*", as a supplement to the *Labour Law*, to guarantee the lawful rights and interests of workers, to increase the costs of law breaking through heavier punishment, to ensure a fair and just environment, and to accelerate the transformation and upgrading of the Chinese economy.

That Li calls for building a "fair and just" environment at the end of his law-making proposal tells us why he links protecting labour rights with a business-friendly environment. To Li, an environment that is good for business, or for his business, is a fair environment where no employer can enjoy labour cost advantage by evading state regulations and violating labour rights. In other words, what Li asks for is fair play. With employers violating labour laws and regulations at little cost, the game can easily become unfair for Li's auto empire, Geely Automobile, which cannot afford to adopt similar practices. Geely, established to produce affordable vehicles for Chinese households at the beginning, now has started to upgrade its products and climb up the value chain. It has taken bold moves to achieve advancements in technology and management, including spending US$1.8 billion to buy Volvo Cars from Ford Motor in 2010 (Volvo News 2010). "Upgrading and Transformation", therefore, are the key words for Geely's production strategy, which explains their repeated appearance in Li's motion. To ensure successful industrial upgrading, Li's Geely has invested heavily in the training and retention of its workforce. In fact, a whole section of Li's motion (which is not cited here) is dedicated to calling for more state investment in vocational education and training. Also, going global means Geely has been put under stricter regulatory frameworks, including those in labour rights. But while industrial upgrading and entering the world market, Geely has continued to compete with other Chinese automobile companies in the domestic market to produce affordable vehicles for Chinese customers, a market where it built its earlier success and which it simply cannot let go. In this situation, Li surely does not want to see his competitors, which may have different production strategies that do not require sophisticated industrial skills from workers, gain labour cost advantage over Geely by ignoring labour rights. Nor does Li wish his workers to leave and join his competitors because they do not want to be forced into localised social protection programmes. One way to deal with all of these concerns, as we have seen in Li's motion, is to urge the state and the union to work together to pass new regulations, which are aimed to strengthen law enforcement so the social protection system can be imposed on all workers and employers. In this way, no employer will be able to gain cost advantage by evading social insurance contributions, and no employee will be lured away by outside employers' promises to let workers stay out of the mobility-limiting local social insurance schemes. The competition in labour markets, therefore, is regulated, and the playing field becomes level. What we see here is not a scenario of "politics against markets", where capitalists attempt to shake off the shackles of a welfare system imposed by the labour and the state, but a case of "politics of the market", where a group of Chinese employers, dictated by their production strategy, ally with the state and the trade union, trying to influence how the regulatory framework is shaped for workers' social rights and to keep competition in the labour and product markets under control. The close link between employers' production strategy and their social policy preferences, as we have seen in the above Chinese case, confirms a central thesis in the Varieties of Capitalism theory that social protection is inherent in the production regime (for two major types of capitalist production regimes, coordinated and uncoordinated/liberal, see Soskice 1990; Soskice 1999; Hollingsworth et al. 1994; Hall and Soskice 2001). Future studies on the political economy of the Chinese welfare state should focus on how Chinese employers' production strategies, which may be determined by socio-economic conditions (like industrial upgrading and labour market tightening), shape their social policy preferences, and to what extent such employer preferences can be translated into government policy through the institutionally regulated interaction between employers and local/national policymakers. In this way, one can find out how the Chinese welfare state fits into China's production regime.

To summarise, the above discussion has shown how Chinese employers perceive the benefits of social insurance programmes in terms of retaining workers and protecting their investments in employee skill formation, and how they form social policy preferences. In the context of labour market tightening, to retain their labour force Chinese employers rely on competitive compensation packages, which include generous, non-portable social insurance schemes. Such a measure for labour retention also serves to protect employer investment in workers' skill development by reducing the attractiveness of offers from outside, poaching employers. On the basis of the economic benefits of social insurance programmes, employers whose production strategy relies on employee skill upgrading support the state to adopt an expansive social policy, which not only serves the employers' purpose of labour retention and skill formation, but also functions as a way to regulate the competition in labour markets, where less skill-intensive firms may lure workers away by helping them evade social insurance contribution and therefore gain labour cost advantage. Without the support from the business sector, the expansion of the Chinese pension system would not be possible.

Summary

This section examines pension policy preferences of Chinese workers and employers, assessing to what extent our theory's assumptions about pension policy preferences of economic agents are an accurate reflection of reality. The survey on Chinese citizens' opinions, CGSS2006, shows that workers in specific skill occupations are in greater need for public pension programmes than workers in general skill occupations, which is consistent with the assumption our theory makes about Chinese workers' pension policy preferences. It is then followed that comprehensive public pension programmes should encourage individuals to choose specific skill occupations through getting a vocational education, a hypothesis that will be tested in the next section. As for the preferences of Chinese employers, in a tightening labour market they compete with each other for workforce and are worried about the problem of poaching. The need for labour retention drives employers, especially those who pursue a production strategy of industrial upgrading, to support the enforcement of expansionary social policies. This helps them share with other employers the costs of social insurance programmes, "deferred wages" that are especially effective for labour retention. It also meant to discipline labour market competition and eliminate labour cost advantage some employers may gain from evading social insurance contribution. With the help of social insurance programmes like pension to regulate the competition in labour markets and alleviate the problem of poaching, the employer can nourish a long-term employment relationship with the employee, which in turn encourages employers to fund on-the-job training programmes. This hypothesis, which predicts a positive impact of pension coverage on job tenure and the incidence of vocational training, will be tested in the third section.

Schooling hypothesis

> If social protection programmes like pension can encourage students to acquire industry specific skills, then regions with high pension coverage rates should have high enrolment rates in vocational education.

This section tests the *Schooling Hypothesis*, which argues that provinces with high pension coverage rates will have high vocational school enrolment rates. The dependent variable is the enrolment rate in vocational education. It is measured as the number of the students who get admitted to secondary vocational schools as a share of all students that get admitted to secondary schools (which include both vocational and general education schools) each year.[3] Clearly this measurement reflects the influx of students attending vocational education. To provide a robustness check, I also measure the dependent variable as the incidence of vocational education, which is the total number of students enroled in secondary vocational schools as a proportion of students enroled in secondary schools. This indicates the stock of vocational education students. The independent variable is the pension coverage rate, which as argued above should have a positive impact on students' willingness to attend vocational education and hence on the enrolment rates in vocational education.

Three control variables are included. The first variable is *Industrialisation*, which is measured as GDP per capita (in logged form) and used to indicate the level of economic development of a province. It is included because economic circumstances should have an impact on individuals' schooling decisions. Compared with those in poor regions, people living in prosperous areas tend to face different economic and educational opportunities, which will affect their education choices. In particular, it is expected that an economy at a higher income level has a higher degree of technological sophistication, which accordingly makes a higher requirement for the skill levels of the industrial worker. This should provide an impetus for individuals to acquire specific industrial skills through vocational education. The level of economic development, therefore, needs to be controlled for, and it should have a positive impact on the enrolment rates of vocational schools.

The second variable is the *Markettisation* index on the labour market, which is one component of the composite marketisation index from the works by Fan Gang and Wang Xiaolu (2011). It measures the integration of the rural-urban labour market with reference to the share of peasant migrant workers in the total urban labour force. The higher this labour market marketisation index is, the fewer the institutional and policy barriers are in place in labour markets that would discriminate against peasant workers working in urban areas. A major strategy of municipal leaders to increase the enrolment rates of vocational schools is to attract peasant students from rural areas through various preferential treatments, like waiving vocational school tuition fees for rural students (Chen and Wang 2009; Wang and Jiang 2012). The countryside then constitutes a major source of students for secondary vocational schools. For example, in 2010 over 80 percent of Beijing's secondary vocational students came from rural backgrounds (Beijing Evening 2010). The willingness of peasant students to have vocational education depends on not only the preferential policies, but also on their access to urban jobs after graduation, which is in turn dependent upon the labour market regulations on the hiring of peasant workers. If such regulations are rigid and discriminate against peasant workers, which can be indicated by a low share of peasant workers in urban labour force, then the employment prospects are not promising for peasant workers, which should discourage rural students from getting a vocational education. On the other hand, if there are few discriminative labour market regulations, then the better employment opportunities in the city should encourage students from rural areas to attend vocational schools. The *Markettisation* index on the labour market, which indicates to what extent rural workers can be integrated into the urban labour markets, should have a positive impact on the enrolment in vocational education.

The third variable is the *Industrial Structure*, which is measured as the share of the secondary industries (whose official definition in China includes the manufacturing and construction sectors) in terms of employment. Arguably peoples' inclination to develop certain kinds of skills depends upon the employment opportunities available in the economy that require such skills. Since construction and manufacturing industries are in great need for specific skills, a strong secondary sector in terms of the huge number of jobs it creates should encourage people to attend vocational schools where they can learn specific skills of value to this sector. To take into account this effect the proportion of secondary industry employment thus should be controlled for.

Drawing on China Statistical Yearbooks (2001–2011) and other statistical yearbooks, the dataset used to test the first hypothesis is a panel of data that covers 31 provincial-level jurisdictions across 10 years. The estimator is the generalised least squares regression with fixed effects.[4] Beck and Katz's (1995) technique of pooled ordinary least squares regression with panel-corrected standard errors (OLS-PCSE) is also used to provide sensitivity checks. Table 5.2 summarises the findings from the regression analysis.

Table 5.2 Testing training hypothesis: determinants of secondary vocational school enrolment rates (2000–2010) Generalised least square regression

Variable	*Model 1*	*Model 2*	*Model 3*	*Model 4*
Pension coverage	.2550331*** (.0700436)	.2257585*** (.0618273)	.1527962** (.0603431)	.1359521** (.0530717)
Industrialisation	.0611158 (.0725266)		.0220435 (.0624822)	
Marketisation (labour market)	.0026771 (.0042652)		.0067773* (.0036745)	
Industrial structure (secondary sector)	.6657374*** (.1888545)		.6260534*** (.1626997)	
Year dummies	Yes	Yes	Yes	Yes
Province fixed effects	Yes	Yes	Yes	Yes
Constant	−.6639438 (.6342176)	.0383793*** (.0444279)	−.185644 (.5463836)	.1623863*** (.0381363)
Observations	217	279	217	279
Probability > F	0.000	0.000	0.000	0.000
Adjusted R-square	0.4579	0.7621	0.4648	0.6480

*, **, ***, stand for $p < 0.1$, $p < 0.05$ and $p < 0.01$ two-tailed test. Standard errors are in parentheses.

In Table 5.2, Model 1 is the baseline estimation, which includes all control variables. It shows that the coverage of pension programmes has a significant and positive impact on the enrolment rates in secondary vocational schools.[5] In other words, the more comprehensive a region's pension scheme is, the more students will be attracted to vocational education. This supports the *Schooling Hypothesis* that social protection programmes like pension induce people's investment in specific skills. Model 2 drops all control variables, and the sign and significance of pension coverage rates stay the same. Model 3 changes the baseline model by measuring the dependent variable as the incidence of vocational education, that is, the total number of students enroled in secondary vocational schools as a proportion of students enroled in secondary schools. The results indicate a positive relationship between the presence of pension programmes and the incidence of vocational education, meaning that the more comprehensive pension programmes a region possesses, the more vocational students it will have. This association remains the same when Model 4 excludes all control variables from Model 3.

It is interesting to examine the effects of the control variables. The employment share of manufacturing sectors has a significant and positive impact on both the enrolment rate in vocational schools and the incidence of vocational education, which is consistent with the expectation that a strong manufacturing economy creates many jobs that require specific skills and thus give students incentives to acquire such skills through vocational education. The coefficients of the other two variables, that is, economic development and rural-urban labour market integration, though showing no statistical significance, display positive signs. This is consistent with our expectations. A technologically sophisticated economy at a higher income level requires more workers with industrial skills, which then motivates people to choose vocational education. The willingness to do so, especially for those from the countryside, hinges upon the prospects of getting employed in the urban manufacturing sector, which are in turn positively linked with the integration of rural-urban labour markets.

Table 5.3 presents the results from robustness checks that use alternative estimation methods. Model 5 and Model 6 use generalised least squares regression with robust variance to replicate the estimation of Model 1 and Model 3, respectively. The procedure of robustisation does not change the coefficients of variables but re-calculates their standard errors, thereby serving to re-examine the statistical significance of variables. The estimations of Model 1 and 3 are also replicated by Model 7 and Model 8, which use pooled ordinary least squares regression with panel-corrected standard errors (OLS-PCSE). It is clear that after the re-estimation of standard errors, the significant and positive impact of pension coverage on vocational education holds across all checking models. The effects of other control variables also remain the same as in the baseline estimation. This gives us more confidence in the validity of the *Schooling Hypothesis* that the presence of comprehensive pension programmes encourages students to invest in specific skills through attending vocational schools.

Table 5.3 Robustness checks: determinants of secondary vocational school enrolment rates (2000–2010) Generalised least squares regression and Prais-Winsten regression with panel-corrected standard errors

Variable	*Model 5*	*Model 6*	*Model 7*	*Model 8*
Pension coverage	.2550331**	.1527962**	.2118817***	.1053349*
	(.0948494)	(.071194)	(.0674097)	(.0570089)
Industrialisation	.0611158	.0220435	.0566402	.0175498
	(.0835445)	(.0815336)	(.0617131)	(.0540604)
Marketisation	.0026771	.0067773	.0014997	.0047609
(labour market)	(.0062043)	(.0049202)	(.0052437)	(.0047844)
Industrial structure	.6657374***	.6260534***	.6359252***	.5835542***
(secondary sector)	(.225365)	(.2115345)	(.152172)	(.1234737)
Year dummies	Yes	Yes	Yes	Yes
Province fixed effects	Yes	Yes	Yes	Yes
Constant	–.6639438	–.185644	–.4992716	-1.189157**
	(.7374758)	(.7168239)	(.6712146)	(.3508201)
Observations	217	217	217	217
Probability > F (Chi-square)	0.000	0.000	0.000	0.000
Adjusted R-square	0.4579	0.4648	0.8651	0.8683

*, **, ***, stand for $p < 0.1$, $p < 0.05$ and $p < 0.01$ two-tailed test. Standard errors are in parentheses.

Training hypothesis

> If localised pension programmes can limit job turnover and hence alleviate the problem of poaching, then workers covered by pension programmes should be more likely to receive trainings offered by employers.

Human capital investment in the acquisition of specific industrial skills is made not only by the students through their decisions on which type of education to get, as examined by the last section, but also by employers. Pension schemes, especially in a localised, non-portable form, reduce labour mobility and therefore give incentives to employers, who are now less worried about workers being poached by outside firms, to invest in the skill development of their employees through trainings on specific skills. This generates the *Training Hypothesis*: If localised pension programmes can limit job turnover and hence alleviate the problem of poaching, workers covered by pension programmes should have longer job tenures and hence be more likely to receive trainings funded by employers. Clearly, this hypothesis has two parts, one concerning the effect of pension programmes on limiting labour mobility and the other concerning the role of pension schemes in inducing employer investment in employee training programmes. This section is accordingly structured into two parts. The first part investigates the relationship between pension coverage and job tenure. The second part examines the association between pension programme and employer-sponsored training.

Pension programme and labour mobility

As have been argued in Chapter 2, China's public pension system, with its localised structure that makes pension packages non-portable across regions, incurs the potential loss of moving to other localities and consequently reduces voluntary labour mobility, thereby prolonging job tenures. This has two implications: One is at the micro level and the other at the macro-level. First, at the micro level, workers that are covered by the public pension programme tend to have longer job tenures, compared with those not covered under such a pension scheme. Secondly, at the macro level, regions with more extensive pension coverage should see less out-migration. The first implication is tested using the micro data from the China Urban Labour Survey (2001), examining at an individual level whether the coverage of public pension schemes prolongs job tenures. The testing of the second implication draws on data at the regional level, aimed to explore whether a region with higher pension coverage rates will have a lower level of out-migration. As shall be clear at the end of this section, statistical analysis of both of the micro- and macro-level data supports the hypothesis that pension coverage lengthens job tenures and lowers migration across localities. Let us start with the testing of the first implication.

To test the first prediction we need data at the individual level, which comes from the China Urban Labour Survey 2001 (CULS2001). This survey was conducted in 2001 by the Institute for Population and Labour Economics at the Chinese Academy of Social Sciences, in collaboration with the provincial and municipal offices of the National Bureau of Statistics. It was administered in five major Chinese cities: Fuzhou, Shanghai, Shenyang, Wuhan and Xi'an. These cities were selected to reflect China's regional diversity as much as possible: Shenyang is the capital city of the northeastern province Liaoning, which has been a base of heavy industries since the socialist years. Wuhan and Xi'an are also traditional industrial bases dominated by state sector enterprises, but they are located in very different places: Wuhan is the capital of Hubei province in central China, while Xi'an serves as the capital city of the Shaanxi province, which lies in the inland area of northwestern China, near several ethnic minority regions. Shanghai, a coastal metropolis that was once home to many large national industries, is now an economic hub dominated by foreign-invested manufacturing companies and financial firms. On the contrary, Fuzhou, the capital city of the coastal province Fujian adjacent to Taiwan, boasts its vibrant, burgeoning homegrown private sector, whose business model of export-led processing trade helps China to earn its name as "the workhouse of the world". A proportional population sampling approach was used. From each of the 70 neighbourhood clusters sampled in each city, 15 registered households were sampled, where all family members older than 16 were interviewed individually. The completed survey covered 8,109 adults above the age of 16, among whom 4,238 were employed in 2001 and 5,787 were under the mandatory retirement age (i.e., 60 for men and 55 for women).

CULS2001 asked questions about the employment history of the individuals, i.e., questions about when they started working for the employer, when they ended the employment relationship, what kind of benefits they received, what their occupations were, etc. To test the first hypothesis on the link between public pension coverage and job tenure, the question on the benefits the respondent received when employed is used to measure the independent variable, *Public Pension*, indicating whether the individual was covered by the public pension scheme (coded as 1 if the respondent was covered under public pension programmes or 0 if the respondent was not covered). Questions on the start and end dates of employment with the same employer are used to calculate the length of job tenure, which is the dependent variable. Several variables on characteristics of respondents and their firms, which may affect the length of job tenure, are controlled for in the regression analysis. There are seven variables that capture individual characteristics, including: *Gender* (1 = Male, 0 = Female), *Age*, *Education* (dummy variables indicating which level of education attainment the respondent has), *Occupation* (dummy variables indicating which role the respondent was serving in the firm: average worker, technician, administrative staff or technocrat who worked both as technician and administrative manager), *Contract* (1 = The respondent had signed a labour contract with his employer, 0 = No labour contract) and *Hukou Status* (1 = The respondent having a urban household registration, 0 = The respondent having a rural household registration). It is possible that a respondent can be covered by the public pension scheme and the firm-based private pension programme at the same time. Since occupational benefits can also reduce labour mobility and prolong the length of employment, it is necessary to control for whether the respondent enjoys the employer-provided pension programme. This is captured by the variable of *Occupational Pension* (1 = Respondent having joined the company pension scheme, 0 = Not having joined such scheme). Three firm characteristics variables are included: *Ownership* (1 = Private sector firms, 0 = State sector work units and enterprises), *Profitability* (dummy variables indicating whether the firm is making a great profit, a moderate profit, a loss or a great loss), and *Sector* (dummy variables indicating which sector the firm belongs to, like the manufacturing, finance, social service sector, etc.). Finally, the regression includes the variable of *City* (dummy variables indicating where the firm is located: Shanghai, Wuhan, Shenyang, Fuzhou or Xi'An), in an attempt to control for unobserved city-level socio-economic factors and institution/policy environments that may affect job tenure of workers. Since the dependent variable, *Job Tenure*, is a continuous variable, the estimator is ordinary least squares (OLS). The regression results are presented in Table 5.4.

The first column of Table 5.4 shows the results of the regression analysis that includes all observations. After other variables that may affect workers' tenure are controlled for, the coverage of public pension schemes displays a positive and

Table 5.4 Determinants of length of job tenure (2001) Ordinary least squares regression

Independent variables	*All cases*	*Sub-sample (workers joining the labour market after 1985)*
Dependent variable: job tenure		
Public pension	2.437*** (.499)	1.374*** (.440)
Occupational pension	4.746*** (.490)	1.191*** (.366)
Gender	.428 (.437)	–.162 (.324)
Age	.521*** (.021)	.066*** (.015)
Contract	.572 (.442)	.754** (.336)
Hukou status	–.671 (1.831)	–.250 (.917)
Ownership	–5.026*** (.797)	–1.695*** (.394)
Education	Yes	Yes
Occupation	Yes	Yes
Profitability	Yes	Yes
Sector	Yes	Yes
City	Yes	Yes
Constant	–10.051*** (2.758)	4.375*** (1.624)
Observations	1606	557
F (β = 0)	27.656***	4.236***
Adjusted R-square	0.495	0.252

*, **, ***, stand for $p < 0.1$, $p < 0.05$ and $p < 0.01$ two-tailed test. Standard errors are in parentheses.

significant impact on the length of job tenure, supporting the hypothesis that being covered by public pension programmes can reduce workers' willingness to change jobs and thus prolong job tenures. The effect of occupational pension schemes on job tenure is also positive with high statistical significance, which is expected since occupation benefits are purposefully designed by employers to retain workers. This may explain why the impact of occupational pension benefits is larger than that of public pension schemes (as both of them are binary variables, to assess their relative importance, we can compare the coefficient of *Occupational Pension* with that of *Public Pension*, which are 4.746 and 2.437, respectively).

The second column of Table 5.4 lists the results of the analysis that uses a sub-sample of workers who started working after 1985. In 1985 China introduced a labour contract system to the rigid socialist personnel management, thereby bringing some market mechanisms into the employment practice especially in the state sector enterprises (White 1987). Since then, whereas old workers who had got employed before 1985 still largely enjoy traditional stable employment, workers who joined the labour force after 1985 have to sign a renewable labour contract with their employers. The result is that the job security of these workers is more likely to be affected by labour market fluctuations. Therefore, to control for the effects of the law change in 1985, the sub-sample is used that only includes workers who entered the labour market after 1985. The regression results are presented in the second column of Table 6.3. The public pension coverage still has the expected positive impact on job tenure. Interestingly, the coefficient of *Public Pension* becomes larger than that of *Occupational Pension*. In other words, for those workers who are employed after 1985 and hence are under the new labour contract system and are more exposed to market fluctuations, public pension schemes matter more than occupational pension benefits in terms of extending job tenure. This may suggest that in more liberal labour markets in the post-1985 years, the localised public pension system becomes more important with respect to reducing labour mobility.

What is also interesting is the effect of *Ownership*, whose negative coefficient indicates that workers in state sector firms tend to have longer job tenure. This is not surprising. Though having been through several rounds of reforms China's state-owned enterprises (SOEs) still have an arrangement of industrial relations that has features inherited from the socialist era. Although there is no lifetime employment that once characterised the socialist employment practice, or "iron rice bowl" as it is called in China, due to organisational inertia in the state sector the pre-reform legacy of personnel management practices tends to foster a long-term employment relationship, especially when compared with the private sector (Ding et al. 2000). This justifies the inclusion of ownership types of firms in the regression analysis, because by doing so we can control for different personnel management practices that may affect workers' job tenure.

The limitations of the above analysis are twofold. First, although its case selection tries to be representative, CULS2001 covers only five cities, which is clearly insufficient to capture China's internal variety and disparity in geographical as well as socio-economic terms. Secondly, the five cities surveyed in CULS2001 are all provincial capitals, where the level of economic development is often higher and therefore the local governments are better financed than the rest of the province. This may overestimate the situations of social benefit provision in China. To examine to what extent the findings from the analysis of CULS2001 can hold valid beyond the five cities, one needs to use macro-level data that include all of the Chinese regions. This makes necessary the testing of our second hypothesis, which predicts a negative association between public pension coverage and regional out-migration.

If the public pension scheme, with its localised structure, can work to extend job tenure and retain labour force, as we have discovered from the analysis of CULS2001, then localities with higher levels of public pension coverage rates should be better at retaining workers and therefore see less out-migration. The rate of out-migration is the number of emigrants (who leave the area to settle in other places) per 1,000 residents of an area in a period of time. The Ministry of Public Security of China reports the annual out-migration rates of provincial jurisdictions in its *Population Statistical Data by County/City of People's Republic of China*. The Chinese data on internal migration are often criticised for problems like underreporting and incompleteness, but one has to use the data provided by the Ministry of Public Security because it is the only government agency in China that regulates population flows. To the author's knowledge, this dataset is the best available data source of China's interregional migration. The interest then is to examine whether the province with higher pension coverage rates (measured as the number of workers covered under public pension schemes as a share of total urban labour force) will have less out-migration as expected. First we take the year of 2001 as an example and draw a dot plot graph in Figure 5.2 to illustrate the relationship between provincial out-migration rates and pension coverage rates.

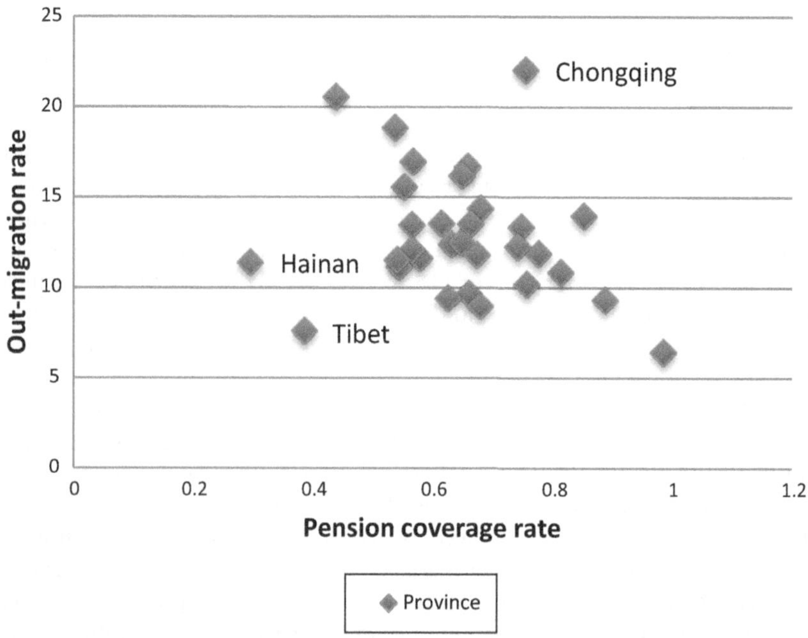

Figure 5.2 Pension coverage rates and provincial out-migration rates (2001)

Source: Data on pension coverage rates comes from the China Statistical Yearbook 2002, and data on out-migration rates from Population Statistical Data by County/City of People's Republic of China (2001), compiled by Ministry of Public Security of China and published by Qunzhong Publishing House (Beijing) in April 2002.

Figure 5.2 shows a negative relationship between a province's out-migration rate and its pension coverage. Three provincial jurisdictions seem to deviate from this general pattern, which are Chongqing, Hainan and Tibet. As discussed earlier in Chapter 5 when we conduct the regression analysis of how the provincial leadership dominated by insiders affects municipal leaders' willingness to expand pension coverage, these three provincial jurisdictions tend to be different from other provinces: Hainan and Chongqing only assumed their provincial rank since 1988 and 1996, while the high political sensitivity of Tibet may distort data on this region for political reasons.

To examine whether the pattern emerging from Figure 5.2 is specific to the year of 2001, whether it is affected by outlier cases, and whether it is actually caused by some other factors, we need to conduct the time-series-cross-sectional regression analysis of all 31 provincial-level units across 10 years (2000–2009), in which pension coverage rate is the independent variable while the out-migration rate is the dependent one. The regression should also control for variables that may affect the out-migration rates. The first control variable is that of *Industrialisation*, measured as the provincial GDP per capita (in logged form). A higher level of economic development provides people with more opportunities like jobs and a higher standard of living and hence makes them less willing to leave, whereas people may be more ready to escape from poor regions. So it is expected that economic development should be negatively related to out-migration rates. The second variable controlled for is *Marketisation* (on the dimension of labour market), which indicates the integration of urban-rural labour markets. It is the same variable used earlier when we examine the association between pension coverage rates and vocational education enrolment rates. This variable is included because intra-provincial migration can be a substitute for inter-provincial migration. Indeed, a peasant worker will first try to find a job in the nearby city centre before he tries his luck in more distant places, like in the localities outside of his home province. The implication is that a province with a more peasant-worker-friendly labour market should see less out-migration of such workers. To include this variable allows us to control for the institutional settings that may affect the migration decisions of peasant workers, who are the major agent in China's long-distance interregional migration. The analysis controls for other variables that may have impacts on out-migration rates by adding province dummy variables. Table 5.5 reports the regression results.

Model 1 in Table 5.5 uses pooled ordinary least squares regression with panel-corrected standard errors (OLS-PCSE), while Model 2 employs a different estimator, the generalised least squares regression (GLS). Both of them include all 31 provincial units. In both of the two models the independent variable, *Pension Coverage*, exhibits a negative impact on provincial out-migration, indicating that provinces with more extensive coverage of pension programmes tend to have lower out-migration rates. This supports our hypothesis and is consistent with the argument that public pension programmes can serve to retain the labour force locally. The coefficients of control variables also show expected signs. The negative impact of the integration of rural-urban labour markets on out-province

Table 5.5 Determinants of provincial out-migration rates (2000–2009) Generalised least square regression and Prais-Winsten regression with panels corrected standard errors

Variable	*Model 1*	*Model 2*	*Model 3*	*Model 4*
Pension coverage	–6.639539** (3.423048)	–7.466706* (4.624119)	–10.61115** (4.424723)	–11.53499** (5.489209)
Industrialisation	–.0000681 (.0001627)	–.0000699 (.0001091)	–.0000861 (.0001648)	–.0000889 (.0001144)
Marketisation (labour market)	–.5897467* (.3478327)	–.6011538* (.3599679)	–.7262727** (.3590279)	–.735005** (.3822332)
Year dummies	Yes	Yes	Yes	Yes
Province fixed effects	Yes	Yes	Yes	Yes
Constant	18.86766*** (6.737911)	19.36445*** (5.951207)	19.09948*** (5.648584)	23.7932*** (6.635446)
Observations	248	248	224	224
Probability > F	0.000	0.000	0.000	0.000
Adjusted R-square	0.5699	0.6160	0.5487	0.5958

*, **, ***, stand for $p < 0.1$, $p < 0.05$ and $p < 0.01$ two-tailed test. Standard errors are in parentheses.

migration rates indicates the trade-off between intra-provincial migration and inter-provincial migration: A more integrated urban-rural labour market with less discrimination against peasant migrant workers may encourage more of them to stay in the province's urban centres instead of moving out of the province. The negative sign of the coefficient of economic development, though having no statistical significance, may suggest the attractiveness of economic wealth: people living in rich provinces are less likely to leave compared with their counterparts in less wealthy provinces. Model 3 and 4 drop the possible outliers, i.e., Chongqing, Hainan and Tibet, from the regression and use OLS-PCSE and GLS as estimation methods, respectively. The regression results remain largely the same, but the coefficients of *Pension Coverage* and other variables become larger than in Model 1 and 2, which include all provincial units. This may suggest that other factors may matter more in terms of affecting out-migration rates in these outlier provinces, which could be explored in future research. For now, the important thing is that from the regression analysis we can see the coverage of the localised public pension schemes can reduce the migration out of a locality, thereby effectively retaining the labour force within the region.

To summarise what has been discussed so far: It has been argued that China's localised public pension system, by incurring the loss of pension benefits to the worker who job-hops to another locality, deters labour mobility across regions and therefore serves to retain the workforce locally. This argument has two implications. One is at the individual level, which predicts that workers covered by public pension schemes should have longer job tenure compared with those who are not covered by such programmes. The other implication is at the macro level, which argues that regions with higher public pension coverage rates will have lower out-migration rates. Both of the two predictions have passed the statistical testing, therefore supporting the argument that the public pension scheme serves the function of limiting the labour mobility across regions. Then what does this imply? It implies that a Chinese local leader, if he sees possibilities of promotion and worries that the flow of skilled workers into the neighbouring localities would enhance the competitiveness of his competitors, will adopt a protectionist policy in the labour market by expanding pension coverage to retain the labour force locally. But this is not our only focus. What we are also interested in is how the localised pension system, which reduces labour mobility, affects employers' willingness to fund employee training programmes.

Pension programme and employer-provided training

This study argues that the presence of pension programmes will induce not only the student's investment in acquiring industry specific skills, but also the employer's investment in training schemes on specific skills. The idea is that by reducing labour mobility with its localised design, as have been demonstrated earlier, the Chinese local pension schemes assure the employer that its employees may not be easily poached by other firms and therefore encourage the current employer to invest in the skill development of their employees. This generates the prediction that workers covered by public pension arrangements are more likely to receive trainings provided by their employers.

The China Urban Labour Survey (CULS) in 2001 provides the opportunity to examine this prediction. It asks the questions of "Have you had any job training or study experience since 1996?" and "What kind of job training or study was this?" Therefore, the dependent variable can be constructed as a binary one. If the respondent had job trainings provided or paid by the employers, then the dependent variable is coded as 1, or 0 if the respondent had training courses paid by himself or had no trainings. The independent variable of interest, *Public Pension*, is also binary, indicating whether the respondent is covered by the public pension programme (coded as 1 if covered and as 0 if not). The analysis controls for several characteristics of the respondent and his firm that may affect the respondent's chances of having employer-provided trainings. The personal characteristics variables include: *Gender* (1 = Male, 0 = Female), *Age*, *Education* (dummy variables indicating which level of education attainment the respondent has), *Occupation* (dummy variables indicating which role the respondent was serving in the firm: average worker, technician, administrative staff or technocrat who worked both as technician and administrative manager) and *Contract* (1 = The respondent had signed a labour contract with her employer, 0 = No labour contract). It is possible that a respondent, in addition to being covered by the public pension scheme, also joined the firm-based private pension programme. Since firm-based benefits can reduce labour mobility and hence encourage employers to invest in employees' career development, it is necessary to control for whether the respondent enjoys the employer-provided pension programme. This is captured by the variable of *Occupational Pension* (1 = Having the firm-based pension scheme, 0 = Not having such a scheme). The firm characteristics are: *Ownership* (1 = Private sector firms, 0 = State-run enterprises), *Profitability* (dummy variables indicating whether the firm is making a great profit, a moderate profit, a loss or a great loss) and *Sector* (dummy variables indicating which sector the firm belongs to, like manufacturing, finance, social service sector, etc.). Finally, in order to control for unobserved socio-economic factors and institution/policy environments, the regression includes the variable of *City* (dummy variables indicating where the firm is located: Shanghai, Wuhan, Shenyang, Fuzhou or Xi'An). Because the dependent variable is dichotomous, the estimation method is logistic regression. Table 5.6 presents the estimation results.

From Table 5.6 we can see a positive relationship between the presence of the public pension scheme and workers' likelihood of attending training programmes provided by employers. This is to say, a worker being covered under the state-run

Table 5.6 Testing training hypothesis: factors affecting the likelihood of attending employer-provided training programmes Logistic regression

Dependent variable: whether or not to have attended employer-provided training programmes		
Independent variables	*Coefficient*	*Marginal effects*
Public pension	.363**	1.438**
	(.171)	(.171)
Occupational pension	.520***	1.683***
	(.177)	(.176)
Gender	–.079	.924
	(.151)	(.151)
Age	–.030***	–.1.026***
	(.007)	(.007)
Contract	.033	1.033
	(.161)	(.161)
Hukou status	–.278	.757
	(.747)	(.747)
Ownership	–.773**	.461**
	(.344)	(.344)
Education	Yes	Yes
Occupation	Yes	Yes
Profitability	Yes	Yes
Sector	Yes	Yes
City	Yes	Yes
Constant	213.941	213.941
	(395081.895)	(395081.895)
Observations	4845	4845
Probability > Chi-square	0.000	0.000
Log likelihood	–1579.273	–1579.273

*, **, ***, stand for $p < 0.1$, $p < 0.05$ and $p < 0.01$ two-tailed test. Standard errors are in parentheses.

pension system increases his chances of receiving trainings organised or paid for by his employer. This association should be a causal relationship because the regression controls for variables that may simultaneously affect workers' chances of having public pension coverage and their probabilities of attending firm-provided trainings, like the worker's education and job position, financial situations of the company and the industrial sector in which the firm operates, etc. The pattern that emerges from the analysis therefore supports the hypothesis that by reducing voluntary labour mobility and hence employers' worries about job-hopping and poaching, the coverage of public pension schemes encourages employers to invest in the skill development of employees. Since such investment is made by the employers, the kind of skills it aims to produce should be those in which the employers have the most interest, which are firm- and industry-specific skills. We have argued that the public pension system contributes to the formation of specific industrial skills by encouraging individuals to invest in skills (who then attend vocational schools), here we find the second mechanism through which the public pension programme induces the production of specific skills, that is, through encouraging employers to invest in employees' skills.

The effects of two control variables are worth discussing. The first is the variable of *Occupational Pension*, whose coefficient exhibits a positive sign with high statistical significance. It shows that having occupational benefits like firm-based pension packages increases the chances of receiving company-provided trainings. This is easy to understand: occupational pension programmes set up by firms, which often are limited in portability, are intentionally designed to retain the labour force, which in turn assures employers about workers' long-term employment and hence encourages them to provide training schemes for employees. So occupational pension packages, given that they are purposely devised by employers for labour retention, should best serve to induce employers' investment in employees' skills. If we compare the marginal effects of *Public Pension* and *Occupational Pension*, which are 1.438 and 1.683, respectively, we can see the impact of the public pension system on encouraging employer investment in employee skills is actually very close to that of the occupational pension arrangement. This is an indication of the effectiveness of the public pension scheme in terms of inducing employers' investment in employees' skills.

The second noteworthy variable is that of *Ownership*, whose negative coefficient suggests that compared with working in the private sector, a worker in the state sector is more likely to receive trainings from the employer. This is unsurprising and consistent with what we have found from Table 6.4 when we explain workers' job tenure. As we have discovered, workers in the state sector tend to have longer job tenure, which can be explained by the socialist human resource management legacy in this sector. Therefore, the pre-reform legacy of personnel management practices nourishes long-term employment in today's state sector and thus encourages firm investment in employee training schemes. Here the key to explaining the incentive of employers to provide trainings is still the institutional capacity to limit labour mobility. The argument of this research is that such capacity can be provided by the institutional arrangement of the localised public pension scheme. As the socialist employment legacy in the state sector can also reduce labour mobility and hence induce employers' investment in workers' skill development, we have to control for firms' ownership type so we can better isolate and capture the capacity of the public pension system to constrain voluntary labour mobility and foster skill formation.

A final note about the above analysis concerns the problem of endogeneity and selection bias. In labour economics this represents the universal challenge where some omitted individual-level and firm-level characteristics may correlate with both independent and dependent variables and therefore may lead the researcher to mistake spurious association for causal relationship. In the case of our analysis, for example, one may argue that the positive relationship between an individual being covered by public pension and him receiving employer-funded training may actually be due to some unobserved individual ability that positively links with the individual's prospensity to receive both pension and training. In other words, since good workers tend to be awarded with pension programmes and training opportunities from their employers, the positive relationship between pension coverage and training incidence is simply spurious and therefore does not suggest any causal association.

There are several approaches in labour economics that one may apply to deal with the issue of endogeneity (Angrist and Krueger 1999: 1284–1309). The most straightforward and common strategy is to control for confounding and theoretically relevant variables. This approach is applied in our analysis, which explains why many firm characteristics such as ownership types and profitability are added in the regression to control for the factors that may affect a worker's chances of receiving pension and training. The second approach is to utilise repeated observations on individuals or firms to control for unobserved characteristics that are constant across time. This implies running fixed-effects regression. This strategy is not applicable here, because we only have data from one year of the China Urban Labour Survey (2001). Even if we had access to other waves of the CULS, we would not be able to use the fixed effects model, because this survey is not longitudinal, meaning that it does not collect data on the same individuals at different points of time. So one has to wait until there is panel survey on the Chinese labour force available to use the fixed effects model to address the endogeneity problem. Finally, one may apply the instrumental variable approach as an identification strategy, which makes it possible to use exogenous variation to approximate randomised trials. This strategy, therefore, requires the survey data to contain a suitable instrumental variable, which should link with the outcome variable but remain unrelated with the independent variable. To the author's best knowledge, there is no such appropriate instrumental variable in our dataset, CULS2001, which only covers a limited number of relevant variables. The limitation on the available data, again, prevents us from implementing a main solution to the endogeneity problem, which is the instrumental variable approach.

Data limitation, therefore, means endogeneity cannot be perfectly eliminated in our analysis. This requires us to use caution in the interpretation of our findings on the positive association between public pension coverage and training incidence. Indeed, as Busemeyer (2007: 595) puts it, "The nature of the data often precludes the application of more complex estimation techniques like instrumental variables estimation, due to a lack of appropriate instruments. The answer to this general problem is to scale down claims of causality", which is the stance this book adopts. It does not argue the public pension system causes employers to fund workplace training in the strictest sense of causality. Instead, this book argues that by limiting labour mobility the localised public pension scheme partly deals with the poaching problem, thereby facilitating the occurrence of firm-funded training. One should understand the positive association between public pension coverage and employer-provided training as indicating the pension programme is a contributing factor in skill formation as opposed to a causal determinant in the process.

Summary

The Chinese public pension system is fragmented along provincial and, more often, municipal borders, with provincial and municipal governments, rather than the central government as in the case of most countries, running the provision and administration of pension programmes. Such fragmentation makes workers' pension packages virtually non-portable across localities. This increases the costs of cross-region job changing and thus reduces labour turnover. The reduced labour mobility, in turn, gives employers assurance that their workers will not be easily poached by outside firms. This assurance encourages employers to invest in training programmes that will equip workers with specific skills. This is the logic behind the *Training Hypothesis.*

The *Training Hypothesis* argues that China's public pension system reduces labour mobility and thus induces firm investment in employee training programmes. This section then is divided into two interrelated parts. The first part tested the hypothesised negative relationship between pension programme coverage and labour mobility, using micro- and macro-level data. The second part evaluated the argument that the public pension scheme, if it constrains labour turnover, should encourage employers to fund on-the-job training programmes, drawing on individual level data from the 2001 China Urban Labour Survey. Evidence shows that China's localised pension system reduces labour mobility and encourages employer-funded trainings. This, therefore, supports the *Training Hypothesis* that by dealing with the poaching programme through its effects on constraining labour mobility, the public pension system in China induces employer-provided trainings.

Extension of analysis: pension coverage and skill profile of the workforce

This section follows King, Gary, Robert, Keohane and Verba's (1994) suggestion that one should derive as many observable implications from his theory as possible and examine the validity of these implications. The preceding two sections have demonstrated that China's pension system contributes to the formation of industry specific skills by encouraging economic agents such as students and employers to make investments in the acquisition of such skills. This is consistent with the labour economics literature and especially with the Varieties of Capitalism theory, which cites high incidences of vocational education in generous welfare states as evidence of the positive role of social protection in skill formation (for example, see Estevez-Abe et al. 2001: 170–173; Iversen 2005: 19). But the Varieties of Capitalism literature stops here. It does not go further to examine more implications of its thesis on the positive impact of social protection on skill formation. If countries with generous social protection programmes have a high level of vocational education incidence, as the VoC literature rightly points out, then these countries should have a high proportion of workers with specific skills in the total labour force. In other words, since social protection programmes encourage people to invest in specific skills, the result of an economy having comprehensive and generous social protection programmes should be that this economy has more workers with specific skills. The Varieties of Capitalism literature has not studied this implication so far. This section tests this implication in the Chinese context.

If China's pension system is conducive to the formation of specific skills by inducing individuals to acquire such skills, as the two preceding sections have demonstrated, then regions with higher levels of pension coverage should have more workers with specific industrial skills. This section exmaines this hypothesised relationship between the presence of public pension schemes and the skill composition of the workforce. The skill profile of the labour force is measured according to Fleckenstein et al.'s (2011) methodology, which categorises major occupation groups classified by the International Standard Occupation Classification 1988 (ISCO-88) into three types of skills, namely specific skills, high-general skills and low-general skills. To apply this methodology to the Chinese context, one has to convert China's National Classification of Occupation 1999 (NCO-99) into ISCO-88, which we have done in the first section of this chapter. On that basis, this section applies Fleckenstein et al.'s (2011) methodology to catergorise the harmonised Chinese occupation classifications into skill types before moving to test the hypothesised relationship between pension programme coverage and the skill profile of the labour force, using provincial-level data from the 2000 and 2010 China Population Censuses. As will be shown in the analysis below, the province with higher pension coverage rates has a larger share of specific skilled workers in the labour force. This result reinforces the argument that China's public pension system is conducive to the formation of specific skills.

Let us begin with the conceptulisation of the workforce skill profile and the method to measure it. The original Varieties of Capitalism argument follows Gary Becker's (1964) formulation, which makes a distinction between general and specific skills, and argues that social protection is negatively associated with the formation of general skills while it can positively induce the production of specific skills. Recent contributions to this literature further differentiate between high-general and low-general skills (Seeleib-Kaiser and Fleckenstein 2009; Fleckenstein et. al 2011), arguing that one should distinguish the two kinds of skills at the two ends of the skill spectrum in the service sector.

No matter how skill is conceptualised, in the literature the specificity of the skills possessed by a worker is indicated by his or her occupation. In other words, the skill specificity is operationalised as workers' occupations, especially the occupations classified in the 1988 version of International Standard Occupation Classification (ISCO-88). We have converted China's National Classification of Occupation (NCO-99) into the ISCO-88, so the methodology of Fleckenstein et al. (2011) to measure skill specificity can be readily applied to the Chinese data.

The harmonised Chinese occupations are then coded as each of the three types of skills using the approach of Fleckenstein et al. (2011). This approach combines Esping-Andersen's (1993) occupational classification with the ISCO-88 major group classification to produce a distinction between high-general, low-general and specific skills. Therefore, following this approach, the Chinese occupations that are equivalent to ISCO-88 major groups 1, 2 and 3 are coded as occupations requiring high-general skills, the Chinese occupations corresponding to major groups 4, 5 and 9 are coded as posts needing low-general skills and the Chinese occupations that are counterparts of major groups 7 and 8 are coded as professions with specific skills (for detailed discussions on the procedure, please refer to Appendix 2).

Having coded the harmonised Chinese occupations on the basis of their skill specificity, we can calculate the number of Chinese workers with each of the three types of skills. Therefore, the skill profile of Chinese provincial jurisdictions can be indicated by the proportion of each type of skilled workers to the total urban workforce. This means each province has three ratios to indicate its skill composition. The data for the calculation come from the Fifth and Sixth Population Census of the People's Republic of China, which were conducted in 2000 and 2010, respectively. The two waves of population census are chosen because it is in these two rounds of population census that the NCO-99 was applied. For both rounds of the Population Census only provincial-level data are available. For each province, the Population Census provides data on Chinese citizens' occupation coded as minor occupation groups of NCO-99. To the best of the author's knowledge, only in the Population Census are Chinese workers' occupations reported systematically across all provinces. So the 2000 and 2010 Population Census are the best datasets to date that can be used to test the hypothesis on the impact of social protection on skill composition in the Chinese context.

Ratios of the workforce with different skills (i.e., high-general, low-general and specific skills) to the total urban labour force, therefore, are the dependent variables. Since the Varieties of Capitalism hypothesis to be tested argues that the different types of skills should have different associations with the presence of social protection programmes like pension, the independent variable is the coverage rate of pension programmes. The goal is to examine whether the presence of pension programmes is positively related to the formation of specific skills and negatively associated with the accumulation of general skills. The estimation method used is multivariate regression, which can estimate more than one dependent variable simultaneously. This suits the purpose here, which is to examine the relationships between three dependent variables (i.e., three types of skills) and one independent variable (i.e., pension programme coverage). The results of the multivariate regression analysis of the cross-sectional data of 31 provincial-level jurisdictions in 2000 and 2010, respectively, without any control variables, are presented in the following Table 5.7.

Table 5.7 Pension coverage and skill profile (2000 and 2010)

Dependent variable: specific skills		
Independent variable	2000 Population census	2010 Population census
Pension coverage	.2269803***	.1966615***
	(.0763845)	(.0689437)
Constant	.2674336***	.2682012***
	(.0551657)	(.0559369)
Observations	31	31
Adjusted R-square	0.2334	0.2191

Dependent variable: high general skills		
Independent variable	2000 Population census	2010 Population census
Pension coverage	–.1508382***	–.0669627**
	(.0408343)	(.0253014)
Constant	.3124047***	.2045918***
	(.029491)	(.0205281)
Observations	31	31
Adjusted R-square	0.3200	0.1945

Dependent variable: low general skills		
Independent variable	2000 Population census	2010 Population census
Pension coverage	–.0761422	–.1296987**
	(.0482107)	(.0523668)
Constant	.4201617***	.5272069***
	(.0348183)	(.0424874)
Observations	31	31
Adjusted R-square	0.0792	0.1746

*, **, ***, stand for $p < 0.1$, $p < 0.05$ and $p < 0.01$ two-tailed test. Standard errors are in parentheses.

It is clear from Table 5.7 that the presence of pension programmes is positively associated with the share of workers with specific skills but is negatively related with the proportion of workers with general skills (be it high-general or low-general skills). This pattern holds for both of the datasets of the 2000 and 2010 Population Censuses (though with the exception in the equation for low-general skills in 2000, where pension coverage displays a negative yet insignificant impact). This supports the Varieties of Capitalism hypothesis that a strong presence of social protection programmes contributes to the formation of specific skills. The reason why this should be the case, as has been discussed earlier, is that a comprehensive social protection system reduces labour market risks related with specific skills and therefore gives agents like the students great incentives to acquire such skills, while in the absence of such social protection system, people choose to acquire the transferable, general skills that may serve as insurance against labour market risks.

Several control variables are added to see whether the pattern that emerges from the above analysis still holds. First, since economic development clearly has an impact on the skill composition of the labour force, the variable ***Industrialisation*** is included, which is the logged form of provincial GDP per capita. Secondly, the skill composition of the labour force is also likely to be affected by the process of marketisation, especially the marketisation process in labour markets. So the index of ***Marketisation*** on the dimension of labour market is controlled for. It is drawn from works by Fan Gang and Wang Xiaolu (2011), as discussed in the previous chapter, and measures the segmentation between urban and rural labour markets. A higher labour market marketisation index indicates a higher proportion of peasant migrant workers in urban labour force and hence a more integrated rural-urban labour market. Finally, peoples' choices on which type of skills to acquire should be influenced by available employment opportunities, which can be indicated by the industrial structure. As Iversen (2005) observes when he investigates the relationship between the process of deindustrialisation and the composition of workforce skills in OECD countries, occupations requiring general skills are most likely to concentrated in the service industries. A province with a strong service sector, if we follow the logic, should offer more employment opportunities that require general skills and therefore encourage people to acquire such skills. Therefore, the share of the tertiary industry in total employment is included to capture this effect. The results of the multivariate regressions that control for the above variables are shown in Table 5.8.

Table 5.8 shows the determinants of the workforce skill profile. After controlling for the other three variables, the pension programme coverage still exhibits the expected impact on skill profile with high statistical significance. In both of the datasets from the 2000 and 2010 Population Censuses, it is positively related with the proportion of specific skilled workers and negatively associated with the share of workers with general skills. This supports the Varieties of Capitalism argument that social protection schemes such as pension programmes can contribute to the accumulation of specific skills. This suggests that pension policy can help Chinese local officials to train an army of specific skilled workers.

The effects of the control variables are worth discussing. First, the employment share of service industries is negatively associated with the share of specific skills and positively with that of general skills. This is consistent with the expectation that general skill occupations are more likely to be found in the tertiary industry and that a strong service economy should induce people to develop general skills. Secondly, the integration of urban-rural labour markets has a positive impact on the formation of specific skills, meaning that the share of peasant migrant workers in the urban labour force is positively related with the proportion of specific skilled workers. This suggests that the peasant workers who pour into city centres in the process of urbanisation are largely absorbed by the specific-skills-intensive manufacturing sector. This is consistent with the consensus that China's comparative advantage on manufacturing industries comes from its relatively low labour costs, which are made possible by the huge amount of peasant workers

Table 5.8 Determinants of skill profile (2000 and 2010)

Dependent variable: specific skills		
Independent variables	2000 Population census	2010 population census
Pension coverage	.2454835***	.1576519***
	(.0790331)	(.0560537)
Industrialisation	.0234303	.0395884
	(.0279573)	(.0283554)
Marketisation	.0171722***	.008965***
(labour market)	(.0039489)	(.0022402)
Industrial structure	–.2492611*	–.0049018***
	(.1490545)	(.0011341)
Constant	.0847706	.0269176
	(.1823045)	(.2449169)
Observations	31	31
Adjusted R-square	0.7029	0.6940

Dependent variable: high general skills		
Independent variables	2000 population census	2010 population census
Pension voverage	–.1176277**	–.0640241***
	(.0459468)	(.0223718)
Industrialisation	–.0134491	.0022884
	(.0162533)	(.011317)
Marketisation	–.0110075***	–.0040021***
(labour market)	(.0022957)	(.0008941)
Industrial structure	.0625649	.0010999**
	(.0866545)	(.0004526)
Constant	.4158692***	.158048
	(.1059847)	(.0977496)
Observations	31	31
Adjusted R-square	0.7196	0.6267

Dependent variable: low general skills		
Independent variables	2000 population census	2010 population census
Pension coverage	–.1278559**	–.0936278*
	(.0572597)	(.0487826)
Industrialisation	–.0099812	–.0418769*
	(.0202551)	(.0246772)
Marketisation	–.0061648**	–.0049629**
(labour market)	(.002861)	(.0019496)
Industrial structure	.1866962*	.0038019***
	(.1079903)	(.000987)
Constant	.4993602***	.8150346***
	(.1320801)	(.2131471)
Observations	31	31
Adjusted R-square	0.4461	0.5754

*, **, ***, stand for $p < 0.1$, $p < 0.05$ and $p < 0.01$ two-tailed test. Standard errors are in parentheses.

coming from the countryside. The reason why peasant workers are more likely to get employed in manufacturing industries is easy to understand. First, as the observation made earlier shows (see Table 6.1), the countryside is a major source of students attending vocational schools, which equip them with industry specific skills that are required by the manufacturing sector. Secondly, it is also likely that peasant workers who used to work in the field may not have the kind of "social skills" (Iversen 2005: 187) required for the urban service sector. This explains the negative association between the integration of urban-rural labour markets and the accumulation of general skills. So peasant workers may have to seek employment in the manufacturing factories, doing the tedious manufacturing jobs that urbanites may be reluctant to take. The implication of the importance of peasant workers to manufacturing industries is clear: If Chinese local leaders hope to foster local industrialisation, then they need to have "something" to retain peasant workers in the urban centres and encourage them to attend vocational schools and training programmes to learn the specific industrial skills required for the manufacturing sector. As we have seen in the analysis of municipal internal speeches, this "something" is the local pension scheme, which can facilitate the integration of peasant workers in the urban labour market and encourage them to attend vocational schools where they can develop specific skills.

Finally, economic development seems to have no significant impact on the skill profile of the labour force. But the signs of its coefficients are noteworthy. Provincial GDP per capita appears to relate positively with the share of specific skilled workers and negatively with that of the general-skilled workers (only with the exception of high-general skills in the 2010 Population Census). This may suggest that to achieve local economic expansion, more specific skilled workers are needed. This is easy to explain because the driving engine of the Chinese economy is the export-led manufacturing industry that relies on specific skills. We will come back to this issue later.

A final noteworthy pattern from Tables 5.6 and 5.7 is that the shares of general-skilled workers are negatively associated with the presence of public pension programmes. The Varieties of Capitalism theory offers one explanation, as we have mentioned earlier, that the *absence* of such a social protection scheme will lead people to acquire general skills as an insurance against income loss risks. This argument, however, falls short of explaining why the *presence* of social protection programmes may reduce the employment share of workers in general skills jobs. Since general skill employment is most likely to be concentrated in the service sector, the recent literature on the expansion of the service economy can shed some light on this issue (for a review on this literature, see Wren 2013). According to this literature, the social security payroll taxes necessary to fund expensive social protection schemes will harm the growth of the labour-intensive private service sector, because this sector is discouraged from hiring people due to the heavy financial burdens imposed by social security taxes (Bradley and Stephens 2007; Nelson and Stephens 2013). This is why we see in Tables 5.6 and 5.7 that the higher the pension system coverage is, the lower the share of people with general skills will be. This has one important implication:

The expansive Chinese social protection system, though contributing to the expansion of the Chinese manufacturing sector, should be partially responsible for the lagged development of the service economy in China. Chapter 7 will elaborate on this idea in detail, discussing the implications of China's extensive pension system for the Chinese government's efforts to unleash the momentum of service sector growth.

This section examines the impact of pension schemes on the skill profile of the labour force. The statistical analysis of the provincial-level data from two recent rounds of population censuses (2000 and 2010), which are harmonised in accordance with ISCO-88, shows that a strong presence of pension schemes contributes to the formation of specific skills. Then how does the pension system achieve this? This research proposes two mechanisms, as analysed in the two preceding sections. First, by reducing lifetime income loss risks associated with specific skills, the social protection programmes of public pension encourage students to invest in acquiring such skills by attending vocational schools. Secondly, by reducing the possibility of worker job-hopping and being poached, the public pension programmes encourage employers to invest in training programmes that equip employees with specific industrial skills. As shown in the two preceding sections, these two hypotheses have received empirical support from the statistical analysis. Therefore, the reason why a comprehensive pension arrangement is associated with a strong specific skilled workforce is that the Chinese public pension system induces the investment in specific skills by workers and employers.

Summarising discussion: skill profile, economic performance and institutional complementarity

How do pension programmes contribute to the formation of industry specific skills? Drawing on the literature on labour economics and Varieties of Capitalism, this study proposes two mechanisms. The first one is the *Schooling Hypothesis*: By reducing the labour market risks of lifetime income loss, which are more likely to be associated with industry specific skills than with general skills, pension programmes encourage students to acquire specific skills through vocational education. The implication is that enrolment rates in vocational education should be high in regions that have a strong presence of pension programmes. The second hypothesis is the *Training Hypothesis*: By making pension packages non-portable across regions, China's localised pension system reduces labour mobility and therefore makes employers less worried about their employees being poached and more motivated to invest in on-the-job training programmes that will equip workers with industry specific skills. This predicts a positive relationship between workers being covered by public pension programmes and them attending training courses provided by their employers. The implication of the two hypotheses is that regions with comprehensive public pension programmes will have a workforce whose skill profile is skewed towards industry specific skills. This chapter has tested all of these hypotheses, drawing on statistical analysis of micro- and macro-level data. The results support the hypotheses, thereby demonstrating the positive impacts of the pension programme on the formation of industry specific skills.

In the discussion on the Chinese pension system being a "beneficial constraint" in Chapter 3, it is argued that having a workforce with a skill profile skewed towards industry specific skills will enhance the overall economic efficiency. Does such positive link between a specific skill profile and a good economic performance exist in the Chinese context? To explore the determinants of the performance of the Chinese economy greatly exceeds the capacity and scope of this book. Nevertheless, this book can examine the relationship between the skill profile of the labour force and the performance of the provincial economy. The interest here is to study whether a specific skills system can lead to better economic performance. Drawing on the provincial-level data from China Population Censuses 2000 and 2010, the best dataset available to measure the skill profile of the provincial economy, this book plots the provincial GDP per capita against the share of workforce with specific skills in 2000 and 2010. The results are presented in Figure 5.3.

Figure 5.3 shows that in both 2000 and 2010, the proportion of specific skilled workers tends to positively link with the provincial GDP per capita, suggesting that specific skills can be a contributing factor to the expansion of the provincial economy. This should not be surprising. As shown in the next chapter, until the recent global recession, the Chinese economic success could be largely attributed to China's comparative advantage in the export-led manufacturing sector. This sector relies on a workforce with industrial specific skills. Therefore, to nourish a workforce with such skills by, for example, expanding social protection programmes like pension is to promote the development of the economic sector in which China has the most comparative advantage. This clearly will enhance economic performance.

But to nourish a specific skilled industrial workforce through extensive social protection is not without cost. As has been discovered by statistical analysis (see Table 5.7), the expansion of pension programmes reduces the share of general-skilled workers. This is because public pension as a social protection programme gives students incentives to proceed to attend vocational schools to acquire industry specific skills, thereby discouraging students to enter labour markets right after their basic education and end up with jobs that only require low-general skills or to continue to prepare for the extremely competitive college entrance examinations to get a general higher education that will equip them with high-general skills. In other words, an expansive pension policy contributes to the accumulation of specific skills at the expense of high- and low-general skills. So in order to see the overall impact of such policy on economic performance, we need to examine how high- and low-general skills may affect the economy. Therefore, I plot the shares of these two types of skills against provincial GDP per capita. Figure 5.4 shows the results.

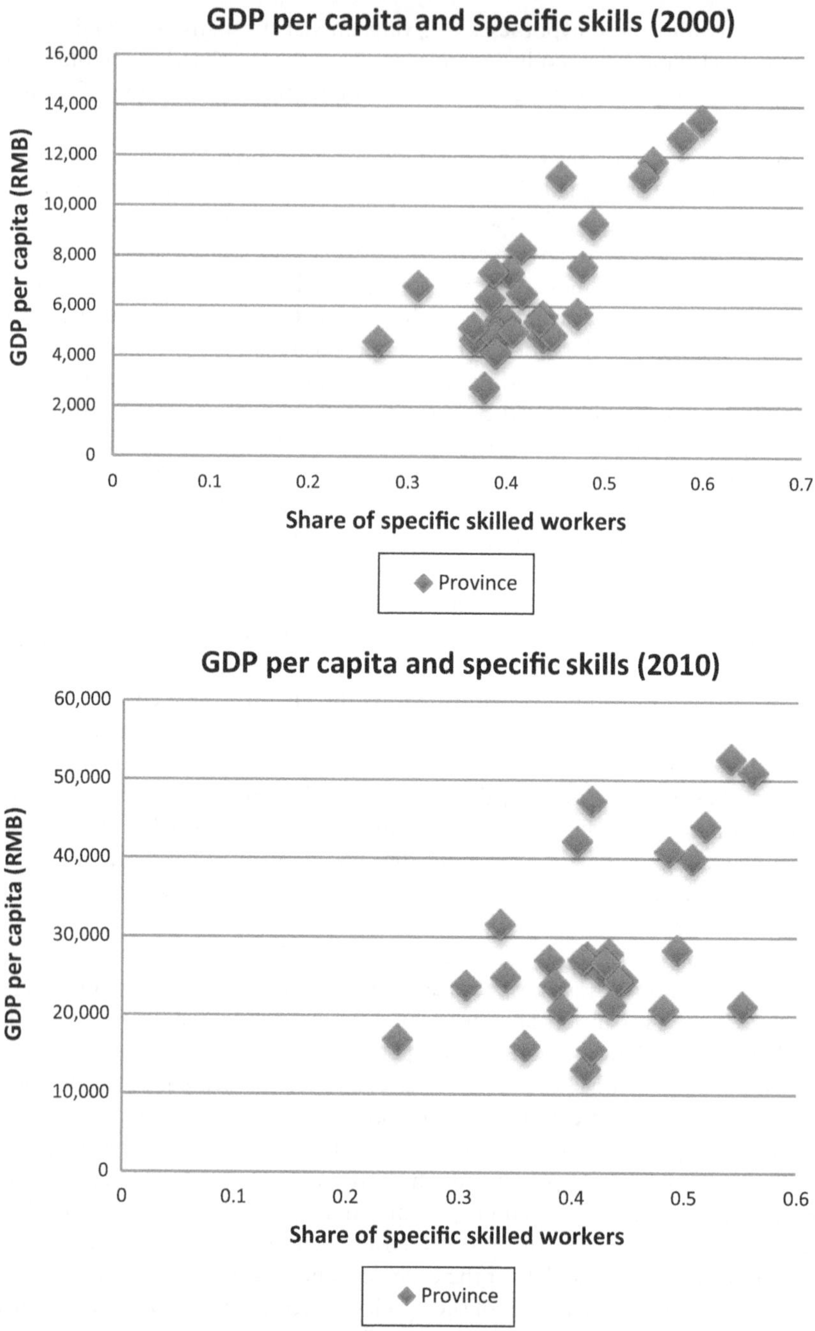

Figure 5.3 Workforce with specific skills and provincial economic development (2000 and 2010)

Source: Data on the share of specific skilled workers come from China Population Censuses 2000 and 2010. Data on provincial GDP per capita come from China Statistical Yearbooks 2001 and 2011.

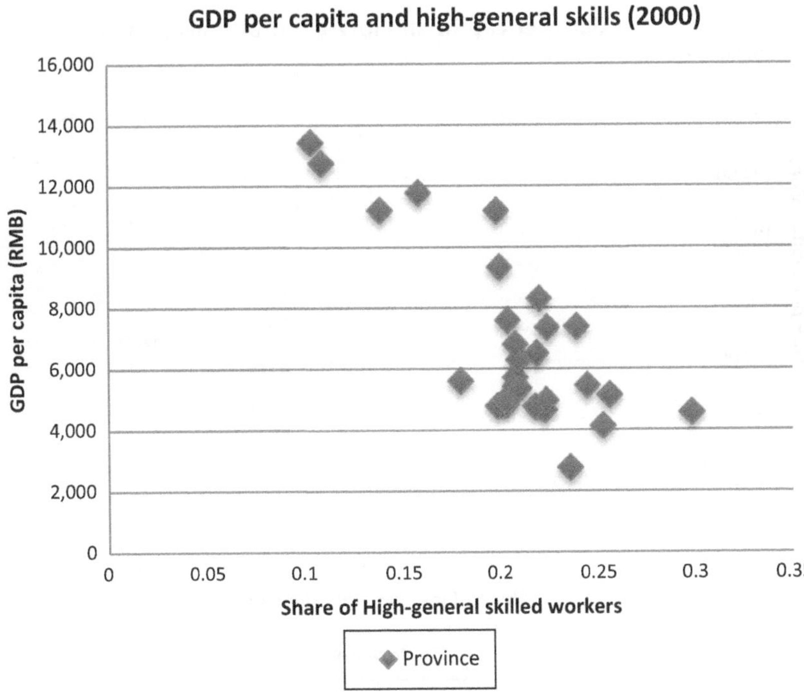

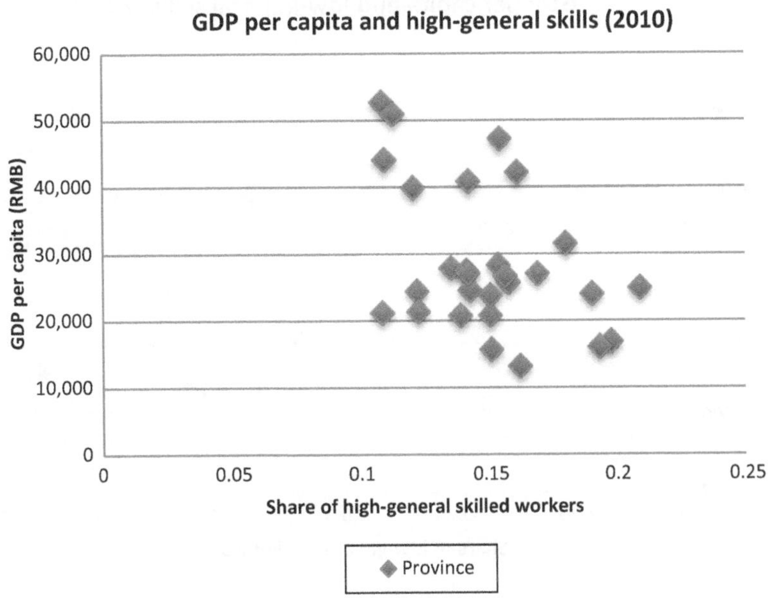

Figure 5.4 Workforce with general skills and provincial economic development (2000 and 2010)

Source: Data on the share of specific skilled workers come from China Population Censuses 2000 and 2010. Data on provincial GDP per capita come from China Statistical Yearbooks 2001 and 2011.

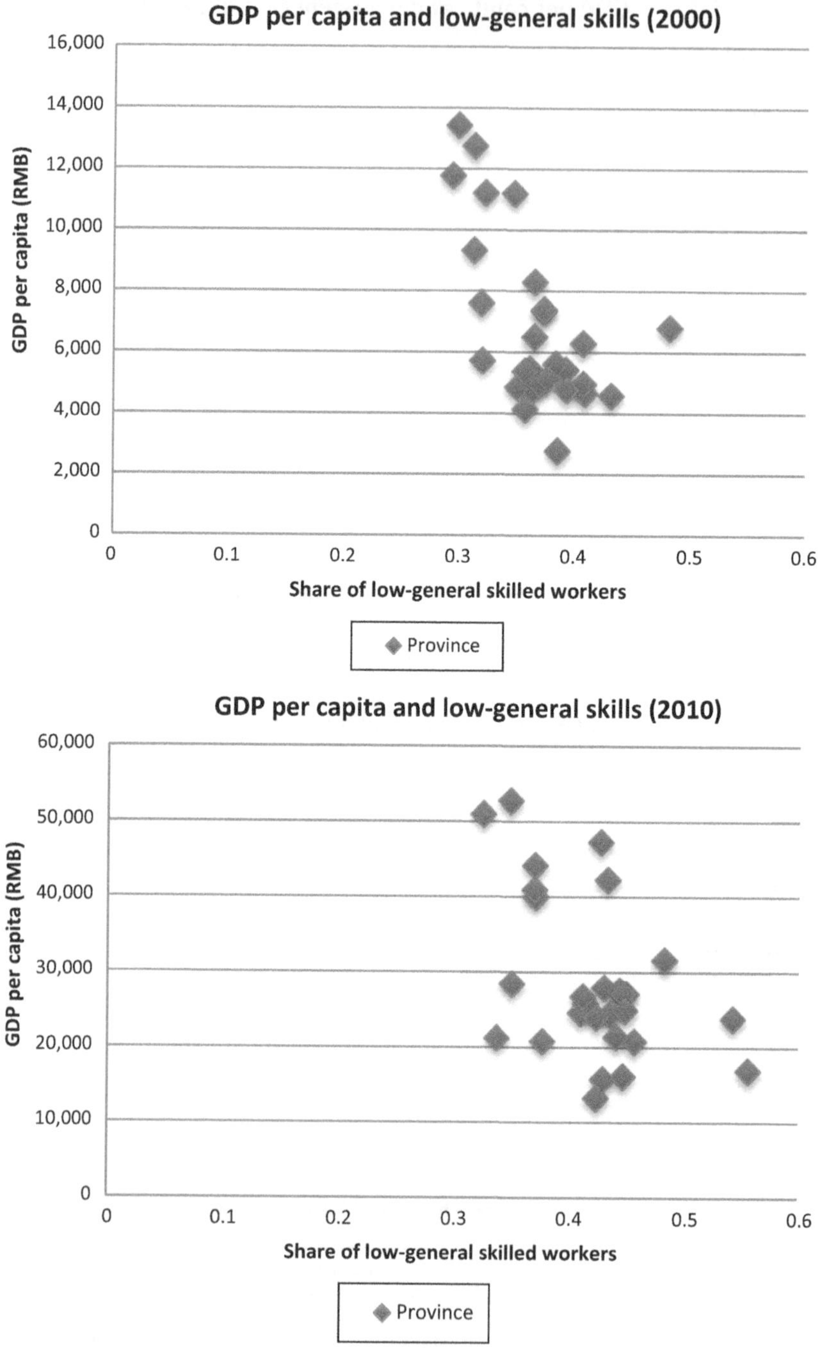

Figure 5.4 Continued

As is clear from Figure 5.4, both types of general skills appear to negatively relate to provincial GDP per capita. It seems that general skills, which are concentrated in service industries, contribute little to China's economic expansion. Two reasons may explain this. First, it may be due to the low productivity of the Chinese service economy, which is still in its adolescence. Secondly, it could be the result of China's low level of urbanisation. Because most services are non-tradable, a vibrant service economy that could sustain continuing economic growth has to be supported by great demand from a huge number of consumers that are geographically concentrated. Without a strong demand for services from the urban centres, which have geographically concentrated populations, the service industries lack momentum to develop and therefore cannot contribute to the growth of the economy at large. This is exactly the situation in China. In 2010, China's urbanisation rate passed 50 percent (Bracken 2012). That is to say, it is only until very recently that China has seen more people live in the cities than in the countryside. This is a great achievement for a country once dominated by an agrarian economy, but it also indicates how far China lags behind the highly urbanised developed world. With a low level of urbanisation, the Chinese service economy simply cannot serve as growth engine of economy like the manufacturing sector does. This explains why general skills, which are most likely to concentrate in the service sector, cannot help to foster the economic expansion in China.

The findings above that the territorial concentration of a workforce with specific industrial skills is positively linked with the level of economic development is consistent with the argument in economics literature that regional specialisation contributes to economic performance. Ever since, Adam Smith economists have argued that division of labour improves productivity. The spatial manifestation of labour division is the regional industrial clusters, which, according to Michael Porter (1998: 78), are "geographic concentrations of interconnected companies and institutions in a particular field". The territorial agglomeration of industries facilitates the utilisation of scale economy, the sharing of a pool of skilled labour force and the spillover of technological know-how. These effects combined together improve economic efficiency. China exemplifies this well. The rise of the Chinese economy is driven by extensive regional specialisation. Notably the industrial agglomerations are based on municipalities, which specialise in the production of certain manufactures (Frattini and Prodi 2013: 6). The establishment of municipal industrial clusters, as has been argued in this study, is the result of the inter-municipal economic competition. The economic rivalry amongst municipalities compels the municipal government to be the developmental agent who seeks to enhance the economic performance by specialising in producing certain commodities and products in the value chain. One strategy to assist this production specialisation is to keep and train an army of workers with industry specific skills. This, as we have seen, is facilitated by the expansive and localised pension system.

This invites us to ponder the institutional underpinnings of China's regional industrial clusters. Indeed, Michael Porter's definition of industrial clusters includes the concept of "institutions", suggesting that an institution is a prerequisite for the territorial concentration of specialised production. The localised pension system, in serving the purpose of local skill formation and labour retention, is one institutional prerequisite for the spatial industrial agglomeration. This raises the question of whether this institution alone is sufficient to support durable local industrial clusters. This leads to the application of the notion of institutional complementarity to the Chinese context.

As discussed in Chapter 2, institutional complementarity refers to the situation where the economic returns from an institution improve when it is coupled with other institutions (Hall and Soskice 2001). The Varieties of Capitalism literature identifies five institutional areas that are interconnected to constitute a production regime: corporate governance, industrial relations, vocational education and trainings, inter-company relations and internal firm structure. As will be shown later, as far as skill formation is concerned, there is a Chinese articulation of institutional complementarity at the municipal level, which can be seen as the foundation of China's local production regime.

Let us start with the area of social protection, the focus of this book. For the localised pension system to function well to encourage investment in industry specific skills, it has to be complemented by other institutions. In Chapter 5, we have seen that the intensity of inter-municipal competition, in addition to increasing the coverage of local pension programmes, also tends to increase public spending on other welfare programmes like unemployment insurance and medical care. That is to say, the expansive and localised pension scheme is often coupled with a more generous unemployment programme. This is easy to understand. The localised pension programme encourages the acquisition of industry specific skills, which however exposes the workers to greater unemployment risks due to the limited transferability of such skills. The concern about the viability of local industries may deter workers from acquiring skills specific for these industries. To deal with this problem, the local government has to establish a comprehensive local unemployment programme so the workers' faith in acquiring industrial skills can be ensured. This demonstrates the complementarity between the localised pension scheme and the local unemployment programme when it comes to skill formation. This complementarity in the Chinese context should be an important subject for future research.

Then what about other institutional areas? The pension system localised along the municipal border makes it costly to move across localities, thereby deterring cross-regional poaching. But this does not exclude the possibility that poaching can happen within the same municipality. If employers in one locality can freely poach workers from each other, then their incentive to provide trainings for employees will be reduced, and therefore the localised pension scheme will become less effective in inducing investment in skills formation. The institutions regulating inter-firm relations come in to solve this problem. As discussed above, poaching is rampant in a tightening labour market. One way Chinese employers have found to cope with this problem involves the collective action among them. This is often achieved through collaboration between business associations and the local government. For example, in the city of Jinjiang in Fujian province, the

Jinjiang Municipal Food Industry Association worked with the Jinjiang Municipal Bureau of Labour and Social Security to monitor and, in some cases, punish the practice of poaching. As Ceng Guochan, head of Jinjiang Municipal Bureau of Labour and Social Security, introduced,

> We work in close cooperation with the Food Industry Association, and target those firms that do not follow the code in labour markets. One of our trump cards is to put the companies on record that engage in vicious poaching and take this into account in the reviewing of their applications for licenses and subsidies.
>
> (*Quanzhou Evening* 2011)

Another example comes from the city of Quanzhou, where in 2008 the Leather Industry Association introduced a tripartite agreement to be signed by the employer, the employee and the Association, requiring that any hiring before a worker's contract with his previous employer ends should be approved by the Association (*Jinjiang Economy News* 2008). Unlike the Food Industry Association in Jinjiang City, whose enforcement of the labour market rules has the backing of local authority, the Quanzhou Leather Industry Association relies on self-discipline and peer pressures that exist in the informal networks among its members. Such reliance on business networks to regulate the competition in labour markets is also discerned by Nee and Opper (2012: 356) in the Yangtze River Delta, where an informal rule exists in the networks among employers that one should "not poach on a friend's business or lure away skilled employees". The important role of employer organisation in regulating labour market competition and addressing the "free ride" problem in the training of skilled workers has long been acknowledged in the literature on industrialised countries. For example, the absence of strong local employer associations has been held responsible for Britain's failure to effectively overcome the poaching problem, which partly explains why Britain was trapped in "low-skills equilibrium" and lacked advantage in high quality product markets in global competition, especially when compared with high-skill economies like Germany (Finegold and Soskice 1988; Soskice 1991). Few studies have looked at the institutional infrastructures for activities of Chinese employers (for example, firm-based training) and the institutional underpinnings of China's competitiveness in the world market. This should be one direction for future study.

To the extent that the business association with the assistance of local government can regulate the poaching activity within one locality, employers should have incentives to fund employee-training programmes. This equips workers with industry specific or even firm-specific skills, which makes the employees less poachable. But this, by limiting workers' outside options and making them more dependent on the employer, reduces their bargaining powers. Therefore, in the area of industrial relations we should expect institutional arrangements to emerge that grant workers more power to offset their weakened bargaining position. This is vindicated by recent changes in China's trade union movement.

Chinese labourers, as introduced in Chapter 1, are represented by the national peak organisation All China Federation of Trade Unions (ACFTU), which has numerous regional and sectoral branches. Many scholars have criticised ACFTU's incompetence, citing its lack of independence from the Chinese Communist Party (Walder 1991; Perry 1995; Chan 1993). But if we observe the dynamics of the Chinese labour movement from a bottom-up perspective, we can discern a different picture under the current economic situation. In 2006 the ACFTU started to require all firms operating on Chinese soil, domestic and foreign, to set up firm-level trade unions. The employers gave in to ACFTU's demand but, unwilling to completely yield the managerial prerogative, often appointed management staff to be chairmen of the shop-floor unions. This "boss union", lacking autonomy and credibility in the eyes of workers, was unable to represent workers' interests in the handling of labour disputes, which increased at an accelerating pace since labour markets have tightened (*Southern Daily* 2012). Disputes therefore often developed into large-scale strikes and stoppages, the most notable of which was the 2010 strike of the Honda workers in the province of Guangdong (*The Economist* 2010b). The strike pressed the local government, along with the local branches of ACFTU, to seek institutional solutions to deal with labour disputes in a more peaceful and institutionalised manner. For example, in 2012, in the city of Shenzhen, Guangdong province, the government and local ACFTU supported the demand of workers at OHMS Electronics (Shenzhen) Co., Ltd., the parts supplier of the Japanese firm Panasonic, to directly elect their firm union chairman and other representatives, who were then entrusted on behalf of the workers to conduct collective negotiations with the employer on issues regarding wages, social insurances and working conditions, etc. With the backing of the municipal government and the local ACFTU, 163 firms in Shenzhen soon followed suit to have their own directly elected trade unions in the same year, including Shenzhen Hailiang Storage Product Co., a subsidiary of Hitachi Global Storage Technologies, Shenzhen Coca Cola and Foxcoon (Shenzhen), Apple's largest OEM (original equipment manufacturer) in mainland China (*The Economic Observers* 2012). It is not just in Shenzhen that the Chinese labour's power has been strengthened and institutionalised. In Shanghai, China's another manufacturing hub, Shanghai Volkswagen, a joint venture between Volkswagen Group and Shanghai Automotive Industry Corporation, set up a works council to discuss with the management "among other things collective bargaining and health and safety issues". This, along with the fact that 80 percent of Volkswagen's 23,000 workers in China were unionised, was applauded as an impressive achievement when the labour and management delegates from Shanghai Volkswagen attended the conference of Volkswagen's World Works Council for the first time in 2010 (International Metalworkers' Federation 2010). Admittedly, the novelty of the above changes and the scarcity of related statistics make it difficult to estimate to what extent industrial relations in China can be characterised by the direct election of grassroots union representatives and the negotiation by works councils. But given the tightening Chinese labour market, which is likely to persist into the near future and thus continue to give Chinese workers more de facto bargaining power, labour disputes between unsatisfactory workers and employers trying to contain costs will tend to increase, and so will the need to keep the disputes in check through institutional measures. Therefore, we have reasons to believe that the approach of electing shop-floor trade union representatives and organising works councils would assume a more important place in the institutional settings of China's industrial relations.

In the area of vocational education, the institutional arrangements reinforce the tendency for employers and workers to invest in the acquisition of industrial skills. China's vocational education system is highly decentralised. The recent decade saw that more than 95 percent of government spending on vocational training happens at the sub-national level (National Bureau of Statistics of China 2011). An even higher share of vocational schools (at the secondary level and above) are either directly administered or regulated by the local government, depending on the ownership type of the vocational school (publicly owned or private). In 2006, Ministry of Education called for the incorporation of working experience in vocational education. This policy guideline, named "work-integrated learning", gave endorsement to the long-standing strategy, called "school-enterprise cooperation", which has been implemented by local governments for vocational education development since 2000 (Wang 2009; Yu 2009; Xu 2009). The "school-enterprise cooperation" refers to the partnership between vocational schools and enterprises, in which the two parties codetermine the content of curriculum, the cultivation of needed workers, the training of the firm's employees, the arrangement of internship, etc. The role of local government in the process is to provide institutional infrastructures for the partnership. The institutions vary among localities, but they mainly consist of two aspects. The first is the incentive structure that encourages the enterprise to join the partnership with vocational schools. For example, the city of Changzhou, in its *Guidelines on Strengthening School-Enterprise Cooperation in Vocational Education and Training* issued in 2007, provides favourable tax conditions and subsidises internship programmes for enterprises that join the partnership (Changzhou Education 2007). The second institutional arrangement provided by the local government is the cooperation platform. In 2011, the city of Wuxi asked that at least half of the board directors for the school-enterprise partnership come from the business sector (Wuxi Daily 2011). The function of the school-enterprise cooperation is to serve the local economy. This is most evident in the arrangement of "order training", in which local employers in the partnership enjoy the rights to place orders for students, who are then educated and trained by the vocational school according to the requirements of the employers. The many classes that bear the name of a firm, like "Siemens Class" and "Audi Class", operate under such arrangement (Zhong 1996). In this way, the skill profile of vocational school graduates is tailored precisely to fit the needs of local industries and even one single firm. The nourishing of a workforce pool with skills that are specifically prepared for the local economy clearly contributes to the formation of regional industrial clusters.

Finally, in the area of corporate governance, the Varieties of Capitalism literature expects the use of industry specific skills is complemented by a reliance on patient capital, which is likely to come from banks rather than securities markets. To figure out how well this prediction fits with the Chinese reality requires us to examine China's financial system. The view that "China's financial system is clearly bank-led" (Witt 2010: 4) is shared by many authors. Walter and Howie (2012: 82) report that in China "the banks are the financial system". An often cited piece of evidence for this comes from Naughton (2007), who found that in 2005 banks accounted for 78.1 percent of funds raised in China, with 6.4 percent coming from corporate bonds and 6 percent from stock issues. What dominate China's bank-led financial system are the state-controlled commercial banks, especially the Big Four, namely Bank of China (BOC), China Construction Bank (CCB), Agricultural Bank of China (ABC) and Industrial and Commercial Bank of China (ICBC). In 2009, as shown in the 2010 Financial Stability Report of PBOC (i.e., People's Bank of China, which is China's central bank), the Big Four accounted for over 70 percent of the US$11 trillion-worth financial assets that were held by the state-controlled bank sector (Naughton 2007). The result of this financial system dominated by state-controlled banks is that bank lending is highly skewed towards the state-owned enterprises (SOEs) and firms that have close links with the government. But does the fact that SOEs rely on loans from state banks mean these banks have control rights over SOEs, as we expect to see in a Coordinated Market Economy (CME)? Witt (2010) says no, on the grounds that state-controlled banks do not hold equity of SOEs or sit in the SOE boardroom as banks in CME normally do. In fact, it is the local government that actively influences the running of local SOEs. It does so through, among other things, controlling the firm's access to financial capital. Ba (2005) trace the evolution of local states' methods to control local supply of financial capital from the early years of the reform era to the present. In the 1980s, when the local government could control the personnel appointment of the local branches of the state-owned banks, local government could easily direct bank lending to fund whatever project or firm they favoured by making administrative orders. This is why several rounds of inflation in the 1980s were caused by reckless local credit expansion (Huang 1996). This arrangement lasted until 1995, when the central government centralised the personnel control in the whole state banking system, which made the local state less able to influence banks' loan decisions. But in what seemed like a compromise gesture, the central government exchanged local governments' support for the banking reform by allowing them to have control over municipal commercial banks, which were transformed from urban credit cooperatives. It dictated that only the local state could hold the majority equity of the municipal commercial bank in its jurisdiction, which virtually gave the municipal government nearly full control of rights. The municipality since then has relied on the municipal commercial bank to influence the credit supply. Therefore, through its control over the local state banks, the municipal government effectively becomes the ultimate source of funds for Chinese firms. It is reasonable to think the capital provided in such an environment to be "patient", because the municipal authority does not require quick returns from the investment. In fact, during economic recession it even helps firms default by putting pressure on the court to bend laws when the bank suits the firm (Ba 2005). Practice like this would cause excess production capacity and bad bank loans, but it also allows local firms to have long-term thinking, which therefore facilitates the accumulation of industry specific skills.

The above discussion does not intend to give a comprehensive assessment of the institutional complementarity in China's local production regime. It only aims to highlight those institutional settings that complement the localised pension system in terms of enabling the buildup of a workforce with industry specific skills. In the presence of these institutional arrangements, the Chinese pension system functions even better to facilitate the skill formation process. To summarise this chapter: If a local leader in China wants to enhance the economic performance of his jurisdiction, then the best he can do is to specialise in certain segments in the manufacturing sector, because this is key to improving the productivity of the local economy. To succeed in the regional specialisation, the local leader has to secure the supply of qualified workers with industry specific skills. As we have argued, this can be achieved by the expansion of social protection programmes like pension. The statistical analysis has demonstrated that a comprehensive pension scheme can induce the formation of industry specific skills, because it encourages workers' and employers' investment in acquiring such skills. Meanwhile, we have also seen that the pension system, with its localised structure, reduces labour mobility across regions and hence helps to retain workers locally. Therefore, with the aid of complementary institutions, the expansive and localised pension system serves to help the training of specific skilled workers and to retain them within the jurisdiction, both of which are crucial to the expansion of local manufacturing industries and hence the growth of the local economy. This is why Chinese local leaders, when perceiving good prospects of promotion, tend to expand pension programmes to better their chances of winning the interregional economic competition. This is the subject of next Chapter.

Notes

1 Acknowledgement: Data analysed in this chapter were collected by the China General Social Survey (CGSS) sponsored by the China Social Science Foundation. This research project was carried out by Department of Sociology, Remin University of China & Social Science Division, Hong Kong Science and Technology University, and directed by Dr. Li Lulu and Dr. Bian Yanjie. The author appreciates the aforementioned institutes' and individuals' assistance in providing data. The views expressed herein are the author's own.

2 Source: official website of Geely Automobile, www.geely.com/news/news/info/5684.html, accessed on Feb 6th, 2013.

3 This study focuses on vocational education at the secondary level because secondary vocational education produces the majority of skilled workers and technicians in China's manufacturing sectors (Yang et al. 2009).

4 For all generalised least squares regression models presented in Tables 5.1 and 5.2, the Hausman test rejects random effects models in favour of fixed effects models. So only results from fixed effects models are reported.

5 Coefficients of variables of Model 1 in Table 5.1 are unstandardised. If we standardise them, which allows us to compare the size of effects of variables, then we can see the standardised coefficient of *Pension Coverage* is 0.35, meaning a 1 standard deviation change in *Insider* results and a 0.35 standard deviation change in the dependent variable. The standardised coefficients of the control variables are: *Industrialisation* (0.34), *Marketisation* (0.73) and *Industrial Structure* (0.53). The effect of pension policy on vocational training, as indicated by the variable of *Pension Coverage*, is sizable.

6 The political story

How do Chinese political institutions shape the pension system?

This chapter examines the political part of the book's central argument, i.e., the two hypotheses derived from our theory, the *Expansion Hypothesis* and *Localisation Hypothesis*. They are about how political institutions of the Chinese state, by structuring the incentives of Chinese municipal leaders, lead to the two prominent features of China's pension system, namely the extensive coverage and the persistent localisation. This chapter follows the structure of Chapter 5, which provides micro-foundations by discovering agents' preferences and behaviours before testing the macro-level associations. That is to say, before testing the two hypotheses using statistical techniques, this chapter first evaluates how well the assumptions the theory makes about the preferences and behaviours of municipal officials capture the reality. As assumed in the leadership selection stage and social policymaking stage of our theory, Chinese municipal leaders compete with each other to promote local economic growth and they tend to apply pension policy as an instrument in the process. The analysis of internal speeches delivered by municipal officials allows us to assess to what extent these behavioural assumptions reflect the actual situation. By examining the perspectives and preferences of individual political agents in the making of developmental strategy and pension policy, this chapter provides the micro-foundations of the hypothesised macro-level associations.

As this chapter will reveal, Chinese municipal officials clearly perceive the pressure to outperform their counterparts in the province in generating economic growth and fiscal revenue. Overtaking one's colleagues in increasing fiscal revenues is a particularly important goal. This is not because municipal bureaucrats seek to manage larger budgets, as Niskanen's budget-maximising assumption would suggest. The reason why Chinese municipal leaders try to generate more revenues than their counterparts is that under China's intergovernmental fiscal system, a large proportion of municipal revenues are required to be remitted to the provincial government, and therefore beating one's colleagues in contributing to the provincial coffer means having more political influence within the province, which will enhance the municipal leaders' promotion chances. Pension policy is instrumental in municipal leaders' efforts to generate fiscal revenues because it serves two local developmental strategies that are applied to fuel economic growth and hence revenue increases. These two strategies are called "industrialisation" and “urbanisation” in the Chinese context. By attracting surplus labourers from the countryside and keeping them trained and retained in the urban centre, an expansive and localising pension policy secures the supply of skilled workforce for local industries and facilitates the urban sprawl into the countryside. The expansion of local pension programmes also assists the restructuring of state enterprises and the cost containment efforts of local employers. This is how Chinese municipal leaders perceive the economic role of pension policy. This picture constitutes the micro-foundations of the two hypotheses to be tested in this chapter. The following sections will first derive the micro-foundations from municipal officials’ conference speeches before applying statistical techniques to test the *Expansion Hypothesis* and *Localisation Hypothesis.*

Micro-foundations: pension policy preferences of municipal leaders

At the micro-level, the theory of this study argues that Chinese municipal leaders engage in a competition with each other to demonstrate good economic performance and employ pension policy to foster local economic development. Is this an accurate description of the political and policy preferences of Chinese municipal officials? This section looks at internal speeches by municipal leaders to reveal their perceptions and preferences. As has been discussed in Chapter 4, internal municipal speeches are delivered by Chinese municipal leaders behind closed doors to the subordinate cadres at work conferences about specific policy issues. Without the need to please the public or their superiors, the municipal leaders are believed to be more likely to express their genuine political and policy preferences in these speeches. Therefore, the analysis of the municipal internal speeches allows us to uncover these preferences of municipal leaders and to examine whether our theory’s assumptions about such preferences accurately capture the situation in the real world.

Local competition

This sub-section examines from the perspective of Chinese local leaders on the competitive nature of the political environment within which municipal governments operate. It reveals the inter-municipal economic competition by decoding the internal speeches of municipal leaders through exploring the economic rationality that underlies these speeches. As will become clear in the following discussion, the starting point of the rational calculation of Chinese municipal leaders is the ranking of their locality relative to other municipalities of the province in terms of several socio-economic developmental goals. The most important socio-economic indicator is the fiscal revenue, which is in turn to be generated through promoting local industrialisation and urbanisation. That is to say, Chinese municipal leaders compete to foster the industrialisation and urbanisation of their jurisdictions so that they can catch up with the pioneer municipalities and eventually move up their rankings in the province, which will enhance their localities' importance to the province and better their prospects of career advancement. The aim of this section is to elaborate this line of reasoning of Chinese municipal leaders, citing their own words in their speeches.

The starting point to reveal the economic calculation of Chinese municipal leaders and to decode their internal speeches is one crucial number, that is, the ranking of the municipality within the province. Municipal leaders in China are obsessed with the place of their cities in relation to neighbouring municipalities with respect to several macroeconomic indicators. In their internal speeches, city bosses very often cite the rankings of their localities, comparing indicators of their jurisdictions with those of other municipalities within the same province to boast about leading positions they vow to retain, or to warn about the danger of falling behind. Interestingly, city leaders would mention explicitly the names of the municipalities they have (or have not) caught up with, suggesting that they are very clear about their competitors in the economic game. This can be clearly seen from the following example. This is a speech given at a municipal economic work conference by Mr. Zhang Yong, major of Fuzhou City in the province of Jiangxi, who summarised the achievements his municipality attained in the year of 2009:

> To catch up and surpass we have to accelerate the pace of development, so moving up our rankings is a test for the result of our development. This year our city has ranked in the top three of the province in terms of the growth rates of six major economic indicators. Among them, gross domestic products, industrial outputs, total fiscal revenues, and revenues of sub-municipal governments have seen their growth rates top the list of the province, while the growth rate of fixed assets investment rank the second in the province and that of foreign trade export volumes rank the third. In terms of absolute number, the rankings of our city on five indicators have moved up this year. For example, on industrial value-added we have moved up by one place, thereby outranking Yingtan; on total fiscal revenue, by one place, outperforming Pingxiang; on sub-municipal government revenues, by one place, surpassing Xinyu; on fixed assets investment, by one place, outstriping Xinyu again; and finally, on volumes of foreign trade export, by two places, surpassing Yichun and Ji'an.[1]

The five cities mentioned in the speech, that is, Yingtan, Pingxiang, Xinyu, Yichun and Ji'an, are municipalities in the Jiangxi province, just like Mayor Zhang's own jurisdiction, Fuzhou. Clearly Mayor Zhang saw them as rivals in the economic race and was proud that his city, Fuzhou, had outperformed them in several aspects like industrial growth and foreign export volumes. But what seems most important to Mr. Zhang is the province-wide position of Fuzhou in the rankings of growth rates of six major macroeconomic indicators, including GDP, industrial output and fiscal revenues etc. Fuzhou ranked in the top three on all these indicators, an impressive performance that placed it in the first group of Jiangxi's municipalities, a place other municipalities would kill to get.

The typical mentality of the municipal leader in economic competition is best captured by the opening line of the above passage: "Moving up rankings is a test for the result of our development". Development, or getting better than yourself, is not enough. You have to be better than others. In the words of Qi Jihui, mayor of Fuxin in Liaoning province, when he warned about self-complacency to municipal government officials,[2] "We can never just compete with ourselves, not to mention have a sense of complacency. Instead, we must compete with advanced regions in our province". To a municipal leader, development becomes meaningful only when it can put his municipality above others, i.e., it can withstand the test of "moving up rankings". When it cannot, municipal leaders can get very upset, as we can tell from the following speech given by Wen Xihao, who addressed it at one municipal industrial economic work conference as vice-mayor of Longyan in Fujian province. He was concerned that Longyan's industrial growth had fallen behind that of the "sibling municipalities" in Fujian. This is another snapshot of the sibling rivalry in the Chinese province:

> We still fall behind our sibling municipalities, so we have to shoulder more responsibilities. Now the situation is threatening: every municipality is doing its best to leap forward to develop. If we don't progress, we will fall behind. If we progress only a little, we will still fall behind. Let's look at the industrial output. The industrial value-added of our city accounts for only 7.1 percent of the provincial industrial value-added and only one fourth of that of Quanzhou. Our growth rate [of industrial value-added] ranks a mere seventh place province-wide. . . . If we look at the number of major industrial projects whose investments are worth more than 1 billion yuan, we only have a few, like the Longgong excavator factory, Longma heavy truck factory and Longyan mini-van factory. Cities in mountainous regions, like Sanming, Ningde and Nanping, they all have more major industrial projects than us.[3]

It is interesting to note the last sentence of the excerpt. Mr. Wen explicitly targeted Sanming, Ningde and Nanping, the municipalities in mountainous areas of the province, his city Longyan being one of them. Mr. Wen did not target the star municipalities like Xiamen, the coastal economic special zone, or Fuzhou, the provincial capital of Fujian. Instead, he aimed to catch up with cities in mountainous regions, which presumably had the similar conditions for economic development as Longyan. In other words, he was not overambitious but set realistic catch-up targets, signalling to his audience the credibility of his words and hence his determination to achieve these catch-up goals.

Chinese municipal leaders' obsession with rankings is clear and evident. Then how can we start from the ranking of a municipality to make sense of the rest of an internal speech? Can we use this number, the ranking, to help us understand the other numbers in a speech? In other words, can we explain the policy actions and targets proposed by municipal leaders from the ranking of their municipality? Let us go back to the speech by Zhang Yong, mayor of Fuzhou in Jiangxi, whose words disclose the mindset of a municipal official when he sets targets and makes policies:

> The effect of the development will be tested by the moving-up of rankings. We must keep a close watch on the sibling municipality that ranks one place higher than us on major economic indicators, and try our best to catch up with it. Next year, our fiscal revenue should surpass that of Xinyu. In this year Xinyu's fiscal revenue is 5.6 billion yuan and it expects to have a 16.8 percent growth rate next year, reaching 6.6 billion yuan. This year the fiscal revenue of our city is 5 billion yuan. So if we can grow by 32 percent next year, then we can overtake Xinyu and thus advance our ranking to the seventh place in the province. Every county, every department and every industrial park should do the same, fixing your targets on the rivalry units that rank one place higher than you and doing all you can for catching-up.[4]

The passage above is revealing. It tells us about the logic behind the seemingly perplexing bunch of numbers contained in Chinese official speeches. The aim of municipal leaders is to move up the rankings of the municipality. If you were a municipal leader, then the starting point of your thinking would be to know your place, which allows you to know which cities to catch up with. Then you would set out to find out the developmental goals, for example fiscal revenues as in the above case, of the city whose ranking is higher than yours. Based on the goals of your target city, you could calculate how much should be achieved on your side in order to get ahead of the target city. This kind of calculation is made not only by the municipal government but also by "every county, every department and every industrial park", all of which are required to know their own places in the province.

It is crucial to note that Zhang Yong particularly mentioned fiscal revenue, rather than GDP, when he designed the strategy for Fuzhou to catch up with Xinyu. It is widely acknowledged that GDP growth is of the utmost importance to Chinese governments at all levels. Many have taken this for granted, but few ask why GDP matters especially for Chinese local leaders. Surely the Chinese local bureaucrats have to demonstrate their capacity to stimulate economic development to their central superiors by showing high GDP growth in their localities. But the official speeches of Chinese local leaders indicate that another equally important reason is due to the tight association between economic development and government revenue. In other words, the expansion of local economy is important to Chinese local officials because it leads to the growth of fiscal revenues of local government, which is a highly prioritised target. For example, when Chen Zhenggao, Mayor of Shenyang in Liaoning province, summed up the economic achievements of his city, he said "the quality of the functioning of our economy has increased impressively. This can be seen from the fact that the hard indicator, that is, the fiscal revenue, has kept a growth rate of 30 percent for four successive years".[5] In all of the official speeches investigated in this study, no other macroeconomic indicator, not even the GDP growth, is labelled as "the hard indicator". Only the fiscal revenue gets called as such. The word "hard" in the Chinese political language, as opposed to "soft" which means flexible, suggests that the target is non-negotiable and therefore must be achieved, as in the famous remark by Deng Xiaoping, which reads "Development is the hard truth". Therefore, only in the case of fiscal revenue would municipal leaders warn their subordinates, i.e., the county and township cadres, that the failure to achieve the target would cost their job. This cannot be clearer in the speech of Qi Jihui, mayor of Fuxin in Liaoning province, who mobilised government officials to achieve the target of generating 5 billion in fiscal revenues by making clear the grave consequences of failing to do so:

> Here I emphasise this again: we have to achieve the target of 5 billion of fiscal revenues this year. We must have this determination . . . The work of our municipality should revolve entirely around this target. We should push forward our work by sticking with this target. For this year's work, the target on fiscal revenues must be achieved. Anyone who fails to meet this single requirement will get dismissed.[6]

Why is fiscal revenue so important to Chinese municipal leaders? Surely municipal government needs money to fund its own functioning and deliver public services to the local community. But this does not justify or explain municipal leaders' obsession with generating more revenues than other cities or their obsession with moving up the ranking of their municipality in terms of generating fiscal revenues. Indeed, if fiscal revenue is mainly for one's own use, then there seems no point of engaging in a competition with others. To understand the importance of fiscal revenue to municipal leaders and the origins of inter-municipal competition in generating fiscal revenue, one needs to look at the fiscal arrangement between the Chinese central and local governments.

The current regime regulating central-local fiscal relations, named the tax-sharing system, which was installed in 1994 and centralised the collecting of government revenues, dictates that the municipal government must remit a portion of its fiscal revenues to the provincial government, which in turn should forward a share of its revenues to the central government (Ahmad et al. 1995; Zheng 2004: 153). Under this arrangement, the fiscal revenues of municipal governments are used for funding the functioning not only of themselves but also of the provincial government and ultimately the central government. The fiscal health of the provincial government, therefore, depends on the contribution of municipal governments, and likewise the fiscal health of the central government on the contribution of provincial governments. The implication is that higher-level governments will tend to award those lower-level governments that make more contributions. The most alluring reward to the leaders of sub-national governments is none other than the promotion to a higher place.

Numerous studies have been made to examine the factors that may affect Chinese local officials' chances of getting promoted. These factors include the economic performance of their localities (in terms of GDP growth), the fiscal contribution to upper-level governments and several personal characteristics like educational background and factional ties with the central leaders. Statistical regressions are run to assess the relative importance of these competing variables. While the effects of other factors remain inconclusive, the positive impact of fiscal contribution on promotion prospects emerges to be consistent across research studies. Bo (2002) examines the mobility of provincial leaders since the founding of the People's Republic of China in 1949. He finds that while better economic performance of jurisdiction helps to keep a provincial leader's job but fails to provide good chances of promotion, the contribution of fiscal revenues to the central governments tends to bring about better prospects of promotion. Guo (2007) studies a dataset of more than one thousand county-level leaders during 1995–2002 and reports that more tax revenues will increase the likelihoods of being promoted, an association which still holds after various "informal factors" like ethnic minority background are controlled for. In a recent paper published in the *American Political Science Review*, Shih et al. (2012) applies a Bayesian estimation method to a newly constructed biographical dataset of members of Chinese Communist Party Central Committee. They discover that the promotion of Communist Party elites to the party centre to a large extent can be explained by three factors: local revenue collection, educational attainment and personal connections with top party leaders.

Given the importance of fiscal revenue to bureaucratic promotion, we can easily understand municipal leaders' preoccupation with outperforming their counterparts in collecting revenues. More fiscal contribution to the province means better chances of promotion. The competition to generate fiscal revenues is essentially the competition to win favours from the province and the party centre. Since the number of offices to be filled by promoted local officials is very limited, it is crucial for a municipal leader to contribute more than his counterparts, i.e., to rank higher than his counterparts in terms of fiscal contribution, if he hopes to win the competition. On the other hand, if a municipal leader falls behind others in the race to collect government revenues, he risks his city and eventually himself being ignored and marginalised in the provincial politics. Municipal leaders themselves are clearly aware of this, as evident in the remarks by Qi Jihui, mayor of Fuxin, and Zhang Yong, major of Fuzhou. Qi Jihui warned that if they failed to achieve the target of collecting 5 billion fiscal revenues, Fuxin would be "neglected in Liaoning province". Similarly, Zhang Yong told his colleagues that without "making it big" in terms of generating economic growth and fiscal revenues, Fuzhou would "have no position in the province". In a word, the direct link between fiscal contribution and municipal leaders' career advancement forces them to focus on surpassing their counterparts in terms of generating fiscal revenues.

After the crucial catch-up objective, fiscal revenue is set and everything else follows. As the authority of the Chinese local government to adjust tax rates is very limited, to generate government revenue municipalities have to expand the tax base (Lou and Wang 2008: 112–113). Unlike advanced countries where the government generates most revenues from income tax, the majority of budgetary revenues of the Chinese municipal government come from industrial and commercial taxation. Then to promote industrialisation becomes one major strategy for local government to expand its tax base. As for the non-budgetary revenue, most of it comes from sales of user-rights to the land owned by the municipality. Lucrative land sales therefore explain Chinese municipal bureaucrats' enthusiasm for property development, an activity they nicely named as "urbanisation". Therefore, the policy to promote industrialisation and urbanisation is logically derived from municipal leaders' pursuit of more fiscal revenues and higher rankings. That is why the mayor of Fuxin in Liaoning province, Qi Jihui, when setting up developmental objectives, explicitly links the growth of industrialisation and urbanisation to that of government revenues.

> Revolving around the target of 5 billion fiscal revenues, in this year the focus of our work should be put on getting breakthroughs in industrialisation and urbanisation. So the growth rates of industrial output and urbanisation should both reach at least 4 percent.[7]

In the case above, the growth rate of industrialisation and urbanisation would have to reach at least 4 percent in the year of 2011. Why? Because that was what would take to guarantee the 5 billion RMB of fiscal revenues. Then why 5 billion? Because according to the mayor, that is how much was needed to prevent Fuxin being "neglected" in the Liaoning province. This is the logic that ties together the indicators and numbers in the municipal internal speeches: The logic starts with the rankings of the municipality in the province, which allow the municipal leader to know which competitor to catch up with, then some "hard" catching-up objective like fiscal revenue is set, so finally instrumental indicators like rates of industrialisation and urbanisation that help to achieve the central aim can be determined.

Following the logic, there are sub-instrumental targets that are set to sustain industrialisation and urbanisation, like fixed asset investment, manufacturing output, electric power supply, etc. These are all interesting aspects of the strategies for local economic development. But what interests this study is the role of pension policy in local economic expansion. Does pension policy serve to facilitate industrialisation and urbanisation? Do municipal leaders see pension policy as a developmental tool in economic competition with other cities? The analysis in the next two sub-sections will suggest affirmative answers to both questions.

Economic benefits of pension policy (1): factor guarantee

The preceding section has shown that Chinese municipalities compete against each other to move up rankings in the province by developing local economy through industrialisation and urbanisation. This section explores the role of pension policy in local developmental strategy. In particular it asks: Do municipal leaders see pension policy as an instrument for local industrialisation and urbanisation? If so, then what economic benefits do pension programmes have? These questions are to be answered in this and the following two sub-sections.

The findings on the economic benefits of pension policy are as follows. As this and the next two sections show, municipal leaders think an expansionary pension policy is able to serve three pro-business functions: (1) to secure the supply of the workforce for urban industries by encouraging the flow of the labour force from the rural to the urban areas, which alleviates the problem of labour shortage and accelerates the process of urbanisation, (2) to improve the allocative efficiency of urban labour markets by facilitating the reallocation of the labour force from the state sector to the private sector and (3) to reduce pension contribution rates, which helps to serve the purpose of cost containment for employers. In a word, public pension scheme is an integral part of local leaders' developmental strategy to build an environment that is attractive to both workers and employers. This is why Lian Weiliang, vice-mayor of Luoyang city in charge of social security, when summarising the economic benefits of social protection at the municipal old-age insurance work conference on October 14th, 2006, explicitly emphasised the role of the social security system in attracting migrant workers and investors:

> To what extent we have a comprehensive social security system concerns our investment environment, entrepreneurial climate and situations of job creation. Without a comprehensive social security system, investors would not invest in our place, because there would be no harmonious industrial relations for them. Without a comprehensive social security system, migrant workers would not work here, because there would be no security for his income and future life. At the same time, we are re-structuring the state-owned enterprise system, and social security is a central issue in the process. So in this sense we can say that a comprehensive social security system is a precondition of the successful restructuring of the state sector.[8]

This section examines how the expansive pension policy facilitates industrialisation and urbanisation by dealing with the problem of labour shortage. We have seen that industrialisation and urbanisation are two major developmental strategies of Chinese municipal leaders to generate fiscal revenues and enhance their influence in the province. An expansive pension policy plays a crucial role in the process. For the aim of industrialisation, municipal leaders use pension and other social protection programmes to attract migrant peasant workers from the countryside. This is meant to secure the labour supply for urban industries in a context of labour market tightening. When municipal leaders search for the source of labour supply, they prefer local peasant workers to "foreign" peasant workers, who migrate from other municipalities. The reason for this is as follows: The jurisdiction of a Chinese municipality is composed of its urban centre and the surrounding countryside, which is home to the local peasant workers. By drawing these local peasant workers into the urban economy, the municipal leaders can seize their farmland and transform it into land for urban property development, provided that these peasant workers can stay in the urban centre and not go back to the countryside. Social protection programmes like pension give peasant workers a safety net for urban living, which is necessary for them to stay permanently in the urban area. The result therefore is successful urbanisation. The following paragraphs elaborate the above logic by citing municipal leaders' speeches.

As discussed in Chapter 1, labour market tightening has been a prominent phenomenon in the Chinese economy since the early 2000s. The implication of a tightening labour market is that Chinese workers now face more employment opportunities and they obtain the power to vote with their feet, meaning they can choose to quit or change positions if they are not happy with the firm or the city for which they work. The strengthening of the bargaining power of workers puts pressures on local employers and eventually local officials, who are concerned about the health of local industrialisation, to attract and retain workers. This is evident in the fact that "guaranteeing labour force supply" has become an important component of the local government's developmental strategy of "factor guarantee".

"Factor guarantee", as municipal leaders call it in their speeches, refers to the municipal government's commitment to secure the supply of various kinds of production input factors for local employers and potential investors. The abundance of production inputs is vital for local industrialisation, and the commitment of their sufficient supply provides crucial assurance to the capital about the viability of the local business environment. Therefore, it is not surprising that "factor guarantee" receives so much attention from local leaders. The production factors concerned normally include: land, bank credit, energy and technology. With the advent of tightening labour markets, securing the supply of the labour force has gradually assumed a prominent priority on municipal leaders' policy agendas. For example, Liu Daoqi, mayor of Sanming in Fujian province, analysed the situation of labour shortage in his city and urged fellow municipal policymakers to tackle this problem at one municipal economic work conference,

> At the moment, the problem of labour shortage is getting serious among all sorts of firms in our city. Four hundred sixty-three firms have reported they have experienced shortage of workers. It is estimated a total number of 18,890 workers are needed. This problem is especially serious in the manufacturing industry. Three manufacturing sectors, like textiles, machinery manufacturing and electric and electronic manufacturing, are reported to run short of 10,150 workers, accounting for 53.8 percent of the total labour shortage.[9]

Local governments have taken all sorts of measures to secure the sufficient supply of production factors. For example, they would go to the provincial government to ask for an increase in their quota of industrial land use. One mayor, in a surprisingly frank manner in his speech, even encouraged the staff of the Municipal Bureau of Land and Resource to treat the provincial officials in charge of land allocation as "good buddies" and to dine with them, obviously in the hope that private networking would lead to the official granting of land use rights. Likewise, local bankers of state-owned and private banks are pushed by municipal leaders to provide credits to local firms, a practice widely applied when China responded to the 2009 credit crisis, and those who succeeded in doing so were publicly praised by local leaders at economic work conferences. But as for the labour force, how to guarantee its adequate supply is less straightforward. After all, human resource is mobile and has its own agency, so no government department or business entity can reasonably control and allocate this kind of production factor as in the case of land and credit. In order to secure labour force supply, municipalities have to appeal to the workforce itself. That is to say, the municipal government has to provide what workers need to attract and retain them in the municipality. Then who are the workers that municipal leaders try to attract, and what do these workers need?

Local leaders primarily recruit the workforce needed from the peasant workers in the local countryside. The local countryside surrounds the urban area of the municipality and hence is part of the municipality in the sense of administrative subordination. In terms of household registration status, the peasant workers from the surrounding countryside are the citizens of this municipality, but they belong to its rural rather than urban sector. For reasons we shall see below, compared with migrant workers from other places, municipal leaders prefer these local peasant workers and take them as the first choice as sources of labour force for local industrialisation. The project to direct these local peasant labourers to work in their home municipalities so the supply of workforce for the urban economy can be secured is called "local transfer of labour force" by local leaders. For example, the aforementioned mayor of Sanming city, Liu Daoqi, saw the "local transfer of labour force" as a major strategy to deal with Sanming's labour shortage problem:

> We should achieve the local transfer of labour force. In the present, in the rural area of our city there are 1.703 million peasant workers. 58.3 percent of them have been transferred away from the countryside to work in urban areas, which are 626,000 people. Among these 626,000 workers 395,000 work for our city, which is only 37 percent of our transferred rural workers, while the rest 63 percent, which is 395,000 people, work outside our city. So we have to guide our rural workers to work within our locality and transfer within our locality . . . We also need to guide employers to have the idea that "treating workers well is treating yourself well", encouraging employers to reasonably raise workers' wages, improve their living conditions and protect their labour rights . . . We should establish long-term mechanisms for benefit sharing between firms and workers, so employment stability can be realised.[10]

From the above passage we can get a sense of competition, that is, the competition for rural workers between the workers' home municipality and other cities. Clearly Mr. Liu was not happy about so many Sanming rural workers choosing to work for other localities rather than his city Sanming, which may exacerbate Sanming's labour shortage problem. But he also sees this presenting a potential solution: The situation of labour shortage may be relieved by bringing back the many Sanming rural workers who chose to leave Sanming and worked somewhere else, i.e., by encouraging them to move from the countryside to the urban centre within the jurisdiction of Sanming. Then how can peasant workers be successfully "locally transferred" to the urban sector? Mr. Liu urged employers to treat their employees well so workers could be attracted and retained by better compensation. This stance was also shared by other municipal leaders, like Liu Keqing, mayor of Zhangzhou in Fujian province, who said that "at the current situation of labour shortage, higher employee income, better employee welfare and better working conditions are especially needed so your working men can stay for better working treatment and living conditions".[11] For a more systematic approach to "local transfer of labour force", we should turn to mayor of Guangzhou in Guangdong province, Su Zhequn. As this approach shows how a local leader views the function of social security in securing labour supply, Mr. Su's words are thus worth quoting at length here:

> To transfer surplus rural workforce, in the present our central aim is to push forward "two integration and one equality" . . . "Two integration" means the integration of rural-urban employment regulation and the integration of rural-urban labour market. It means to extend the networks of the city's employment service agency and labour market services to the countryside. . .
>
> "One equality" refers to the equality of several labour rights between rural and urban workers. I think it should involve equalities in the following aspects. The first is the equal rights between urban and rural workers to get registered in the employment service agency . . . The second is the equal rights to employment. Under the state regulation, as long as the worker has qualification issued by state institutions, he should be taken as qualified for this job no matter he is from the countryside or the city. The third is the equal rights of rural and urban workers to labour protection. That is, no matter the worker is a peasant or an urban resident, he should receive equal protection from labour laws as others. The fourth aspect is the equality of rights to social protection. Once the peasant workers get employed in the city, employers should buy them whatever social insurance urban workers enjoy. Finally it is the equality of rights to vocational training. Peasant workers should have access to whatever training services provided to urban workers.[12]

Mr. Su's approach to "local transfer of labour force" seeks to facilitate labour mobility between rural and urban areas by integrating the labour markets fragmented between the two sectors. It puts a great emphasis on the "equality of social protection" between urban and peasant workers, urging to bring migrant workers into the urban social security programmes. Why would social protection be a selling point to peasant workers? The reason is similar to that in the case of solving the overstaffing problem in state sector, which we will discuss shortly in the next section: To attract the surplus labour force in state enterprises to move to the private sector, the redundant workers have to be assured that they will be covered by social protection schemes once they work for the private firms. Likewise, to direct the workforce from the rural sector to the urban sector and make them stay in the urban economy, these peasant workers have to believe that they will be looked after by the urban social security arrangements. It is in this sense that social protection programmes can attract peasant workers to urban economies and thus serve to facilitate the labour mobility between the rural and urban sector.

A tightening labour market has changed the power balance between the labour and the government. To attract and retain the labour force, a production factor that is crucial for local industrialisation, municipal leaders have to take measures that are appealing to workers, like covering workers with a more comprehensive social security scheme. Under the conditions of labour scarcity, municipal leaders' pursuit of economic development and peasant workers' claim to social rights eventually coincide. In the words of Liu Keqing, mayor of Zhangzhou city, "improving people's livelihood is equal to developing the economy".[13] Paradoxically, it is the need to commodify Chinese peasant workers that delivers them rights to de-commodificating social programmes. In this respect the power of competition works better than any diligent labour rights lawyers or job inspectors.

But as mentioned earlier, not every peasant worker is lucky enough to benefit from the situation of labour scarcity. To find labour supply for the urban economy, municipal leaders generally turn to peasant workers from the surrounding countryside, which is administratively subordinated to the municipality and whose villagers are in principle its citizens albeit only with rural household registration status. But for the non-local migrant workers from places that do not fall into the municipality's jurisdiction, the attitudes of municipal officials are quite different. They prefer native peasants over "foreign" migrant workers. In fact, they see it as a problem that, in the words of a Guangzhou mayor, "numerous migrant workers from other provinces pour into our city, taking up positions and leaving many of our own peasants with nothing to do".[14] They make regulations that favour the interests of native workers and encourage firms to employ these local peasants. For example, in a speech by the Guangzhou mayor Su Zhequn, a section was dedicated to "preferential policies to encourage Guangzhou firms to recruit local peasant workers". These policies include government subsidies to the work-related injury insurance for native peasant workers and a pre-tax deduction of expenses on the training programme for these workers. In addition to ensuring the employment of local peasant workers from the demand side, from the supply side Mr. Su went further to suggest that the villagers' committee, the governing body in the countryside, should be awarded 100 RMB for every local peasant worker it sent out to work in Guangzhou city, and if the committee was "too rich to care for the mere 100 yuan", more straightforward incentives could be provided like "giving the money directly to individual village cadres".

The reason why Chinese municipal leaders care passionately about bringing native peasants rather than non-local migrants into the urban economy is that this strategy facilitates the process of urbanisation. As we have discussed earlier, along with industrialisation, urbanisation, with its implication on property development and other related construction industries, is a major engine of local economic development, which is crucial for generating government fiscal revenues and moving up the rankings of the municipality. Urbanisation in China, as in most developing countries, mainly takes the form of urban sprawl, meaning that urban areas spread outward incorporating the suburban and rural area into the urban territory. In the process, the municipal government can acquire the village land. Making peasants leave the countryside surrounding the city and taking them into the urban economy, therefore, facilitates land acquisition by the municipal government, because every couple of years in land reallocation the villagers' committee often takes back a proportion of the land left uncultivated from the peasants who are employed in the city. The land taken by the villagers' committee is often sold to the municipal government. Then we can understand why Mr. Su, mayor of Guangzhou, asked local cadres to "put the issue of transferring the rural labour force in the perspective of the urbanisation process of Guangzhou". In the first ten months of 2003, according to him, the urban area of Guangzhou had expanded from "tens of square kilometers" to "hundreds of square kilometres", with more industrial parks in the north and south of Guangzhou being put on the municipal government's development plan.[15] Against the background of municipal officials' pursuit of rapid urbanisation, it is not difficult to understand their enthusiasm for bringing local peasants into the urban economy.

For the local government, one essential way to prepare local peasant workers for urban jobs is to equip them with relevant skills that are required by the urban economy. This is most likely to be achieved through vocational education and training. As we shall see in Chapter 6, which deals with the issue of vocational education, the expansion of social protection programmes like pension plays an important role in the development of vocational education, because it encourages individuals to attend vocational schools by assuring them about the stability of future income and induces employer investment into employee training programmes by reducing labour turnover. Thus, vocational education is an indispensable supplement to the strategy of "local transfer of labour force", because it equips local peasant workers with industrial skills and therefore enhances the chances of peasant workers getting employed in the urban centre, which keeps them out of the way in the process of urbanisation. The issue of local vocational training and education will be examined in greater detail in Chapter 6.

"Local transfer of labour force", therefore, is not only aimed to secure sufficient supply for local industrialisation, but also meant to accelerate the process of urbanisation. It is a strategy that kills two birds with one stone. Under the pressure of a tightening labour market, the pursuit of industrialisation dictates municipal leaders to find and retain a source of workforce for local employers. Their enthusiasm for urbanisation then directs them to turn to local peasants rather than non-local migrants for the source of labour supply. To achieve the "local transfer of labour force", urban social security programmes like pension should be expanded to cover peasant workers, because that is the way to reduce the risks of losing welfare coverage that face peasant workers when they move out of the countryside and settle in urban areas. It is also the way, as we shall discuss in Chapter 6, to encourage the peasant workers to attend vocational schools to acquire specific industrial skills, which are needed if they are to get employed in the urban economy and settle down in the city permanently. This is the reason why, if we go back to the remarks of Mr. Lian Weiliang, vice-mayor of Luoyang city, "[w]ithout a comprehensive social security system, migrant workers would not work [in the municipality], because there would be no security for his income and future life".

Economic benefits of pension policy (2): state-sector restructuring

The speech by Mr. Lian Weiliang also reveals another economic benefit of pension policy, when he said that "a comprehensive social security system is a precondition of the successful restructuring of the state sector". Why are comprehensive social security programmes like pension a prerequisite of the successful state sector reform? This concerns the second economic function of pension policy, that is, to facilitate the allocation of workers from the state sector to the private economy, which improves the efficiency of labour force utilisation that is crucial for rapid industrialisation.

China's pension reform coincided with the reform of the state sector in the urban areas, which started tentatively in mid-1980s and saw more fundamental restructuring launched in 1997. During the socialist era, when there was no labour market in China, the Chinese state allocated labour force to state-owned enterprises. State-run companies could not dismiss urban workers, who effectively enjoyed the right to lifetime job security, a major embodiment of socialist ideals and an important component of the contract between the socialist state and the urban proletariat. Lacking the authority to optimise their employment structure, state-owned enterprises were consequently burdened with surplus labour, which inevitably led to economic inefficiency. The reform on the state sector, aiming to restore the efficiency of the allocation of economic resources such as the labour force, commenced in 1985, when a labour contract system was introduced, allowing state enterprise managers to recruit workers on a contract basis and renew the contract on the basis of workers' productive performance. This arrangement, despite granting managers more authority on personnel decisions, failed to solve the problem of overstaffing, because it was only applied to new labour market entrants while leaving the permanent employment status of old workers intact. To deal with the problem of inefficient workforce utilisation, the Chinese government then sought to enhance the mobility of the surplus labour in state-owned enterprises. In other words, the issue of overstaffing should be addressed through the channelling of abundant workers in the state sector to somewhere else. But to where?

The answer is that the surplus labour in state-run enterprises should be directed to and absorbed by the non-state enterprises, like private and foreign-invested companies, which emerged after the launch of economic reform. This is where pension reform can be economically beneficial. One obstacle to the labour reallocation from the state to the non-state sector is the potential loss of welfare packages, like housing, healthcare and pension. Workers were often reluctant to move to work for private enterprises, fearing that their welfare rights accumulated over the years at the state work units would be lost. So unless the emerging private sectors are also covered by some social security arrangement, the voluntary labour mobility between enterprises of different ownership types would be very low, which prevents solving the overstaffing problem in the state sector and impedes the flourishing of the private economy. Therefore, extending the pension programmes to cover the non-state sector can have enormous economic benefits. That is, it can enhance the overall efficiency of industrialisation by increasing the efficiency of state enterprises and fostering the growth of private firms. Chinese municipal leaders are clearly aware of these benefits of pension programmes, as we can tell from the words of Shen Bonian, vice-mayor of Guangzhou in the Guangdong province, who gave the following speech at a work conference on extending pension coverage when he explained the importance of pension expansion:

> With the deepening of the reforms on economic structure and labour employment system and the maturity of labour market, workers have become increasingly mobile across firms of different types of ownership. Whether they can have old-age income security, therefore, has become an important factor that affects their job choice. If our social insurance arrangement cannot cover every type of firms regardless of their ownership, then it will impede the prospects for job creation, inhibit the optimal allocation of labour force, and hinder the development of private economic sector. Now due to the economic restructuring and reforms on the state-owned enterprise, we have more and more laid-off workers. We are under a great pressure to ensure their reemployment. To address this issue, we have to create jobs not just in the state sector. This thus requires social insurance programmes to cover all kinds of economic sector. To free them from worries about their future life social insurance should follow workers to whatever economic sector they want to go to.[16]

It is worth noting that in his speech Mr. Shen saw extending pension coverage could benefit the private sector by improving the allocative efficiency of the labour force. As we have discussed, expanding pension programmes to cover the private sector can help to solve the problem of overstaffing in state-owned enterprises by increasing labour mobility across firms of different ownership. In the process the private sector absorbs from the state sector a large number of workers who have been well trained. In other words, being covered by the social security programmes helps private enterprises get the human resources that are needed for their expansion and growth. That is why Mr. Shen reckoned that if social security programmes could not be extended to enterprises of all types of ownership, the development of the private sector could be snuffed.

Indeed, to ensure private firms have the human capital they need is always an integral part of the strategy of Chinese local leaders to bolster the growth of private economy. For example, Lin Shusen, mayor of Guangzhou in Guangdong province, at one private sector economic work conference in 1998, made it clear that a crucial step to help private businesses was to "encourage graduates from colleges and vocational schools and technicians to flow to individual employers and private enterprises".[17] Another example is given at a municipal non-state economic work conference in 2003, by Zheng Zhongli, mayor of Xiamen in Fujian province, who charged the Municipal Bureau of Labour and Social Security to "help private enterprises to break the boundaries of enterprise ownership so they can attract the talent they need".[18] One way to increase the attractiveness of the private sector relative to the state enterprise, as we have seen, is to make sure employees in the private firm are also covered by social security programmes like public pension, which means pension programmes have to be extended to cover the private sector.

Therefore, against the backdrop of state-sector restructuring that has unfolded on a large scale since 1997, pension policy has been used by municipal leaders as a tool to smooth the restructuring process and enhance the growth of the private sector. A central aim of the reforming of the Chinese state sector is to solve its overstaffing problem, which means the surplus labour that has been accumulated in the state sector during the period of planned economy has to be directed to other sectors of the economy. An obstacle to achieving this goal is the lack of incentives to join the private sector of the state sector workers, who are worried about losing their enterprise-based welfare benefits after they leave their state work units. By building a public pension scheme and extending it to cover the private sector, the municipal government then assures state sector workers about the availability and stability of welfare entitlements in the private sector, which therefore encourages these workers to move to the private business. The result is that the state sector shrugs off the surplus labour, which improves its efficiency, and the private sector also benefits from being staffed by well-trained workers who come from the state enterprises. In other words, with an expansive pension programme that covers all enterprises regardless of their ownership type, the overall allocative efficiency of the labour force can be improved, which is important for local industrialisation and economic expansion.

Economic benefits of pension policy (3): cost containment

The final economic benefit of the expansionary pension policy concerns its contribution to cost containment for employers. This may seem paradoxical. Indeed, pension programmes are expensive. If we consider the costs of funding the public pension schemes, then there could be a potential dilemma. On the one hand, as we have seen, an extensive pension system can be conducive to local industrialisation and urbanisation, which help municipal leaders to generate fiscal revenues, their major concern in their plan for career advancement. On the other hand, a comprehensive pension scheme means a huge financial burden imposed on employers, who normally have to pay 20 percent of workers' wages to contribute to the pension programme. This reduces employers' profits and therefore is likely to discourage investment and deter potential investors, the last thing the local leaders obsessed with economic growth would like to see. With the possibility that pension programmes may harm local businesses, will municipal leaders still choose to adopt an expansive pension policy?

The following analysis shows that although local leaders do have concerns about the problem of pension contribution being a financial burden on local firms, they see the expansion of the pension programme as a solution to this problem. That is to say, an expansive pension policy, rather than being the cause of firm's financial burden, is seen as a tool to ease such burden. This is because the more people are covered under the pension programme, the more contribution the programme will receive from an enlarged pool of programme participants, and the lower the contribution rates will be that are required to fund a given level of benefits for a given number of pensioners. In other words, the expansion of pension programmes, by bringing in new active contributing workers and employers, increases the total contribution and therefore eases the financial burden on individual workers and employers.

It is conventionally believed that the expensive welfare state threatens the flourishing of business. One way \ the welfare state can harm business is by imposing tax burdens on employers, which adds to labour costs and distorts investment incentives. In other words, the welfare state sacrifices economic efficiency when it redistributes wealth for the sake of social equality. It then follows that employers, whose pursuit of maximised profit depends upon the unchecked functioning of the market, will try to shed the shackles imposed by the welfare state whenever possible. This argument, which views the welfare state as a manifestation of "politics against markets" (Esping-Andersen 1985), has one important implication: In a world where the capital becomes increasingly mobile and hence the business sector possesses more bargaining power, the employers can force the government to reduce regulations because now they can issue credible threats of exiting. Faced with the credible intimidations from the employers, the government, which needs investment for economic growth, has no choice but to yield to the demands of the capital, retreating its market interventions, including those concerning citizens' social security. The result of government competing for mobile capital is a "race to the bottom" of welfare provision, or "social dumping" (see Chapter 2 for detailed discussion on the literature on the "social dumping" thesis).

As far as China's pension programme is concerned, the "social dumping" argument seems even more pertinent. Pension provision is the biggest component of the Chinese welfare state and the bulk of it is financed by the payroll tax imposed on employers. In other words, pension represents the heaviest financial burden on Chinese employers, which accounts for at least 20 percent of the taxable payroll. Then pension should be a most likely case of the "social dumping" thesis in China. If there is one social programme Chinese employers would oppose, then it should be the public pension programme. If Chinese local leaders care about the health of local economy, which hinges upon the activities of the business sector, then presumably they would share employers' concern about the huge costs of pension contributions and should be most reluctant to push for pension reform and expanding the coverage of pension programmes. This is the expectation of the "social dumping" argument when it is applied to the case of Chinese pension reform.

As one may have already realised, this prediction fails to account for what has really happened. In fact, the coverage rates of China's pension system have increased rapidly especially since the early 2000s, and the agency of Chinese local officials, particularly those working at the municipal level, contributes a lot in the process. It is not that Chinese local leaders are not aware of the huge costs of funding the increasingly expanding pension programmes. Nor are they indifferent to the financial burden the pension programmes impose on employers. In fact, the costs of pension programmes and the resultant financial burdens on the business sector are real concerns of Chinese municipal leaders, as we can tell from the following passage of the internal speech delivered by Mr. Lian Weiliang, mayor of Luoyang city, at the municipal work conference on extending pension coverage:

> [T]he contribution rate of pension programme in our city is 31 percent, with employers paying 23 percent and workers paying 8 percent. This means firms in Luoyang, under the current policy framework, have to pay an extra 3 percent in pension contribution, compared with firms in other municipalities. An extra of 3 percent amounts to an extra of 90 million yuan. So compared with firms in other places, firms in Luoyang face higher costs, and therefore the scope for their profitability of investing in Luoyang becomes narrower. This has a bad effect on the competitiveness of Luoyang.[19]

The above passage reveals that Mr. Lian did think the high contribution rate of pension programme was a huge burden on the employers in Luoyang. The use of the term "competitiveness" suggests that he saw this issue against the background of the economic competition between Luoyang and other municipalities in the province. This is not surprising given the high priority of winning the inter-municipal economic race on Chinese municipal leaders' political agenda. Given the political importance of this issue, obviously Mr. Lian would seek to enhance his city's competitiveness by easing the financial burden of firms, which he believed could be done through the reduction of the pension contribution rate:

> So the municipal party committee and municipal government have made a strategic decision to bring the pension contribution rate down. This is meant to improve Luoyang's environment of economic development. Originally we planned to bring firm's contribution rate right down to 20 percent, thereby saving almost 100 million yuan and leaving it to the firms, which should enhance their competitiveness. But the provincial government thought it would be too much because it would lead to a large fall in pension contribution, so they suggested that we should make it step by step. We pushed for

> our cause and finally we decided to first bring down 2 percent, which reduces costs for firms of nearly 60 million yuan. Indeed we will see a corresponding funding gap of 60 million in our pension programme. But this is well worth it. This is because we believe that creating an investment environment better than other cities is an important responsibility of our municipal party committee and municipal government. Where we are not as well as others, we catch up with them. Where we are equals of others, we seek to outperform them. Only in this way can our firms have a good environment to grow and thrive.[20]

Viewed in isolation, this passage may serve as exactly a piece of evidence showing that Chinese local officials engage in social dumping. Indeed, to contain costs for firms and improve their competitiveness at the expense of social programme funding is a defining measure of social dumping. But Mr. Lian would really have dumped workers "socially" if he had left funding gaps in pension programmes unattended and hence let pension benefits fall. But as we have discussed, in the first decade of the twenty-first century, with the labour market tightening, Chinese local leaders simply cannot afford to ignore the wellbeing of workers, otherwise they will face even more severe labour shortage, which harms local businesses even more than pension contribution fees. Therefore, Chinese local leaders have to ensure the stability of welfare benefits while also easing firm's financial burdens. That is why Mr. Lian, having asked to bring down pension contribution rates, moved quickly to discuss how to deal with the resulting 60 million funding gap in pension programme:

> Surely we had different views when we made the decision [to bring down employer pension contribution rate to 21 percent]. Many colleagues were worried about the 60 million gap after the reduction of contribution rate. Having this funding gap, we may have to put money from local finance into it [i.e., the pension programme], which will put a huge pressure on municipal treasury in the future. As many people questioned, could we afford to do so?[21]

Clearly Mr. Lian had no intention to leave the problem of the funding gap in the pension programme unaddressed. Pumping public money into the pension programme may be one way to solve this problem. But Mr. Lian shared his colleagues' concern about it putting financial stresses on the local public purse. At this point Mr. Lian introduced a viable way to deal with the funding gap, that is, to extend the coverage of pension programme,

> [B]ut if we can well enforce the expansion of pension programme and the collection of pension contribution, then there is no need to use local finance money to subsidise pension programme. This is because we still have huge potentials for increasing the participation of pension programme and

> collecting the arrears of pension contribution fees. So in this year we reduce pension contribution rate for employers by 2 percent, and next year, if possible, we will still bring down the extra 1 percent. . . . This requires us to do our job well to expand the coverage of pension programme and to settle the pension contribution fees due, otherwise we cannot realise the improving of business environment and the safeguarding of the rights of pension programme participants and pensioners.[22]

The last sentence of the above passage indicates that Mr. Lian did not see that the cultivating of a pro-business atmosphere conflicts with the guaranteeing of citizens' rights to social security. In other words, one does not have to "socially dump" workers to improve the investment environment. Mr. Lian was confident that his municipality could achieve the two things at the same time, which are developing a business-friendly environment and achieving the old-age income security for citizens. This confidence came from the municipality's capacity to solve the problem of the 60 million funding gap in the pension programme, which is in turn dependent upon the "huge potentials" for expanding the pension programme coverage. What does this mean? What are the potential sources of new pension programme participants? Like many municipal leaders we have seen earlier, Mr. Lian, mayor of Luoyang city, also urged to bring in peasant workers from the countryside surrounding Luoyang and cover them with public pension programmes. So the "potentials" for expanding pension coverage and thus establishing a financially sustainable pension programme came from the inflow of young and productive peasant workers, who could make a great amount of net contributions to the local pension programme for years before retiring to claim their benefits. Therefore, expanding the municipal pension programme to cover these peasant workers can help to offset the funding gap in the pension scheme, which is caused by the reduction of employers' contribution rates, and to maintain the stability of workers' welfare benefits, which is required to alleviate labour shortage when the labour market becomes increasingly tightened. Considering such "potentials", one can understand why Mr. Lian believed that cost containment for employers did not conflict with ensuring social security for workers. Mr. Lian is not alone in holding this belief. Mr. Chen Zhenggao, mayor of Shenyang in Liaoning province, expressed a similar view when he gave orders on the exact number of people needed to participate in the pension programme to improve the investment environment and ensure social security rights:

> Regarding extending the coverage of pension programme, our goal is to have 1.6 million people covered in the programme. This is a difficult task, but it must be done. If we achieve this goal, then we will have more pension funds to provide old age security for the working people. Also, it will create conditions for us to lower employer pension contribution rate by a further 2 percent, and then by that time Shenyang will have better investment environment.[23]

Therefore, the analysis of the internal speeches by Chinese municipal leaders reveals what the "social dumping" thesis is right and wrong about the Chinese case. It is correct to point out the local government's concern about the huge costs imposed on employers by the expensive pension programme. Indeed, as we have seen, Chinese municipal officials have tried to ease the financial burden on firms, mostly by reducing the pension contribution rate at which they have to pay. But the "social dumping" argument is wrong in assuming that this cost containment for employers has to be done at the expense of workers' social security. In fact, in the Chinese context, the municipal leaders respond to the employers' demand for cost containment, not by cutting social benefits so firms can bear fewer social costs, but by expanding the social programmes to cover new active contributors so the contribution from firms can be reduced without diminishing the total funds for social programmes. The expansion of social programmes, in other words, is not the cause of employers' financial burden, but on the very contrary, it is its remedy. The new contributors to social programmes, as we have seen, come from the surplus labour released from the countryside in the process of urbanisation.

It is the neglect of this point that may render it misleading to apply the "social dumping" thesis to the Chinese context. The "social dumping" thesis is originally formulated on the historical experience of advanced countries and mature welfare states. In the context of the well-established welfare state, where social programmes have virtually covered all citizens, there is no source of new participants that can be brought into social programmes. Without any new blood to bring in, if the government has to trim some of the social costs for employers, the total contribution to social programmes has to fall, which will inevitably lead to a corresponding cut in social benefits. This is the scenario where social dumping happens. But in China the historical context is different. Unlike the industrialised countries, China is still transforming itself into an urban society while it tries to establish its own welfare state. The coincidence of the two ongoing processes, urbanisation and welfare state building, means that they can reinforce each other. As we have discussed earlier, the expansion of social programmes like pension brings peasant workers into the urban areas and facilitates their vocational education that will give them industrial skills required for the urban economy, which helps the peasant workers to permanently settle down in the city centre. This is a case of how welfare state building assists urbanisation. What we have seen in this section is how urbanisation contributes to the building of the welfare state. The process of urbanisation releases a massive number of surplus labour from the countryside. This surplus labour from rural areas then becomes sources of funding for China's urban welfare programmes. So when the Chinese local state hopes to relieve some of employers' social burdens, it need not reduce the total contribution to the social programmes or the benefit levels, because it can always extend the coverage of these programmes to cover peasant workers for extra contribution. So even if the Chinese local state seeks to nourish an investment-friendly environment, "social dumping" may not necessarily happen. This is an example of how urbanisation aids welfare state formation. Applying the "social dumping" argument to the Chinese case of welfare state building without paying attention to China's specific historical context, in which welfare state formation coincides with urbanisation, would yield a misleading conclusion that the Chinese state's desire to attract investment would jeopardise China's welfare regime, especially its most expensive component, the pension programme. The above analysis has shown that when Chinese local leaders adopt pro-business measures like reducing employers' share in the funding of pension programmes, they avoid endangering the financial viability of the public pension scheme by expanding the programme to cover more active contributors.

Summary

The preceding discussions provide micro-foundations for the two hypotheses derived from our theory, which are the *Expansion Hypothesis* and *Localisation Hypothesis*, by citing the internal speeches of municipal leaders to show how they perceive the political and economic competition between municipalities and the role of pension policy in the process. The assumptions made in the theory that Chinese municipal leaders compete with each other to promote local economic growth and adopt pension policy as an instrument to achieve this goal receive empirical support from municipal leaders' own words. Our theory, therefore, accurately captures the political and policy preferences of Chinese municipal leaders in the real world.

No passage is better than the following one to conclude this section. It is an excerpt of the speech at the municipal old-age insurance work conference made by Cai Guangxin, Head of Social Security Bureau of Sanming City in Fujian province:

> Extending the coverage of [old-age] social insurance is an old issue as well as an important issue . . . We are not only to compare ourselves to ourselves with respect to extending [pension] coverage rates, examining whether we have reached the target. We also should compare our city to other cities in this respect. Last year we had municipalities that had coverage rates of more than 90 percent. In comparison though our city reached the target our ranking is still relatively low. This puts great pressures on this year's work of extending coverage rates . . . So we have to promptly track how neighbouring cities approach to extend their coverage rates, learn from their experience, know what to focus on in our work, and never hold our city back.[24]

The above passage shows how the inter-municipal economic competition can "spill over" to the field of pension policy. Cai was concerned that Sanming had lagged behind in extending pension coverage compared with the neighbouring cities and urged his staff to learn from them and to catch up. The reason why Chinese municipal officials care about the local economy and hence local pension schemes is that they are motivated by the political institutions of the Chinese state. Building on the micro-level preferences and behaviours of Chinese municipal leaders, our theory generates two predictions on how political institutions, through shaping the preferences and behaviours of Chinese municipal leaders, shape the structure of China's pension system. The next two sections are dedicated to testing the two hypotheses using statistical techniques.

Expansion hypothesis

> Other things being equal, the province more often governed by insider leadership will have a higher level of pension coverage because its municipal leaders are motivated to make more efforts to promote local economic development by expanding the coverage of pension programmes.

In this hypothesis, the independent variable is the *insider* index, an institution variable reflecting the incentive structure facing municipal leaders. The dependent variable is the coverage rate of pension programmes, which is measured as the ratio of the number of urban employees and retirees covered by pension schemes to the total number of urban workers and pensioners. The estimation applies Beck and Katz's (1995) technique of ordinary least squares with panel-corrected standard errors (OLS-PCSE) to a panel of data on 31 provincial-level jurisdictions from 2000 to 2009. The year 2000 was chosen because data on provincial pension coverage rates are not available until this year. In all models, the independent variable and all of the control variables are lagged by one year to eliminate possible reversed causality.

The independent variable, the *insider* index, measures the degree to which the top provincial leadership post (i.e., the provincial party secretary) is presided by officials recruited from within the province, i.e., promoted from the municipalities of this province. It is an indicator of the chances of the current municipal leaders being promoted to the provincial posts and hence the credibility of central government regarding promotion, which as this book has argued will affect the motivation of municipal leaders to bolster local economic development through the expansive and localising pension policy. This variable, the *insider*, is coded as 1 for the year when the office of provincial party secretary is presided by insiders (i.e., officials who build their career from below within the province) or 0 if otherwise. This book uses a cumulative measure from 1978 to each year in the period of 2000–2009, meaning that for a given province the value on the *insider* variable for each individual year in the period concerned is obtained by summing up its scores on this variable in previous years since 1978. Following the convention in contemporary China studies, the year 1978 was chosen because this is when China entered the reform era. One can understand measuring the *insider* variable in a cumulative manner as a way to reflect the calculation of municipal leaders when they speculate the possibility of the next provincial party secretary being an insider (i.e., being one of them): They must have gone through the backgrounds of all top provincial leaders in the past three decades (in total there are 18–20 top provincial leaders for each province during this period) before they come up with the prospects of the next provincial governor being an insider.

After all, to make a prediction about the future one often has to rely on the past. Also, measuring the *insider* variable cumulatively is to follow the convention in the comparative political economy literature to measure, for example, the prominence of leftist parties. For example, in their study on the extent of redistribution among major OECD countries in postwar years, Bradley et al. (2003) measure the party government share of the leftist party and Christian democratic party by using a cumulative measure from 1946. Similar application of historically cumulative measures to indicate the prominence of political actors can also be found in Huber and Stephens (2000). The career paths of provincial party secretaries are traced by examining their resumes, which are available on official websites of the Central People's Government of the People's Republic of China (www.gov.cn) and the provincial governments of the 31 provincial-level jurisdictions.

Three variables are controlled for in addition to year and region dummies (see Chapter 4 for reasons for adding region dummies). The first one is *Industrialisation*, measured as provincial GDP per capita (in logged form), indicating the level of economic development. For two reasons this variable is controlled for. First, according to the literature on the logic of industrialism (Cutright 1965; Wilensky and Lebeaux 1958; Wilensky 1975), economic modernisation should push the provincial and ultimately the municipal government (who receive pressures from their provincial bosses) to respond to demographic pressures associated with modernisation by expanding pension programmes. Also, economic development generates material resources that are necessary for the expansion of social programmes such as public pension. Secondly, as argued in this study, China's pension reform unfolds in a context of industrial upgrading and labour market tightening. Chapter 1 has cited China's export product composition to indicate the level of industrial upgrading and the demand-supply ratio in urban labour markets to show the degree of labour scarcity. Unfortunately, there are no data that measure the two indicators at the provincial level. But it is reasonable to assume that both industrial upgrading and labour market tightening are positively associated with the level of economic development. Indeed, the coastal provinces, which are the most prosperous regions in China, first see their manufacturing industries climbing up the value chain, while the less developed inland provinces still largely rely on exporting raw materials for economic growth. It is also in those coastal, developed provinces, for example Guangdong, that labour shortage was first reported, which was in 2003 (Southern Weekly 2004). So the level of economic development, measured as GDP per capita, can be a proxy of industrial upgrading and labour scarcity. Therefore, the variable *Industrialisation*, indicating the material resources available to the government as well as the likelihood to have industrial upgrading and labour shortage, is hypothesised to be positively associated with pension coverage rates.

The second control variable is that of *Marketisation*, which measures how far a province has gone in the transition from a planned economy to a market-oriented one. It reflects the relative importance of the private sector to the state sector in terms of employment and economic output. This variable is taken from the works by two prominent Chinese economists, Fan Gang and Wang Xiaolu (2011).

They measure the degree of marketisation of Chinese provinces on five dimensions and construct a composite index.[25] The higher the index is, the more developed the market economy and the stronger the private sector is in the province. As the analysis of municipal speeches has revealed, in order to foster local economic development, municipal leaders expand pension coverage to facilitate the moving of workers from state-owned enterprises to private firms. The motivation of urban officials to do so should increase with the strength of the private sector, meaning a positive relationship between *Marketisation* and pension coverage rates. In addition, a market-oriented environment should see more intensified competition for the labour force, which facilitates the expansion of localised pension programmes as a tool for labour retention. So this also predicts the degree of marketisation to be positively associated with pension coverage rates. On the other hand, it is conventionally held that one obstacle to the expansion of pension coverage is the resistance from the private sector, which sees participating in pension programmes as a financial burden because having private firms pay pension contribution fees is a redistribution of wealth from the younger private sector to the state sector with older workers. This view echoes the "politics against markets" thesis that holds capitalists as antagonists of the welfare state. Mark Frazier (2010) and many others have this view but none of them have offered convincing evidence. Thus, it is important to test this competing hypothesis here by adding the variable *Marketisation*, which according to the above argument should have a negative impact on pension coverage.

Finally, I control for the variable of *Central Subsidy*, which is the fiscal subsidy to local social insurance programmes from the central government as a share of the total provincial government revenue. This intends to capture the impact of central government in the process of local pension expansion. A large amount of fiscal transfers from the central government should ease the financial burden for local governments to run pension programmes and consequently make them more capable to carry out pension expansion. Thus, the variable of *Central Subsidy* is expected to positively relate to pension coverage rate.

The regression results in Table 6.1 show that in the baseline estimation Model 1 all variables exhibit expected impacts. That is to say, a province tends to have a higher level of pension coverage if it has been more often governed by locally promoted insider leaders, enjoys a higher level of economic development, has deeper market-oriented reforms and receives more subsidises to social protection programmes from the central government.[26] All variables show statistical significance, except for *Industrialisation*, measured as logged provincial GDP per capita, whose coefficient has the hypothesised sign but fails to show statistical significance. But if this variable is measured as logged GDP rather than logged GDP per capita, then without altering the signs and significance of the coefficients of other variables, it shows the expected effect that is statistically significant at the 0.05 level (this result is omitted here for presentational economy). It may be that GDP per capita is not a good indicator of industrial upgrading and labour scarcity. One may need more specific and precise measurements for the two structural factors. It may also suggest a more general issue in the research on the Chinese

Table 6.1 Testing expansion hypothesis: determinants of pension coverage rates (2000–2009) Prais-Winsten regression, heteroskedastic panels corrected standard errors

Variable	*Model 1*	*Model 2*
Insider	.0037785*** (.0010458)	.0051699*** (.0012299)
Industrialisation	.0208315 (.027583)	
Marketisation	.0283438*** (.0079433)	
Central subsidy	.0068366*** (.0017551)	
Year dummies	Yes	Yes
Region dummies	Yes	Yes
Constant	.6522925*** (.125221)	.5627745*** (.0179054)
Observations	279	279
Probability > Chi-square	0.000	0.000
Adjusted R-square	0.8197	0.8172

*, **, ***, stand for $p < 0.1$, $p < 0.05$ and $p < 0.01$ two-tailed test. Standard errors are in parentheses. All variables are lagged by one year.

political economy. In studies on policy decisions in Western countries, when economic development should be taken into account, the usual indicator to look at is GDP per capita. Like the present study, the majority of the political economy literature on contemporary China follows this norm. Looking at GDP per capita makes sense in the Western context, because in the democratic decision-making process it is the preference of individual voters, which is largely shaped by the material resources each individual enjoys, that dictates the government policy. But in China where such electoral pressure is absent, the developmental state can concentrate the economic resources on a few chosen social engineering projects through industrial policies in an authoritative manner without worrying too much about the popular preference. Therefore, in the Chinese context it seems that total amount of economic resources matters more than such resources averaged at the individual level in terms of giving the state the fiscal capacity to achieve developmental goals such as industrial upgrading.[27] To fully explore this issue exceeds the capacity of this dissertation, so it has to be left for future research.

What is also worth noting is that *Marketisation* actually increases pension coverage rates, which is consistent with this study's argument that the expansion of pension programmes is a response to the growth of the private sector and the intensified competition for workers in the labour market. This is very contrary to the common wisdom that Chinese private firms competing in an increasingly liberal market reject pension programmes as an unnecessary financial burden. Even if we replace the variable *Marketisation* with the share of the private sector in terms of industrial output, the result is the same (which is not shown here, for presentational economy). This finding should cast some doubts on the "politics against markets" argument in the Chinese context, suggesting that the employer preferences should be further explored. Indeed, as one will see in Chapter 6, the statements made by business leaders show that private employers whose production strategies rely on skill upgrading of employees actually urge the government to strengthen the enforcement of social protection regulations so no employers can evade social insurance contributions to have labour cost advantages. Therefore, there are segments of private employers who support the expansion of social insurance programmes, and the regression results here show that they are not a minority.

At the moment it is important to note that the independent variable of interest, i.e., *insider*, is positively associated with pension coverage rates with statistical significance, even after all control variables are dropped from the equation as in Model 2. This supports the *Expansion Hypothesis* that the provincial leadership dominated by insiders effectively demonstrates the credibility of the central government on personnel promotion and therefore gives municipal leaders incentives to expand pension programmes to facilitate local skill formation and retain skilled workers locally.

Several robustness checks are conducted to examine how the results from the baseline Model 1 hold to different model specification. The results are shown in Table 5.2. From Table 5.2 we can see that across all models the independent variable, *insider*, shows significant and expected impacts on pension coverage rates, which should reinforce our confidence in the theory of this study. Model 3 controls for the insider/outsider profile of the provincial governor. The provincial party secretary, who leads the party-apparatus that supervises, if not dictates, the government policy, is the undisputable top leader of a province. So who is appointed by the central government to this post, compared with any other posts in the provincial party-state, conveys more messages about the central government's credibility to municipal leaders. This is the reason why the insider/outsider composition of provincial party secretary is chosen as the independent variable in this study. Nevertheless, one may think that the appointment of provincial governor, the number two official of a province and head of the provincial government, can also send important information to municipal officials. Therefore, the insider/outsider profile of provincial governor may need to be controlled for.

Model 4 measures the dependent variable, the pension coverage rate, by having the number of pension-covered urban workers divided by the total number of urban workers, thereby excluding the number of retirees from the calculation. To take retirees into consideration, the variable of *Retiree Dependency Ratio*, measured as the ratio of retirees to urban labour force, is included in this model. This ratio is expected to have a positive impact on pension coverage rates, because a higher dependency ratio of pensioners should present greater pressures on local governments to take care of them through pension programme expansion, which is meant to relieve such pressure by incorporating more young contributors and thus increasing the financial viability of pension schemes.

Model 5 drops from the dataset Chongqing, Hainan and Tibet, three provincial units that are not often included in cross-provincial research in the field of contemporary China studies. Data on Tibet, due to the high political sensitivity of this region, is often confidential or unreliable when made publicly. Hainan and Chongqing only became provincial-level units in 1988 and 1996, respectively, and thus may not be truly comparable with other provinces that have existed since 1949. In this study, for example, few of the party secretaries of these two provincial-level jurisdictions are insiders, which may reflect the fact that they simply lack enough time to produce home-grown provincial leaders.

The previous models use Beck and Katz's (1995) technique of pooled ordinary least squares regression with panel-corrected standard errors (OLS-PCSE). Model 6 uses a different estimation method. Beck and Katz (1995) suggests that OLS-PCSE had better be used in panel data settings where the number of time points (T) is greater than that of units (N). Although Beck and Katz do not specify the ratio of time points to units that is most suitable for OLS-PCSE, one should be cautious when applying this technique to a dataset with relatively large N and small T, which is the case in this research, which studies 31 provinces across a period of 10 years. Therefore, Model 6 uses pooled ordinary least squares regression with Driscoll and Kraay's (1998) standard errors, which does not place any restrictions on the number of panel units and therefore can be used even when the number of N is much larger than T.

Finally, Model 7 adds another control variable to the baseline model, namely *Inter-municipal Disparity*, which is the inequality in economic development in terms of GDP per capita among municipalities within a province. This variable is included for the following reason: The bureaucratic promotion tournament model has an implication that the more equal municipalities are in economic terms, the fiercer the inter-municipal competition is, because equal economic capacity to compete among municipalities means that no one will be too weak to give up competing. A higher level of pension coverage rate could therefore be caused by a fiercer inter-municipal competition induced by a low degree of inter-municipal disparity rather than by the central government's credibility regarding promotion. This is a competing hypothesis to our theory and thus needs to be taken into account. The inter-municipal disparity is measured by the coefficient of variation (c.v.) that measures the dispersion of the GDP per capita of municipalities within one given province. Coefficient of variation is a distribution's standard deviation divided by its mean. A higher coefficient of variation means a higher level of disparity between the municipalities of a given province. Its limitation is that it is not weighted and thus is not immune to outliers. With that said, the inter-municipal disparity is expected to be negatively associated with pension programme coverage rates.

As is clear from Table 6.2, these robustness check models show largely similar results as the baseline estimation. In particular, across all models, the independent variable, *insider*, as predicted by our theory, is significantly and

Table 6.2 Robustness checks: determinants of pension coverage rates (2000–2009) Prais-Winsten regression, heteroskedastic panels corrected standard errors (except for Model 6, which uses pooled OLS with Driscoll and Kraay's (1998) standard errors)

Variable	*Model 3*	*Model 4*	*Model 5*	*Model 6*	*Model 7*
Insider	.0037656***	.0027893***	.004834***	.0026719***	.0041077***
	(.0011129)	(.0006261)	(.0011237)	(.000298)	(.0010713)
Industrialisation	.0214669	–.0215086	.0443591	–.005447	.080803***
	(.028892)	(.0426853)	(.0279079)	(.01763)	(.0260449)
Marketisation	.0270634***	.0357262***	.0069914	.0493952***	.0079907
	(.0079216)	(.0066258)	(.0076173)	(.0038731)	(.0066425)
Central subsidy	.0065133***	.0061582***	.0027779*	.0156095***	.0020298
	(.0017655)	(.0023545)	(.0016227)	(.0017253)	(.0015558)
Governor	.0002145				
	(.0010976)				
Retiree dependency		.2232316***			
		(.0540162)			
Inter-municipal disparity					–.0190049
					(.0252335)
Year dummies	Yes	Yes	Yes	Yes	Yes
Region dummies	Yes	Yes	Yes	Yes	Yes
Constant	.6376213***	.3752011	.1143918	.9419738***	.3466703***
	(.1367104)	(.3950054)	(.261924)	(.065642)	(.093606)
Observations	279	279	252	279	234
Probability > Chi-square	0.000	0.000	0.000	0.000	0.000
Adjusted R-square	0.8223	0.7132	0.8393	0.6971	0.8547

*, **, ***, stand for $p < 0.1$, $p < 0.05$ and $p < 0.01$ two-tailed test. Standard errors are in parentheses. All variables are lagged by one year.

positively associated with coverage rates of pension programmes, thereby supporting the *Expansion Hypothesis.*

Localisation hypothesis

> Other things being equal, the province more often governed by insider leadership is less likely to have its pension scheme integrated at the provincial level because its municipal leaders will try to keep the pension programmes localised along the municipal border.

In the *Localisation Hypothesis*, the independent variable is still the institution variable *insider*, which indicates the degree of domination by locally promoted officials in provincial leadership. The dependent variable is the level of risk pooling of pension programmes. If a province has given the authority of pension provision and administration solely to the provincial government, then this province is said to have an integrated provincial pension scheme and it is coded as 1. But if a province leaves such authority to its municipalities, then this province has a municipally fragmented pension arrangement and it is coded as 0. Given the dichotomous nature of the dependent variable, I choose the probit model, which is used to model binary outcome variables. I also chose the logistic model to do the robustness checks.

In addition to year and region dummies, the model for *Localisation Hypothesis* includes the same three control variables used in the testing of *Expansion Hypothesis.* Two of them, that is, *Industrialisation* (measured as logged GDP per capita) and *Central Subsidy*, are hypothesised to positively affect the likelihood of a province achieving pension integration. This is because both economic development and the fiscal aid from the central government will give the provincial governments more material resources to implement pension integration. The third variable, *Marketisation*, is expected to be negatively associated with a province's chances of having an integrated pension system. This is because a higher level of labour mobility in a more marketised environment will intensify the local competition for labour force, and this will make municipal leaders more dependent on keeping pension packages non-portable as an instrument to retain workers within their jurisdictions and hence more reluctant to comply with the central directive on pension integration.

Table 6.3 presents regression results that are largely consistent with the *Localisation Hypothesis.* The baseline Model 1 shows that the variable of *insider* has a significant, negative impact on the likelihood of a province having pension pooling arrangement integrated at the provincial level. In other words, other things being equal, insider-dominant provinces are more likely to have a fragmented pension scheme because in these provinces the economic competition among municipal leaders is more intensive and hence they tend to apply local protectionist measures like resisting the integration of pension programmes at the provincial level so they can retain locally skilled workers that are crucial for local economic growth. All control variables show expected signs of coefficients,

Table 6.3 Testing localisation hypothesis: determinants of level of pension pooling (2000–2009)

Variable	*Model 1 (Probit)*	*Model 2 (Probit)*
Insider	–.2010748***	–.2047195***
	(.0682113)	(.0690453)
Industrialisation	8.981657***	8.804506***
	(1.668305)	(1.724159)
Marketisation	–.6815531*	–.6917569*
	(.4227314)	(.4198304)
Central subsidy	.091119	.0708227
	(.1320815)	(.1532669)
Retiree dependency		2.261283
		(6.673607)
Year dummies	Yes	Yes
Region dummies	Yes	Yes
Constant	-71.84268***	-70.53785***
	(13.58777)	(13.99267)
Observations	279	279
Wald Chi-square	38.57	38.23
Probability > Chi-square	0.000	0.000
Log Likelihood	-19.202842	-19.167463

*, **, ***, stand for $p < 0.1$, $p < 0.05$ and $p < 0.01$ two-tailed test. Standard errors are in parentheses. All variables are lagged by one year.

but only *Industrialisation* and *Marketisation* are statistically significant. Model 2 controls for *Retiree Dependency Ratio*, which displays a positive yet insignificant impact on the chances of a province having a provincial-level pension scheme. This positive sign is easy to explain: Mounting demographic pressures clearly give the provincial government more incentive to achieve pension integration, which helps to share old-age income risks more efficiently among municipalities within the province.

As shown in Table 6.4, another five models are estimated for checking the robustness of the above findings. It is clear that across all of them the independent variable, *Insider*, exhibits statistically significant effect as expected by the *Localisation Hypothesis.* Model 3 controls for the insider profile of provincial governor. Model 4 excludes Tibet, Chongqing and Hainan from the data. Models 5, 6 and 7 follow a similar checking procedure but estimate the regression equations with logistic models. All of the models yield largely the same results with respect to the signs and statistical significance of the coefficients of the variables. Most importantly, the independent variable, *Insider*, shows hypothesised impacts with statistical significance consistently across all models. The *Localisation Hypothesis* then survives the sensitivity tests, so we can safely conclude that this prediction has received ample support from the data on 31 provincial jurisdictions from 2000 to 2009.

Table 6.4 Robustness checks: determinants of level of pension pooling (2000–2009)

Variable	*Model 3 (Probit)*	*Model 4 (Probit)*	*Model 5 (Logit)*	*Model 6 (Logit)*	*Model 7 (Logit)*
Insider	–.1603807**	–.1948408**	–.4318516*	–.836482*	–.6955496***
	(.0796645)	(.080455)	(.2532217)	(.4455747)	(.2399461)
Industrialisation	17.01937***	8.251873***	37.45499***	28.72431***	52.09224***
	(2.905575)	(1.856587)	(6.301854)	(7.917972)	(8.82107)
Marketisation	-1.367455**	–.6735188	–2.154433	–1.516186	–4.554872***
	(.5987074)	(.5629994)	(1.666606)	(1.569315)	(1.719492)
Central subsidy	–.1961248	.1059878	.2432893	.2665537	–.4198277
	(.1672682)	(.164768)	(.5181264)	(.5576318)	(.4105393)
Governor	–.4282784*				–1.181447***
	(.1016081)				(.2533183)
Retiree dependency				28.33832	
				(28.93658)	
Year dummies	Yes	Yes	Yes	Yes	Yes
Region dummies	Yes	Yes	Yes	Yes	Yes
Constant	–130.7072***	–66.07366***	–302.951***	–233.7836***	–399.9172***
	(22.11781)	(15.15014)	(51.17836)	(62.81341)	(70.7388)
Observations	279	252	279	279	279
Wald Chi-square	39.14	26.05	47.04	19.02	50.74
Probability > Chi-square	0.000	0.025	0.000	0.212	0.000
Log likelihood	–13.78427	–17.862171	–17.867564	–17.960295	–14.020847

*, **, ***, stand for $p < 0.1$, $p < 0.05$ and $p < 0.01$ two-tailed test. Standard errors are in parentheses. All variables are lagged by one year.

Extension of analysis: political institutions and welfare efforts

This section follows the advice of King, Keohane and Verba (1994) that one should test as many observable implications of a theory as possible to assess its validity. Up to this point we have tested two predictions of our theory. The results have shown that the incentive structure facing municipal leaders, as indicated by the insider profile of provincial leadership, has a significant impact on the shaping of the Chinese pension system. The explanatory power of our theory is not limited to the area of pension policy. In fact, this theory can generate more predictions concerning a wide range of social policies. This section extends the application of our theory to examine a phenomenon of major interest to political economists, that is, the welfare efforts of government. If its additional prediction can be supported by quantitative analysis, then we can be more confident in the validity of our theory.

How much in economic resources a society allocates to welfare programmes through its public authority has been a central question in the comparative political economy of the welfare state. It is interesting and important to explore this issue in the Chinese context. If we follow the Varieties of Capitalism theory, which argues that social policy is conducive to economic growth via its contribution to skill formation, then we should expect that the Chinese local leaders, who are obsessive with the economic expansion of their jurisdictions, tend to enhance their regions' economic performance by making more welfare efforts. Such tendency, as suggested by our theory, is mediated by the incentive structure facing Chinese municipal leaders. That is to say, only when the promise about bureaucratic career advancement becomes credible can the office-seeking municipal officials be motivated to promote local economy through expansive social policy that helps to build up a local stock of skilled workers. Therefore, concerning the welfare efforts of the Chinese local state, our theory generates the following prediction:

> Other things being equal, municipal leaders working in provinces with more insider-domination have more motivation to spend on human-capital related social programmes like education, healthcare and social protection to foster local economic development.

For this prediction, the independent variable is *insider*, indicating how credible the promise of bureaucratic promotion seems to municipal leaders. The dependent variable, *Social Spending*, is operationalised as the ratio of public spending on education, healthcare and social protection, i.e., the sort of social programmes that would have an impact on the local stock of human capital, to total public expenditure. This book calls such expenditure human capital-related social spending. This study measures the government efforts on human capital-related social spending by using the ratio of such social spending to total public spending rather than to provincial GDP. This is for two reasons. First, as Chinese provinces have to remit a significant proportion of fiscal revenues to the central government, the total provincial GDP does not reflect the economic resources that a province is free to use. Secondly, given the high GDP growth rate of the Chinese economy, using total GDP may suppress the government welfare efforts.

To test the welfare efforts prediction, this book uses Beck and Katz's (1995) method of pooled ordinary least squares with panel-corrected standard errors (OLS-PCSE). The baseline regression has three control variables in addition to the region and year dummies. *Industrialisation* and *Marketisation*are are included, and both are expected to have positive effects on government welfare efforts. The reasons are twofold. First, the process of industrialisation and marketisation generates social risks that call for government intervention through social policy. Secondly, as suggested by the analysis of the internal municipal speeches, Chinese local leaders tend to foster the growth of the private sector by directing human resources to this sector. To achieve this the private sector has to be covered by the state-funded social programmes. So a strong and rapidly growing private sector, as indicated by a high degree of marketisation, should be associated with a high level of welfare efforts by the government. The third control variable is *Retiree Dependency Ratio*. It has to be controlled for because the structural trend of population ageing naturally increases government social spending. It is possible that a high level of welfare efforts is the result of demographic pressures rather than of the inter-municipal competition to build up human capital stock. Therefore, to deal with this alternative hypothesis the variable of *Retiree Dependency Ratio* has to be added to the regression model.

The results of regression models are shown in Table 6.5. In the baseline estimation Model 1 where the independent variable of *insider* and all control variables

Table 6.5 Determinants of human capital-related social spending as percent of total public expenditure (2000–2009) Prais-Winsten regression, heteroscedastic panels corrected standard errors

Variable	*Model 1*	*Model 2*
Insider	.098176[4]** (.0486441)	.0877458* (.0539961)
Industrialisation	–5.936726*** (1.012983)	
Marketisation	.0217844 (.2952482)	
Retiree dependency	8.940669** (3.832028)	
Year dummies	Yes	Yes
Region dummies	Yes	Yes
Constant	89.36122*** (8.956947)	34.38534*** (.9783329)
Observations	279	279
Probability > Chi-square	0.000	0.000
Adjusted R-square	0.8265	0.8133

*, **, ***, stand for $p < 0.1$, $p < 0.05$ and $p < 0.01$ two-tailed test. Standard errors are in parentheses. All variables are lagged by one year.

are included in the regression equation, there is a positive and statistically significant association (at the level of 0.01) between the insider index and the share of human capital-related social spending in total public expenditure. This is consistent with our prediction, which argues an insider-dominant provincial leadership, suggesting the credibility of the central government regarding promotion, will motivate its municipal leaders to increase social spending. This pattern still holds, though with less statistical significance, when all control variables except year and region dummies are dropped from the regression equation, as shown in Model 2. It is interesting to examine the effects of the control variables in Model 1. Coefficients of the variables *Marketisation* and *Retiree Dependency Ratio* show expected signs, but the impact of *Marketisation* bears no statistical significance.

Industrialisation has a significant but unexpectedly negative impact on government efforts on social spending. This is not hard to understand: The dependent variable is measured as the ratio of social spending to total public expenditure. Other things being equal, a more industrialised province should have more fiscal revenues and hence more total public expenditure, which therefore reduces the share of social expenditure in total public spending. If we measure *Industrialisation* as total provincial GDP and add total public expenditure as a control variable to the model, then the variable of *Industrialisation* shows a positive sign, which is consistent with the argument that economic modernisation increases government welfare efforts.

More models are run to assess the robustness of the findings from the above baseline estimation, largely following the procedure used earlier when the *Expansion Hypothesis* was tested. The results are listed in Table 6.6. With the independent variable of *Insider* displaying the expected and significant impacts on human capital-related social spending across all models, the welfare efforts prediction is further supported. Model 3 controls for the insider profiles of provincial governors. Model 4 re-measures the dependent variable by excluding social assistance, because one may argue that it does not serve any productive purposes, although it may be very important for someone to survive in urban China without regular income before he finishes his un-paid apprenticeship and becomes a worker with some skills. Model 5 drops Tibet, Chongqing and Hainan from the dataset. Model 6 uses a different estimator, which is the pooled OLS regression with Driscoll and Kraay's (1998) standard errors. Model 7 tries to capture the role of central government in local welfare efforts by adding to the equation the variable of *Central Subsidy*.

Therefore, the results of the quantitative analysis of time-series-cross-section data on public welfare efforts support our theory's prediction that the more credible the central government's commitment regarding bureaucratic promotion is, the more economic resources local governments will allocate to social programmes that are conducive to the accumulation of human capital. In addition to the *Expansion Hypothesis* and *Localisation Hypothesis*, one more implication of our theory has survived the quantitative test. If we adopt the criteria set by King, Gary, Robert, Keohane and Verba (1994), then this should give us more confidence in the validity of our theory.

Table 6.6 Robustness checks: determinants of human capital-related social spending as percent of total public expenditure (2000–2009) Prais-Winsten regression, heteroscedastic panels corrected standard errors

Variable	*Model 3*	*Model 4*	*Model 5*	*Model 6*	*Model 7*
Insider	.1400429***	.0851828*	.1113444**	.0946492***	.0626627*
	(.0465178)	(.045343)	(.2532217)	(.0195566)	(.0373429)
Industrial-isation	−5.180665***	−5.646561***	−1.0734***	−7.17683***	−5.59609***
	(.9031352)	(.9640316)	(.2417311)	(.4811556)	(.8185271)
Marketi-sation	.0548302	.0540836	−2.154433***	.4434054***	.3404745
	(.2678597)	(.2843775)	(1.666606)	(.1094831)	(.2614749)
Retiree de-pendency	5.257707	8.700354**	1.046385	12.7493***	4.283346
	(3.68301)	(3.687073)	(3.366594)	(1.80969)	(3.410372)
Governor	Yes	No	No	No	No
Central subsidy					.3212548***
					(.0761177)
Year dummies	Yes	Yes	Yes	Yes	Yes
Region dummies	Yes	Yes	Yes	Yes	Yes
Constant	5.133036	86.63075	92.58804***	29.90994**	35.74587***
	(24.95627)	(7.647417)	(8.656496)	(12.25951)	(5.819642)
Observations	279	279	252	279	279
Probability > Chi-square	0.000	0.000	0.000	0.000	0.000
Adjusted R-square	0.8246	0.8542	0.8596	0.6635	0.7980

*, **, ***, stand for $p < 0.1$, $p < 0.05$ and $p < 0.01$ two-tailed test. Standard errors are in parentheses. All variables are lagged by one year.

Summary

The theory of this study generates two predictions concerning the shaping of China's pension system, which argue that the credibility of the central government's commitment regarding bureaucratic promotion is positively related with the coverage rates of public pension programmes but negatively associated with the pension programmes' level of risk pooling. To provide micro-foundations for the hypothesised associations, this chapter first conducts qualitative analysis of the internal speeches by Chinese municipal leaders to reveal their political and policy preferences. The micro picture shows that Chinese municipal leaders adopt the expansionary pension policy to foster local industrialisation in the inter-municipal competition in economic development. This is consistent with the assumptions made in our theory about the preferences and behaviours of Chinese municipal leaders. Aggregated from the micro preferences and behaviours are two macro phenomena, which are the expansive and localised characteristics of China's pension system. This chapter then tests two hypotheses on how the two features are shaped by China's political institutions, drawing on statistical analysis of time-series-cross-section data that cover China's 31 provincial jurisdictions during the period from 2000 to 2009. After controlling for other socio-economic variables that identified in the literature as being able to affect the shaping of the pension system, the results of statistical analysis support our predictions. Also supported by the data is an additional hypothesis derived from our theory, which predicts a positive relationship between the central government's credibility on bureaucratic promotion and local governments' welfare efforts. With our theory's implications supported by qualitative materials and surviving the quantitative analysis, we can say in confidence that the political institutions of the Chinese state, which constitute an incentive structure, do have an impact on local officials' policy behaviours concerning social programmes like public pension.

Notes

1 Zhang Yong: Speech for Municipal Economic Work Conference (Fuzhou of Jiangxi province, 30/12/2009) [江西抚州张勇在全市经济工作会议上的讲话, 2009年12月30日]
2 Qi Jihui: Speech for Municipal Government Plenary Session (Fuxin of Liaoning province, 3/3/2011) [辽宁阜新市长齐继慧在市政府全体会议上的讲话 2011年3月3日]
3 Wen Xihao: Speech for Municipal Industry Work Conference (Longyan of Fujian province, 16/2/2011) [福建龙岩副市长温锡浩在全市工业工作会议上的讲话要点 2011年2月16日]
4 Zhang Yong: Speech for Municipal Economic Work Conference (Fuzhou of Jiangxi province, 30/12/2009) [江西抚州张勇在全市经济工作会议上的讲话 2009年12月30日]
5 Chen Zhenggao: Speech for Municipal Economic Work Conference (Shenyang of Liaoning province, 17/2/2005) [辽宁沈阳市长陈政高在全市经济工作会议上的讲话 2005年2月17日]
6 Qi Jihui: Speech for Municipal Government Plenary Session (Fuxin of Liaoning province, 3/3/2011) [辽宁阜新市长齐继慧在市政府全体会议上的讲话 2011年3月3日]

7 Qi Jihui: Speech for Municipal Government Plenary Session (Fuxin of Liaoning province, 3/3/2011) [辽宁阜新市长齐继慧在市政府全体会议上的讲话 2011年3月3日]
8 Lian Weiliang: Speech for Municipal Pension Coverage Expansion Work Conference (Luoyang of Henan province, 14/10/2006) [河南洛阳副市长连维良在全市养老保险扩面征缴工作会议上的讲话 2006年10月14日]
9 Liu Daoqi: Speech for Municipal Economic Work Conference (Sanming of Fujian province, 17/1/2011) [福建三明市长刘道崎在全市经济工作会议上的讲话 2011年1月17日]
10 Liu Daoqi: Speech for Municipal Economic Work Conference (Sanming of Fujian province, 17/1/2011) [福建三明市长刘道崎在全市经济工作会议上的讲话 2011年1月17日]
11 Liu Keqing: Speech for Municipal Economic Work Conference (Zhangzhou of Fujian province, 31/12/2010) [福建漳州市长刘可清在全市经济工作会议上的讲话 2010年12月31日]
12 Su Zhequn: Speech for Municipal Surplus Agricultural Worker Transfer and Employment Work Conference (Guangzhou of Guangdong province, 11/11/2003) [广东广州市长苏泽群在广州市农村富余劳动力转移就业工作现场会上的讲话2003年11月11日]
13 Liu Keqing: Speech for Municipal Economic Work Conference (Zhangzhou of Fujian province, 31/12/2010) [福建漳州市长刘可清在全市经济工作会议上的讲话 2010年12月31日]
14 Su Zhequn: Speech for Municipal Surplus Agricultural Worker Transfer and Employment Work Conference (Guangzhou of Guangdong province, 11/11/2003) [广东广州市长苏泽群在广州市农村富余劳动力转移就业工作现场会上的讲话2003年11月11日]
15 Ibid.
16 Shen Bonian: Speech for Municipal Pension Coverage Expansion Work Conference (Guangzhou of Guangdong province, 10/11/1998) [广东广州副市长沈柏年在扩大养老保险覆盖面工作会议上的讲话 1998年11月10日]
17 Lin Shusen: Speech for the Third Municipal Individual and Private Business Work Conference (Guangzhou of Guangdong province, 29/5/1998) [广东广州市长林树森在广州市第三次个体、私营经济工作会议上的讲话 1998年5月29日]
18 Lin Shusen: Speech for Municipal Private Business Work Conference (Xiamen of Fujian province, 30/7/2003) [福建厦门市长郑中立在全市民营经济工作会议上的讲话2003年7月30日]
19 Lian Weiliang: Speech for Municipal Pension Coverage Expansion Work Conference (Luoyang of Henan province, 14/10/2006) [河南洛阳副市长连维良在全市养老保险扩面征缴工作会议上的讲话 2006年10月14日]
20 Ibid.
21 Ibid.
22 Ibid.
23 Chen Zhenggao: Speech for Municipal Economic Work Conference (Shenyang of Liaoning province, 17/2/2005) [辽宁沈阳市长陈政高在全市经济工作会议上的讲话 2005年2月17日]
24 Cai Guangxin: Speech for Municipal Pension Work Conference (Sanming of Xiamen province, 8/5/2008) [福建三明社保局长蔡光信在全市养老保险工作会议上的讲话 2008年5月8日]
25 The five dimensions are: (1) state-market relations in terms of, for example, the proportion of commodities whose prices are regulated by the government; (2) the development of the non-state sector; (3) maturity of the commodity market; (4)

maturity of the factor market; and (5) the development of market intermediary organisations like law firms and trade associations.

26 Coefficients of variables of Model 1 in Table 5.1 are unstandardised. If we standardise them, which allows us to compare the size of effects of variables, then we can see the standardised coefficient of *Insider* is 0.16, meaning a 1 standard deviation change in *Insider* results in a 0.16 standard deviation change in the dependent variable. The standardised coefficients of the control variables are: *Industrialisation* (0.08), *Marketisation* (0.39) and *Central Subsidy* (0.20). It is clear that the effect of political institutions, as indicated by the variable of *Insider*, is close to, if not larger than, that of the socio-economic factors.

27 To concentrate economic resources authoritatively on certain projects presumes that the state has some knowledge on where to put these resources. Where does such knowledge come from? Often the state gets it by learning from pioneering countries, an activity captured by the notion of "backwardness advantage". This therefore relates to the issue of late-industrialisation we discussed in the literature review in Chapter 2.

7 Conclusion

Economic rebalancing and the future of China's pension system

This book explores the political-economic logic of China's welfare state, drawing on its pension system as an example. By studying the Chinese pension system in light of the political-economic framework, this book shows how it is shaped by the interaction between political institutions, economic developmental strategy through welfare policy and human capital investments in labour markets. This approach sees China's pension system as an integral part of the Chinese political economy, thereby avoiding the common mistake of treating the pension arrangement as a separate, self-contained entity. This gives us the opportunity to examine some of China's greatest economic issues through the lens of the political-economic logic of China's pension arrangement. Indeed, if China's welfare state is often designed for developmental purposes, as discovered by this study, then it is bound to have impacts on the Chinese economy. Drawing on the political-economic framework of this study, this chapter shows how China's welfare state is partially responsible for its imbalanced economic growth model, characterised by an overreliance on export-led manufacturing industries and the laggard development of the service economy. It argues that the expansive Chinese pension system facilitates the expansion of the manufacturing sector by subsidising the training of workers with industrial specific skills, as this system is designed to do, but it has an unintended consequence: The social security taxes required to fund the pension programmes are likely to harm the growth of the service economy by imposing heavy financial burdens on the service firms (Bradley and Stephens 2007; Nelson and Stephens 2013), which suffer productivity stagnation and therefore cannot compensate the social security costs through productivity growth. Rebalancing the Chinese economy, the overriding priority in Chinese government's post-crisis macroeconomic policy, therefore requires adjustments to the Chinese pension system. To the contrary of the popular policy prescription that advocates pension centralisation, the political-economic framework of this study suggests that certain elements of the current pension system's decentralised structure should be maintained. Only with a decentralised structure can we harness the Chinese polity's most dynamic element, namely the interregional competition, to achieve the target of economic rebalancing. Therefore, in this final chapter this study engages with the literature on the expansion of service sector employment (Iversen and Wren 1998; Wren 2013; Nelson and Stephens 2013) and the policy debate on

China's economic rebalancing (Blanchard and Giavazzi 2006; Deer and Song 2012; Fukumoto and Muto 2012). Let us begin by summarising the findings of this research, that is, the political-economic logic of China's pension system.

The political-economic logic of China's pension system

This book aims to reveal the political-economic nexus underlying the Chinese welfare state. "Political-economic nexus" means the interconnection and complementarity between the political institutions (that provides the incentive structure facing political actors), the welfare policy (that is chosen by politicians under the incentive structure) and the economic decisions in labour markets (that are made by economic agents such as workers and employers in response to the welfare policy). This interaction produces a self-reinforcing equilibrium in the sense that institutions generate policy, the policy shapes economic decisions and economic decisions produce outcomes that make economic actors constituents of the policy and the institutions. Only in light of this equilibrium can we have a full understanding of the political and economic forces that shape the welfare state. To uncover the political-economic logic of the Chinese welfare state, this study focuses on its urban pension system, because it is the most important component of China's welfare regime in terms of expenditures. In other words, the fact that the Chinese welfare regime is "pension-dominant" warrants the central place of the public pension system in the study of China's welfare state (Frazier 2010).

The Chinese urban pension system has two prominent yet puzzling features in international comparison. First, the authoritarian Chinese state abolished the socialist occupational pensions for state sector workers and has applied an inclusive approach to pension reform that extends the coverage of pension programmes, while democracies in the developing world largely retained their corporatist welfare arrangements that entrench special interests. Secondly, while almost all large countries have integrated pension systems at the national level, China has its public old-age pension system fragmented on a regional basis, despite the authoritarian central government's efforts to consolidate this system for more than one decade. How can we explain these two characteristics within one theoretical framework?

To solve our puzzles, this study puts China's pension reform in the context of two structural changes in the Chinese economy, namely industrial upgrading and labour market tightening. These two trends have gained momentum since the early 2000s, coinciding with the pension reform that fully started in 1997. Industrial upgrading sees the Chinese economy climbing up the value chain and producing more technologically sophisticated products. The upgrading of the industrial structure and technology requires a corresponding improvement of workforce skills. The condition of labour market tightening, on the other hand, intensifies the labour market competition for skilled labour force among employers and raises the issue of retaining skilled workers. Both of the structural changes point to the importance of a skilled workforce to economic development. Under such circumstances, social protection programmes like public pension can serve crucial economic functions.

On the basis of statistical analysis of quantitative data at the micro and macro level, this book finds that in China the presence of public pension programmes is positively linked with students' willingness to join vocational education and employers' inclination to provide vocational trainings, while it is negatively related with workers' disposition to change jobs. The qualitative materials, drawn from newspaper data on views of workers and employers, reveal the reason why this is the case. It seems that the localised Chinese pension system, by insuring the covered workers against the loss of lifetime income, encourage individuals to acquire skills that are specific for certain industries, and, by incurring extra costs to cross-locality job changing, deters job turnover and poaching, thereby giving employers incentives to invest in workers' skill development. Therefore, pension policy is beneficial for the skill formation of Chinese workers, which is of crucial importance to economic growth under the circumstances of industrial upgrading and labour market tightening.

Given the economic benefits of pension policy, it can be expected that Chinese municipal bureaucrats, who are passionate about outperforming their counterparts in generating economic growth, will resort to pension policy for developmental purposes. This is supported by qualitative analysis of internal speeches by Chinese municipal leaders. The inter-municipal economic competition is driven by institutional arrangements of China's decentralised authoritarianism, notably the bureaucratic promotion tournament and the Chinese-style political decentralisation. When the central government's promise to promote the best-performing officials is credible, municipal leaders will be motivated to compete with each other to foster local economic development through various measures, including adopting an expansionary pension policy for the purpose of skill formation. They also tend to keep the pension programmes localised along the municipal borders, because this could prevent skilled workers from leaving their locality and joining the labour force of the competing municipalities. These predictions have been supported by statistical analysis of macro-level data on Chinese provinces. Therefore, we can conclude that the competition between Chinese political actors to utilise the economic benefits of pension programmes, among other things, is responsible for the expansive and localised nature of China's pension system.

The above political-economic interaction is modelled as a three-stage process. First, the central government appoints the provincial leadership in accordance with the institutional rules of bureaucratic promotion tournament and Chinese-style political decentralisation. Next, under the career incentive structure shaped by these institutional arrangements, municipal leaders move to adopt and implement pension policy. In the final stage economic agents such as workers and employers respond to such policy by making human capital investment decisions. The interactions among economic and political agents constitute an equilibrium in the sense that there exists a feedback loop between institutions, policies and economic outcomes.

Having discovered the political-economic logic of China's pension system, this study has clear theoretical implications. First, it contributes to the Varieties of Capitalism theory by empirically testing the hypothesised positive impacts of social protection on skill formation in the Chinese context. Given the political weakness of the Chinese trade unions, one can identify economic efficiency, rather than the redistributive cause championed by labour movements, as the major rationale for welfare expansion. In this sense, this study also demonstrates the crucial role of economic considerations in welfare state development. Secondly, by revealing the economic functions of social policy, this study adds to the Statist account of welfare state formation. The state-centred theory on welfare politics normally sees social policy as a tool utilised by state actors and ruling bureaucrats to appease challenging social groups. This study shows that, in the case of Chinese bureaucrats, considerations of economic performance and career advancement also drive state actors to push for welfare state building. Finally, this book contributes to the institutionalist model of welfare politics. The institutionalist account of social policymaking focuses on how political competition is regulated by institutional settings in electoral democracies and what impacts such institutionally structured competition has on welfare politics. By showing how institutions in an authoritarian state (i.e., China) regulate political competition and affect social policymaking, this study broadens our understanding of the institutional underpinnings of welfare politics.

In addition to contributing to the existing literature, the political-economic framework of this study is also able to shed light on some of the most pressing economic challenges confronting China today. Indeed, designed for developmental purposes, China's pension system is deeply embedded in the Chinese economy and has shaped the economy in profound ways. The next section examines the structure of the Chinese economy through the lens of this study's political-economic framework.

Pension system and China's economic imbalance

The political-economic logic has shown that China's pension system is dictated by the need of the Chinese economy. Through the lens of this political-economic framework we can make sense of some of the most important aspects of the Chinese economy. The most critical issue about the Chinese economy after the financial crisis (i.e., after 2007) was its imbalanced structure. In March 2007, at the press conference after the annual meeting of the National People's Congress, China's former Premier Wen Jiabao warned that the economic development in China was "unsteady, imbalanced, uncoordinated, and unsustainable" (People's Daily 2007). At that time Mr Wen's remarks were only interpreted as his characteristic rhetoric and few took it seriously. Indeed, since 1978 the Chinese economy has expanded at a near double-digit the average annual rate. Moreover, after 2007, when the global economy plunged into the greatest recession in decades, China weathered the financial crisis fairly well after launching a multi-billion stimulus plan. Entering 2012, however, the optimism about the health of the Chinese economy has turned sour. With the effects of the stimulus plan fading away and a swift recovery of the global demand not in evidence, China's economic growth started to slow. The growth rate for the first quarter of 2013 slowed to a record low of 7.5 percent, which led Paul Krugman (2013) to comment in *New York Times* that "Just the other day we were afraid of the Chinese. Now we're afraid for them". What's wrong with the Chinese economy?

The answer points to Mr. Wen's diagnosis of the Chinese economy, which emphasises its imbalanced structure. According to Nicholas Lardy (2012), there are two main approaches to measuring the extent to which an economy is balanced. The first is the production approach, which examines the relative share of different sectors (i.e., agriculture, industry and service) in total output. While this approach looks at the economy from the supply side, the second approach, called the expenditure approach, observes the economy from the demand side. The expenditure approach examines the composition of aggregate demand by investigating the respective share of consumption, investment, government spending and net exports.

Figure 7.1 displays the changing structure of the Chinese economy from the production perspective. As shown in the graph, there was a constant decline in the share of agricultural sector in the past three decades, which reflects the unceasing industrialisation and urbanisation of the Chinese economy. The service sector expanded rapidly, but its share never exceeded that of the industry (i.e., the manufacturing and construction sector), which accounted for almost half of

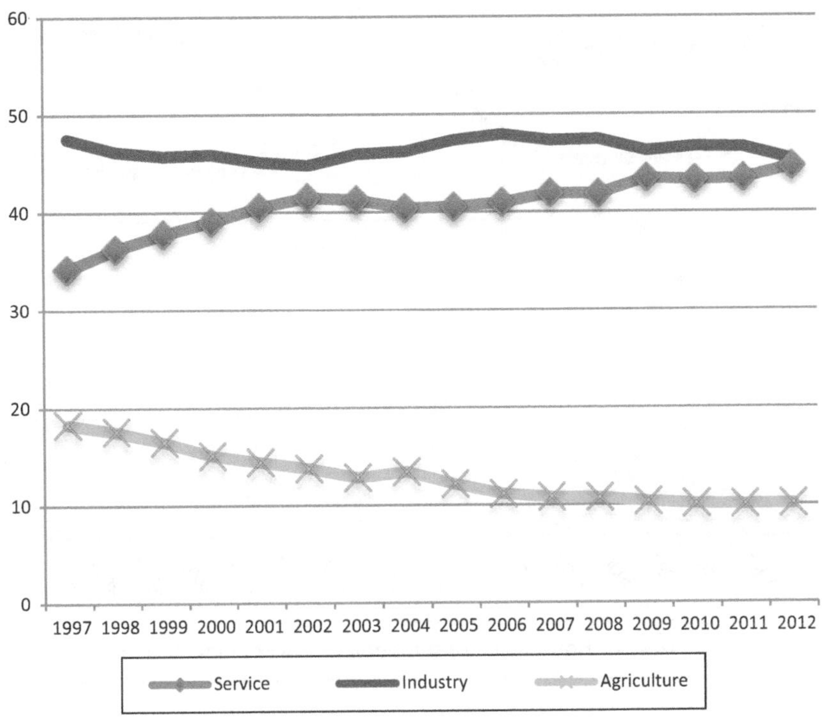

Figure 7.1 China's economic structure: production approach (% of GDP, 1997–2012)
Source: China Statistical Yearbooks (1998–2012)

the overall output for the past decade. It is revealing to note that China's service economy kept growing steadily until 2002, after which its development became stagnant, only to have a weak recovery after 2008, when the export-led industrial sector was hit hard by the global recession. As mentioned in Chapter 1, the year of 2002 was the first time China saw labour shortage, which intensified the competition for workers in the labour market. This gave the pension programmes, designed for the purpose of labour retention, real momentum to expand. It is no coincidence that the ceasing of the service sector expansion and the growth of the pension system happened in the same year, 2002. As shall be discussed in detail below, the expensive social insurance schemes like public pension are partially responsible for the stagnant development of the Chinese service economy.

Given the dominant status of the manufacturing and construction industries and the fact that capital investment is disproportionately concentrated in these sectors, it is not surprising to find the importance of investment to China's aggregate demand. Figure 7.2 examines the Chinese economy from the expenditure

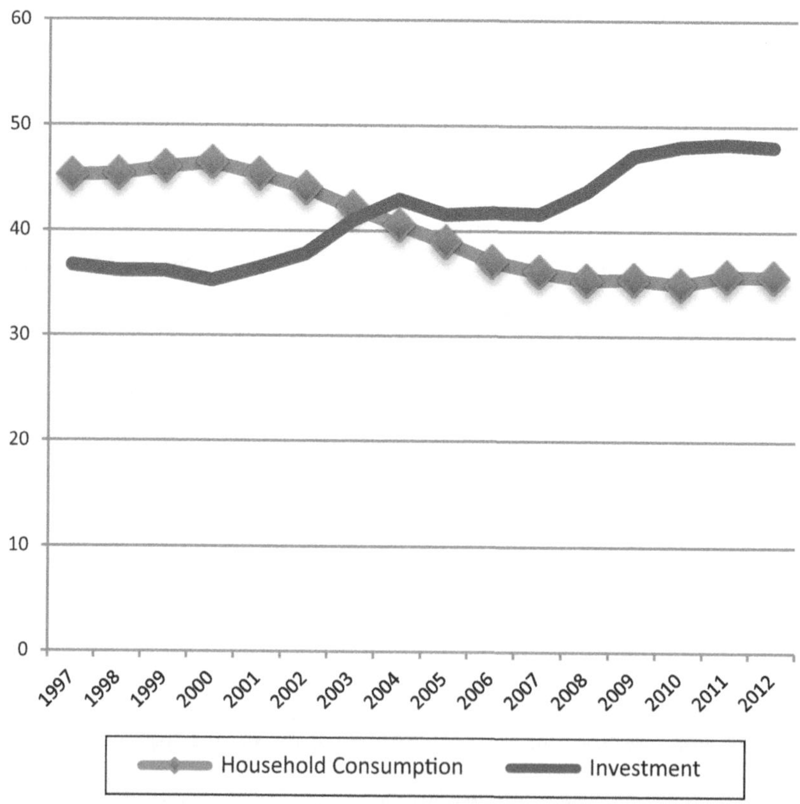

Figure 7.2 China's economic structure: expenditure approach (Percent of GDP, 1997–2012)

Source: China Statistical Yearbooks (1998–2012)

perspective. It shows a continuing drop in the share of private consumption in China's GDP and an accelerating surge in the ratio of investment, which surpassed that of household consumption in 2002, the year when the service sector stopped expanding and the share of industrial sectors in the economy started to rise. The share of household consumption, which stood at around 35 percent, is the lowest among the world's major economies (Lardy 2012).

The dominance of the industry and the relative weakness of the service sector, which is responsible for the overreliance on investment to sustain aggregate demand, is the clearest indication of China's economic imbalance (Pettis 2013). The imbalanced growth model is a prominent feature of the Chinese economy. The share of industrial sector in China is higher than would be expected in a country at a comparable level of economic development, while the contribution of the service sector to the Chinese economy is much lower than in other countries at China's GDP level.

The imbalanced growth model, with an overemphasis on the export-led industrial sector and capital investment, served the Chinese economy well when the external demand was strong (Zheng 2010). Indeed, when the domestic consumption is weak, the production capacity built through excessive investments in the industrial sector has to be absorbed elsewhere. The extra demand is most likely to come from the external, i.e., the global market. So when the economies in advanced countries and emerging markets were booming and craving Chinese products, as they did before the current recession, the Chinese economy fared quite well. But when the world economy was hit by the financial crisis, which led to a plummet in global demand, surplus production capacity in the Chinese economy had nowhere to go and became a serious liability. This is a perfect illustration of the renowned Harrod – Domar model of economic growth (Harrod 1939; Domar 1946). In this model, investment has a dual role in an economy: In the short run, investment is a major source of demand. In the long run, investment will become the source of production capacity on the supply side. An economy that relies on investment to boost demand in the short run, like China, therefore faces the challenge of dealing with the extra production capacity that is gradually built up over the long run. If it fails to release the excess capacity, then the problem of overcapacity will lead to an imbalanced economy that has no sufficient demand to match the supply. The result is the economic slowdown. This is the situation we see in China today.

To get China out of this trouble, therefore, the Chinese authorities have to rebalance the economy, i.e., to make China's economic development dependent less upon the capital-intensive industrial sector and more on the consumption-led service economy. To this aim, they should be aware of the causes of China's overreliance on the industrial sector. The finding of this book, i.e., the political-economic logic of China's pension system, offers one explanation of why China's economy is dominated by the industry. The prominence of the industrial economy, or alternatively, the weakness of the service sector, owes much to China's extensive social insurance system that serves the purpose of local industrial skill formation for the competing regional governments. The reason is twofold. First, as this book has demonstrated through qualitative and quantitative analysis, China's localised social protection programmes like pension, by insuring individuals against the risks of lifetime income loss and helping employers deal with the problem of labour retention, encourage investment in the acquisition of industrial skills. Chinese municipal authorities, by funding the expansion of local pension programmes under the pressure of interregional economic competition, are essentially bestowing subsidies to the supply of skilled labour force, the production factor that is essential for the development of the industrial sector. With the crucial input (i.e., a skilled workforce) underpriced, the unusually strong growth of the industrial sector in the Chinese economy should not be surprising. This is consistent with the argument in the economics literature that China's manufacturing-biased production structure can be attributed to the Chinese state's deliberate downward distortion of the prices for several key industrial inputs, like credit, land, energy, environmental charges, etc. (Huang and Wang 2011).

Secondly, in addition to facilitating the expansion of the manufacturing industry, China's social insurance system directly limits the growth of the service sector. As we have discussed above, the expansion of social insurance programmes like public pension, which is spurred by the interregional race for industrialisation, promotes the growth of the manufacturing sector by facilitating the training of skilled workers this sector needs. But the social insurance contribution fees, which are indiscriminately imposed on firms in all sectors, pose a financial burden to employers of the service economy, which suffers a stagnation of productivity growth and thus cannot compensate the costs of social insurance contribution by increasing productivity as the manufacturing sector does. The lack of productivity gains in the service sector was first identified by Baumol and Bowen (1966) and has since been widely accepted by economists (for example, see Gordon 1987), despite the difficulty to measure productivity in the service industry. The service economy's productivity stagnation becomes a centrepiece in the analysis of its employment expansion (for instance, see Iversen and Wren 1998). One result of the stagnation of productivity in the service sector is that payroll taxes may hamper the development of the services industry, especially that of its low-end segment,[1] by discouraging the labour-intensive service firms to expand through employing more service workers.

The adverse effects of social security payroll taxes on service economy growth have been documented in the literature on the service transition in advanced economies (Wren 2013). The statistical analysis by Bradley and Stephens (2007) on a pooled dataset of 17 industrialised democracies across 1974–1999 shows that social security taxes dampen national employment performance, suggesting that with the end of employment expansion in the industrial sector, the employment growth comes from the service employment expansion and therefore depends on how the service expansion is facilitated or constrained by institutional settings like the social protection system. Nelson and Stephens (2013) find a similar pattern, extending the work by Huo et al. (2008) to an updated dataset of 18 advanced economies from 1972 to 2004.

There is not much literature on the service expansion in China and how it is related with the welfare regime, perhaps due to the fact that China has not reached the stage of deindustrialisation, but Chinese policymakers and employers know well that social security taxes may have harmed the service business. It is reported that the head of municipal labour and social security bureau of Maoming City, Guangdong province once warned "[i]f we impose[d] social insurance fees forcibly on local business, then our service firms like restaurants and hotels would all go bankrupt" (*Guangzhou Daily* 2007). This view echoes employers like Zhou Zhongyi (2011), general manager of Chengdu Security Service Company, who expresses to CGBA (China's national private security employers association) his concern about the fact that the passage and enforcement of *Social Insurance Law* has raised the social security costs for security service firms, often resulting in frontline security workers getting laid off. The adverse impact of social security taxes is felt not only in the service economy's low-end segment but also in the high-end service business. In June 2013, Ma Yiming, CEO of Camelot Information System Inc., the Chinese branch of the U.S. Camelot Business Inc. that offers business IT solutions and consultancy, complained at the Shanghai Smart City Forum that "Shanghai's current social security system harms the development of modern service industries" (Dongfang Daily 2013). According to him, social security taxes reduce the income of employees, which makes it hard for services firms like his to attract high-skilled talents from other domestic regions and foreign countries. Given the harmful effects of social security fees on the growth of the service sector, it is not surprising to find that Chinese local governments, when they are to foster the service economy expansion, will subsidise service workers on the participation in social programmes, as the Ningbo municipal government did when it offered a 50 percent discount on social insurance contribution fees to all household service workers (Ningbo Evening Post 2012).

China's extensive social insurance system, therefore, is likely to have contributed to an imbalanced model of economic growth, which is highly skewed towards manufacturing industries and lagging behind in terms of service economy development. This is why there is a positive relationship between the coverage of urban pension programmes and the share of industrial workers with specific skills in the labour force and a negative association between that coverage and the ratio of service workers with general skills, as we have seen in Chapter 6 (please refer to Tables 5.7 and 5.8). This is a clear indication of the Chinese welfare state's positive effects on manufacturing expansion and its adverse impacts on service development.[2]

Does China need a nationally unified pension system? A case for the decentralised structure

China's imbalanced growth model, which remains one of the greatest challenges for Chinese policymakers to address in the coming years, owes much to its welfare regime. Thus, to rebalance the growth formula so the industrial and service sectors could have healthy and sustainable proportions in the economy requires adjustments on the Chinese welfare state, especially on its most expensive component, the public pension system. Then what reform measures are needed? The fact that expensive social insurance programmes obstruct the growth of the service sector may suggest the retrenchment of the Chinese welfare state. This would be a self-defeating option. Cutting welfare benefits and hence employer social insurance contributions could ease the financial burdens on firms, but it will equally reduce the perceived wealth of workers and will in no way lead them to form stable expectations about the future. This will increase their disposition to make savings and reduce their willingness to consume (Horioka and Wan 2007). Indeed, there is extensive literature on how social benefit programmes, including age-related schemes, serve the role as the smoother of consumption and hence the stabiliser of aggregate demand during recessions (Darby and Melitz 2008; Prasad and Gerecke 2010; Jochem 2011). Reducing welfare benefits, therefore, will not help to transform the investment-led economy in China into a consumption-fuelled one. Strengthening welfare provision, on the other hand, is what's needed after the 2008 financial crisis, when the aggregate demand has to be maintained at a certain level to sustain economic growth.

It is therefore not surprising to find the Chinese central authority has devised several strategies to reinforce various social insurance programmes since 2009 (The Economist 2012). In the case of public pension, the measures range from injecting more public money into the pension funds to raising the compulsory benefit level. Of particular relevance to this study is the move to unify the localised pension system at the national level in the near future, which has been codified in the 2010 *Social Insurance Law*. The Chinese central authorities hope that the centralisation of the public pension system will improve the efficiency of pension funds allocation across localities, thereby addressing the problem of regional disparities in benefit levels and contribution rates (Reuters 2013).

This study acknowledges the importance of tackling regional inequalities and the crucial role of pension centralisation in addressing this problem. Indeed, Chinese citizens' rights to old-age income security should not depend upon where they choose to work or retire. The integration of the public pension system at the national level, by allowing the central government to pool and allocate pension resources countrywide, ensures that every Chinese citizen should enjoy equal pension rights no matter where he or she happens to be born or decides to work and live. However, public policymaking is about making trade-offs. The policy of pension centralisation does not generate those benefits without paying prices. This study, based on the political-economic logic of China's pension system, argues that the centralisation of the pension system, while ensuring equal pension rights among Chinese citizens, would snuff out the potential of China's decentralised political institutions to strengthen the country's welfare state and tackle the issue of economic imbalance.

That China's decentralised political institutions have the potential to enhance its welfare state is the most important policy implication of this study. The political-economic framework of this book shows that under the economic conditions of industrial upgrading and labour market tightening, China's decentralised authoritarianism motivates the local authorities to better their regional pension programmes for the purpose of skill formation and labour retention. Striping local governments of the authority over pension programmes and entrusting such authority solely with the central government will undoubtedly deprive local officials of a crucial policy tool in the labour market and therefore reduce local officials' enthusiasm about pension policy. Surely the resistance to pension integration will fade away, but so will the passion for pension expansion. Unless the central ministry in charge of running the integrated, national pension system could offer its local branches enough incentives equal to those generated by the economic competition under the decentralised regime, the prospects of further active pension reform initiatives and implementations at the local level would not be bright. At worst, in a centralised pension system, there could be a moral hazard problem, in which local governments, in anticipation that the central government would take full responsibility of pension provision and would cease to actively extend the pension coverage or to collect sufficient funds for benefit distribution but instead count on transfers or even bail out from the central government. Without the participation and contribution of local authorities, the sustainability of the pension system and the Chinese welfare state at large would be in danger.

Therefore, this study argues that while certain pension centralisation is worth pursuing, we should keep some elements of the decentralised structure of the pension system. That is to say, in addition to establishing a nationally integrated pension programme, China should allow its municipal governments to run their own pension schemes and retain the authority to set the parameters of their pension programmes, like contribution rate and benefit level, according to their local conditions. The municipal pension scheme would be like the employer-provided occupational pension, but instead of being funded by a firm, it is funded by a locality, or precisely, funded by a combination of funding sources from local government, employers and workers within one locality. Financial aids from higher levels of government should be cut off in order to have the municipal government solely responsible for the provision of the municipal pension, thereby avoiding the moral hazard problem.

Retaining the decentralised structure of the pension system is meant to allow the municipal government to utilise pension policy as a strategy in the inter-municipal competition. Nothing motivates Chinese local officials better than the competition for economic performance and career advancement. With pension policy as a useful labour market tool at hand, the municipal government can set the related parameters to shape the skill profile of the labour force in its jurisdiction to match the municipality's comparative advantage. If the municipality, due to its natural endowments and geographical location for example, has the potential to develop manufacturing industries, then the municipal government can adopt an expansive pension policy to encourage the acquisition of industry specific skills, which is vital to realise that potential. But if the municipality has no comparative advantage in the manufacturing sector but is well placed to develop the service economy, then the municipal government has the option to adjust the related parameters to have a modest pension programme so the financial burdens would not be too much to snuff out the growth of service firms. That is to say, the municipal government should have the authority to adjust the generosity of local pension schemes to fit the chosen path of development. In this way, municipalities are allowed to pursue developmental strategies that suit their local comparative advantages.

This has important implications for the rebalancing of the Chinese economy. As discussed earlier, with surplus capacity becoming a burden in an era of global recession, China has to abandon the old development formula that is characterised by an overreliance on investment and manufacturing expansion. But no one, or no ministry, can tell how much manufacturing and services China should have. The economic rebalancing cannot be calculated or planned, not least because China is no longer a command economy. Then how can the rebalancing be achieved? This book suggests that we should let the inter-municipal competition do the job. The production structure of an economy, ideally, should be derived from its comparative advantage. The comparative advantage, by definition, is revealed through competition, in which all participants find out what they do best. China, due to its internal diversity, is composed of many regional economies, each with its own factor endowment and geographical location, which gives them different potentials for developing production structures (i.e., the combination of manufacturing and service industries). For regional economies to exploit their comparative advantages and realise their respective potentials, they should be left to compete freely without being intervened, as they have been doing for the past three decades. Such intervention is likely to come from the proposed centralised pension system in which a standardised pension policy would be imposed by the central government on all localities regardless of their different local conditions.[3] Local governments can be free of such outside intervention if they are entrusted with the authority to run their own pension schemes. Moreover, they can tailor the local pension programmes to suit their developmental strategies that follow their comparative advantages. With an effective policy tool at their disposal and in an environment with less central intervention, Chinese regional authorities, driven by the career incentives generated by the decentralised authoritarian polity, will exploit the comparative advantages of their jurisdictions in the economic competition. When all regions follow their comparative advantages to develop production structures accordingly, the Chinese economy, as a whole, can reach the point where it has the "right" proportion of manufacturing and service industries. This right point, instead of being designed and ordered by the central government, should emerge from the "laboratory" of interregional competition (for the literature on laboratory federalism in the Western context, see Oates (2008) for the U.S. case and Manatschal (2011) for the Swiss case).

Seen from this perspective, the interregional economic competition, shaped by China's political institutions, can be an "automatic balancer" in the functioning of the Chinese economy. Unlike the automatic stabiliser in macroeconomics like the fiscal policy, which serves as a counter-cyclical macro-control measure to dampen economic fluctuations, the interregional competition operates as an automatic mechanism that balances the economic structure. As discussed above, the production structure of an economy is based upon its comparative advantage. But comparative advantage is not fixed. It not only comes from factor endowments that are given by nature and gained through accumulation, but also depends on the fluctuating market conditions. Before the financial crisis, the global economy was booming and the demand for Chinese manufactures strong. So a surplus workforce, well-maintained industrial bases and a depreciating currency, which were good conditions for developing export-led manufacturing industries, allowed China to have the comparative advantage in industrial production and export. This is the reason why many of the Chinese regions, when under the competitive pressure to pursue economic expansion, focused on the manufacturing sector in their developmental strategies. These local manufacturing-centred strategies combined gave China an economic structure dominated by industrial production and investment. This structure, one has to admit, was based on China's comparative advantage before the financial crisis and therefore served China quite well, which is evident in the nearly double-digit growth rates of the Chinese economy before the credit crunch. The resultant imbalanced growth model only became a serious concern when the global recession changed the world market and redefined China's comparative advantage. The post-crisis global market sees a slumping demand for manufactures. The conditions favourable for manufacturing expansion ceased to be China's advantages but became a liability, or "excess capacity" as it is called. Under the new circumstances, China's local states should be allowed the freedom, through competition, to reveal China's new comparative advantage on a regional basis and adjust the production structure according to the newly emerging advantage, as they were allowed to build the previous production structure before the crisis. The production structure can be "automatically" rebalanced through a new round of interregional economic competition.

The implication is that the intervention of central government in the course of economic rebalancing is unnecessary, if not harmful. When the central state takes policy autonomy away from the local government and imposes a national policy on all regions, as would be in the case of the proposed centralisation of pension schemes, it will effectively interrupt the process of economic rebalancing through interregional competition. This is not unlike the state intervening in market competition. The inevitable result will be distortion. If the central government adopts an expensive national pension system, then regions that have comparative advantages in developing manufacturing industries, and hence are in greater need for social protection programmes for industrial skill formation purposes, will essentially receive subsidies from other regions that have no such advantages and thus have to develop other sectors like the service industry. A nationally standardised pension policy will therefore lead to the underpricing of the industrial skilled workforce and the taxing of service workers. The net result of such distortion of factor price will be an even more imbalanced production structure, with the manufacturing sector assuming a more prominent status.

Therefore, the central government should not apply centralising policies to intervene in the automatic rebalancing through interregional economic competition. What the central government should do, instead, is deal with the negative consequences of competition. Competition is itself a regulating mechanism that will prevent the local government from doing harm to social welfare. This is because any local authority that pursues economic growth at the expense of social welfare will eventually harm its economic performance and therefore lose in competition. But this never excludes the possibility that in the short run competition could have undesirable side effects. For example, under the competitive pressure, local government could be overambitious and take too many risks, which would easily lead to the failure of local projects. Such failure could also result from mistakes or bad luck. In cases like this, the loss of local citizens' welfare is inevitable, which therefore requires the central government to step in to protect citizens' wellbeing. This is not meant to let the central authority bail out the failing local government, because this will cause the moral hazard problem, which will lead the local government to be even more careless when making investment decisions in the future. On the contrary, local officials responsible for bad decisions should be held accountable, either explicitly through the administrative and organisational laws that punish incompetence, or implicitly through the bureaucratic promotion rules that deprive ineffective officials of the promotion chances. But in the process local citizens should not be punished for officials' mistakes. For the sake of social welfare and stability, the central government should provide a safety net for all Chinese citizens to guarantee their basic rights to a socially acceptable standard of living. This is why this book, while arguing a case for keeping the decentralised structure of the pension system, also supports a certain degree of pension centralisation.

Therefore, our proposal to maintain the decentralised pension system should be coupled with a certain form of national integration. The centralisation of pension system is desirable to the extent that it allows the central government to ensure Chinese citizens' basic pension rights in cases of the bankruptcy of regional pension programmes. In this way, even if the local pension scheme goes bust, local citizens' rights to basic old-age income security will still be protected under the central programme. At the same time, the central government should avoid interfering with the local autonomy in pension policymaking. A balance should be stricken between protecting citizens' pension rights from power abuses and incompetence of local officials and motivating local governments to take initiatives in pension reform and economic rebalancing. The decentralised structure of China's pension system and the decentralised structure of the Chinese state in general generate the most dynamic element in Chinese politics, namely the inter-regional competition. This element should be preserved and harnessed to deal with some of the toughest challenges China faces and will face in years to come.

Notes

1 Recent research suggests that advances in information and communications technologies (ICT) allow high-end service segments like financial intermediation and business services to enjoy productivity growth comparable to, if not higher than, that in the manufacturing sector (for example, please refer to Table 1.1 in Wren (2013: 7), which compares the growth rates of productivity in different economic sectors). Having said that, the growth of productivity in the high-end service industry has been mostly observed in postindustrial economies, while due to the

lack of literature it remains unclear whether ICT leads to productivity gains in the high-end service sector in developing countries like China. But it is certain that in the low-end segment of the service economy there is productivity stagnancy, no matter at what developmental stage the national economy is.

2 Another phenomenon that may indicate the adverse impact of the Chinese social security system on the service economy, which may be studied in future research, is the informalisation of employment in China's labour market. By "informal" it means the atypical employment that is based on the temporary contract and insufficient labour protection. After comprehensively surveying various official data sources, Park and Cai (2011) report that almost 39 percent of Chinese urban workers are employed informally, concluding that the informalisation of the Chinese labour market has been "significant over the past two decades". This trend can be understood if we take China's social insurance system into account. As argued above, this system discourages the employment of low-skilled workers. But when economic conditions require employers in the service sector to hire more workers, they resort to several types of informal employment practices to contain the costs imposed by the social insurance system. The most widespread practice is called "labour dispatching" (*laowu paiqian*), which is most common among the urban service firms. It refers to a kind of atypical employment relationship in which "workers employed by a contractor are sent to work at client firms on a contingent basis" (Gallagher et al. 2011: 2). It is a practice that aims to help employers reduce costs incurred by social insurance contributions. This is because it is the contractor, rather than the client firm, that pays the social insurance fees for the workers. Given the localised nature of China's social insurance system, the contractor then can register its business at a locality where the social insurance contribution fee rates are low and send its workers to employers in regions with high contribution fee rates. By doing so it saves the client employers the difference in social insurance fees between the two localities. No wonder service sector employers, who have to contain labour costs, are so fond of using dispatch workers. The fact that Chinese employers in the service sector go to all that trouble, like extensively employing dispatched workers, for the purpose of saving labour costs imposed by the social insurance contribution fees, is an indication of the financial burden on the service firms imposed by China's welfare state. Such burden undoubtedly constrains the development of China's service economy.

3 Admittedly, centralised policies are not necessarily standardised. Indeed, in many large, federal countries like the U.S. and India, federal policies leave ample room for interpretation to subnational governments. But China is not a federal country. Instead, China is a unitary country governed by an authoritarian party-state. This means once the local autonomy in a certain policy area is taken from regional governments, as in the case of the proposed pension centralisation, the resultant central policy is likely to be standardised. In other words, in the Chinese political context, centralised policies often mean standardised policies.

Appendix 1

Administrative structure of the Chinese government

The above chart shows the five-level administrative divisions of the Chinese state, descending from the national level to the township level. At village level there is the villager self-government, staffed by officials elected by local villagers. Therefore, the village-level government is not accountable to the township government but to the villagers, so it is not counted as part of the state administrative hierarchy.

The unit of analysis of this dissertation is the provincial-level jurisdictions. I do not include one type of provincial-level jurisdiction in my study: the special administrative zones (Hong Kong and Macau). This is because Hong Kong and Macau, with their different political and economic systems, are not comparable to other Chinese provincial-level jurisdictions. This study, therefore, looks at the other three kinds of provincial-level jurisdictions: provinces, autonomous regions (established for ethnic minorities living in a relatively compact region) and municipalities directly under the central government (Beijing, Tianjin, Shanghai and Chongqing).

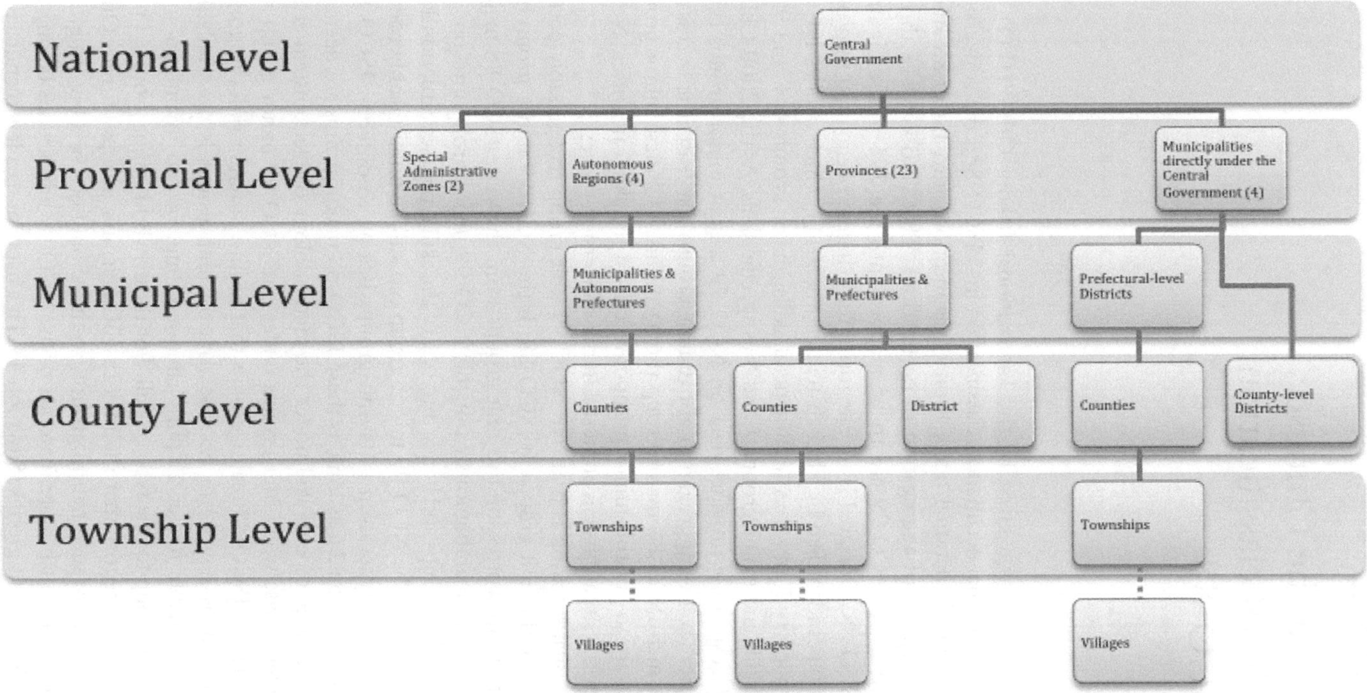

Figure A.1.1 Administrative structure of the Chinese government

Source: Drawn by the author according to the introduction to China's administrative structure at the official website of the Chinese central government (http://english.gov.cn/about/politics.htm)

Appendix 2
Converting the Chinese occupational classification into ISCO-88

Following the instruction given by the International Labour Office (ILO) on how to convert national occupation classification into ISCO-88,[1] the conversion of NCO-99 (China's national occupational classification) into ISCO-88 starts from the lowest level of aggregation of occupations. That is to say, 413 three-digit unit groups in NCO-99 are to be mapped into the 391 four-digit unit groups in ISCO-88. Our goal is to categorise the Chinese occupation into one of three skill types identified by Fleckenstein et al. (2011), which defines ISCO-88 major groups 1, 2 and 3 as high-general skills, major groups 4, 5 and 9 as low-general skills and major groups 7 and 8 as specific skills. As the 2000 China Population Census only provides data on NCO-99 2-digit minor groups (i.e., the next higher level of aggregation above unit groups), at least it is necessary to know to which ISCO-88 major group the harmonised Chinese minor group belongs if we are to put this minor group into one of the skill categories. Next, we discuss several situations encountered in the conversion process.

The most usual situation is that one NOC-99 unit group recognisably corresponds to one of the unit groups in ISCO-88. If the NCO-99 minor group has all of its unit groups correspond to unit groups from the same ISCO-88 major group, then we can unambiguously put this NCO-99 minor group into one of the ISCO-88 major groups and hence into one of the skill types (see Situation 1 in the following table). The NCO-99 minor group can still be unmistakably coded into one of the skill types even if its unit groups belong to different ISCO-88 major groups (Situation 2), as long as these ISCO-88 major groups are deemed as requiring the same type of skill under the methodology of Fleckenstein et al. (2011). Problems arise when unit groups under one NCO-99 minor group are coded into different ISCO-88 major groups that fit into different skill categories (Situation 3). This is a problem because data on unit groups is not available, which makes us unable to get a "pure" minor group, i.e., to unambiguously assign this minor group to one type of skill. For these hybrid minor groups, I put them into the skill category that the majority of their unit groups fit into. Only three minor groups are such hybrid groups, so this should not be a big issue.

There are cases in which more than one of the NCO-99 unit groups belong to one of the ISCO-88 unit groups (Situation 4). This happens to a few manufacturing occupations, which NCO-99 classifies in terms of not only the skill required but also their final products. So in NCO-99 we have occupations that require the same kind of skill but are classified into different unit groups on the basis of the final products. These unit groups therefore are assigned to the same ISCO-88 major groups and hence the same skill type category. There are also situations where one NCO-99 unit group covers more than one ISCO-88 unit group (Situation 5). Such an "overarching" NCO-99 unit group can still be assigned to one type of skill so long as the ISCO-88 unit groups it covers require the same kind of skill.

Situation	*NCO-99 examples*	*ISCO-99 four-digit unit group examples*	Skill type of *Fleckenstein et al. (2011)*
1	**25 Literary and art related workers**		
	251 Literary writers and critics 252 Directors and music conductors 253 Actors (actresses) 254 Instrument players 255 Movie and TV producers 256 Artists	2,451 Authors, journalists and other writers 2,455 Film, stage and related actors and directors 2,455 Film, stage and related actors and directors 2,453 Composers, musicians and singers 2,455 Film, stage and related actors and directors 2,452 Sculptors, painters and related artists	High-general Skills
2	**61 Quarry workers**		
	611 Mining and stone gathering workers 612 Mineral and stone processing workers 613 Drilling workers 614 Oil and natural gas mining workers 615 Salt mining workers	7,111 Miners and quarry workers 7,113 Stone splitters, cutters and carvers 8,111 Mining-plant operators 8,113 Well drillers and borers and related workers 7,111 Miners and quarry workers	Specific Skills
3	**27 Journalism and culture related Staff**		
	271 Journalist 272 Editors 273 Proofreaders 274 Broadcasters 275 Translators 276 Library and information personnel 277 Archaeologists and workers associated with historical relics	2,451 Authors, journalists and other writers 2,451 Authors, journalists and other writers 4,143 Coding, proofreading and related clerks 3,472 Radio, television and other announcers 2,444 Philologists, translators and interpreters 2,431 Archivists and curators; 2,432 Librarians and related information professionals	High-general Skills

(*Continued*)

Situation	*NCO-99 examples*	*ISCO-99 four-digit unit group examples*	Skill type of *Fleckenstein et al. (2011)*
		2,442 Sociologists, anthropologists and related professionals	
4	623 Ferroalloy smelting related workers 624 Heavy non-ferrous metal smelting related workers 625 Light non-ferrous metal smelting related workers 626 Precious and rare metal smelting related workers	8,121 Ore and metal furnace operators	Specific Skills
5	311 Administrative management staff of practical affairs	3,441 Customs and border inspectors 3,442 Government tax and excise officials 3,443 Government social benefits officials 3,444 Government licensing officials 3,449 Customs, tax and related government associate professionals not elsewhere classified	High-general Skills

The discussion above suggests that the lack of information on NCO-99 unit groups will pose an obstacle to the harmonisation of NCO-99 in accordance with ISCO-88. Without such information, given the existence of the "hybrid" minor group that is composed of several unit groups that can be put under different ISCO-88 major groups, it is almost impossible to map accurately such "hybrid" minor group into any ISCO-88 minor or even major group without making sacrifices like applying certain kinds of rules to get rid of some unit groups. Even with the data on NCO-99 unit groups, we still do not know to which ISCO-88 major group we should assign the "overarching" NCO-99 unit group that covers more than one of the ISCO-88 unit groups from different major groups. Despite the learning from ISCO-88 in the making of NCO-99, the conceptual and structural differences between the two systems are still very much evident, posing challenge to any attempt of harmonisation between NCO-99 and ISCO-88. Fortunately the aim of this study is recoding NCO-99 not so much into ISCO-88 as into one of the three skill types specified by Fleckenstein et al. (2011). So the problems discussed above present less of a threat. But these problems are the reason why this study does not adopt the harmonisation procedure used by previous research (for example, the one used by the Minnesota Population Center, available at https://cps.ipums.org/cps/), which seems to have produced neatly harmonised Chinese occupational data according to ISCO-88 but neither specifies the sources of the unit group level data nor the rules used to deal with the "overarching" unit groups. Clearly, there is still work to do before we can satisfactorily map China's national occupational classification into ISCO-88.

Note

1 For the instruction, please see www.ilo.org/public/english/bureau/stat/isco/isco88/publ7.htm.

References

Acemoglu, Daron. 1996. "A Microfoundation for Social Increasing Returns in Human Capital Accumulation." *The Quarterly Journal of Economics* 111(3): 779–804.

Acemoglu, Daron, and Jorn-Steffen Pischke. 1999. "Beyond Becker: Training in Imperfect Labour Markets." *The Economic Journal* 109(February): F112–F142.

Acemoglu, Daron, and Jorn-Steffen Pischke. 2000. "Certification of Training and Training Outcomes." *European Economic Review* 44(4–6): 917–927.

Achen, Christopher H. 1986. *The Statistical Analysis of Quasi-Experiments.* Los Angeles: University of California Press.

Agarwala, Ramgopal. 1998. "Unification of Pension System in China: Lessons of Experience from Other Countries." *Paper Presented at the International Conference on Old-Age Security Reform and Pension Funds Management,* Beijing: Economic Science Press.

Ahmad, Ehtisham, Vito Tanzi, and Qiang Gao. 1995. *Reforming China's Public Finances.* Washington, DC: International Monetary Fund.

Akerlof, George A. 1982. "Labor Contracts as Partial Gift Exchange." *The Quarterly Journal of Economics* 97(4): 543–569.

Akerlof, George A. 1984. "Gift Exchange and Efficiency-Wage Theory: Four Views." *American Economic Review* 74(2): 79–83.

Alber, Jens, and Guy Standing. 2000. "Social Dumping, Catch-up or Convergence? Europe in a Comarative Global Context." *Journal of European Social Policy* 10(2): 99–119.

Alesina, Alberto, Vittorio Grilli, and Gian Maria Milesi-Ferretti. 1994. "The Political Economy of Capital Controls." In *Capital Mobility: The Impact on Consumption, Investment and Growth.* Cambridge: Cambridge University Press, pp. 678–706.

Allen, Franklin, Jun Qian, and Meijun Qian. 2008. "China's Financial System: Past, Present, and Future." In *China's Great Economic Transformation.* Cambridge: Cambridge University Press, pp. 506–568.

Allianz International Pensions. 2013. "What's Happening in India." http://projectm-online.com/new-perspectives/indias-pension-puzzle. (Accessed October 22, 2013).

Allison, Paul D. 1984. *Event History Analysis: Regression for Longitudinal Event Data.* London: SAGE.

Alvarez, R. Michael, Geoffrey Garrett, and Peter Lange. 1991. "Government Partisanship, Labor Organization, and Macroeconomic Performance." *American Political Science Review* 85(2): 539–556.

Amsden, Alice H. 1989. *Asia's Next Giant: South Korea and Late Industrialization.* Oxford: Oxford University Press.

Anderson, Perry. 2010. "Two Revolutions." *New Left Review* 61: 71–87.

Andrietti, Vincenzo. 2001. "Portability of Supplementary Pension Rights in the European Union." *International Social Security Review* 54(1): 59–83.

Angrist, Joshua D., and Alan B. Krueger. 1999. "Empirical Strategies in Labor Economics." In *Handbook of Labor Economics, Elsevier*, pp. 1277–1366.

Aoki, Masahiko. 1994. "The Contingent Governance of Teams: Analysis of Institutional Complementarity." *International Economic Review* 35(3): 657–676.

Aoki, Masahiko. 2001. *Toward a Comparative Institutional Analysis.* New York: MIT Press.

Armingeon, Klaus., and Bonoli, Giuliano. 2006. *The Politics of Post-Industrial Welfare States.* London: Routledge.

Arrow, Kenneth. 1951. *Social Choice and Individual Values.* New Haven: Yale University Press.

Arrow, Kenneth. 1973. "Higher Education as Filter." *Journal of Public Economics* 2(3): 193–216.

Avato, Johanna, Johannes Koettl, and Rachel Sabates-Wheeler. 2009. "Definitions, Good Practices, and Global Estimates on the Status of Social Protection for International Migrants." *The World Bank Social Protection Discussion Paper Series No. 49172.* Washington, D.C.: The World Bank.

Ba, Shusong. 2005. "Challenges Confronting Banking Sector." *Business Weekly China*, 7 Feb. 2005.

Babbie, Earl. 1992. *The Practice of Social Research.* New York: Cengage Learning.

Baldacci, Emanuele, Benedict Clements, Sanjeev Gupta, and Cui Qiang. 2008. "Social Spending, Human Capital, and Growth in Developing Countries." *World Development* 36(8): 1317–1341.

Banting, Keith. 1987. *Welfare State and Canadian Federalism.* Montreal: McGill-Queen's University Press.

Barr, Nicholas. 1989. "Social Insurance as an Efficiency Device." *Journal of Public Policy* 9(1): 59–82.

Barro, Robert J. 1991. "Economic Growth in a Cross Section of Countries." *The Quarterly Journal of Economics* 106(2): 407.

Barro, Robert J. 1996. "Determinants of Economic Growth: A Cross-Country Empirical Study." *NBER Working Paper 5698.* Cambridge, MA: National Bureau of Economic Research.

Barron, John, Mark Berger, and Dan Black. 1997. "How Well Do We Measure Training." *Journal of Labour Economics* 15(3): 507–528.

Barron, John, Mark Berger, and Dan Black. 1999. "Replacing General Training with Specific Training: Why Restricting Alternatives Makes Sense." *Research in Labor Economics* 18: 281–302.

Barron, John, Dan Black, and Mark Loewenstein. 1989. "Job Matching and On-the-Job Training." *Journal of Labor Economics* 7(1): 1–19.

Barzel, Yoram. 2002. *A Theory of the State: Economic Rights, Legal Rights, and the Scope of the State.* Cambridge: Cambridge University Press.

Baumol, William J., and William G. Bowen. 1966. *Performing Arts – The Economic Dilemma: A Study of Problems Common to Theater, Opera, Music, and Dance.* New York: Twentieth Century Fund.

Beck, Nathaniel, and Jonathan N. Katz. 1995. "What to do (and not to do) with Time-Series Cross-Section Data." *American Political Science Review* 89(3): 634–647.
Beck, Nathaniel, and Jonathan N. Katz. 1996. "Nuisance vs. Substance: Specifying and Estimating Time-Series-Cross-Section Models." *Political Analysis* 6(1): 1–36.
Beck, Nathaniel, and Jonathan N. Katz. 1997. "The Analysis of Binary Time-Series-Cross-Section Data and/or The Democratic Peace." *Paper Presented at the Annual Meeting of the Political Methodology Group,* Columbus, Ohio, 23-27 July.
Beck, Nathaniel, Jonathan N. Katz, and Richard Tucker. 1998. "Taking Time Seriously: Time-Series-Cross-Section Analysis with a Binary Dependent Variable." *American Journal of Political Science* 42(4): 1260–1288.
Becker, Gary S. 1962. "Investment in Human Capital: A Theoretical Analysis." *Journal of Political Economy* 70(5): 9–49.
Becker, Gary S. 1964. *Human Capital: A Theoretical and Empirical Analysis, with Special Reference to Education.* Chicago: University of Chicago Press.
Beijing Evening. 2010. "80% of Beijing Secondary Vocational Education Students Come From The Countryside (北京中等职业学校80%生源全来自农村)." http://bjwb.bjd.com.cn/html/2010-08/24/node_4.htm. (Accessed November 11, 2010).
Beramendi, Pablo. 2012. *The Political Geography of Inequality: Regions and Redistribution.* Cambridge: Cambridge University Press.
Bian, Morris L. 2009. *The Making of the State Enterprise System in Modern China: The Dynamics of Institutional Change.* Cambridge: Harvard University Press.
Birchfield, Vicki, and Markus Crepaz. 1998. "The Impact of Constitutional Structures and Collective and Competitive Veto Points on Income Inequality in Industrialized Democracies." *European Journal of Political Research* 34(2): 175–200.
Blanchard, Olivier, and Francesco Giavazzi. 2006. "Rebalancing Growth in China: A Three-Handed Approach." *China & World Economy* 14(4): 1–20.
Bland, Daniel, and Ka Man Yu. 1999. "A Long Financial March: Pension Reform in China." *Journal of Social Policy* 33(2): 267–288.
Blecher, Marc J., and Vivienne Shue. 1996. *Tethered Deer: Government and Economy in a Chinese County.* Stanford: Stanford University Press.
Bloom, Howard S. 2008. "The Core Analytics of Randomized Experiments for Social Research." In *The SAGE Handbook of Social Research Methods.* London: SAGE, pp. 169–193.
Bloomberg News. 2010. "China's Stock Markets Are Most Immature in Asia, Goldman (GS) Says." http://hedgefundmgr.blogspot.co.uk/2010/06/friday-watch_25.html. (Accessed June 26, 2012).
Blossfeld, Hans-Peter, Katrin Golsch, and Gotz Rohwer. 2007. *Event History Analysis With Stata.* New York: Psychology Press.
Blyth, Mark. 2002. *Great Transformations: Economic Ideas and Institutional Change in the Twentieth Century.* Cambridge: Cambridge University Press.
Bo, Zhiyue. 2002. *Chinese Provincial Leaders: Economic Performance and Political Mobility Since 1949.* New York: M. E. Sharpe Incorporated.
Bonoli, Giuliano. 2007. "Time Matters: Postindustrialization, New Social Risks, and Welfare State Adaptation in Advanced Industrial Democracies." *Comparative Political Studies* 40(5): 495–520.

Booth, Alison, and Mark Bryan. 2002. "Who Pays for General Training? New Evidence for British Men and Women." *IZA Discussion Paper* 486. Available at SSRN: https://ssrn.com/abstract=311759. (Accessed June 16, 2013).

Borjas, George J. 1999. "Immigration and Welfare Magnets." *Journal of Labor Economics* 17(4): 607–637.

Bracken, Gregory. 2012. *Aspects of Urbanization in China*. Amsterdam: Amsterdam University Press.

Bradley, David et al. 2003. "Distribution and Redistribution in Postindustrial Democracies." *World Politics* 55(2): 193–228.

Bradley, David H., and John D. Stephens. 2007. "Employment Performance in OECD Countries: A Test of Neoliberal and Institutionalist Hypotheses." *Comparative Political Studies* 40(12): 1486–1510.

Brady, David, Jason Beckfield, and Martin Seeleib-Kaiser. 2005. "Economic Globalization and the Welfare State in Affluent Democracies, 1975–2001." *American Sociological Review* 70: 921–948.

Brandt, Loren, Thomas Rawski, and John Sutton. 2008. "China's Industrial Development." In *China's Great Economic Transformation*, Loren Brandt and Thomas Rawski eds. Cambridge University Press, pp. 930.

Brandt, Loren, and Eric Thun. 2010. "The Fight for the Middle: Upgrading, Competition, and Industrial Development in China." *World Development* 38(11): 1555–1574.

Breznitz, Dan, and Michael Murphree. 2011. *Run of the Red Queen: Government, Innovation, Globalization, and Economic Growth in China*. New Haven: Yale University Press.

Broadman, Harry G., and Xiaolun Sun. 1997. "The Distribution of Foreign Direct Investment in China." *The World Economy* 20(3): 339–361.

Bruno, Amable. 2003. *The Diversity of Modern Capitalism*. Oxford: Oxford University Press.

Buchanan, James M., and Gordon Tullock. 1962. *The Calculus of Consent: Logical Foundations of Constitutional Democracy*. Ann Arbor: The University of Michigan Press.

Buchinsky, Moshe et al. 2010. "Interfirm Mobility, Wages and the Returns to Seniority and Experience in the United States." *Review of Economic Studies* 77(3): 972–1001.

Busemeyer, Marius R. 2007. "Determinants of Public Education Spending in 21 OECD Democracies, 1980–2001." *Journal of European Public Policy* 14(4): 582–610.

Busemeyer, Marius R. 2009. "Asset Specificity, Institutional Complementarities and the Variety of Skill Regimes in Coordinated Market Economies." *Socio-Economic Review* 7(3): 375–406.

Busemeyer, Marius R. 2013. "Education Funding and Individual Preferences for Redistribution." *European Sociological Review* 29(6): 1122–1133.

Busemeyer, Marius R., Achim Goerres, and Simon Weschle. 2009. "Attitudes Towards Redistributive Spending in An Era of Demographic Ageing: the Rival Pressures from Age and Income in 14 OECD Countries." *Journal of European Social Policy* 19(3): 195–212.

Busemeyer, Marius R., Maria Alejandra Cattaneo, and Stefan C. Wolter. 2011. "Individual Policy Preferences for Vocational versus Academic Education : Micro Level Evidence for the Case of Switzerland." *Journal of European Social Policy* 21(3): 253–273.

Busemeyer, Marius R., and Christine Trampusch. 2012. *The Political Economy of Collective Skill Formation*. Oxford: Oxford University Press.

Cahuc, Pierre, and Andre Zylberberg. 2004. *Labor Economics*. Cambridge: MIT Press.

Cai, Fang, John Giles, Philip O'Keefe, and Dewen Wang. 2012. *The Elderly and Old Age Support in Rural China*. Washington, DC: World Bank Publications.

Cai, Fang, and Meiyan Wang. 2010. "Growth and Structural Changes in Employment in Transition China." *Journal of Comparative Economics* 38(1): 71–81.

Campbell, Donald T. 1975. "'Degrees of Freedom' and the Case Study." *Comparative Political Studies* 8(2): 178–185.

Campbell, Donald T., and Julian Stanley. 1963. *Experimental and Quasi-Experimental Designs for Research*. Chicago: Rand McNally.

Cary, William L. 1974. "Federalism and Corporate Law: Reflections upon Delaware." *The Yale Law Journal* 83(4): 663–705.

Casey, Bernard. 1991. "Recent Developments in the German Apprenticeship System – Casey." *British Journal of Industrial Relations* 29(2): 205–222.

Cates, Jerry Ray. 1983. *Insuring Inequality: Administrative Leadership in Social Security, 1935–54*. Ann Arbor: University of Michigan Press.

Chan, Anita. 1993. "Revolution or Corporatism? Workers and Trade Union in Post-Mao China." *The Australian Journal of Chinese Affairs* 29: 31–61.

Chang, Chun, and Yijiang Wang. 1996. "Human Capital Investment under Asymmetric Information: The Pigovian Conjecture Revisited." *Journal of Labor Economics* 14(3): 505–519.

Changzhou Education. 2007. "Changzhou Takes New Measures on Promoting School-Enterprise Cooperation in Vocational Education (江苏常州出台职业教育校企合作办学新举措)." www.gxnews.com.cn/staticpages/20070914/newgx46e9dafc-1224524.shtml. (Accessed August 11, 2013).

Charlot, Olivier, Bruno Decreuse, and Pierre Granier. 2005. "Adaptability, Productivity, and Educational Incentives in a Matching Model." *European Economic Review* 49(4): 1007–1032.

Chen, Aimin, and N. Edward Coulson. 2002. "Determinants of Urban Migration: Evidence from Chinese Cities." *Urban Studies* 39(12): 2189–2197.

Chen, Shengxiang, and Wang Qiuping. 2009. "The Impact of Free Secondary Vocational Education Policy On Educational Investment Preferences of Peasant Household (农村中职免费政策对农户教育投资偏好的影响)." *Journal of Jiangsu Technical College (江苏技术师范学院学报)* (7): 44–56.

Chen, Xi. 2010. "State-Generated Data and Contentious Politics in China." In *Contemporary Chinese Politics : New Sources, Methods, and Field Strategies*, A Carlson et al. eds. New York: Cambridge University Press, pp. 15–32.

Chen, Ye, Hongbin Li, and Li-An Zhou. 2005. "Relative Performance Evaluation and the Turnover of Provincial Leaders in China." *Economics Letters* 88(3): 421–425.

China Economic Weekly. 2011. "Snatching People! An Investigation into Labour Shortage in Western and Central Provinces (抢人！ 中西部'民工荒'调查)." http://paper.people.com.cn/zgjjzk/html/2011-05/02/content_812194.htm?div=-1. (Accessed May 10, 2013).

China Vocational and Technical Education. 2009a. "On the Attractiveness of Vocational Education: An Interview with Li Zhong'an (职业教育吸引力访谈 – 访民盟中央副主席李重庵)." www.cvae.com.cn/www/yj/zhyj/09-12-15/5055.html. (Accessed February 25, 2013a).

China Vocational and Technical Education. 2009b. "On the Attractiveness of Vocational Education: An Interview with Zhao Weiliang (职业教育吸引力问题 – 访重庆教委副主任赵为良). " www.cvae.com.cn/www/yj/zhyj/09-12-15/5059.html. (Accessed March 1, 2013b).

Collier, David. 1993. "The Comparative Method." In *Political Science: The State of the Discipline*, Washington, DC: American Political Science Association.

Collier, David, and Richard E. Messick. 1975. "Prerequisites Versus Diffusion: Testing Alternative Explanations of Social Security Adoption." *American Political Science Review* 69(4): 1299–1315.

Cornelius, Wayne A., Todd A. Eisenstadt, and Jane Hindley. 1999. *Subnational Politics and Democratization in Mexico.* San Diego, CA: Center for Us-Mexican Studies.

Cusack, Thomas, Torben Iversen, and Philipp Rehm. 2006. "Risks at Work: The Demand and Supply Sides of Government Redistribution." *Oxford Review of Economic Policy* 22(3): 365–389.

Cutright, Phillips. 1965. "Political Structure, Economic Development, and National Social Security Programs." *American Journal of Sociology* 70(5): 537–550.

d'Addio, Anna Cristina, and Maria Chiara Cavalleri. 2013. "Labour Mobility and the Portability of Social Rights in the EU." *CESifo Working Paper: Social Protection 4153.* Munich, Germany: Center for Economic Studies and Ifo Institute (CESifo).

Darby, Julia, and Jacques Melitz. 2008. "Social Spending and Automatic Stabilizers in the OECD." *Economic Policy* 23(56): 715–756.

David, Paul A. 1985. "Clio and the Economics of QWERTY." *American Economic Review* 75(2): 332–337.

Dazong Daily. 2008. "If You Ask Me to Join Social Insurance Programmes, I Will Quit! ('要让我缴社会保险，马上辞职换个不缴的企业！')." http://insurance.cnfol.com/080428/135,1518,4087268,00.shtml. (Accessed March 7, 2013).

de Vaus, David. 2001. *Research Design in Social Research.* London: SAGE.

Decreuse, Bruno, and Pierre Granier. 2007. "Labor Market Institutions and the Divide of Schooling Investment Between General and Specific Skills." *MPRA Paper 6948,* University Library of Munich, Germany.

Deer, Luke, and Ligang Song. 2012. "China's Approach to Rebalancing: A Conceptual and Policy Framework." *China & World Economy* 20(1): 1–26.

Derthick, Martha. 1979. *Policymaking for Social Security.* Washington, DC: Brookings Institute Press.

Ding, Daniel Z., Keith Goodall, and Malcolm Warner. 2000. "The End of the 'Iron Rice-Bowl': Whither Chinese Human Resource Management?" *The International Journal of Human Resource Management* 11(2): 217–236.

Domar, Evsey D. 1946. "Capital Expansion, Rate of Growth, and Employment." *Econometrica* 14(2): 137–147.

Dongfang Daily. 2013. "Shanghai's Social Protection Arrangement "Harms Service Sector Development"(上海现行社保制度"不利服务业发展")." http://epaper.dfdaily.com/dfzb/html/2013-06/24/content_783105.htm. (Accessed September 2, 2013).

Downs, Anthony. 1957. *An Economic Theory of Democracy.* Boston: Addison-Wesley.

Dreze, Jean, and Amartya Sen. 2013. *An Uncertain Glory: India and its Contradictions.* Penguin.

Driscoll, John, and Aart Kraay. 1998. "Consistent Covariance Matrix Estimation With Spatially Dependent Panel Data." *The Review of Economics and Statistics* 80(4): 549–560.

Dube, Arindrajit, Oeindrila Dube, and Omar Garcia-Ponce. 2013. "Cross-Border Spillover: U.S. Gun Laws and Violence in Mexico." *American Political Science Review* 107(3): 397–417.

Duckett, Jane. 1998. *The Entrepreneurial State in China: Real Estate and Commerce Departments in Reform Era Tianjin.* London: Routledge.

Easterly, William. 2001. *The Elusive Quest for Growth: Economists' Adventures and Misadventures in the Tropics.* New York: MIT Press.

Eckstein, Harry. 1992. "Case Study and Theory in Political Science." In *Regarding Politics: Essays on Political Theory, Stability, and Change.* New York: University of California Press, pp. 117–178.

Economic Analytical Unit. 2005. "Unlocking China's Services Economy." *Department of Foreign Affairs and Trade, Australian Government.* Barton, A.C.T. : Department of Foreign Affairs and Trade

The Economic Observer. 2012. "Workers Elect Trade Union Reps." www.eeo.com.cn/ens/2012/0618/228497.shtml. (Accessed August 11, 2013).

The Economist. 2010a. "China's Economy: Hello, America." www.economist.com/node/16834943. (Accessed December 21, 2011a).

The Economist. 2010b. "Unions in China: Strike Breakers." www.economist.com/node/16282233. (Accessed July 11, 2013b).

The Economist. 2012. "Asian Welfare States: New Cradles to Graves." www.economist.com/node/21562210. (Accessed July 9, 2013).

Edin, Maria. 2003. "State Capacity and Local Agent Control in China: CCP Cadre Management from a Township Perspective." *The China Quarterly* (173): 35–52.

Elias, Peter. 1997. "Occupational Classification (ISCO-88): Concepts, Methods, Reliability, Validity and Cross-National Comparability." OECD Labour Market and Social Policy Occasional Papers.

Elster, Jon. 1982. "The Case for Methodological Individualism." *Theory and Society* 11(4): 453–482.

Emmenegger, Patrick, Bruno Palier, and Martin Seeleib-Kaiser. 2012. *The Age of Dualization.* New York: Oxford University Press.

Esping-Andersen, Gøsta. 1985. *Politics against Markets: The Social Democratic Road to Power.* Princeton: Princeton University Press.

Esping-Andersen, Gøsta. 1993. *Changing Classes: Stratification and Mobility in Post-Industrial Societies.* London: SAGE.

Esping-Andersen, Gøsta. 1996. *Welfare States in Transition: National Adaptations in Global Economies.* London: SAGE.

Esping-Andersen, Gøsta. 1999. *Social Foundations of Postindustrial Economies.* Oxford: Oxford University Press.

Estevez-Abe, Margarita. 2008. *Welfare and Capitalism in Postwar Japan: Party, Bureaucracy, and Business.* Cambridge: Cambridge University Press.

Estevez-Abe, Margarita, Torben Iversen, and David Soskice. 2001. "Social Protection and the Formation of Skills: A Reinterpretation of the Welfare State." In *Varieties of Capitalism: The Institutional Foundations of Comparative Advantage*, Peter Hall and David Soskice eds. Oxford: Oxford University Press, pp. 145–183.

Evans, Peter B., Dietrich Rueschemeyer, and Theda Skocpol. 1985. *Bringing the State Back in.* Cambridge: Cambridge University Press.

Farbera, Henry S., and Joanne Gowa. 1997. "Common Interests or Common Polities? Reinterpreting the Democratic Peace." *The Journal of Politics* 59(2): 393–417.

Fenge, Robert, and Jakob von Weizsäcker. 2010. "Public Pension Systems and Distortions of Intra-EU mobility: the Lodge Test." *Journal of Pension Economics and Finance* 9(2): 263–275.

Ferrera, Maurizio. 1996. "The 'Southern Model' of Welfare in Social Europe." *Journal of European Social Policy* 6(1): 17–37.

Finegold, David, and David Soskice. 1988. "The Failure of Training in Britain: Analysis and Prescription." *Oxford Review of Economic Policy* 4(3): 21–53.

Finer, Catherine Jones. 2003. *Social Policy Reform in China: Views from Home and Abroad*. Washington, DC: Ashgate Publishing, Ltd.

Fleckenstein, Timo, Adam Saunders, and Martin Seeleib-Kaiser. 2011. "The Dual Transformation of Social Protection and Human Capital: Comparing Britain and Germany." *Comparative Political Studies* 44(12): 127–156.

Fleisher, Belton, Haizheng Li, and Min Qiang Zhao. 2010. "Human capital, economic growth, and regional inequality in China." *Journal of Development Economics* 92(2): 215–231.

Flora, Peter, and Jens Alber. 1981. "Modernization, Democratization, and the Development of Welfare States in Western Europe." In *The Development of Welfare States in Europe and America*, Peter Flora and Arnold J. Heidenheimer eds. London: Transaction Books.

Florini, Ann, Hairong Lai, and Yeling Tan. 2012. *China Experiments: From Local Innovations to National Reform*. Washington, DC: Brookings Institution Press.

Flyvbjerg, Bent. 2006. "Five Misunderstandings About Case-Study Research." *Qualitative Inquiry* 12(2): 219–245.

Forteza, Alvaro. 2010. "The Portability of Pension Rights: General Principles and the Caribbean Case." *Development Policy Review* 28(2): 237–255.

Frattini, Federico, and Giorgio Prodi. 2013. "Industrial clusters in China: Policy tools for further and more balanced development." *European Review of Industrial Economics and Policy* (5): 3–11.

Frazier, Mark. 2004. "China's Pension Reform and Its Discontents." *Unknown* (51): 97–114.

Frazier, Mark. 2006. "The International Sources of Social Policy Reconsidered: Foreign and Local Influence on China's Pension Reforms." *Paper Presented in the Annual Meeting of the American Political Science Association*, Marriott, Loews Philadelphia, and the Pennsylvania Convention Center, Philadelphia, PA, August 31, 2006.

Frazier, Mark. 2010. *Socialist Insecurity: Pensions and the Politics of Uneven Development in China*. Ithaca, NY: Cornell University Press.

Freedman, David A. 1987. "As Others See Us: A Case Study in Path Analysis." *Journal of Educational and Behavioral Statistics* 12(2): 101–128.

Freeman, David A. 1991. "Statistical Models and Shoe Leather." In *Sociological Methodology*. San Francisco: Jossey-Bass.

Friedman, Milton. 1953. "The Methodology of Positive Economics." In *Essays in Positive Economics*. Chicago: University of Chicago Press.

Frye, Timothy, and Andrei Shleifer. 1997. "The Invisible Hand and the Grabbing Hand." *American Economic Review Papers and Proceedings* 87(2): 354–358.

Fujita, Shigeru, and Garey Ramey. 2009. "The Cyclicality of Separation and Job Finding Rates." *International Economic Review* 50(2): 415–430.

Fukumoto, Tomoyuki, and Ichiro Muto. 2012. "Rebalancing China's Economic Growth: Some Insights from Japan's Experience." *China & World Economy* 20(1): 62–82.

Gallagher, Mary E., Ching Wan Lee, and Sarosh Kuruvilla. 2011. "Introduction and Argument." In *From Iron Rice Bowl to Informalization: Markets, Workers, and the State in a Changing China*, Ithaca, NY: Cornell University Press, pp. 1–39.

Gang, Fan, and Wang Xiaolu. 2011. *NERI Index of Marketization Of China's Provinces 2011 Report.* Beijing: Economic Science Press.

Garrett, Geoffrey. 1995. "Capital Mobility, Trade, and the Domestic Politics of Economic Policy." *International Organization* 49(4): 657–687.

Garrett, Geoffrey. 1998. *Partisan Politics in the Global Economy.* Cambridge: Cambridge University Press.

Gautier, Pieter A., Coen N. Teulings, and Aico Van Vuuren. 2010. "On-the-Job Search, Mismatch and Efficiency." *Review of Economic Studies* 77(1): 245–272.

Geddes, Barbara. 2003. *Paradigms and Sand Castles: Theory Building and Research Design in Comparative Politics.* Ann Arbor: University of Michigan Press.

George, Alexander L., and Timothy J. McKeown. 1985. "Case Studies and Theories of Organizational Decision Making." In *Advances in Information Processing in Organizations.* Santa Barbara: JAI Press, pp. 26–57.

Gerschenkron, Alexander. 1962. *Economic Backwardness in Historical Perspective: A Book of Essays.* Cambridge: Belknap Press of Harvard University Press.

Goodman, David. 1986. *Centre and Province in the People's Republic of China.* London: Cambridge University Press.

Gordon, Andrew. 1988. *The Evolution of Labor Relations in Japan.* Cambridge: Harvard University Asia Center.

Gordon, Robert J. 1987. "Productivity, Wages, and Prices Inside and Outside of Manufacturing in the U.S., Japan, and Europe." *European Economic Review* 31: 112–139.

Granick, David. 1990. *Chinese State Enterprises : A Regional Property Rights Analysis.* Chicago: University of Chicago Press.

Green, Donald, and Ian Shapiro. 1994. *Pathologies of Rational Choice Theory.* New York: Yale University Press.

Gu, Edward. 2001. "Dismantling the Chinese mini-welfare state? Marketization and the politics of institutional transformation, 1979–1999." *Communist and Post-Communist Studies* 34(1): 91–111.

Guangzhou Daily. 2007. "Maoming Labour and Social Security Bureau: Social Insurance Contributions Bancrupt the Service Sector (广东茂名市劳保局：强征社保费 服务业就得倒闭)." http://gzdaily.dayoo.com/html/2007-04/06/content_24270220.htm. (Accessed August 13, 2013).

Guo, Gang. 2007. "Retrospective Economic Accountability under Authoritarianism: Evidence from China." *Political Research Quarterly* 60(3): 378–390.

Gustman, Alan, and Thomas L. Steinmeier. 1993. "Pension Portability and Labor Mobility Evidence from the Survey of Income and Program Participation." *Journal of Public Economics* 50(3): 299–323.

Hagopian, Frances. 1996. *Traditional Politics and Regime Change in Brazil.* Cambridge: Cambridge University Press.

Hall, Peter A., and Rosemary C. R. Taylor. 1996. "Political Science and the Three New Institutionalisms." *Political Studies* 44(5): 936–957.

Hall, Peter A., and David Soskice. 2001. *Varieties of Capitalism: The Institutional Foundations of Comparative Advantage.* Oxford: Oxford University Press.

Hall, Robert E. 2005. "Employment Fluctuations with Equilibrium Wage Stickiness." *American Economic Review* 95(1): 50–65.

Hampel, Frank R. et al. 1987. *Robust Statistics: The Approach Based on Influence Functions*. New York: John Wiley & Sons.

Harrod, Roy F. 1939. "An Essay in Dynamic Theory." *The Economic Journal* 49(193): 14–33.

Hashimoto, Masanori. 1981. "Firm-Specific Human Capital as a Shared Investment." *American Economic Review* 71(3): 475–482.

He, Zhou, and Jian-hua Zhu. 2002. "The Ecology of Online Newspapers: the Case of China." *Media, Culture & Society* 24(1): 121–137.

Heckman, James J. 2005. "China's Human Capital Investment." *China Economic Review* 16(1): 50–70.

Heckman, James J., Lance J Lochner, and Petra E. Todd. 2011. "Earnings Functions, Rates of Return and Treatment Effects: The Mincer Equation and Beyond." In *Handbook of the Economics of Education*, Eric A Hanushek and Finis Welch eds. London: Elsevier, pp. 310–458.

Heclo, Hugh. 1974. *Modern Social Policies in Britain and Sweden: From Relief to Income Maintenance*. New Haven: Yale University Press.

Herrigel, Gary, Volker Wittke, and Ulrich Voskamp. 2013. "The Process of Chinese Manufacturing Upgrading: Transitioning from Unilateral to Recursive Mutual Learning Relations." *Global Strategy Journal* 3(1): 109–125.

Hicks, Alexander. 1994. "Introduction to Pooling." In *The Comparative Political Economy of the Welfare State*, Thomas Janoski and Alexander Hicks eds. Cambridge: Cambridge University Press, pp. 31–53.

Hicks, Alexander. 1999. *Social Democracy and Welfare Capitalism: A Century of Income Security Politics*. Ithaca, NY: Cornell University Press.

Hicks, Alexander, and William D. Patterson. 1989. "On the Robustness of the Left Corporatist Model of Economic Growth." *The Journal of Politics* 51(3): 662–675.

Holliday, Ian. 2002. "Productivist Welfare Capitalism: Social Policy in East Asia." *Political Studies* 48(4): 706–723.

Holliday, Ian, and Linda Wong. 2003. "Social Policy under One Country, Two Systems: Institutional Dynamics in China and Hong Kong Since 1997." *Public Administration Review* 63(3): 269–282.

Hollingsworth, Joseph R., Philippe C. Schmitter, and Wolfgang Streeck. 1994. *Governing Capitalist Economies: Performance and Control of Economic Sectors*. New York: Oxford University Press.

Holzmann, Robert, and Johannes Koettl. 2012. "Portability of Pension, Health, and Other Social Benefits: Facts, Concepts, and Issues." *CESifo Working Paper Series No. 4002*. Munich, Germany: Center for Economic Studies and Ifo Institute (CESifo).

Holzmann, Robert, Johannes Koettl, and Taras Chernetsky. 2005. "Portability Regimes of Pension and Health Care Benefits for International Migrants: An Analysis of Issues and Good Practices." *The World Bank Social Protection Discussion Paper Series No. 0519*. Washington, D.C.: World Bank.

Hopkin, Jonathan. 2002. "Comparative Methods." In *Theory and Methods in Political Science*. David Marsh and Gerry Stoker eds. London: Palgrave Macmillan.

Horioka, Charles, and Junmin Wan. 2007. "The Determinants of Household Saving in China: A Dynamic Panel Analysis of Provincial Data." *Journal of Money, Credit and Banking* 39(8): 2077–2096.

Hsieh, Hsiu-Fang, and Sarah E Shannon. 2005. "Three Approaches to Qualitative Content Analysis." *Qualitative Health Research* 15(9): 1277–1288.
Huang, Yasheng. 1996. *Inflation and Investment Controls in China.* Cambridge: Cambridge University Press.
Huang, Yiping, and Xun Wang. 2011. "Does Financial Repression Inhibit or Facilitate Economic Growth? A Case Study of Chinese Reform Experience." *Oxford Bulletin of Economics and Statistics* 73(6): 833–855.
Hubacek, Klaus, Dabo Guan, and Anamika Barua. 2007. "Changing Lifestyles and Consumption Patterns in Developing Countries: A Scenario Analysis for China and India." *Futures* 39(9): 1084–1096.
Huber, Evelyne, Charles Ragin, and John D. Stephens. 1993. "Social Democracy, Christian Democracy, Constitutional Structure, and the Welfare State." *American Journal of Sociology* 99(3): 711–749.
Huber, Evelyne, and John D. Stephens. 2000. "Partisan Governance, Women's Employment, and the Social Democratic Service State." *American Sociological Review* 65(3): 323–342.
Huber, Evelyne, and John D. Stephens. 2001. *Development and Crisis of the Welfare State: Parties and Policies in Global Markets.* Chicago: University of Chicago Press.
Huo, Jingjing, Moira Nelson, and John D. Stephens. 2008. "Decommodification and Activation in Social Democratic Policy: Resolving the Paradox." *Journal of European Social Policy* 18(1): 5–20.
Immergut, Ellen M. 1992. *Health Politics: Interests and Institutions in Western Europe.* Cambridge: Cambridge University Press.
International Metalworkers' Federation. 2010. "VW World Works Council Welcomes China." www.imfmetal.org/index.cfm?c=24550&l=2. (Accessed July 29, 2013).
Iversen, Torben. 2005. *Capitalism, Democracy, and Welfare.* Cambridge: Cambridge University Press.
Iversen, Torben, and Thomas Cusack. 2000. "The Causes of Welfare State Expansion: Deindustrialization or Globalization?." *World Politics* 52(3): 313–349.
Iversen, Torben, and David Soskice. 2001. "An Asset Theory of Social Policy Preferences." *American Political Science Review* 95(4): 875–893.
Iversen, Torben, and David Soskice. 2006. "Electoral Institutions and the Politics of Coalitions: Why Some Democracies Redistribute More than Others." *American Political Science Review* 100(2): 165–181.
Iversen, Torben, and David Soskice. 2009. "Distribution and Redistribution: The Shadow of the Nineteenth Century." *World Politics* 61(03): 438.
Iversen, Torben, and David Soskice. 2010. "Real Exchange Rates and Competitiveness: The Political Economy of Skill Formation, Wage Compression, and Electoral Systems." *American Political Science Review* 104(3): 601–623.
Iversen, Torben, and John Stephens. 2008. "Partisan Politics, the Welfare State, and Three Worlds of Human Capital Formation." *Comparative Political Studies* 41(4): 600–637.
Iversen, Torben, and Anne Wren. 1998. "Equality, Employment, and Budgetary Restraint: The Trilemma of the Service Economy." *World Politics* 50(4): 507–546.
Jackman, Robert W. 1987. "The Politics of Economic Growth in the Industrial Democracies, 1974–80: Leftist Strength or North Sea Oil?." *The Journal of Politics* 49(1): 242–256.
Jackman, Robert W. 1989. "Politics of Economic Growth, Once Again." *The Journal of Politics* 51(3): 646–661.

Jackson, John. 1992. "Estimation of Models with Variable Coefficients." In *Political Analysis*. Ann Arbor: University of Michigan Press, pp. 21–50.

Jackson, Richard, and Neil Howe. 2004. *The Graying of the Middle Kingdom: The Demographics and Economics of Retirement Policy in China*. New York: Center for Strategic & Internatonal Relations.

Janoski, Thomas, and Alexander Hicks. 1994. *The Comparative Political Economy of the Welfare State*. Cambridge: Cambridge University Press.

Jiangnan Metropolis. 2013. "Nanchang Entrance Requirement for General and Vocational High Schools Determined (南昌普高和职高分数线划定)." http://jiangxi.jxnews.com.cn/system/2013/08/06/012556278.shtml. (Accessed September 26, 2014).

Jin, Hehui, Yingyi Qian, and Barry R. Weingast. 2005. "Regional De-Centralization and Fiscal Incentives: Federalism, Chinese Style." *Journal of Public Economics* 89 (9–10): 1719–1742.

Jinjiang Economy News. 2008. "Quanzhou Leather Industry Association Introduces Tripartite Agreement on Hiring (规范用工环境，泉州皮革协会发起'三方人才公约')." www.jjjjb.com.cn/html/2008-07/01/content_110774.htm. (Accessed July 15, 2013).

Jochem, Sven. 2011. "Nordic Employment Policies – Change and Continuity Before and During the Financial Crisis." *Social Policy & Administration* 45(2): 131–145.

Johnson, Chalmers. 1982. *MITI and the Japanese Miracle: the Growth of Industrial Policy, 1925–1975*. California: Stanford University Press.

Joseph, William A. 2010. *Politics in China*. Oxford: Oxford University Press.

Katz, Eliakim, and Adrian Ziderman. 1990. "Investment in General Training: The Role of Information and Labour Mobility." *The Economic Journal* 100(403): 1147–1158.

Katzenstein, Peter J. 1985. *Small States in World Markets: Industrial Policy in Europe*. Ithaca, NY: Cornell University Press.

Keidel, Albert. 2009. "China's Financial Sector: Contributions to Growth and Downside Risks." In *The Milken Institute Series on Financial Innovation and Economic Growth 1571–4772*, James R. Barth, John A. Tatom, and Glenn Yago eds. Boston: Springer, pp. 111–125.

Kennedy, Peter. 1998. *A Guide to Econometrics*. Cambridge: MIT Press.

Kerr, Clark, John Dunlop, Frederick Harbison, and Charles Myers. 1960. *Industrialism and Industrial Man*. Cambridge: Harvard University Press.

King, Gary, Robert O. Keohane, and Sidney Verba. 1994. *Designing Social Inquiry: Scientific Inference in Qualitative Research*. Princeton University Press.

King, Gary, Jennifer Pan, and Molly Roberts. 2013. "How Censorship in China Allows Government Criticism But Silences Collective Expression." *American Political Science Review* 107(2): 1–18.

Kmenta, Jan. 1971. *Elements of Econometrics*. Ann Arbor: University of Michigan Press.

Knight, John, Deng Quheng, and Li Shi. 2011. "The Puzzle of Migrant Labour Shortage and Rural Labour Surplus in China." *China Economic Review* 22(4): 585–600.

Kohli, Atul. 2012. *Poverty Amid Plenty in the New India*. New Delhi: Cambridge University Press.

Korpi, Walter. 1983. *The Democratic Class Struggle*. London: Routledge.

Korpi, Walter. 2006. "Power Resources and Employer-Centered Approaches in Explanations of Welfare States and Varieties of Capitalism: Protagonists, Consenters, and Antagonists." *World Politics* 58(2): 167–206.

Korpi, Walter, and Joakim Palme. 2003. "New Politics and Class Politics in the Context of Austerity and Globalization: Welfare State Regress in 18 Countries, 1975–95." *American Political Science Review* 97(3): 425–446.
Kotlikoff, Laurence J., and Jagadeesh Gokhale. 1992. "Estimating a Firm's Age-Productivity Profile Using the Present Value of Workers' Earnings." *The Quarterly Journal of Economics* 107(4): 1215–1242.
Krueger, Anne O. 1974. "The Political Economy of the Rent-Seeking Society." *The American Economic Review* 64(3): 291–303.
Krug, Barbara. 2012. "Political Embeddedness in China: Strengths and Limitations." In *Capitalisms and Capitalism in the Twenty-First Century*, Glenn Morgan and Richard Whitley eds. Oxford: Oxford University Press, pp. 345–365.
Krugman, Paul. 2013. "Hitting China's Wall." *New York Times.* www.nytimes.com/2013/07/19/opinion/krugman-hitting-chinas-wall.html?_r=0.
Kung, James Kai-sing, and Justin Yifu Lin. 2003. "The Causes of China's Great Leap Famine, 1959–1961." *Economic Development and Cultural Change* 52(1): 51–73.
Landry, Pierre F. 2008. *Decentralized Authoritarianism in China: The Communist Party's Control of Local Elites in the Post-Mao Era.* Cambridge and New York: Cambridge University Press.
Lange, Peter, and Geoffrey Garrett. 1985. "The Politics of Growth: Strategic Interaction and Economic Performance in the Advanced Industrial Democracies, 1974–1980." *The Journal of Politics* 47(3): 791–827.
Lanzhou Morning Post. 2010. "High Employment Rates of Vocational School Graduates Does Not Encourage Enrolment When Low Wages Push Off Students and Parents (中职高就业率难掩招生困难 工资低让学生家长皆顾虑)." http://gansu.gansudaily.com.cn/system/2010/12/06/011799388_01.shtml. (Accessed February 10, 2013).
Lardy, Nicholas. 2012. *Sustaining China's Economic Growth: After the Global Financial Crisis.* New York: Peterson Institute.
Lazarsfeld, Paul F. 1955. "Interpretation of Statistical Relations as a Research Operation." In *The Language of Social Research*, Paul F. Lazarsfeld and Morris Rosenberg eds. New York: Free Press, pp. 110–136.
Lazear, Edward P. 1979. "Why Is There Mandatory Retirement?." *Journal of Political Economy* 87(6): 1261–1284.
Lazear, Edward P. 1981. "Agency, Earnings Profiles, Productivity, and Hours Restrictions." *American Economic Review* 71(4): 606–620.
Lazear, Edward P. 1989. "Pay Equality and Industrial Politics." *Journal of Political Economy* 97(3): 561–580.
Lazear, Edward P., and Robert L. Moore. 1984. "Incentives, Productivity, and Labor Contracts." *The Quarterly Journal of Economics* 99(2): 275.
Lazear, Edward P., and Sherwin Rosen. 1981. "Rank-Order Tournaments as Optimum Labor Contracts." *Journal of Political Economy* 89(5): 841–864.
Lee, Ching Kwan. 2007. "Is Labor A Political Force in China?." In *Grassroots Political Reform in Contemporary China*, Elizabeth J. Perry and Merle Goldman eds. Cambridge: Harvard University Press, pp. 228–252.
Lemieux, Thomas. 2010. "The 'Mincer Equation' Thirty Years After Schooling, Experience, and Earnings." In *Jacob Mincer: A Pioneer of Modern Labor Economics.* Shoshana Grossbarded. London: Springer.

Lenski, Gerhard. 1966. *Power and Privilege: A Theory of Social Stratification*. London: McGraw-Hill.

Leung, Joe C B. 2003. "Social Security Reforms in China: Issues and Prospects." *International Journal of Social Welfare* 12(2): 73–85.

Levi, Margaret. 1988. *Of Rule and Revenue*. Los Angles: University of California Press.

Li, Hongbin, and Li-An Zhou. 2005. "Political Turnover and Economic Performance: The Incentive Role of Personnel Control in China." *Journal of Public Economics* 89: 1743–1762.

Li, Yiqiong, and Peter Sheldon. 2010. "HRM Lives Inside and Outside the Firm: Employers, Skill Shortages and the Local Labour Market in China." *The International Journal of Human Resource Management* 21(12): 2173–2193.

Liao, Qi, and Ling Qing. 2011. "Personnel File System in Harmonious Labour Relations (和谐劳动关系中的人事档案系统)." *Journal of Sichuan Administration College (四川行政学院学报)* (3): 36–45.

Lieberthal, Kenneth. 2004. *Governing China: From Revolution to Reform*. New York: W. W. Norton.

Lieberthal, Kenneth, and David Lampton. 1992. *Bureaucracy, Politics, and Decision Making in Post-Mao China*. Los Angeles: University of California Press.

Lijphart, Arend. 1971. "Comparative Politics and the Comparative Method." *American Political Science Review* 65(3): 682–693.

Lijphart, Arend, and Markus M. L. Crepaz. 1991. "Corporatism and Consensus Democracy in Eighteen Countries: Conceptual and Empirical Linkages." *British Journal of Political Science* 21(2): 235–246.

Lin, Justin Yifu. 2003. "Development Strategy, Viability, and Economic Convergence." *Economic Development and Cultural Change* 51(2): 277–308.

Lindert, Peter H. 2004. *Growing Public: Social Spending and Economic Growth Since the Eighteenth Century*. Cambridge: Cambridge University Press.

Liu Mingwei. 2010. "Union Organizing in China: Still a Monolithic Labor Movement?" *Industrial and Labor Relations Review* 64(1): 30–52.

Loewenstein, Mark, and James Spletzer. 1998. "Dividing the Costs and Returns to General Training." *Journal of Labor Economics* 16(1): 79–93.

Loewenstein, Mark, and James Spletzer. 1999. "General and Specific Training: Evidence and Implications." *The Journal of Human Resources*, 34(4): 710–733.

Lou, Jiwei, and Shuilin Wang. 2008. *Public Finance in China: Reform and Growth for a Harmonious Society*. Washington, DC: World Bank Publications.

Lucas, Robert E., Jr. 1988. "On the Mechanics of Economic Development." *Journal of Monetary Economics* 22(1): 3–42.

Maioni, Antonia. 1998. *Parting at the Crossroads: The Emergence of Health Insurance in the United States and Canada*. Princeton: Princeton University Press.

Manatschal, Anita. 2011. "Taking Cantonal Variations of Integration Policy Seriously – or How to Validate International Concepts at the Subnational Comparative Level." *Swiss Political Science Review* 17(3): 336–357.

Mann, Michael. 1987. "Ruling Class Strategies and Citizenship." *Sociology* 21(3): 339–354.

Mares, Isabela. 2001. "Firms and the Welfare State: When, Why, and How Does Social Policy Matter to Employers?." In *Varieties of Capitalism: The Institutional Foundations of Comparative Advantage*, Peter Hall and David Soskice eds. Oxford: Oxford University Press.

Mares, Isabela. 2003. "The Sources of Business Interest in Social Insurance: Sectoral versus National Differences." *World Politics* 55(2): 229–258.

Marimon, Ramon, and Fabrizio Zilibotti. 1999. "Unemployment vs. Mismatch of Talents: Reconsidering Unemployment Benefits." *The Economic Journal* 109(455): 266–291.

Markula, Pirkko, and Michael Silk. 2011. *Qualitative Research for Physical Culture.* London: Palgrave Macmillan.

Marshall, Thomas H. 1950. *Citizenship and Social Class, and Other Essays.* Cambridge: Cambridge University Press.

Martin, Cathie Jo. 1995. "Nature or Nurture? Sources of Firm Preference for National Health Reform." *American Political Science Review* 89(4): 898–913.

Martin, Cathie Jo. 2000. *Stuck in Neutral: Business and the Politics of Human Capital Investment Policy.* Princeton: Princeton University Press.

Martin, Cathie Jo, and Duane Swank. 2012. *The Political Construction of Business Interests: Coordination, Growth, and Equality.* Cambridge: Cambridge University Press.

McCall, Leslie, and Lane Kenworthy. 2009. "Americans' Social Policy Preferences in the Era of Rising Inequality." *Perspectives on Politics* 7(3): 459–484.

McGuire, Thomas, Michael Coiner, and Larry Spancake. 1979. "Budget-Maximizing Agencies and Efficiency in Government." *Public Choice* 34(3/4): 333–357.

McKinnish, Terra. 2007. "Welfare-Induced Migration at State Borders: New Evidence from Micro-Data." *Journal of Public Economics* 91(3–4): 437–450.

Mehmet, Ozay. 2002. *Westernizing the Third World: The Eurocentricity of Economic Development Theories.* London: Routledge.

Mei, Ciqi. 2009. "Brings the Politics Back in: Political Incentive and Policy Distortion in China." *PhD dissertation, Univesity of Maryland, College Park.*

Meisner, Maurice J. 1999. *Mao's China and After: A History of the People"s Republic.* New York: Free Press.

Menard, Scott. 2010. *Logistic Regression: From Introductory to Advanced Concepts and Applications.* London: SAGE.

Metcalf, David, and Jianwei Li. 2005. *Chinese Unions: Nugatory or Transforming? An 'Alice' Analysis.* London: Centre for Economic Performance, London School of Economics and Political Science.

Michels, Robert. 1962. *Political Parties: A Study of the Oligarchical Tendencies of Modern Democracy.* New York: Simon and Schuster.

Migdal, Joel S. 1988. *Strong Societies and Weak States: State-Society Relations and State Capabilities in the Third World.* Princeton: Princeton University Press.

Mill, John Stuart. 1843. *A System of Logic, Ratiocinative and Inductive.* New York: Harper & Brothers.

Miller, Gary J., and Terry M. Moe. 1983. "Bureaucrats, Legislators, and the Size of Government." *American Political Science Review* 77(2): 297–322.

Mincer, Jacob. 1974. *Schooling, Experience and Earnings.* New York: National Bureau of Economic Research (Distributed by Columbia University Press).

Ministry of Labour and Social Security. 2001. *China Implicit Pension Debt Projection and Pension Management.* Beijing: Economic Science Publishing House.

Mitchell, Olivia S. 1982. "Fringe Benefits and Labor Mobility." *The Journal of Human Resources* 17(2): 286–298.

Modern Logistics. 2010. "How to Solve the Training Problem for Logistics Firms? (如何解决物流企业培训难题)." www.kesum.com/zx/jqzxrd/201005/112605.html. (Accessed March 7, 2013).

Moen, Espen R., and Åsa Rosén. 2004. "Does Poaching Distort Training?" *Review of Economic Studies* 71(4): 1143–1162.

Molina, Oscar, and Martin Rhodes. 2002. "Corporatism: The Past, Present, and Future of a Concept." *Annual Review of Political Science* 5(1): 305–331.

Monroe, Kristen R. 2001. "Paradigm Shift: From Rational Choice to Perspective." *International Political Science Review* 22(2): 151–172.

Montinola, Gabriella, Yingyi Qian, and Barry R. Weingast. 1995. "Federalism, Chinese Style: The Political Basis for Economic Success in China." *World Politics* 48(1): 50–81.

Moran, Michael. 1999. *Governing the Health Care State: A Comparative Study of the United Kingdom, the United States, and Germany.* Manchester: Manchester University Press.

Mosley, Herbert. 1995. "The 'Social Dumping' Threat of European Integration: A Critique." In *Convergence or Diversity? Internationalization and Economic Policy Response*, Brigitte Unger and Frans Van Waarden eds. Avebury: Aldershot, pp. 182–199.

Mosteller, Frederick, and John Wilder Tukey. 1977. *Data Analysis and Regression: A Second Course in Statistics.* Reading, MA: Addison-Wesley.

Mueller, Dennis C. 2003. *Public Choice III.* Cambridge: Cambridge University Press.

Myles, John, and Jill Quadagno. 2002. "Political Theories of the Welfare State." *Social Service Review* 76(1): 34–57.

Nagel, Ernest. 1961. *The Structure of Science: Problems in the Logic of Scienific Explanation.* New York: Hackett Publishing Company.

National Audit Office. 2012. "No. 34 of 2012 (General Serial No.141): Audit Results of the National Social Security Funds." www.cnao.gov.cn/main/articleshow_ArtID_1270.htm (Accessed May 6, 2013).

National Bureau of Statistics of China. 2011. *China Statistical Yearbook.* Beijing: China Statistics Press.

Naughton, Barry. 1995. *Growing Out of the Plan: Chinese Economic Reform, 1978–1993.* Cambridge: Cambridge University Press.

Naughton, Barry. 2007. *The Chinese Economy: Transitions and Growth.* Cambridge: MIT Press.

Nee, Victor, and Sonja Opper. 2012. *Capitalism from Below: Markets and Institutional Change in China.* Cambridge: Harvard University Press.

Nelson, Moira, and John D. Stephens. 2013. "The Service Transition and Women's Employment." In *The Political Economy of the Service Transition*, Anne Wren ed. Oxford: Oxford University Press, pp. 147–170.

Nelson, Richard R., and Edmund S. Phelps. 1966. "Investment in Humans, Technological Diffusion, and Economic Growth." *American Economic Review* 56(1/2): 69–75.

Ningbo Evening Post. 2012. "Household Service Firms Can Apply for Social Insurance Subsidy (员工制家政企业可申请社保补贴)." http://daily.cnnb.com.cn/nbwb/html/2012-08/07/node_61.htm. (Accessed March 6, 2013).

Niskanen, William A. 1971. *Bureaucracy and Representative Government.* Chicago: Transaction Publishers.

North, Douglas. 1986. "A Neoclassical Theory of the State." In *Rational Choice*, Jon Elster ed. New York: New York University Press, pp. 248–260.

North, Douglass. 1990. *Institutions, Institutional Change, and Economic Performance.* Cambridge: Cambridge University Press.

Oates, Wallace E. 2008. "On The Evolution of Fiscal Federalism: Theory and Institutions." *National Tax Journal* 61(2): 313–334.
Oatley, Thomas. 1999. "How Constraining is Capital Mobility? The Partisan Hypothesis in an Open Economy." *American Journal of Political Science* 43(4): 1003–1027.
Obinger, Herbert, Stephan Leibfried, and Francis G. Castles. 2005. *Federalism and the Welfare State: New World and European Experiences.* Cambridge: Cambridge University Press.
Offe, Claus. 1984. *Contradictions of the Welfare State.* London: Hutchinson.
Oi, Jean C. 1992. "Fiscal Reform and the Economic Foundations of Local State Corporatism in China." *World Politics* 45(01): 99–126.
Oi, Jean C. 1999. *Rural China Takes Off: Institutional Foundations of Economic Reform.* Los Angeles: University of California Press.
Olson, Mancur. 1965. *The Logic of Collective Action.* Cambridge: Harvard University Press.
Oneal, John R., and Bruce M. Russet. 1997. "The Classical Liberals Were Right: Democracy, Interdependence, and Conflict, 1950–1985." *International Studies Quarterly* 41(2): 267–294.
O'Neill, Jim. 2001. "Building Better Global Economic BRICs." *Goldman Sachs Global Economics Paper No: 66.* London: Goldman Sachs Economic Research Group.
Ordeshook, Peter. 1990. "The Emerging Discipline of Political Economy." In *Perspectives on Positive Political Economy,* James E. Alt and Kenneth A. Shepsle eds. Cambridge: Cambridge University Press, pp. 9–30.
Orloff, Ann Shola, and Theda Skocpol. 1984. "Why Not Equal Protection? Explaining the Politics of Public Social Spending in Britain, 1900–1911, and the United States, 1880s-1920." *American Sociological Review* 49(6): 726–750.
Pampel, Fred C. 2000. *Logistic Regression: A Primer.* London: SAGE.
Pampel, Fred C., and Jane A. Weiss. 1983. "Economic Development, Pension Policies, and the Labor Force Participation of Aged Males: A Cross-National, Longitudinal Approach." *American Journal of Sociology* 89(2): 350–372.
Pampel, Fred C., and John B. Williamson. 1989. *Age, Class, Politics, and the Welfare State.* Cambridge: Cambridge University Press.
Pan, Yao. 2012. "The Effect of Labor Mobility Restrictions on Human Capital Accumulation in China." *Working Papers,* The George Washington University, Institute for International Economic Policy.
Park, Albert. F., and Fang Cai. 2011. "The Informalization of the Chinese Labor Market." In *From Iron Rice Bowl to Informalization: Markets, State and Workers in a Changing China,* Sarosh Kuruvilla, Mary Gallagher, and Ching-kwan Lee eds. Ithca, NY: Cornell University Press, pp. 17–35.
Parks, Richard W. 1967. "Efficient Estimation of a System of Regression Equations when Disturbances are Both Serially and Contemporaneously Correlated." *Journal of the American Statistical Association* 62(318): 500–509.
Patton, Michael Quinn. 2002. *Qualitative Research & Evaluation Methods.* London: Sage.
People's Daily. 2007. "Officials Have No Power Except for the People." http://english.people.com.cn/200703/19/eng20070319_358925.html. (Accessed January 6, 2013).
Perry, Elizabeth J. 1995. "Labour's Battle for Political Space: The Role of Worker Associations in Contemporary China." In *Urban Spaces in Contemporary China,* Deborah Davis ed. Cambridge: Cambridge University Press, pp. 302–325.

Perry, Elizabeth J., and Merle Goldman. 2007. *Grassroots Political Reform in Contemporary China*. Los Angeles: University of California Press.

Persson, Petra, and Ekaterina Zhuravskaya. 2012. "Elite Influence as a Substitute for Local Democracy: Evidence from Backgrounds of Chinese Provincial Leaders." *Working Paper*. www.stanford.edu/~perssonp/China_Fiscal_Federalism.pdf.

Persson, Torsten, and Guido Tabellini. 2000. *Political Economics: Explaining Economic Policy*. Cambridge: MIT Press.

Pettis, Michael. 2013. *Great Rebalancing: Trade, Conflict, and the Perilous Road Ahead for the World Economy*. Princeton: Princeton University Press.

Pierson, Paul. 1993. "When Effect Becomes Cause: Policy Feedback and Political Change." *World Politics* 45(4): 595–628.

Pierson, Paul. 1996. "The New Politics of the Welfare State." *World Politics* 48(2): 143–179.

Pierson, Paul. 2000. "Increasing Returns, Path Dependence, and the Study of Politics." *American Political Science Review* 94(2): 251–267.

Pierson, Paul. 2001. *The New Politics of the Welfare State*. Oxford: Oxford University Press.

Pigou, Arthur Cecil. 1912. *Wealth and Welfare*. London: Macmillan.

Plumper, Thomas, Vera Troeger, and Philip Manow. 2005. "Panel Data Analysis in Comparative Politics: Linking Method to Theory." *European Journal of Political Research* 44: 327–354.

Poirier, Dale J., and Paul A. Ruud. 1988. "Probit with Dependent Observations." *The Review of Economic Studies* 55(4): 593–614.

Porter, Michael. 1998. "Clusters and the New Economics of Competition." *Harvard Business Review* (November-December): 77–90.

Prasad, Naren, and Megan Gerecke. 2010. "Social Security Spending in Times of Crisis." *Global Social Policy* 10(2): 218–247.

Przeworski, Adam. 1987. "Methods of Cross-National Research, 1970–1983: An Overview." In *Comparative Policy Research: Learning from Experience*, Meinolf Dierkes ed. Brookfield: Gower Publishing Company, Limited.

Przeworski, Adam, and Henry Teune. 1970. *The Logic of Comparative Social Inquiry*. New York: Wiley-Interscience.

Qian, Xiaolei, and Russell Smyth. 2006. "Growth Accounting for the Chinese Provinces 1990–2000: Incorporating Human Capital Accumulation." *Journal of Chinese Economic and Business Studies* 4(1): 21–37.

Qian, Yingyi, and Barry R. Weingast. 1997. "Federalism as a Commitment to Perserving Market Incentives." *The Journal of Economic Perspectives* 11(4): 83–92.

Quadagno, Jill. 1987. "Theories of the Welfare State." *Annual Review of Sociology* 13: 109–128.

Quadagno, Jill. 1988. *The Transformation of Old Age Security: Class and Politics in the American Welfare State*. Chicago: University of Chicago Press.

Quanzhou Evening. 2011. "Hostile Poaching Will Be Punished by Credit Limits (恶意挖人 融资受限)." http://szb.qzwb.com/qzwb/html/2011-10/09/content_321504.htm. (Accessed May 2, 2013).

Quinn, Dennis P., and Carla Inclan. 1997. "The Origins of Financial Openness: A Study of Current and Capital Account Liberalization." *American Journal of Political Science* 41(3): 771–813.

Ragin, Charles C. 1987. *The Comparative Method: Moving Beyond Qualitative and Quantitative Strategies*. Los Angeles: University of California Press.

Ragin, Charles C. 2008. *Redesigning Social Inquiry: Fuzzy Sets and Beyond.* Chicago: University of Chicago Press.

Razin, Assaf, and Jackline Wahba. 2011. "Welfare Magnet Hypothesis, Fiscal Burden and Immigration Skill Selectivity." *NBER Working Paper No. 17515.*Cambridge, MA: National Bureau of Economic Research.

Redding, Gordon, and Michael A. Witt. 2008. "China's Business System and its Future Trajectory." *Asia Pacific Journal of Management* 26(3): 381–399.

Rein, Shaun. 2012. *The End of Cheap China: Economic and Cultural Trends That Will Disrupt the World.* Hoboken: John Wiley & Sons.

Reuters. 2013. "China Set to Announce Reforms of Creaking Pension System." http://uk.reuters.com/article/2013/10/17/uk-china-pensions-idUKBRE99G1BF20131017. (Accessed November 3, 2013).

Rhodes, Martin. 1996. "Globalization and West European Welfare States: a Critical Review of Recent Debates." *Journal of European Social Policy* 6(4): 305–327.

Riker, William H. 1962. *The Theory of Political Coalitions.* New Haven: Yale University Press.

Rithmire, Meg E. 2014. "China's "New Regionalism": Subnational Analysis in Chinese Political Economy." *World Politics* 66(1): 165–194.

Rodrik, Dani. 1997. *Has Globalization Gone Too Far?* Washington, D.C: Institute for International Economics.

Rodrik, Dani. 2005. "Growth Strategies." In *Handbook of Economic Growth*, Philippe Aghion and Steven Durlauf eds. London: Elsevier.

Romer, Paul M. 1986. "Increasing Returns and Long-Run Growth." *Journal of Political Economy* 95(5): 1002–1037.

Romer, Thomas, and Howard Rosenthal. 1978. "Political Resource Allocation, Controlled Agendas, and the Status Quo." *Public Choice* 33(4): 27–43.

Rosenzweig, M. R., and Junsen Zhang. 2009. "Do Population Control Policies Induce More Human Capital Investment? Twins, Birth Weight and China's "One-Child" Policy." *Review of Economic Studies* 76: 1149–1174.

Rudra, Nita. 2002. "Globalization and the Decline of the Welfare State in Less-Developed Countries." *International Organization* 56(2): 411–445.

Rueda, David. 2007. *Social Democracy Inside Out: Partisanship and Labor Market Policy in Industrialized Democracies.* New York: Oxford University Press.

Sartori, Giovanni. 1970. "Concept Misformation in Comparative Politics." *American Political Science Review* 64(4): 1033–1053.

Saw, Swee-Hock, and John Wong. 2009. *Regional Economic Development in China.* Singapore: Institute of Southeast Asian Studies.

Schmidt, Manfred G. 1997. "Determinants of Social Expenditure in Liberal Democracies: The Post World War II Experience." *Acta Politica* 32(2): 153–173.

Schneider, Carsten Q., and Claudius Wagemann. 2012. *Set-Theoretic Methods for the Social Sciences: A Guide to Qualitative Comparative Analysis.* Cambridge: Cambridge University Press.

Schreier, Margrit. 2012. *Qualitative Content Analysis in Practice.* London: SAGE.

Schwartz, Herman M. 1994. *States Versus Markets: The Emergence of a Global Economy.* Houndmills, Basingstoke, Hampshire: Palgrave Macmillan.

Seeleib-Kaiser, Martin, and Timo Fleckenstein. 2009. "The Political Economy of Occupational Family Policies." *British Journal of Industrial Relation* 47(4): 741–764.

Segal, Adam. 2003. *Digital Dragon: High-technology Enterprises in China.* Ithca, NY: Cornell University Press.

Shapiro, Carl, and Joseph Stiglitz. 1984. "Equilibrium Unemployment as a Worker Discipline Device." *American Economic Review* 74(3): 433–444.

Shefter, Martin. 1977. "Party and Patronage: Germany, England, and Italy." *Politics & Society* 7: 403–451.

Sheldon, Peter, and Yiqiong Li. 2013. "Localized Poaching and Skills Shortages of Manufacturing Employees among MNEs in China." *Journal of World Business* 48(2): 186–195.

Shen, Kunrong, and Yuan Tian. 2002. "Human Capital and Location Choice of Foreign Direct Investment (人力资本与外商直接投资的区位选择)." *Management World (管理世界)* (11).

Sheng, Yumin. 2010. *Economic Openness and Territorial Politics in China*. New York: Cambridge University Press.

Shepsle, Kenneth A., and Mark S. Bonchek. 1997. *Analyzing Politics: Rationality, Behavior, and Instititutions*. New York: W. W. Norton.

Shi, Shih-Jiunn. 2009. "The Territorial Politics of Social Protection in China: Local Governments as an Emerging Locomotive of Policy Learning and Diffusion." *Paper Presented at the Annual Conference of the International Sociological Association, RC 19*, Montreal, Canada, August 20–22, 2009. Available at www.cccg.umontreal.ca/rc19. (Accessed November 26, 2012).

Shih, Victor. 2008. *Factions and Finance in China: Elite Conflict and Inflation*. New York: Cambridge University Press.

Shih, Victor, Christopher Adolph, and Mingxing Liu. 2012. "Getting Ahead in the Communist Party: Explaining the Advancement of Central Committee Members in China." *American Political Science Review* 106(1): 166–187.

Shirk, Susan. 1993. *The Political Logic of Economic Reform in China*. Oxford: University of California.

Sinn, Hans-Werner. 2001. "Social Dumping in the Transformation Process?" *NBER Working Paper No. 8364*. Cambridge, MA: National Bureau of Economic Research.

Skocpol, Theda. 1979. *States and Social Revolutions: A Comparative Analysis of France, Russia and China*. Cambridge: Cambridge University Press.

Skocpol, Theda. 1984. *Vision and Method in Historical Sociology*. Cambridge: Cambridge University Press.

Skocpol, Theda. 1985. "Bringing the State Back In: Strategies of Analysis in Current Research." In *Bringing the State Back in*. Cambridge: Cambridge University Press.

Skocpol, Theda. 1995. *Protecting Soldiers and Mothers: The Political Origins of Social Policy in United States*. Cambridge: Harvard University Press.

Skocpol, Theda, and Edwin Amenta. 1986. "States and Social Policies." *Annual Review of Sociology* 12: 131–157.

Skocpol, Theda, and Kenneth Finegold. 1982. "State Capacity and Economic Intervention in the Early New Deal." *Political Science Quarterly* 97(2): 255–278.

Skocpol, Theda, and Jerry Ikenberry. 1983. "The Political Formation of the American Welfare State in Historical and Comparative Perspective." *Comparative Social Research* 6: 87–148.

Skocpol, Theda, and Margaret Somers. 1980. "The Uses of Comparative History in Macrosocial Inquiry." *Comparative Studies in Society and History* 22(2): 174–197.

Skowronek, Stephen. 1982. *Building a New American State: The Expansion of National Administrative Capacities, 1877–1920*. Cambridge: Cambridge University Press.

Snyder, Richard. 2001. "Scaling Down: The Subnational Comparative Method." *Studies in Comparative International Development* 36(1): 93–110.

Solow, Robert. 1956. "A Contribution to the Theory of Economic Growth." *The Quarterly Journal of Economics* 70(1): 65–94.

Soskice, David. 1990. "Reinterpreting Corporatism and Explaining Unemployment: Co-ordinated and Uncorordinated Market Economies." In *Labour Relations and Economic Performance*, Renato Brunetta and Carlo Dell'Aringa eds. London: Palgrave Macmillan.

Soskice, David. 1991. "The Institutional Infrastructure for International Competitiveness: A Comparative Analysis of the UK and Germany." In *Economics for the New Europe*, Anthony Barnes Atkinson and Renato Brunetta eds. Basingstoke: Macmillan in association with the International Economic Association.

Soskice, David. 1999. "Divergent Production Regimes: Coordinated and Uncoordinated Market Economies in the 1980s and 1990s." In *Continuity and Change in Contemporary Capitalism*, Herbert Kitschelt et al. eds. Cambridge: Cambridge University Press.

Southern Daily. 2012. "Over Sixty Percent of Company Unions are "Boss Unions" (超六成企业工会仍是'老板工会')." http://epaper.nfdaily.cn/html/2012-11/14/content_7142224.htm. (Accessed July 26, 2013).

Southern Weekly. 2004. "China Has Labour Shortage For The First Time in 20 Years (中国遭遇20年来首次' 民工荒')." www.southcn.com/weekend/top/200407150009.htm. (Accessed November 19, 2012).

Spence, Michael. 1973. "Job Market Signaling." *The Quarterly Journal of Economics* 87(3): 355–374.

Steinmo, Sven. 1994. "The End of Redistribution? International Pressures and Domestic Tax Policy Choices." *Challenge* 37(6): 9–17.

Stephens, John, and Evelyne Huber. 2001. "Welfare State and Production Regimes in the Era of Retrenchment." In *The New Politics of the Welfare State*. Oxford: Oxford University Press, pp. 107–145.

Stevens, Margaret. 1994. "An Investment Model for the Supply of Training by Employers." *The Economic Journal* 104(424): 556–570.

Stevens, Margaret. 1996. "Transferable Training and Poaching Externalities." In *Acquiring Skills: Market Failures, Their Symptoms and Policy Responses*, Alison L Booth and Dennis J Snower eds. Cambridge: Cambridge University Press, pp. 19–40.

Stevens, Margaret. 1999. "Human Capital Theory and UK Vocational Training Policy." *Oxford Review of Economic Policy* 15(1): 16–32.

Stiglitz, Joseph E. 1974. "Alternative Theories of Wage Determination and Unemployment in LDC's: The Labor Turnover Model." *The Quarterly Journal of Economics* 88(2): 194.

Storz, Cornelia et al. 2013. "Bringing Asia into the Comparative Capitalism Perspective." *Socio-Economic Review* 11(2): 217–232.

Strange, Susan. 1996. *The Retreat of the State: The Diffusion of Power in the World Economy*. Cambridge: Cambridge University Press.

Streeck, Wolfgang. 1997. "Beneficial Constraints: On the Economic Limits of Rational Voluntarism." In *Contemporary Capitalism: The Embeddedness of Institutions*, J. Rogers Hollingsworth and Boyer, Robert eds. Cambridge: Cambridge University Press, pp. 197–218.

Swank, Duane. 1992. "Politics and the Structural Dependence of the State in Democratic Capitalist Nations." *American Political Science Review* 86(1): 38–54.

Swank, Duane. 1998. "Funding the Welfare State: Globalization and the Taxation of Business in Advanced Market Economies." *Political Studies* 46(4): 671–692.

Swenson, Peter. 1991. "Bringing Capital Back in, or Social Democracy Reconsidered: Employer Power, Cross-Class Alliances, and Centralization of Industrial Relations in Denmark and Sweden." *World Politics* 43(4): 513–544.

Swenson, Peter. 2002. *Capitalists Against Markets: The Making of Labor Markets and Welfare States in the United States and Sweden.* New York: Oxford University Press.

Tanzi, Vito. 1995. *Taxation in an Integrating World.* Washington, D.C.: Brookings Institution Press.

Tarrow, Sidney. 2004. "Bridging the Quantitative-Qualitative Divide." In *Rethinking Social Inquiry: Diverse Tools, Shared Standards.* Lanham: Rowman & Littlefield Publishers.

Thelen, Kathleen. 1999. "Historical Institutionalism in Comparative Politics." *Annual Review of Political Science* 2(1): 369–404.

Thelen, Kathleen, and Marius R. Busemeyer. 2012. "Institutional Change in German Vocational Training: From Collectivism towards Segmentalism." In *The Political Economy of Collective Skill Formation*, Marius R. Busemeyer and Christine Trampusch eds. Oxford: Oxford University Press.

Thun, Eric. 2006. *Changing Lanes in China: Foreign Direct Investment, Local Governments, and Auto Sector Development.* Cambridge: Cambridge University Press.

Tilly, Charles. 1993. *European Revolutions: 1492–1992.* Oxford: Wiley-Blackwell.

Tong, Jingrong. 2009. "Press Self-censorship in China: a Case Study in the Transformation of Discourse." *Discourse & Society* 20(5): 593–612.

Treisman, Daniel. 2007. *The Architecture of Government: Rethinking Political Decentralization.* Cambridge: Cambridge University Press.

Tsai, Lily. 2007. *Accountability Without Democracy: Solidary Groups and Public Goods Provision in Rural China.* Cambridge: Cambridge University Press.

Tsebelis, George. 1990. *Nested Games: Rational Choice in Comparative Politics.* Los Angeles: University of California Press.

Tsebelis, George. 2002. *Veto Players: How Political Institutions Work.* Princeton: Princeton University Press.

Tsui, Kai-yuen, and Youqiang Wang. 2004. "Between Separate Stoves and a Single Menu: Fiscal Decentralization in China." *The China Quarterly* (177): 71–90.

Tu, Edward Jow-Ching, Jersey Liang, and Shaomin Li. 1989. "Mortality Decline and Chinese Family Structure Implications for Old Age Support." *Journal of Gerontology* 44(4): 157–168.

Vanhuysse, Pieter. 2006. *Divide and Pacify: Strategic Social Policies and Political Protests in Post-Communist Democracies.* Budapest: Central European University Press.

Varshney, Ashutosh. 2002. *Ethnic Conflict and Civic Life: Hindus and Muslims in India.* New Haven: Yale University Press.

Vaughan-Whitehead, Daniel. 2003. *EU Enlargement Versus Social Europe? The Uncertain Future of the European Social Model.* Cheltenham: Edward Elgar Publishing.

Verba, Sidney. 1967. "Dilemmas in Comparative Research." *World Politics* 20(1): 111–127.

Verscheuren, Hirshman. 2009. "Regulation 883/2004 and Invalidity and Old-Age Pensions." *European Journal of Social Security* 11(1–2): 143–162.

Volvo News. 2010. "Zhejiang Geely Completes Acquisition of Volvo Car Corporation." www.volvocars.com/uk/top/about/news-events/pages/default.aspx?item id=52. (Accessed November 29, 2012).

Walder, Andrew. 1991. "Workers, Managers and the State: The Reform Era and the Political Crisis of 1989." *The China Quarterly* 127: 467–492.

Walder, Andrew G. 1995. "Local Governments as Industrial Firms: An Organizational Analysis of China's Transitional Economy." *American Journal of Sociology* 101(2): 263–301.

Walter, Carl, and Fraser Howie. 2012. *Red Capitalism: The Fragile Financial Foundation of China's Extraordinary Rise*. Singapore: John Wiley & Sons.

Wang, Meng-yun. 2009. "An Analysis of the Current Problems and the Effective Development of Vocational Education: On the Transition of Vocational Education from School-based Model to School-Enterprise Cooperation Model." *Journal of Shanxi University (Philosophy and Social Science Edition)* (3): 17–29.

Wang, Shuying, and Jiang Li. 2012. "A Study On The Free Secondary Vocational Education Policy（中等职业教育实施免费政策现状研究）." *Research on Vocational Education (职业教育研究)* (7): 31–43.

Wang, Yan, and Yudong Yao. 2003. "Sources of China's economic growth 1952–1999: incorporating human capital accumulation." *China Economic Review* 14(1): 32–52.

Wang, Zheng. 2008. "Employers Should Not Violate the Rights of Job Choice." Labor Security World (劳动保障世界) (6): 7–13.

Wasmer, Etienne. 2006. "General versus Specific Skills in Labor Markets with Search Frictions and Firing Costs." *American Economic Review* 96(3): 811–831.

Wedeman, Andrew. 2003. *From Mao to Market: Rent Seeking, Local Protectionism, and Marketization in China*. Cambridge: Cambridge University Press.

Weingast, Barry R. 1995. "The Economic Role of Political Institutions: Market-Preserving Federalism and Economic Development." *Journal of Law, Economics, & Organization* 11(1): 1–31.

Weir, Margaret, and Theda Skocpol. 1983. "State Structures and Social Keynesianism: Responses to the Great Depression in Sweden and the United States." *International Journal of Comparative Sociology* 24(1–2): 4–29.

Weiss, Andrew. 1980. "Job Queues and Layoffs in Labor Markets with Flexible Wages." *Journal of Political Economy* 88(3): 526–538.

Weiss, Andrew. 1990. *Efficiency Wages: Models of Unemployment, Layoffs, and Wage Dispersion*. New York: Princeton University Press.

West, Loraine. 1999. "Pension reform in China: Preparing for the future." *Journal of Development Studies* 35(3): 153–183.

White, Gordon. 1987. "The Politics of Economic Reform in Chinese Industry: The Introduction of the Labour Contract System." *The China Quarterly* 111: 365–389.

White, Tyrene. 2006. *China's Longest Campaign: Birth Planning in the People's Republic, 1949–2005*. Ithaca, NY: Cornell University Press.

Whiteford, Elaine A. 1996. *Adapting to Change: Occupational Pensions Schemes, Women and Migrant Workers : an Examination of the Extent to Which Occupational Pension Schemes in the UK, the Netherlands and Germany Enable Women and Migrant Workers to Accrue Adequate Pensions*. London: Kluwer Law International.

Whyte, William Foote. 1943. *Street Corner Society: The Social Structure of an Italian Slum*. Chicago: University of Chicago Press.

Wilensky, Harold L. 1975. *The Welfare State and Equality: Structural and Ideological Roots of Public Expenditures*. Los Angeles: University of California Press.

Wilensky, Harold L., and Charles Lebeaux. 1958. *Industrial Society and Social Welfare*. New York: Russell Sage Foundation.

Wilkinson, Steven I. 2006. *Votes and Violence: Electoral Competition and Ethnic Riots in India*. Cambridge: Cambridge University Press.

Williamson, Oliver E. 1979. "Transaction-Cost Economics: The Governance of Contractual Relations." *Journal of Law and Economics* 22(2): 233–261.

Wilson, Jeanne. 2006. "China's Transformation towards Capitalism." In *Varieties of Capitalism in Post-Communist Countries*, David Lane and Martin Myant eds. London: Palgrave Macmillan.

Witt, Michael A. 2010. "China: What Variety of Capitalism." *INSEAD Faculty & Research Working Paper*. Available at SSRN: https://ssrn.com/abstract=1695940. (Accessed Dec 20, 2013).

Witt, Michael A., and Gordon Redding. 2013. "Asian Business Systems: Institutional Comparison, Clusters and Implications for Varieties of Capitalism and Business Systems Theory." *Socio-Economic Review* 11(2): 265–300.

World Bank. 1994. *Averting the Old Age Crisis*. Washington, DC: World Bank Publications.

World Bank. 1997. "Old Age Security: Pension Reform in China." In *China 2020 Series*, Washington, DC: World Bank.

World Health Organisation. 2011. "WHO Database: Life Expectancy by Country." http://apps.who.int/gho/data/node.main.688?lang=en. (Accessed January 29, 2012).

Wren, Anne. 2013. *The Political Economy of the Service Transition*. Oxford: Oxford University Press.

Wuxi Daily. 2011. "A Brief on Wuxi Local Government Promoting Higher Vocational Education (无锡市开展地方政府促进高等职业教育发展综合改革试点情况的汇报)." www.tech.net.cn/web/articleview.aspx?id=20110729142331496&cata_id=N163. (Accessed August 23, 2013).

Xihai Metropolis. 2012. "They Do Not Want Social Insurance: It Is Kind of Hard to Use Social Protection to Keep Workers (三险五险他不要 社保留人有点难)." http://epaper.tibet3.com/xhdsb/html/2012-10/19/node_43.htm. (Accessed May 10, 2013).

Xu, Jian-hua. 2009. "Historical Evolution of Cooperation between School and Enterprise in China and Its Development Trends." *Vocational and Technical Education (职业技术教育)* (7): 33–39.

Yang, Dali. 1996. *Calamity and Reform in China: State, Rural Society, and Institutional Change*. Stanford: Stanford University Press.

Yang, Jing, Zhao Zhiqun, and Liu Jie. 2009. *Vocational Education and Manufacturing Industry Development in China (职业教育与中国制造业发展研究)*. Higer Education Press (高等教育出版社).

Yin, Robert K. 2009. *Case Study Research: Design and Methods*. Beverly Hill: SAGE.

Young, Doug. 2012. *The Party Line: How The Media Dictates Public Opinion in Modern China*. New York: John Wiley & Sons.

Yu, Zhong-en. 2009. "Discussion on the Role of Government in Cooperation of School and Enterprise." *Vocational and Technical Education (职业技术教育)* (22): 36–41.

Zhang, Bochun et al. 2004. *Technology Transfer from Soviet Union to People's Republic of China (1949–1966)*. Jinan: Shandong Education Publishing House.

Zhang, Yuanting, and Franklin Goza. 2006. "Who will care for the elderly in China? A Review of the Problems Caused by China's One-Child Policy and Their Potential Solutions." *Journal of Aging Studies* 20(2): 151–164.

Zhao, Dingxin. 2009. "The Mandate of Heaven and Performance Legitimation in Historical and Contemporary China." American Behavioral Scientist 53(3): 416–433.

Zheng, Bingwen. 2010. "The Policy Analysis for the Lagging behind of Enterprise Annuity in China (中国企业年金发展滞后的政策因素分析)." *China Population Science (中国人口科学)* 10(2): 2–23.

Zheng, Yongnian. 2004. *Globalization and State Transformation in China*. Cambridge: Cambridge University Press.

Zheng, Yongnian. 2007. *De Facto Federalism in China: Reforms and Dynamics of Central-Local Relations.* Singapore: World Scientific Publishing Company.

Zhong, Wuqiang. 1996. "Audi Class: Thoughts on China's Vocational Education (奥迪班: 对中国职业教育的思考)." *Adult Education (成人教育)* (1): 7–12.

Zhou, Zhongyi. 2011. "How Security Service Responds to the Impact of the Social Security Law (浅谈保安服务业如何应对《社会保险法》实施的冲击)." *China Security Service (中国保安)* (11): 12–16.

Index

Note: Page numbers in *italic* indicate figures; those in **bold** indicate tables.